# ACCA

## PAPER F6

TAXATION (UK)

FA 2013

FOR EXAMS IN 2014

BPP
LEARNING MEDIA

PRACTICE & REVISION KIT

First edition 2007
Eighth edition January 2014
ISBN 9781 4727 5304 5
(previous ISBN 9781 4453 6646 3)
ebook ISBN 9781 4727 0251 7

British Library Cataloguing-in-Publication Data
A catalogue record for this book
is available from the British Library

Published by

BPP Learning Media Ltd
BPP House, Aldine Place
London W12 8AA

www.bpp.com/learningmedia

Printed in the United Kingdom by Ricoh

Ricoh House
Ullswater Crescent
Coulsdon
CR5 2HR

We are grateful to the Association of Chartered Certified
Accountants for permission to reproduce past
examination questions. The suggested solutions in the
exam answer bank have been prepared by BPP Learning
Media Ltd, except where otherwise stated.

Your learning materials, published by BPP Learning
Media Ltd, are printed on paper obtained from
traceable, sustainable sources.

# Contents

# A note about copyright

Dear Customer

What does the little © mean and why does it matter?

Your market-leading BPP books, course materials and e-learning materials do not write and update themselves. People write them: on their own behalf or as employees of an organisation that invests in this activity. Copyright law protects their livelihoods. It does so by creating rights over the use of the content.

Breach of copyright is a form of theft – as well as being a criminal offence in some jurisdictions, it is potentially a serious breach of professional ethics.

With current technology, things might seem a bit hazy but, basically, without the express permission of BPP Learning Media:

- Photocopying our materials is a breach of copyright

- Scanning, ripcasting or conversion of our digital materials into different file formats, uploading them to facebook or emailing them to your friends is a breach of copyright

You can, of course, sell your books, in the form in which you have bought them – once you have finished with them. (Is this fair to your fellow students? We update for a reason.) Please note the e-products are sold on a single user licence basis: we do not supply 'unlock' codes to people who have bought them second-hand.

And what about outside the UK? BPP Learning Media strives to make our materials available at prices students can afford by local printing arrangements, pricing policies and partnerships which are clearly listed on our website. A tiny minority ignore this and indulge in criminal activity by illegally photocopying our material or supporting organisations that do. If they act illegally and unethically in one area, can you really trust them?

# Using your BPP Learning Media products

This Kit gives you the question practice and guidance you need in the exam. Our other products can also help you pass:

- **Learning to Learn Accountancy** gives further valuable advice on revision

- **Passcards** provide you with clear topic summaries and exam tips

- **Success CDs** help you revise on the move

- **i-Pass CDs** offer tests of knowledge against the clock

You can purchase these products by visiting http://www.bpp.com/acca

# Question index

The headings in this checklist/index indicate the main topics of questions, but questions often cover several different topics.

Questions set under the old syllabus exam are included in this Kit (labelled BTX) because their style and content are similar to those that appear in the current syllabus exam. The questions have been amended as appropriate to reflect the current syllabus exam format.

| | | Time allocation | | Page number | |
|---|---|---|---|---|---|
| | | Marks | Mins | Question | Answer |

## Part A: Taxation of individuals

### Income tax computation

| | | Marks | Mins | Question | Answer |
|---|---|---|---|---|---|
| 1 | Brad, Lauren, Tom, Sarah and Louise | 22 | 40 | 3 | 61 |
| 2 | Domingo, Erigo and Fargo (TX 06/09) | 25 | 45 | 4 | 64 |
| 3 | The Wind Family (TX 12/11) | 25 | 45 | 5 | 67 |
| 4 | Joe Jones (TX 12/10) | 25 | 45 | 6 | 71 |
| 5 | Sam and Kim White (TX 06/08) | 25 | 45 | 7 | 74 |
| 6 | Sammi Smith (TX 12/10) | 15 | 27 /247 | 9 | 78 |

### Property income

| | | Marks | Mins | Question | Answer |
|---|---|---|---|---|---|
| 7 | Edmond Brick (TX 12/07) | 15 | 27 | 9 | 79 |
| 8 | Peter Chic (TX 12/08) | 25 | 45 | 10 | 81 |
| 9 | Leticia Stone (TX 12/11) | 15 | 27 /99 | 11 | 85 |

### Pensions

| | | Marks | Mins | Question | Answer |
|---|---|---|---|---|---|
| 10 | Peach, Plum and Pear (TX12/08) | 10 | 18 /18 | 12 | 87 |

### Sole trader businesses

| | | Marks | Mins | Question | Answer |
|---|---|---|---|---|---|
| 11 | Na Style (TX 12/09) | 25 | 45 | 13 | 88 |
| 12 | Simon House (TX 12/09) | 15 | 27 | 14 | 91 |
| 13 | Bayle Defender (TX 06/11) | 30 | 54 | 15 | 94 |
| 14 | Samantha Fabrique (TX 12/07) | 10 | 18 | 17 | 97 |
| 15 | Michael and Sean (TX 06/12) | 15 | 27 /171 | 17 | 99 |

### Partnerships

| | | Marks | Mins | Question | Answer |
|---|---|---|---|---|---|
| 16 | Ae, Bee, Cae, and Eu (TX 12/08) | 10 | 18 | 18 | 100 |
| 17 | Auy Man and Bim Men (TX 06/10) | 30 | 54 | 19 | 102 |
| 18 | Flick Pick (TX 06/12) | 30 | 54 /126 | 21 | 105 |

### Administration

| | | Marks | Mins | Question | Answer |
|---|---|---|---|---|---|
| 19 | Pi Casso (TX 06/08) | 15 | 27 | 22 | 109 |
| 20 | Ernest Vader (TX 06/10) | 15 | 27 /54 | 22 | 110 |

≈ 12h

≈ 13 h

## Planning your question practice

Our guidance from page xxv shows you how to organise your question practice, either by attempting questions from each syllabus area or **by building your own exams** – tackling questions as a series of practice exams.

≈13,5 h

BPP
LEARNING MEDIA

# Topic index

Listed below are the key Paper F6 syllabus topics and the numbers of the questions in this Kit covering those topics.

If you need to concentrate your practice and revision on certain topics or if you want to attempt all available questions that refer to a particular subject, you will find this index useful.

| Syllabus topic | Question numbers |
|---|---|
| Administration of tax – individuals | 2, 4, 11, 13, 19, 20, ME1 Qu 1, ME3 Qu 1 |
| Administration of tax – companies | 31, 34, 35, 37, 43, 45, 48, ME1 Qu2, ME3 Qu 2 |
| Capital allowances | 16, 17, 18, 31, 32, 33, 36, 37, 41, 43, 47, 48, ME1 Qu 1, ME1 Qu 2, ME2 Qu 2, ME2 Qu 4, ME3 Qu 1, ME3 Qu 2 |
| Chargeable gains – reliefs | 21, 22, 23, 24, 25, 39, 40, ME1 Qu 3, ME2 Qu 3, ME3 Qu 3 |
| Chargeable gains – companies | 22, 31, 32, 38, 39, 40, ME1 Qu 3, ME3 Qu 2 |
| Chargeable gains – individuals | 12, 21, 22, 23, 24, 25, 40, ME1 Qu 4, ME2 Qu 3, ME2 Qu 5, ME3 Qu 3 |
| Companies – calculation of taxable total profits | 6, 31, 32, 33, 34, 36, 37, 38, 39, 40, 41, 42, 43, 44, 45, 46, 47, 48, ME1 Qu 2, ME2 Qu 2, ME2 Qu 4, ME3 Qu 2 |
| Companies – calculation of tax | 6, 31, 32, 34, 35, 36, 37, 38, 40, 43, 44, 45, 46, 48, ME1 Qu 2, ME1 Qu 4, ME2 Qu 2, ME3 Qu 2 |
| Companies – groups | 33, 44, 45, 46, 47, 48, ME2 Qu 2, ME3 Qu 2 |
| Companies – losses | 37, 41, 42, 43, ME1 Qu 3 |
| Income tax computation | 1, 2, 3, 4, 5, 6, 8, 11, 12, 13, 33, ME1 Qu 1, ME1 Qu 4, ME1 Qu 5, ME2 Qu 1, ME2 Qu 5, ME3 Qu 4 |
| Individuals – employment income | 2, 3, 4, 5, 6, 8, 13, 18, ME1 Qu 1, ME1 Qu 4, ME2 Qu 1 |
| Individuals – property income | 7, 8, 9, 18, ME1 Qu 1, ME2 Qu 1, ME2 Qu 5 |
| Individuals – trading income | 2, 3, 5, 11, 12, 13, 16, 17, 18, ME1 Qu 1, ME3 Qu 1, ME3 Qu 4 |
| Individuals – losses | 14, 15, ME3 Qu 4 |
| Inheritance tax | 26, 27, 28, 29, 30, 44, ME1 Qu 5, ME2 Qu 5, ME3 Qu 5 |
| National insurance contributions | 3, 6, 8, 12, 13, 17, 18, 33, ME1 Qu 4, ME2 Qu 1, ME3 Qu 1 |
| Partnerships | 13, 16, 17, 18, ME 3 Qu 4 |
| Pensions | 2, 3, 10, ME1 Qu 5, ME2 Qu 1 |
| Value added tax | 17, 18, 32, 41, 43, 49, 50, 51, 52, 53, ME1 Qu 2, ME2 Qu 2, ME3 Qu 1 |

ME1 is Mock Exam 1, ME2 is Mock Exam 2 and ME3 is Mock Exam 3

# Helping you with your revision

## BPP Learning Media Approved Learning Partner – content

As ACCA's **Approved Learning Partner – content**, BPP Learning Media gives you the **opportunity** to use revision materials reviewed by the ACCA examination team. By incorporating the examination team's comments and suggestions regarding syllabus coverage, the BPP Learning Media Practice and Revision Kit provides excellent, **ACCA-approved** support for your revision.

## Tackling revision and the exam

You can significantly improve your chances of passing by tackling revision and the exam in the right ways. Our advice is based on feedback from ACCA examiners.

- We look at the dos and don'ts of revising for, and taking, ACCA exams
- We focus on Paper F6; we discuss revising the syllabus, what to do (and what not to do) in the exam, how to approach different types of question and ways of obtaining easy marks

## Selecting questions

We provide signposts to help you plan your revision.

- A full **question index**
- A **topic index** listing all the questions that cover key topics, so that you can locate the questions that provide practice on these topics, and see the different ways in which they might be examined
- **BPP's question plan** highlighting the most important questions and explaining why you should attempt them
- **Build your own exams**, showing how you can practise questions in a series of exams

## Making the most of question practice

At BPP Learning Media we realise that you need more than just questions and model answers to get the most from your question practice.

- Our **Top tips** included for certain questions provide essential advice on tackling questions, presenting answers and the key points that answers need to include
- We show you how you can pick up **Easy marks** on some questions, as we know that picking up all readily available marks often can make the difference between passing and failing
- We include **marking guides** to show you what the examiner rewards
- We include **examiners' comments** to show you where students struggled or performed well in the actual exam
- We refer to the **FA 2013 Study Text** (for exams in 2014) for detailed coverage of the topics covered in questions

## Attempting mock exams

There are three mock exams that provide practice at coping with the pressures of the exam day. We strongly recommend that you attempt them under exam conditions. **Mock exams 1** and **2** reflect the question styles and syllabus coverage of the exam and **Mock exam 3** is the December 2013 paper.

# Revising F6

Firstly we must emphasise that you will need a good knowledge of the **whole syllabus.**

That said, you must have **sound knowledge in the following fundamental areas** if you are to stand a chance of passing the exam. You should therefore **revise the following areas particularly well.**

- **Income tax computation** including the personal allowance and the tax bands and rates.

- The **calculation of benefits from employment**, such as company car and/or fuel, use of an employer's asset and low cost loans. Make sure you can spot tax free benefits too.

- **Capital allowances proforma** paying particular attention to the availability of annual investment allowance. Note particularly the difference in the calculation rules between individuals (sole traders and partners) and companies.

- **Calculation of taxable total profits**, in relation to companies. Be aware that you may need to calculate the various elements that make up the taxable total profits such as property business income, interest income, gains and so on.

- **Computation of chargeable gains** paying attention to whether the disposal is made by an individual or a company, particularly for aspects such as indexation allowance and annual exempt amount.

- **Inheritance tax computations**, including lifetime transfers and the death estate.

- How to calculate **VAT payable or repayable** depending on the type of supply (ie standard rated, zero rated or exempt).

- The **different classes of NIC** payable by employees and their employers compared to those due from self employed individuals or partners.

## Reading articles

The examiner has stressed the importance of reading the technical articles published in *Student Accountant* that relate to F6. The **Finance Act 2013 article** is particularly relevant as it highlights topical aspects which are likely to be tested in the 2014 exams.

## Question practice

You should use the Passcards and any brief notes you have to revise the syllabus, but you mustn't spend all your revision time passively reading. **Question practice is vital**; doing as many questions as you can in full will help develop your ability to analyse scenarios and produce relevant discussion and recommendations. The question plan on page xxi tells you what questions cover so that you can choose questions covering a variety of syllabus areas.

# Passing the F6 exam

## Displaying the right qualities

The examiner expects students to display the following qualities.

| Qualities required | |
|---|---|
| **Knowledge development** | Questions will test your knowledge of underlying principles and major technical areas of taxation, as they affect the activities of individuals and businesses, across the breadth of the F6 syllabus. You will also be expected to apply this knowledge to the facts of each particular question and also to identify the compliance issues for your client. |
| **Computation skills** | Although you will be expected to be able to calculate the tax liability, note that you will also be marked on the methods you use. So, if your numbers are not perfect you will not necessarily lose too many marks so long as your method is correct and you have stated any assumptions you have made. |
| **Ability to explain** | Whilst the main focus of the exam is on the computation of tax liabilities, you may also be required to explain rules and conditions, so take care to practise the written elements of the answers also. |
| **Identification capability** | You must know who you are calculating tax liabilities for – is the client a company or an individual? Be sure who you are advising as this will seriously impact your answers. |

You will not always produce the exact same answer as we have in our answer section. This does not necessarily mean that you have failed the question, but if you do use the suggested proformas and methods you will maximise the number of marks you can achieve.

## Avoiding weaknesses

We give details of the examiner's comments and criticisms throughout this Kit. These have hardly varied over the last few years. His reports always emphasise the need for thorough preparation for the exam, but there are various things you can do on the day of the exam to enhance your chances. Although these all sound basic, the examiner has commented that many scripts don't:

- Make the most of the information given in the question
- Follow the question requirements
- Set out workings clearly

## Using the reading time

You will have 15 minutes' reading time for Paper F6. Here are some helpful tips on how to best utilise this time.

- Speed read through the question paper, jotting down any ideas that come to you about any of the questions.

- Decide the order which you're likely to tackle questions (probably easiest questions first, most difficult questions last).

- Spend the remainder of reading time reading the question(s) you'll do first in detail jotting down proformas and plans (any plans or proformas written on the question paper should be reproduced in the answer booklet).

- When you can start writing, get straight on with the question(s) you've planned in detail.

If you have looked at all of the questions during the reading time, this should hopefully mean that you will find it easier to answer the more difficult questions when you come to them, as you will have been generating ideas and remembering facts while answering the easier questions.

# Choosing which questions to answer first

There are five compulsory questions, with a larger number of marks awarded for the first two questions.

- Many students prefer to answer the questions with the largest number of allocated marks first. Others prefer to answer a question on their most comfortable topic.

- Whatever the order, make sure you leave yourself **sufficient time** to tackle all the questions. Don't get so bogged down in the calculations in the first question you do, especially if it's your favourite topic, that you have to rush the rest of the paper.

- Allocate your time carefully between different question parts. If a question is split into a number of requirements, use the number of marks available for each to allocate your time effectively.

# Tackling questions

You'll improve your chances by following a step-by-step approach along the following lines.

### Step 1    Read the requirement

Identify the knowledge areas being tested and see precisely what the examiner wants you to do. This will help you focus on what's important in the question.

### Step 2    Check the mark allocation

This helps you allocate time.

### Step 3    Read the question actively

You will already know which knowledge area(s) are being tested from having read the requirement so whilst you read through the question underline or highlight key words and figures as you read. This will mean you are thinking about the question rather than just looking at the words blankly, and will allow you to identify relevant information for use in your calculations.

### Step 4    Plan your answer

You may only spend five minutes planning your answer but it will be five minutes well spent. Identify the calculations you will need to do and whether you have appropriate proformas to assist in these. If there is a written element to the question, determine whether you can you use bullet points or if you need a more formal format.

### Step 5    Write your answer

Stick carefully to the time allocation for each question, and for each part of each question.

# Gaining the easy marks

There are two main ways to obtain easy marks in the F6 exam.

## Proformas

There will always be basic marks available for straightforward tasks such as putting easy figures into proformas, for example putting the cost figure for an addition into a capital allowances proforma. Do not miss out on these easy marks by not learning your proformas properly. Make it easy for yourself to pick up the easy marks.

## Deadlines and dates

An important component of your knowledge of the different taxes is the administrative, or compliance, details such as filing deadlines and tax payment dates. This element of the requirement can often be answered even before you make any calculations, for example stating the submission deadline for an individual's self assessment tax return.

# Exam information
# The exam paper

The syllabus is assessed by a three-hour paper-based examination.

The paper will be predominantly computational and will have five questions, all of which will be compulsory.

- Question one will focus on income tax and question two will focus on corporation tax. The two questions will be for a total of 55 marks, with one of the questions being for 30 marks and the other being for 25 marks.

- Question three will focus on chargeable gains (either personal or corporate) and will be for 15 marks.

- Questions four and five will be on any area of the syllabus, can cover more than one topic, and will be for 15 marks each.

There will always be at a minimum of 10 marks on value added tax. These marks will normally be included within question one or question two, although there might be a separate question on value added tax.

There will always be between 5 and 15 marks on inheritance tax. Inheritance tax can be included within questions three, four or five.

National insurance contributions will not be examined as a separate question, but may be examined in any question involving income tax or corporation tax.

Groups may be examined in either question two, question four or question five.

A small element of chargeable gains may be included in questions other than question three.

Any of the five questions might include the consideration of issues relating to the minimisation or deferral of tax liabilities.

## December 2013

| | | *Question in this Kit* |
|---|---|---|
| 1 | Adjustment of profit for sole trader. Employer's national insurance contributions. Filing of tax return. Compliance check. Registration for VAT. Ethical considerations on client refusal to register for VAT. VAT simplified invoice. Filing of VAT return and payment of VAT. | ME3 Qu 1 |
| 2 | Computation of taxable total profits. Property business income. Loan relationships. Capital allowances. Groups of companies. | ME3 Qu 2 |
| 3 | Capital gains reliefs for business assets. Transfer between spouses. Principal private residence relief. Disposal of shares. Basic capital gains tax planning. | ME3 Qu 3 |
| 4 | Basis of assessment for sole trader on commencement. Pre-trading expenditure. Relief for trading loss against income and gains. Partnership income. Basis of assessment on cessation. | ME3 Qu 4 |
| 5 | Inheritance tax on lifetime transfers and death estate. Payment of tax. | ME3 Qu 5 |

# June 2013

| | | *Question in this Kit* |
|---|---|---|
| 1 | Employment income. Personal pension contributions. Computation of income tax. National insurance contributions. Restriction of personal allowances. Furnished holiday lettings. | ME2 Qu 1 |
| 2 | Adjustment of trading profit. Capital allowances. Associated companies. Corporation tax computation. VAT payable. Input tax not recoverable. Late submission of VAT return and late payment of VAT. Group registration for VAT. | ME2 Qu 2 |
| 3 | Use of annual exempt amount. Replacement of business assets. Disposal of shares with and without entrepreneurs' relief. | ME2 Qu 3 |
| 4 | Part (a) and (b) no longer in syllabus. Part (c) long period of account for company. | ME2 Qu 4(c) |
| 5 | Inheritance tax on lifetime tax and death estate. Capital gains tax on disposal of house. Income tax on property business income. | ME2 Qu 5 |

## Examiner's comments

The vast majority of candidates attempted all five questions, and there was little evidence of time pressure.

Overall, this was a particularly impressive performance. Candidates performed particularly well on questions 1a, 1b, 1c, 2a, 2b(i), 2b(iii), 2c(i), 2c(iii), 3b, 3c, 4c, 5a(i) and 5b. The questions candidates found most challenging were questions 1d, 2b(ii), 2c(ii), 3a and 5a(ii).

# December 2012

| | | *Question in this Kit* |
|---|---|---|
| 1 | Trading income assessment. Employment income. Property business income, investment income. Calculation of income tax payable. Payment of income tax under self-assessment. | ME1 Qu 1 |
| 2 | Computation of taxable total profits, capital allowances. Submission of corporation tax returns. VAT cash accounting scheme and annual accounting scheme. VAT overseas aspects. | ME1 Qu 2 |
| 3 | Chargeable gains for company. Share pool, part disposal and compensation for destruction of asset. | ME1 Qu 3 |
| 4 | Part (a) extracting profits from company as salary or dividends. Part (b) no longer in syllabus. | ME1 Qu 4(a) |
| 5 | Pensions. Individual savings accounts. Inheritance tax on lifetime transfers. | ME1 Qu 5 |

## Examiner's comments

The vast majority of candidates attempted all five questions, but question four was often left to last and answered under time pressure. This problem often arose because the workings for parts 1a and 2a were far too detailed.

Question 4 was the most difficult of the three 15-mark questions, although the calculations themselves were quite straightforward. What candidates needed to do with this question was to spend several minutes thinking their answer through and making sure that basic concepts were not overlooked. Many candidates appeared to be rushing, and making basic mistakes, such as calculating NIC in respect of dividend income.

Candidates performed particularly well on questions 1a, 1b(i), 1b(ii), 2a, 2c(i), 3a, 3b, 5a, 5b and 5c. The questions candidates found most challenging were questions 2b(i), 2b(ii), 2c(ii) 2b, and 4a.

A number of common issues arose in candidate's answers:

- Failing to read the question requirement clearly. For example, calculating the CGT liability in question 3(b) despite being told that only chargeable gains were required.

- Poor time management. For example, the 1 mark requirement for part 2b(i) needed just a date, so time was wasted by writing a whole paragraph.

- Poor use of workings. The workings for parts 1a and 2a were often far too detailed. Many of the calculations could have been included within the main computation, and once something such as the exempt premium bond prize was shown once there was no need for further explanation. However, when it came to the share pool in part 3b there was often a complete lack of workings for the indexation calculations – making marking extremely difficult.

## June 2012

|   |   | Question in this Kit |
|---|---|---|
| 1 | Employee. Partnership profits. Property income. Classes of national insurance contributions. Choice of accounting date. VAT flat rate scheme. Tax point. | 18 |
| 2 | Two companies, adjustment of trading profits. Capital allowances. Long period of account. Calculation of corporation tax. | 36 |
| 3 | Liability to tax on chargeable gains. Calculation of CGT at different rates. Chargeable gain for company with rollover relief. | 22 |
| 4 | Government tax policies. Trading losses in early years and on cessation. | 15 |
| 5 | Inheritance tax transfer of nil band. Death estate with prior lifetime transfers. | 27 |

### Examiner's comments

The vast majority of candidates attempted all five questions, and there was little evidence of time pressure. Where questions were left unanswered by candidates, this appeared to be due to a lack of knowledge or poor exam technique, as opposed to time pressure.

Question 4 was the most difficult of the three 15-mark questions, so it was a sensible strategy to leave this question until last. If time was running out, it would have been much easier and quicker to score marks on question 5.

Candidates performed particularly well on questions 1a, 1b, 1d(i), 2a, 3a, 3b, 3c(i), 4a, 5a and 5b. The questions candidates found most challenging were questions 1c, 1d(ii), 1d(iii), 2b, 3c(ii), 4b and 5c – approximately one-third of the paper. This is mainly due to candidates not covering the entire syllabus as part of their studies

A number of common issues arose in candidate's answers:

- Failing to read the question requirement clearly. For example, calculating the income tax in question 1(a) despite being told that only the taxable income figure was required.

- Poor time management. For example, the 1 mark questions should have been answered with a brief sentence rather than a long paragraph.

- Not learning lessons from earlier examiner's reports and hence making the same mistakes. For example, the necessity of learning basic rules (such as where there is a long corporation tax period of account) has previously been highlighted several times.

- Poor layout of answers. For example, the two sections of question 2 were sometimes combined into one long very confusing answer. The same with question 3(b) where it was often not clear which of the two sections was being answered.

# December 2011

### Examiner's comments

This was another good performance, although many candidates achieved a pass mark without particularly excelling. There are two aspects that are worth mentioning. The first is that candidates should sometimes stand back and think about their answers to see whether they make sense. For example, for question 5 part (c) it should have been fairly obvious that an answer with six marks attached to it was not simply that no inheritance tax was due. The second aspect is that candidates should give particular attention to the requirements, especially any guidance that is given. In this paper they would have seen that in question 3 there was no need to calculate any CGT liability, in question 4 they were given advice on how to layout their answer, and in question 5 they were told to ignore annual exemptions - making their answer much more straightforward.

# June 2011

### Examiner's comments

This was a very good performance and it was pleasing to see how well the first Paper F6 inheritance tax question was answered. One particular problem at this sitting was that candidates wasted quite a bit of time where something should have been obvious without having to produce detailed calculations, and also where more calculations were done than was necessary because the requirements were not read properly. This is where the reading time should be put to good use.

# December 2010

## Examiner's comments

This paper continued in the same style as that of the June paper, with the aim of being less predictable and required candidates to think a bit more in order to achieve a pass mark. Although the overall result was satisfactory, the performance was not quite as good as expected. The main problems were that candidates were obviously not expecting a question on PAYE, and question 4, although not being particularly difficult, required some careful planning before doing the computations.

# June 2010

## Examiner's comments

This style of this paper was slightly different from recent papers, with more smaller sub-parts enabling more of the syllabus to be covered: Some of the other changes were that the VAT information needed for question 1 part (d) was not shown separately (instead being included within the main text), and in question 2 the group relief and capital allowance aspects were in separate sections (requiring explanations instead of straightforward computations) rather than being examined computationally as part of the main corporation tax question. Candidates cannot expect to have an easy income tax or benefits computation in every paper. The pass rate achieved was quite satisfactory.

# December 2009

|  |  | Question in this Kit |
|---|---|---|
| 1 | Basis periods; adjustment of profit for sole trader. Calculation of income tax. Administration for self assessment. | 11 |
| 2 | Residence of company. Capital allowances. Calculation of corporation tax. VAT registration. Pre-registration input tax and errors. | n/a |
| 3 | CGT for three individuals. Part (a) no longer in syllabus. Part (b) gift relief and part (c) principal private residence relief. | 25(b), (c) |
| 4 | Badges of trade. Calculation of tax liability if trading or realising capital gain. | 12 |
| 5 | Corporate loss relief. | 42 |

## Examiner's comments

This was another good performance, and well prepared candidates had no difficulty in achieving a pass mark. Questions 3 (capital gains tax (CGT)) and 5 (corporate loss relief) caused the most problems, and the value added tax (VAT) aspects of question 2 were also not particularly well answered.

# June 2009

|  |  | Question in this Kit |
|---|---|---|
| 1 | Calculation of income tax liabilities. Filing dates and record retention. | 2 |
| 2 | Calculation of company's adjusted trading profit. Corporation tax. Interest. Capital gains group and use of election. | 48 |
| 3 | Calculation of capital gains tax liabilities. Use of losses b/f. | 24 |
| 4 | Calculation of VAT payable. Cash accounting scheme. VAT registration and output VAT on piecemeal sale of fixed assets or TOGC. | 53 |
| 5 | Factors indicating employment. Income tax and national insurance as employee and self employed. | ME1 Qu 4(b) |

## Examiner's comments

This was another exceptionally good performance with many candidates achieving high marks. The simplification of capital gain tax for individuals, having a separate VAT question, and a fairly straightforward question 5 all contributed to the good pass rate. In addition, candidates seemed very well prepared for this examination. Areas, such as NIC, which a few diets ago were causing problems, are now handled with ease.

# December 2008

|  |  | Question in this Kit |
|---|---|---|
| 1 | Employment income. Property income. Calculation of income tax. National insurance. | n/a |
| 2 | Calculation of loss for company. Use of loss. Penalties for late submission of return. VAT default surcharge. Annual accounting scheme. | 43 |
| 3 | Chargeable gains for company. Shares. Part disposal. Relief for replacement of business assets. | 38 |
| 4 | Partnership. Cessation of sole trade. | 16 |
| 5 | Pension provision. | n/a |

## Examiner's comments

This was an exceptionally good performance with many candidates achieving high marks. None of the questions caused any problems, and even candidates who did not do particularly well with questions 1, 2 and 3, often managed to achieve a pass mark by scoring good marks on questions 4 and 5.

# June 2008

## Examiner's comments

This was a reasonable performance. The main problem was caused by question 4, which many candidates found surprisingly difficult. This question was usually left until last, and it was often obvious that insufficient time had been left to attempt it properly.

# December 2007

## Examiner's comments

This was a very good performance for the first sitting of this paper. Those candidates who marginally failed to achieve a pass mark generally did so because of poor time management. Also, many candidates that were obviously running out of time surprisingly opted to attempt question 5, which was quite the most technically demanding on the paper, rather than question 4 where it was relatively easy to score 9 or 10 marks. Practicing questions under timed, exam-style conditions prior to sitting the examination would have helped as regards time management.

# Pilot paper

# Analysis of past papers

The table below provides details of when each element of the syllabus has been examined and the question number and section in which each element appeared.

| Covered in Text chapter | | Dec 2013 | June 2013 | Dec 2012 | June 2012 | Dec 2011 | June 2011 | Dec 2010 | June 2010 | Dec 2009 |
|---|---|---|---|---|---|---|---|---|---|---|
| | **UK TAX SYSTEM** | | | | | | | | | |
| 1 | Introduction to the UK tax system | 1d | | | 4a | | | | | |
| | **INCOME TAX AND NATIONAL INSURANCE CONTRIBUTIONS** | | | | | | | | | |
| 2 | The computation of taxable income and the income tax liability | 4b | 1a, 1c, 5b | 1a, 4a, 5b | 1a | 1a | 1a | 1a | 1a, 2d | 1c, 4b |
| 3 | Employment income | 1b | 1a | 1a, 4a | | 1a | | 1a | | |
| 4 | Taxable and exempt benefits. The PAYE system | | 1a | 1a | 1a | 1a | | 1a, 4 | | |
| 5 | Pensions | | 1a | 5a | | 1c | | 1a | | |
| 6 | Property income | 2a | 1d, 5b | 1a | 1a | 4 | 2a | | | |
| 7 | Computing trading income | 1a | 2a, 5b | 1a | | | 1a | | 1b | 1b, 4a, 4b |
| 8 | Capital allowances | 1a, 2a | 2a, 4b, 4c | 1a, 2a | 2a | | 2a | | 2c | |
| 9 | Assessable trading income | 4a, 4c | 4a, 4b | 1a | 1c | | | | | 1a |
| 10 | Trading losses | 4b | | | 4b | | 5 | | | |
| 11 | Partnerships and limited liability partnerships | 4c | | | 1a | | 1b | | 1b | |
| 12 | National insurance contributions | 1b | 1b | 4a | 1b | 1b | 1b | 4 | 1c, 2d | 4b |
| | **CHARGEABLE GAINS FOR INDIVIDUALS** | | | | | | | | | |
| 13 | Computing chargeable gains | 3a, 3b, 3c | 3a, 3b, 3c, 5b | | 3b | 3 | 3b | 3 | | 3a, 3b, 3c, 4b |
| 14 | Chattels and the principal private residence exemption | 3b | | | | 3 | | | | 3c |
| 15 | Business reliefs | 3a | 3a, 3b, 3c | 4b | 3b | 3 | 3a | 3 | | 3a, 3b |
| 16 | Shares and securities | 3c | | | | | 3b | 3 | | 3b |
| | **TAX ADMINISTRATION FOR INDIVIDUALS** | | | | | | | | | |
| 17 | Self assessment and payment of tax by individuals | 1c | | 1b | | | 1a | 1a | 4 | 1c, 1d |
| | **INHERITANCE TAX** | | | | | | | | | |
| 18 | Inheritance tax: scope and transfers of value | 5 a-c | 5a | 5c | 5a-c | 5c | 5a-c | n/a | n/a | n/a |
| | **CORPORATION TAX** | | | | | | | | | |
| 19 | Computing taxable total profits | 2a | 2a, 4c | 2a, 4a | 2a, 2b | 2a, 2b | 2a | 2a, 4 | 2a | 2a |
| 20 | Computing the corporation tax liability | 2a | 2b | 2a, 4a | 2a, 2b | 5b | 2a | 2a, 4 | 5 | 2a |
| 21 | Chargeable gains for companies | | | 3 | 3a, 3c | | | 3 | 3a, 3b | |
| 22 | Losses | | | | | 2c | | | 2a | 5 |
| 23 | Groups | 2c | 2b | | | 5a | | | 2b | |
| 24 | Self assessment and payment of tax by companies | 2b | | 2b | | | 2b | | | |
| | **VALUE ADDED TAX** | | | | | | | | | |
| 25 | An introduction to VAT | 1d | 2c | | 1d | 2d | 4a | 2b | 1d | 2b |
| 26 | Further aspects of VAT | 1d | 2c | 2c | 1d | 2d | 4b-e | 2b | 1d | 2b |

# Useful websites

The websites below provide additional sources of information of relevance to your studies for F6 *Taxation*.

- www.accaglobal.com

    ACCA's website. The students' section of the website is invaluable for detailed information about the qualification, past issues of *Student Accountant* (including technical articles) and even interviews with the examiners.

- www.bpp.com

    Our website provides information about BPP products and services, with a link to the ACCA website.

# Planning your question practice

We have already stressed that question practice should be right at the centre of your revision. Whilst you will spend some time looking at your notes and Paper F6 Passcards, you should spend the majority of your revision time practising questions.

We recommend two ways in which you can practise questions.

- Use **BPP Learning Media's question plan** to work systematically through the syllabus and attempt key and other questions on a section-by-section basis

- **Build your own exams** – attempt questions as a series of practice exams

These ways are suggestions and simply following them is no guarantee of success. You or your college may prefer an alternative but equally valid approach.

# BPP Learning Media's question plan

The BPP Learning Media plan below requires you to devote a **minimum of 30 hours** to revision of Paper F6. Any time you can spend over and above this should only increase your chances of success.

Step 1    For each section of the syllabus, **review your notes** and the relevant chapter summaries in the Paper F6 **Passcards**.

Step 2    **Answer the key questions** for that section. These questions have boxes round the question number in the table below and you should answer them in full. Even if you are short of time you must attempt these questions if you want to pass the exam. You should complete your answers without referring to our solutions.

Step 3    **Answer the other questions** for that section, if you have time. You must make sure that you attempt a variety of questions from the whole syllabus and not just concentrate on a few aspects.

Step 4    Once you have worked through all of the syllabus sections attempt **Mock exam 1** under strict exam conditions. Then have a go at **Mock exam 2**, again under strict exam conditions. Just before the exam, if you have time, attempt **Mock exam 3**, again under strict exam conditions. This is the December 2013 paper.

| Syllabus section | Passcards chapters | Questions in this Kit | Comments | Done ☑ |
|---|---|---|---|---|
| **Revision period 1**<br>Introduction to the UK tax system<br><br>Income tax computations | 1, 2 | 1 | Work through this question carefully. It covers the basic income tax computation you will have to do in the exam. | ☐ |
| **Revision periods 2/3**<br>Employees | 3, 4 | 3, 4 | Q3 covers some basic aspects of income tax computation and benefits. It also includes an element of tax planning which is becoming more important in the F6 exam. Q4 is a great question on employment income presenting two different jobs with different remuneration packages. It also covers the PAYE system and gives an idea how simple this will be when examined. | ☐ |
|  |  | 2, 5 | Q2 and Q5 give you extra practice in the type of question set as Q1 in the exam. | ☐ |
| **Revision period 4**<br>Pensions and property income | 5 | 10 | Q10 tests the topical area of pensions. | ☐ |
|  | 6 | 9 | Q9 shows how property income can be tested in a full 15 mark question. | ☐ |
|  |  | 7, 8 | Q7 is another full question on property income. Q8 shows how property income can be examined as part of a longer question. | ☐ |
| **Revision periods 5/6**<br>Trading profits and losses for individuals |  |  |  |  |
| Adjustment of profits | 7 | 13 | Q13 includes an adjustment of profit computation and also tests employment income. You may want to do part (b) in revision period 7. | ☐ |
| Assessable trading income | 9 | 11 | Q11 is a good example of a typical Q1 in the exam. It covers basic adjustment of profit and the basis of assessment rules. | ☐ |
| Trading losses | 10 | 15 | Q15 covers early years loss relief and terminal loss relief. Part (a) is a theory question which is becoming more common in the F6 exam. | ☐ |
|  |  | 14 | Q14 is another question on losses and includes interaction with chargeable gains. | ☐ |

| Syllabus section | Passcards chapters | Questions in this Kit | Comments | Done ☑ |
|---|---|---|---|---|
| **Revision period 7**<br>Partnerships | 11 | 16, 18 | Q16 shows how partnerships can be tested with other rules on basis periods. Q18 has an element of partnerships as part of a longer question – this is common format for the examiner to use. | ☐ |
| | | 17 | Q17 is an other example of partnership as part of a longer question. | ☐ |
| **Revision period 8**<br>National insurance contributions | 12 | 6 | Q6 requires you to work out the tax implications of a director leasing a car or being provided with a company car. This type of question is increasingly being asked at F6 so make sure you are prepared. | ☐ |
| **Revision period 9**<br>Computing chargeable gains | 13 | 12 | Gains will be tested in Question 3 in the exam and may also be tested in any of the other questions. The gains rules are therefore key for your exam. Q12 a good question covering both trading income and capital gains. Again, this is making you think about tax planning, not just doing computations. | ☐ |
| **Revision period 10**<br>Chattels and PPR | 14 | 23 | Q23 is great question covering PPR relief and a number of other aspects of CGT. | ☐ |
| **Revision period 11**<br>Capital gains reliefs | 15 | 22, 25 | Q22 deals with CGT liability and the effect of entrepreneurs' relief. Q25 is a good question to practice a number of reliefs. | ☐ |
| **Revision period 12**<br>Shares and securities | 16 | 21 | Q21 covers aspects of disposals of shares and the effect of takeovers. | ☐ |
| | | 24 | Q24 covers a number of aspects of CGT. | ☐ |
| **Revision period 13**<br>Self assessment and payment of tax by individuals | 17 | 20 | Don't neglect administrative aspects in your F6 revision. Q20 covers the topical issue of tax evasion and tax avoidance. | ☐ |
| | | 19 | Q19 covers some basic administration rules. | ☐ |
| **Revision periods 13/14**<br>Inheritance tax (IHT) | 18 | 27, 29 | You will be asked between 5 and 15 marks on inheritance tax so this is an important topic to revise. Q27 tests how to deal with lifetime transfers and a simple death estate. Don't forget the easy administration mark in part (b). Q29 focuses on a more complicated death estate. | ☐ |
| | | 26, 28, 30 | Q26, 28 and 30 give you extra practice in IHT. | ☐ |

| Syllabus section | Passcards chapters | Questions in this Kit | Comments | Done ☑ |
|---|---|---|---|---|
| **Revision periods 14/15** Computing corporation tax | | | | |
| Capital allowances | 8 | | These are usually tested in detail in the corporation tax question. But you also need to make sure you understand the rules for unincorporated businesses. | |
| Computation of taxable total profits and corporation tax liability | 19, 20 | 31, 33, 36 | Q31 gives you practice in the style of question which is usually set as Q2 in the exam. Q33 is a slightly unusual style of question which covers basic corporation tax and also requires you to give tax advice on a number of matters. Q36 includes a long period of account. | ☐ |
| | | 34, 37 | Q34 deals with a long period of account. Q37 gives you extra practice in a long question with capital allowances. | ☐ |
| **Revision period 16** Chargeable gains for companies | 21 | 39, 40 | Q39 shows how company gains may be tested in Q3. Q40 is a typical of a question testing a mixture of company and individual gains. | ☐ |
| | | 38 | Q38 is another example of a whole question on company gains. | ☐ |
| **Revision period 17** Corporation tax losses | 22 | 41, 42 | Q41 shows how trading losses may be examined in Q2 in the exam. Q42 is an example of a shorter losses question. | ☐ |
| | | 43 | Q43 is another example of a longer question including losses. | ☐ |
| **Revision period 18** Groups | 23 | 47, 48 | Q47 covers group relief. Q48 includes capital gains groups. | ☐ |
| | | 44, 45, 46 | Q 44 covers a number of topics, including group relief. Q45 is a short question giving you more practice on group relief. Q46 similarly is a short question on capital gains groups. | ☐ |
| **Revision period 19** Self assessment and payment of tax by companies | 24 | 35 | Q35 is a useful reminder about the payment of corporation tax in instalments. | ☐ |
| **Revision periods 20/21** Valued added tax (VAT) | | | There will be at least 10 marks for VAT in your paper so be prepared. | |
| | 25, 26 | 32, 50, 53 | Q32 shows how VAT may be tested as part of a longer question. Q50 and Q53 are 15 mark questions on VAT. | ☐ |
| | | 49, 51, 52 | Q49, Q51 and Q52 give you extra practice on VAT topics. | ☐ |

# Build your own exams

Having revised your notes and the BPP Passcards, you can attempt the questions in the Kit as a series of practice exams. You can organise the questions in the following ways.

- Either you can attempt complete past exam papers; recent papers are listed below:

|  | June 13 Questions in Kit | December 12 Questions in Kit | June 12 Questions in Kit | December 11 Questions in Kit | June 11 Questions in Kit |
|---|---|---|---|---|---|
| 1 | ME2 Qu 1 | ME1 Qu 1 | 18 | 3 | 13 |
| 2 | ME2 Qu 2 | ME1 Qu 2 | 36 | 41 | 31 |
| 3 | ME2 Qu 3 | ME1 Qu 3 | 22 | 23 | 21 |
| 4 | ME2 Qu 4 | ME1 Qu 4 | 15 | 9 | 50 |
| 5 | ME2 Qu 5 | ME1 Qu 5 | 27 | 44 | 29 |

- Or you can make up practice exams, either yourself or using the suggestions we have listed below.

|  | Practice Exam | | | | | |
|---|---|---|---|---|---|---|
|  | 1 | 2 | 3 | 4 | 5 | 6 |
| 1 | 3 | 18 | 11 | 13 | 5 | 2 |
| 2 | 32 | 33 | 41 | 31 | 43 | 48 |
| 3 | 38 | 21 | 40 | 22 | 23 | 24 |
| 4 | 30 | 27 | 20 | 28 | 15 | 29 |
| 5 | 45 | 19 | 26 | 50 | 46 | 49 |

# Questions

**TAXATION OF INDIVIDUALS**

Questions 1 to 18 cover the taxation of individuals and their income from employment and self-employment, the subject of Part B of the BPP Study Text for Paper F6. Questions 19 and 20 cover tax administration for individuals, the subject of Part D of the BPP Study Text for Paper F6.

# 1 Brad, Lauren, Tom, Sarah and Louise          40 mins

(a)  Brad (born in 1968), an advertising executive, and his wife Lauren (born in 1970), an IT consultant, have one son. Having made a large gain on the sale of a property when they got married, they have acquired a considerable number of investments. They now require assistance in preparing their taxation returns for tax year 2013/14 and have listed out their income and expenditure:

**Brad**

|  | £ |
|---|---|
| Salary (before deduction of PAYE) | 104,500 |
| Building society interest (Joint account – total net interest credited) | 4,400 (net) |

**Lauren**

|  | £ |
|---|---|
| Salary (before deduction of PAYE) | 45,975 |
| Interest received on ISA account | 350 |
| Dividend received on Virgin plc shares | 2,250 |
| Building society interest (Joint account – total net interest credited) | 4,400 (net) |
| Interest received on 2025 5% Treasury Stock (received gross) | 2,000 |
| Gift Aid payment to Dogs Trust (a registered charity) (actual amount paid) | 1,000 |

*Required*

Calculate Brad and Lauren's income tax liability for tax year 2013/14. You should indicate by the use of zero any items that are non-taxable/exempt from tax.          **(9 marks)**

(b)  Lauren's father, Tom, a widower, who was born in 1944, has the following income for tax year 2013/14.

|  | £ |
|---|---|
| State retirement pension | 4,926 |
| Pension from former employer (before deduction of PAYE) | 7,890 |
| Building society interest (net interest credited) | 14,320 |

Tom gave £3,200 to Oxfam (a registered charity) on 21 September 2013 under Gift Aid. This was the actual amount paid.

*Required*

Calculate Tom's income tax liability for tax year 2013/14.          **(5 marks)**

(c)  Sarah, Brad's sister, was born in 1966. She is self-employed and has the following income for tax year 2013/14:

|  | £ |
|---|---|
| Trading profits | 164,000 |
| Bank interest received from Santander (net interest credited) | 8,000 |
| Dividends from BP plc (actual amount received) | 4,950 |

Sarah paid £16,000 (net) into her personal pension scheme during 2013/14.

*Required*

Calculate Sarah's income tax liability for tax year 2013/14.          **(5 marks)**

(d) Louise, Lauren's sister, is a single mother and has one child, aged four. She has net income of £59,000 in the tax year 2013/14. Louise paid £4,000 (net) into her personal pension scheme during 2013/14. This was the actual amount paid. Louise receives child benefit of £1,056 in 2013/14.

*Required*

Calculate Louise's child benefit income tax charge for 2013/14. **(3 marks)**

**(Total = 22 marks)**

# 2 Domingo, Erigo and Fargo (TX 06/09)       45 mins

Domingo, Erigo and Fargo Gomez are three brothers. The following information is available for the tax year 2013/14:

**Domingo Gomez**

(1) Domingo was born in 1946.

(2) During the tax year 2013/14 he received the state pension of £4,500 and a private pension of £3,400.

(3) In addition to his pension income Domingo received building society interest of £15,520 and interest of £600 on the maturity of a savings certificate from National Savings and Investments during the tax year 2013/14. These were the actual cash amounts received.

(4) During the tax year 2013/14 Domingo made donations of £300 (gross) to local charities. These were not made under the gift aid scheme.

**Erigo Gomez**

(1) Erigo was born in 1957.

(2) He is employed as a business journalist by Economical plc, a magazine publishing company. During the tax year 2013/14 Erigo was paid a gross annual salary of £36,000.

(3) During the tax year 2013/14 Erigo used his private motor car for business purposes. He drove 18,000 miles in the performance of his duties for Economical plc, for which the company paid an allowance of 25 pence per mile.

(4) During June 2013 Economical plc paid £11,400 towards the cost of Erigo's relocation when he was required to move his place of employment. Erigo's previous main residence was 140 miles from his new place of employment with the company. The £11,400 covered the cost of disposing of Erigo's old property and of acquiring a new property.

(5) Erigo contributed 6% of his gross salary of £36,000 into Economical plc's HM Revenue and Customs' registered occupational pension scheme.

(6) During the tax year 2013/14 Erigo donated £100 (gross) per month to charity under the payroll deduction scheme.

**Fargo Gomez**

(1) Fargo was born in 1960.

(2) He commenced self-employment as a business consultant on 6 July 2013. Fargo's tax adjusted trading profit based on his draft accounts for the nine-month period ended 5 April 2014 is £64,775. This figure is before making any adjustments required for:

    (i) Advertising expenditure of £2,600 incurred during May 2013. This expenditure has not been deducted in calculating the profit of £64,775.

    (ii) Capital allowances.

(3) The only item of plant and machinery owned by Fargo is his motor car. This cost £11,000 on 6 July 2013 and had $CO_2$ emissions of 125g/km. During the nine-month period ended 5 April 2014 Fargo drove a total of 24,000 miles, of which 8,000 were for private journeys.

(4)   During the tax year 2013/14 Fargo contributed £5,200 (gross) into a personal pension scheme, and made gift aid donations totalling £2,400 (net) to national charities.

## Tax returns

For the tax year 2013/14 Domingo wants to file a paper self-assessment tax return and have HM Revenue and Customs prepare a self-assessment on his behalf. Erigo also wants to file a paper tax return but will prepare his own self-assessment. Fargo wants to file his tax return online.

*Required*

(a)   Calculate the respective income tax liabilities for the tax year 2013/14 of:

  (i)    Domingo Gomez                                                        **(6 marks)**
  (ii)   Erigo Gomez                                                          **(6 marks)**
  (iii)  Fargo Gomez                                                          **(7 marks)**

(b)   Advise Domingo, Erigo and Fargo Gomez of the latest dates by which their respective self-assessment tax returns for the tax year 2013/14 will have to be submitted given their stated filing preferences.   **(3 marks)**

(c)   Advise Domingo, Erigo and Fargo Gomez as to how long they must retain the records used in preparing their respective tax returns for the tax year 2013/14, and the potential consequences of not retaining the records for the required period.                                        **(3 marks)**

**(Total = 25 marks)**

# 3 The Wind Family (TX 12/11)                          45 mins

Philip, Charles and William Wind are grandfather, father and son. The following information is available for the tax year 2013/14:

## Philip Wind

Philip was born in 1935. During the tax year 2013/14 he received pensions of £13,140.

In addition to his pension income, Philip received building society interest of £13,280 during the tax year 2013/14.

This was the actual cash amount received.

## Charles Wind

Charles was born in 1964. He is self-employed as an architect, and his tax adjusted trading profit for the year ended 31 December 2013 was £111,400.

During the tax year 2013/14 Charles made a gift aid donation of £800 (gross) to a national charity.

## William Wind

William was born in 1990. He is employed as a security consultant by Crown plc, a company that supplies security services.

During the tax year 2013/14 William was paid a gross annual salary of £181,335.

During the tax year 2013/14 William contributed £7,300 into Crown plc's HM Revenue and Customs' registered occupational pension scheme. The company contributed a further £10,950 on his behalf.

Throughout the tax year 2013/14 Crown plc provided William with a petrol-powered motor car which has a list price of £83,100. The motor car cost Crown plc £78,800, and it has an official $CO_2$ emission rate of 222 grams per kilometre. Crown plc also provided William with fuel for private journeys. During the tax year 2013/14 William made contributions of £8,000 to Crown plc in respect of the motor car. This consisted of £4,800 for the use of the motor car, and £3,200 towards the cost of fuel for private journeys. The total cost of the fuel for private journeys was £4,400.

*Required*

(a) Calculate the respective income tax liabilities for the tax year 2013/14 of:

    (i)    Philip Wind     **(4 marks)**
    (ii)   Charles Wind     **(4 marks)**
    (iii)  William Wind     **(7 marks)**

(b) Calculate the respective national insurance contributions, if any, suffered by Philip, Charles and William Wind for the tax year 2013/14.     **(4 marks)**

(c) Explain to Charles and William Wind, with supporting calculations, how their respective income tax liabilities for the tax year 2013/14 would have been reduced if:

    (i)    Charles Wind had contributed £10,600 (gross) into a personal pension scheme during the tax year 2013/14     **(3 marks)**

    (ii)   William Wind's contributions of £8,000 to Crown plc in respect of the company motor car for the tax year 2013/14 had been allocated on a more beneficial basis     **(3 marks)**

**(Total = 25 marks)**

# 4 Joe Jones (TX 12/10)     45 mins

On 31 December 2013 Joe Jones (born in 1955) resigned as an employee of Firstly plc, and on 1 January 2014 commenced employment with Secondly plc. Joe was employed by both companies as a financial analyst. The following information is available for the tax year 2013/14:

**Employment with Firstly plc**

(1) From 6 April 2013 to 31 December 2013 Joe was paid a salary of £6,360 per month. In addition to his salary, Joe was paid a bonus of £12,000 on 12 May 2013. He had become entitled to this bonus on 22 March 2013.

(2) Joe contributed 6% of his monthly gross salary of £6,360 into Firstly plc's HM Revenue and Customs' registered occupational pension scheme.

(3) On 1 May 2013 Firstly plc provided Joe with an interest free loan of £120,000 so that he could purchase a holiday cottage. Joe repaid £50,000 of the loan on 31 July 2013, and repaid the balance of the loan of £70,000 when he ceased employment with Firstly plc on 31 December 2013.

(4) During the period from 6 April 2013 to 31 December 2013 Joe's three-year-old daughter was provided with a place at Firstly plc's workplace nursery. The total cost to the company of providing this nursery place was £11,400 (190 days at £60 per day).

(5) During the period 6 April 2013 to 31 December 2013 Firstly plc paid gym membership fees of £1,650 for Joe.

(6) Firstly plc provided Joe with a home entertainment system for his personal use costing £4,400 on 6 April 2013. The company gave the home entertainment system to Joe for free, when he left the company on 31 December 2013, although its market value at that time was £3,860.

**Employment with Secondly plc**

(1) From 1 January 2014 to 5 April 2014 Joe was paid a salary of £6,565 per month.

(2) During the period 1 January 2014 to 5 April 2014 Joe contributed a total of £3,000 (gross) into a personal pension scheme.

(3) From 1 January 2014 to 5 April 2014 Secondly plc provided Joe with living accommodation. The property has an annual value of £10,400 and is rented by Secondly plc at a cost of £2,250 per month. On 1 January 2014 Secondly plc purchased furniture for the property at a cost of £16,320. The company pays for all of the running costs relating to the property, and for the period 1 January 2014 to 5 April 2014 these amounted to £1,900.

(4) During the period 1 January 2014 to 5 April 2014 Secondly plc provided Joe with 13 weeks of childcare vouchers costing £100 per week. Joe used the vouchers to provide childcare for his three-year-old daughter at a registered nursery near to his workplace.

(5) During the period 1 January 2014 to 5 April 2014 Joe used Secondly plc's company gym which is only open to employees of the company. The cost to Secondly plc of providing this benefit to Joe was £340.

(6) During the period 1 January 2014 to 5 April 2014 Secondly plc provided Joe with a mobile telephone costing £560. The company paid for all of Joe's business and private telephone calls.

*Required*

(a) Calculate Joe Jones' taxable income for the tax year 2013/14. **(17 marks)**

(b) (i) Briefly explain the basis of calculating Joe Jones' PAYE tax code for the tax year 2013/14, and the purpose of this code. **(2 marks)**

(ii) For each of the PAYE forms P45, P60 and P11D, briefly describe the circumstances in which the form will be completed, state who will provide it, the information to be included, and the dates by which they should have been provided to Joe Jones for the tax year 2013/14. **(6 marks)**

*Note:* your answer to both sub-parts (i) and (ii) should be confined to the details that are relevant to Joe Jones. **(Total = 25 marks)**

# 5 Sam and Kim White (TX 06/08)                                       45 mins

Sam and Kim White are a married couple. Sam was born in 1977 and Kim was born in 1979. The following information is available for the tax year 2013/14:

**Sam White**

(1) Sam is self-employed running a retail clothing shop. His statement of profit or loss for the year ended 5 April 2014 is as follows:

|  | Note | £ | £ |
|---|---|---|---|
| Gross profit | | | 138,823 |
| Depreciation | | 6,123 | |
| Motor expenses | 2 | 8,800 | |
| Patent royalties | 3 | 700 | |
| Professional fees | 4 | 1,860 | |
| Other expenses | 5 | 71,340 | |
| | | | (88,823) |
| Net profit | | | 50,000 |

(2) During the year ended 5 April 2014 Sam drove a total of 25,000 miles, of which 5,000 miles were driven when he visited his suppliers in Europe. The balance of the mileage is 25% for private journeys and 75% for business journeys in the United Kingdom.

(3) During the year ended 5 April 2014 Sam paid patent royalties of £700 (gross) in respect of specialized technology that he uses when altering clothes for customers.

(4) The figure for professional fees consists of £1,050 for legal fees in connection with an action brought against a supplier for breach of contract and £810 for accountancy. Included in the figure for accountancy is £320 in respect of personal capital gains tax advice for the tax year 2012/13.

(5) The figure for other expenses of £71,340 includes £560 for gifts to customers of food hampers costing £35 each and £420 for gifts to customers of pens carrying an advertisement for the clothing shop costing £60 each.

(6) Sam uses one of the eight rooms in the couple's private house as an office for when he works at home. The total running costs of the house for the year ended 5 April 2014 were £5,120. This cost is not included in the statement of profit or loss expenses of £88,823.

(7) Sam uses his private telephone to make business telephone calls. The total cost of the private telephone for the year ended 5 April 2014 was £1,600, and 25% of this related to business telephone calls. The cost of the private telephone is not included in the statement of profit or loss expenses of £88,823.

(8) During the year ended 5 April 2014 Sam took goods out of the clothing shop for his personal use without paying for them and no entry has been made in the accounts to record this. The goods cost £820 (an amount which has been deducted when calculating gross profit), and had a selling price of £1,480.

(9) The tax written down values for capital allowance purposes at 6 April 2013 were as follows:

|  | £ |
| --- | --- |
| Main pool | 18,500 |
| Motor car | 20,200 |

The motor car has $CO_2$ emissions of 175 g/km and is used by Sam.

## Kim White

(1) Kim is employed as a sales person by Sharp-Suit plc, a clothing manufacturing company. During the tax year 2013/14 she was paid a gross annual salary of £23,730.

(2) On 1 June 2013 Sharp-Suit plc provided Kim with an interest free loan of £12,000 so that she could purchase a new motor car.

(3) During the period from 1 June 2013 to 5 April 2014 Kim used her private motor car for business and private purposes. She received no reimbursement from Sharp-Suit plc for any of the expenditure incurred. Kim's mileage during this period included the following:

|  | Miles |
| --- | --- |
| Normal daily travel between home and permanent workplace | 3,400 |
| Travel between permanent workplace and Sharp-Suit plc's customers | 11,200 |
| Travel between home and a temporary workplace for a period of one month | 1,300 |

(4) During the tax year 2013/14 Kim paid interest of £140 (gross) on a personal loan taken out on 1 January 2012 to purchase a laptop computer for use in her employment with Sharp-Suit plc.

## Joint income – Building society deposit account

The couple have savings of £25,000 in a building society deposit account which is in their joint names.

During the tax year 2013/14 Sam and Kim received building society interest of £1,200 in total from this joint account.

This was the actual cash amount received.

*Required*

(a) Calculate Sam's tax adjusted trading profit for the year ended 5 April 2014.

*Note:* your computation should start with net profit for the period of £50,000 and should list all of the items in the statement of profit or loss indicating by the use of a zero (0) any items that do not require adjustment.

**(11 marks)**

(b) Calculate Sam and Kim's respective income tax liabilities for the tax year 2013/14.

*Note:* you should ignore any capital allowances that Kim might be entitled to. **(10 marks)**

(c) Explain to Sam and Kim how their overall income tax liability could be reduced if they were to either:
(i)    transfer their joint building society deposit account into individual savings accounts (ISAs); or

**(2 marks)**

(ii)    transfer their joint building society deposit account into Kim's sole name. **(2 marks)**

**(Total = 25 marks)**

# 6 Sammi Smith (TX 12/10)

**27 mins**

You should assume that today's date is 20 March 2013.

Sammi Smith is a director of Smark Ltd. The company has given her the choice of being provided with a leased company motor car or alternatively being paid additional director's remuneration and then privately leasing the same motor car herself.

### Company motor car

The motor car will be provided throughout the tax year 2013/14, and will be leased by Smark Ltd at an annual cost of £26,380. The motor car will be petrol powered, will have a list price of £80,000, and will have an official $CO_2$ emission rate of 300 grams per kilometre.

The lease payments will cover all the costs of running the motor car except for fuel. Smark Ltd will not provide Sammi with any fuel for private journeys.

### Additional director's remuneration

As an alternative to having a company motor car, Sammi will be paid additional gross director's remuneration of £26,000 during the tax year 2013/14. She will then privately lease the motor car at an annual cost of £26,380.

### Other information

The amount of business journeys that will be driven by Sammi will be immaterial and can therefore be ignored.

Sammi's current level of director's remuneration is over £150,000 which means that she will pay income tax at the additional rate of 45% in 2013/14. Smark Ltd prepares its accounts to 5 April, and pays corporation tax at the main rate of 23%. The lease of the motor car will commence on 6 April 2013.

*Required*

(a) Advise Sammi Smith of the income tax and national insurance contribution implications for the tax year 2013/14 if she (1) is provided with the company motor car, and (2) receives additional director's remuneration of £26,000. **(5 marks)**

(b) Advise Smark Ltd of the corporation tax and national insurance contribution implications for the year ended 5 April 2014 if the company (1) provides Sammi Smith with the company motor car, and (2) pays Sammi Smith additional director's remuneration of £26,000.

*Note:* you should ignore value added tax (VAT). **(5 marks)**

(c) Determine which of the two alternatives is the more beneficial from each of the respective points of view of Sammi Smith and Smark Ltd. **(5 marks)**

**(Total = 15 marks)**

# 7 Edmond Brick (TX 12/07)

**27 mins**

Edmond Brick owns four properties which are let out. The following information relates to the tax year 2013/14:

### Property one

This is a freehold house that qualifies as a trade under the furnished holiday letting rules. The property was purchased on 6 April 2013. During the tax year 2013/14 the property was let for eighteen weeks at £370 per week. Edmond spent £5,700 on furniture and kitchen equipment during April 2013. Due to a serious flood £7,400 was spent on repairs during November 2013. The damage was not covered by insurance. The other expenditure on this property for the tax year 2013/14 amounted to £2,710, and this is all allowable.

### Property two

This is a freehold house that is let out furnished. The property was let throughout the tax year 2013/14 at a monthly rent of £575, payable in advance. During the tax year 2013/14 Edmond paid council tax of £1,200 and insurance of £340 in respect of this property. He claims the wear and tear allowance for this property.

### Property three

This is a freehold house that is let out unfurnished. The property was purchased on 6 April 2013, and it was empty until 30 June 2013. It was then let from 1 July 2013 to 31 January 2014 at a monthly rent of £710, payable in advance. On 31 January 2014 the tenant left owing three months rent which Edmond was unable to recover. The property was not re-let before 5 April 2014. During the tax year 2013/14 Edmond paid insurance of £290 for this property and spent £670 on advertising for tenants. He also paid loan interest of £6,700 in respect of a loan that was taken out to purchase this property.

### Property four

This is a leasehold office building that is let out unfurnished. Edmond pays an annual rent of £6,800 for this property, but did not pay a premium when he acquired it. On 6 April 2013 the property was sub-let to a tenant, with Edmond receiving a premium of £15,000 for the grant of a five-year lease. He also received the annual rent of £4,600 which was payable in advance. During the tax year 2013/14 Edmond paid insurance of £360 in respect of this property.

### Furnished room

During the tax year 2013/14 Edmond rented out one furnished room of his main residence. During the year he received rent of £5,040, and incurred allowable expenditure of £1,140 in respect of the room. Edmond always computes the taxable income for the furnished room on the most favourable basis.

*Required*

(a)     State the tax advantages of property one being treated as a trade under the furnished holiday letting rules.

**(3 marks)**

(b)     Calculate Edmond's furnished holiday letting loss in respect of property one for the tax year 2013/14.

**(3 marks)**

(c)     Calculate Edmond's property business profit in respect of the other three properties and the furnished room for the tax year 2013/14.                                                                                       **(9 marks)**

**(Total = 15 marks)**

# 8 Peter Chic (TX 12/08)                                       45 mins

Peter Chic is employed by Haute-Couture Ltd as a fashion designer. He was born on 10 September 1948. The following information is available for the tax year 2013/14:

### Employment

(1)     During the tax year 2013/14 Peter was paid a gross annual salary of £44,260 by Haute-Couture Ltd. Income tax of £14,270 was deducted from this figure under PAYE.

(2)     In addition to his salary, Peter received two bonus payments from Haute-Couture Ltd during the tax year 2013/14. The first bonus of £4,300 was paid on 30 April 2013 and was in respect of the year ended 31 December 2012. Peter became entitled to this first bonus on 10 April 2013. The second bonus of £3,600 was paid on 31 March 2014 and was in respect of the year ended 31 December 2013. Peter became entitled to this second bonus on 25 March 2014.

(3)     Throughout the tax year 2013/14 Haute-Couture Ltd provided Peter with a diesel powered motor car which has a list price of £22,500. The motor car cost Haute-Couture Ltd £21,200, and it has an official $CO_2$ emission rate of 207 grams per kilometre. Peter made a capital contribution of £2,000 towards the cost of the motor car when it was first provided to him. Haute-Couture Ltd also provided Peter with fuel for private journeys.

(4)     Haute-Couture Ltd has provided Peter with living accommodation since 1 January 2011. The company had purchased the property in 2008 for £160,000, and it was valued at £185,000 on 1 January 2011. Improvements costing £13,000 were made to the property during June 2012. The annual value of the property is £8,225.

(5)     Throughout the tax year 2013/14 Haute-Couture Ltd provided Peter with two mobile telephones. The telephones had each cost £250 when purchased by the company in January 2013.

BPP
LEARNING MEDIA

(6)     On 5 January 2014 Haute-Couture Ltd paid a health club membership fee of £510 for the benefit of Peter.

(7)     During February 2014 Peter spent five nights overseas on company business. Haute-Couture Ltd paid Peter a daily allowance of £10 to cover the cost of personal expenses such as telephone calls to his family.

### Property income

(1)     Peter owns two properties, which are let out. Both properties are freehold houses, with the first property being let out furnished and the second property being let out unfurnished.

(2)     The first property was let from 6 April 2013 to 31 August 2013 at a monthly rent of £500, payable in advance. On 31 August 2013 the tenant left owing two months' rent which Peter was unable to recover. The property was not re-let before 5 April 2014. During March 2014 Peter spent £600 repairing the roof of this property.

(3)     The second property was purchased on 1 July 2013, and was then let from 1 August 2013 to 5 April 2014 at a monthly rent of £820, payable in advance. During July 2013 Peter spent £875 on advertising for tenants. For the period 1 July 2013 to 5 April 2014 he paid loan interest of £1,800 in respect of a loan that was taken out to purchase this property.

(4)     Peter insured both of his rental properties at a total cost of £660 for the year ended 30 June 2013, and £1,080 for the year ended 30 June 2014. The insurance is payable annually in advance.

(5)     Where possible, Peter claims the wear and tear allowance.

### Other information

(1)     During the tax year 2013/14 Peter received building society interest of £1,760 and dividends of £720. These were the actual cash amounts received.

(2)     On 4 August 2013 Peter received a premium bond prize of £100.

(3)     During the tax year 2013/14 Peter made Gift Aid donations totaling £2,400 (net) to national charities.

*Required*

(a)     Calculate the income tax payable by Peter Chic for the tax year 2013/14. You should indicate by the use of zero any items that are non-taxable/exempt from tax.                                    **(21 marks)**

(b)     Calculate the total amount of national insurance contributions that will have been paid by Peter Chic and Haute-Couture Ltd in respect of Peter's earnings and benefits for the tax year 2013/14.        **(4 marks)**

**(Total = 25 marks)**

# 9 Leticia Stone (TX 12/11)                                          27 mins

Leticia Stone owns three properties which are let out. The following information relates to the tax year 2013/14:

### Property one

This is a freehold house that qualifies as a trade under the furnished holiday letting rules. Leticia purchased this property on 1 July 2013 for £282,000. The purchase price included £4,600 for furniture and kitchen equipment.

Leticia borrowed £220,000 to purchase this property. During the period 1 July 2013 to 5 April 2014 she made loan repayments totalling £14,300, of which £12,700 was in respect of loan interest.

The property was let for 22 weeks at £425 per week during the period 1 July 2013 to 5 April 2014.

Due to a fire, £12,200 was spent on replacing the roof of the house during March 2014. Only £10,900 of this was paid for by Leticia's property insurance.

During the tax year 2013/14 Leticia drove 1,170 miles in her motor car in respect of the furnished holiday letting business. She uses HM Revenue and Customs' authorised mileage rates to calculate her expense deduction. The mileage was for the following purposes:

|  | *Miles* |
| --- | --- |
| Purchase of property | 160 |
| Running the business on a weekly basis | 880 |
| Property repairs | 130 |

The other expenditure on this property for the period 1 July 2013 to 5 April 2014 amounted to £3,770, and this is all allowable.

### Property two

This is a leasehold shop that is let out unfurnished. The property was acquired on 1 May 2013 and was immediately let to a tenant, with Leticia receiving a premium of £45,000 for the grant of a five-year lease. During the period 1 May 2013 to 5 April 2014 Leticia received four quarterly rental payments of £2,160 per quarter, payable in advance.

Leticia pays a monthly rent of £1,360 for this property, but did not pay a premium when she acquired it.

### Property three

This is a freehold house that is let out unfurnished. The property was let from 6 April 2013 to 31 January 2014 at a monthly rent of £580. On 31 January 2014 the tenant left, owing three months rent. Leticia recovered two months of the outstanding rent by retaining the tenant's security deposit, but was unable to recover the balance.

On 1 March 2014 a new tenant paid Leticia a security deposit of £1,200, being two months rent, although the new tenancy did not commence until 15 April 2014.

During the tax year 2013/14 Leticia paid loan interest of £9,100 in respect of a loan that was taken out to purchase this property.

### Other expenditure

The other expenditure on properties two and three for the tax year 2013/14 amounted to £36,240, and this is all allowable.

### Furnished room

During the tax year 2013/14 Leticia rented out one furnished room of her main residence. During the year she received rent of £3,170, and incurred allowable expenditure of £4,840 in respect of the room. Leticia always uses the most favourable basis as regards the tax treatment of the furnished room.

*Required*

(a)     Calculate Leticia Stone's property business loss for the tax year 2013/14.

   *Note:* your answer should separately identify the furnished holiday letting loss.          **(13 marks)**

(b)     Advise Leticia Stone as to the possible ways in which her property business loss for the tax year 2013/14 can be relieved.          **(2 marks)**

**(Total = 15 marks)**

# 10 Peach, Plum and Pear (TX 12/08)          18 mins

You are a trainee accountant and your manager has asked for your help regarding three taxpayers who have all made personal pension contributions during the tax year 2013/14.

### Ann Peach

Ann, born in 1984, is self-employed as an estate agent. Her trading profit for the year ended 5 April 2014 was £46,065. Ann made contributions of £49,000 (gross) into a personal pension scheme during the tax year 2013/14. This was the first year that she had been a member of a pension scheme.

**Basil Plum**

Basil, born in 1972, is employed by the Banana Bank plc as a fund manager. During the tax year 2013/14 Basil was paid a gross salary of £330,000. Basil made contributions of £60,000 (gross) into a personal pension scheme during the tax year 2013/14. This was the first year that he had been a member of a pension scheme.

**Chloe Pear**

Chloe, born in 1960, lets out unfurnished property. For the tax year 2013/14 her property business profit was £26,630. Chloe made contributions of £8,200 (gross) into a personal pension scheme during the tax year 2013/14. This was the first year that she had been a member of a pension scheme.

*Required*

For each of the three taxpayers Ann Peach, Basil Plum and Chloe Pear, state, giving reasons, the amount of personal pension contributions that will have qualified for tax relief for the tax year 2013/14, and calculate their income tax liabilities for the year, assuming that they have no other income.

*Note:* marks are allocated: Ann Peach, 3 marks; Basil Plum, 5 marks; and Chloe Pear, 2 marks.       **(10 marks)**

# 11 Na Style (TX 12/09)       45 mins

Na Style (born in 1976) commenced self-employment as a hairdresser on 1 January 2011. She had tax adjusted trading profits of £25,200 for the six-month period ended 30 June 2011 and £21,600 for the year ended 30 June 2012.

The following information is available for the tax year 2013/14:

**Trading profit for the year ended 30 June 2013**

(1)    Na's statement of profit or loss for the year ended 30 June 2013 is as follows:

|  | Note | £ | £ |
|---|---|---|---|
| Income |  |  | 63,635 |
| Expenses |  |  |  |
| Depreciation |  | 2,635 |  |
| Motor expenses | 2 | 2,200 |  |
| Professional fees | 3 | 1,650 |  |
| Property expenses | 4 | 12,900 |  |
| Purchases | 5 | 4,700 |  |
| Other expenses | 6 | 16,550 |  |
|  |  |  | (40,635) |
| Net profit |  |  | 23,000 |

(2)    Na charges all the running expenses for her motor car to the business. During the year ended 30 June 2013 Na drove a total of 8,000 miles, of which 7,000 were for private journeys.

(3)    The figure for professional fees consists of £390 for accountancy and £1,260 for legal fees in connection with the grant of a new five-year lease of parking spaces for customers' motor cars.

(4)    Na lives in a flat that is situated above her hairdressing studio, and one-third of the total property expenses of £12,900 relate to this flat.

(5)    During the year ended 30 June 2013 Na took goods out of the hairdressing business for her personal use without paying for them, and no entry has been made in the accounts to record this. The goods cost £250 (an amount that has been deducted under 'purchases') and had a selling price of £450.

(6)    The figure for other expenses of £16,550 includes £400 for a fine in respect of health and safety regulations, £80 for a donation to a political party and £160 for a trade subscription to the Guild of Small Hairdressers.

(7)    Na uses her private telephone to make business telephone calls. The total cost of the private telephone for the year ended 30 June 2013 was £1,200, and 20% of this related to business telephone calls. The cost of the private telephone is not included in the statement of profit or loss expenses of £40,635.

(8)    Capital allowances for the year ended 30 June 2013 are £810.

**Other information**

(1) During the tax year 2013/14 Na received dividends of £1,080, building society interest of £560, interest of £310 from an individual savings account (ISA), interest of £1,100 on the maturity of a savings certificate from the National Savings & Investments Bank and interest of £1,440 from government stocks (gilts). These were the actual cash amounts received in each case.

(2) Na's payments on account of income tax in respect of the tax year 2013/14 totalled £3,200.

*Required*

(a) Calculate the amount of trading profits that will have been assessed on Na Style for the tax years 2010/11, 2011/12 and 2012/13 respectively, clearly identifying the amount of any overlap profits.          **(5 marks)**

(b) Calculate Na Style's tax adjusted trading profit for the year ended 30 June 2013.

   *Note:* your computation should commence with the net profit figure of £23,000, and should list all of the items referred to in notes (1) to (8) indicating by the use of zero (0) any items that do not require adjustment.          **(8 marks)**

(c) (i) Calculate the income tax payable by Na Style for the tax year 2013/14.

   *Note:* you should indicate by the use of zero any items that are non-taxable/exempt from tax.          **(6 marks)**

   (ii) Calculate Na Style's balancing payment for the tax year 2013/14 and her payments on account for the tax year 2014/15, stating the relevant due dates.

   *Note:* you should ignore national insurance contributions.          **(3 marks)**

(d) Advise Na Style of the consequences of not making the balancing payment for the tax year 2013/14 until 31 May 2015.

   *Note:* your answer should include calculations as appropriate.          **(3 marks)**

   **(Total = 25 marks)**

# 12 Simon House (TX 12/09)          27 mins

On 26 April 2013 Simon House (born in 1980) purchased a derelict freehold house for £127,000. Legal fees of £1,800 were paid in respect of the purchase.

Simon then renovated the house at a cost of £50,600, with the renovation being completed on 6 August 2013. He immediately put the house up for sale, and it was sold on 26 August 2013 for £260,000. Legal fees of £2,600 were paid in respect of the sale.

Simon financed the transaction by a bank loan of £150,000 that was taken out on 26 April 2013 at an annual interest rate of 6%. The bank loan was repaid on 26 August 2013.

Simon had no other income or capital gains for the tax year 2013/14 except as indicated above.

Simon has been advised that whether or not he is treated as carrying on a trade will be determined according to the six following 'badges of trade':

(1) Subject matter of the transaction
(2) Length of ownership
(3) Frequency of similar transactions
(4) Work done on the property
(5) Circumstances responsible for the realisation
(6) Motive

*Required*

(a) Briefly explain the meaning of each of the six 'badges of trade' listed in the question.

   *Note:* you are not expected to quote from decided cases.          **(3 marks)**

(b)  Calculate Simon House's income tax liability and his Class 2 and Class 4 national insurance contributions for the tax year 2013/14, if he is treated as carrying on a trade in respect of the disposal of the freehold house.

**(8 marks)**

(c)  Calculate Simon House's capital gains tax liability for the tax year 2013/14, if he is not treated as carrying on a trade in respect of the disposal of the freehold house.

**(4 marks)**

**(Total = 15 marks)**

# 13 Bayle Defender (TX 06/11)                                 54 mins

(a)  **You should assume that today's date is 20 November 2013.**

Bayle Defender, who was born in 1967, is self-employed as a lawyer. She is also a director of Acquit & Appeal Ltd. The following information is available for the tax year 2013/14:

**Self-employment**

(1)  Bayle's statement of profit or loss for the year ended 30 September 2013 is as follows:

|  | Note | £ | £ |
|---|---|---|---|
| Revenue | 2 |  | 318,987 |
| Expenses |  |  |  |
| Gifts and donations | 3 | 8,680 |  |
| Lease of motor car | 4 | 4,345 |  |
| Professional fees | 5 | 3,240 |  |
| Property expenses | 6 | 46,240 |  |
| Travel expenses | 7 | 16,770 |  |
| Other expenses | 8 | 66,410 |  |
|  |  |  | (145,685) |
| Net profit |  |  | 173,302 |

(2)  Revenue includes £2,800 received during May 2013 in respect of an impairment loss that Bayle had written off when calculating her trading profit for the year ended 30 September 2011.

(3)  Gifts and donations are as follows:

|  | £ |
|---|---|
| Gifts to customers (clocks costing £110 each and displaying Bayle's name) | 3,300 |
| Gifts to customers (bottles of champagne costing £40 each and displaying Bayle's name) | 2,480 |
| Donations to political parties | 2,900 |
|  | 8,680 |

(4)  The lease commenced on 1 May 2013, and is in respect of a motor car with $CO_2$ emissions of 244 grams per kilometre. There is no private use of the motor car.

(5)  The figure of £3,240 for professional fees is in respect of accountancy services, of which £600 is for inheritance tax planning advice.

(6)  Bayle lives in an apartment that is situated above her office, and two-fifths of the total property expenses of £46,240 relate to this apartment.

(7)  The figure of £16,770 for travel expenses includes £520 for parking fines incurred by Bayle.

(8)  The figure for other expenses of £66,410 includes £670 for Bayle's professional subscription to the Law Society, and £960 for her golf club membership fee.

**Director's remuneration**

(9)  Bayle will be paid gross director's remuneration of £42,000 by Acquit & Appeal Ltd during the tax year 2013/14.

(10) In addition to her director's remuneration, Bayle received two bonus payments of £6,000 from Acquit & Appeal Ltd during June 2013, both of which were in respect of the year ended 31 December 2012. Bayle became entitled to the first bonus payment of £6,000 on 10 March 2013, and to the second bonus payment of £6,000 on 20 April 2013.

(11) Acquit & Appeal Ltd deducts PAYE at a flat rate of 45% from all of Bayle's earnings.

**Other information**

(12) During the tax year 2013/14 Bayle will receive dividends of £9,900, interest of £5,240 on the maturity of a savings certificate issued by National Savings & Investments (NS&I), and interest of £3,600 from government stocks (gilts). These are the actual cash amounts that will be received.

(13) Bayle's payments on account of income tax in respect of the tax year 2013/14 will total £50,607.

*Required*

(i) Calculate Bayle Defender's tax adjusted trading profit for the year ended 30 September 2013.

*Note:* your computation should commence with the net profit figure of £173,302, and you should also list all of the items referred to in notes (2) to (8) indicating by the use of zero (0) any items that do not require adjustment. **(6 marks)**

(ii) Calculate the income tax payable by Bayle Defender for the tax year 2013/14. **(8 marks)**

(iii) Calculate the amount of income tax that will be due for payment by Bayle Defender on 31 January 2015, and advise her of the consequences if this amount is not paid until 31 August 2015.

*Note:* you should ignore national insurance contributions. **(5 marks)**

(b) On 1 December 2013 Bayle Defender is planning to bring a newly qualified lawyer, Fyle Guardian, into her business. Fyle will either be taken on as an employee, being paid a gross monthly salary of £3,300, or join Bayle as a partner, receiving a 20% share of the new partnership's profits.

Bayle has forecast that her tax adjusted trading profit will be £216,000 for the year ended 30 September 2014, and £240,000 for the year ended 30 September 2015.

Fyle does not have any other income for the tax year 2013/14.

*Required*

(i) Assuming that Fyle Guardian is employed from 1 December 2013, calculate the total amount of national insurance contributions that will be paid by Bayle Defender and Fyle Guardian, if any, in respect of his earnings for the tax year 2013/14;

Note: You are not expected to calculate the national insurance contributions that will be paid in respect of Bayle Defender's earnings. **(4 marks)**

(ii) Assuming that Fyle Guardian becomes a partner from 1 December 2013:

(1) Calculate his trading income assessments for the tax years 2013/14 and 2014/15.

*Note:* you are not expected to calculate any overlap profits. **(4 marks)**

(2) Calculate the total amount of national insurance contributions that will be paid by Bayle Defender and Fyle Guardian, if any, in respect of his trading income assessment for the tax year 2013/14.

*Note:* you are not expected to calculate the national insurance contributions that will be paid in respect of Bayle Defender's trading income assessment. **(3 marks)**

**(Total = 30 marks)**

# 14 Samantha Fabrique (TX 12/07)

**18 mins**

Samantha Fabrique, who was born in 1971, has been a self-employed manufacturer of clothing since 2001. She has the following gross income and chargeable gains for the tax years 2011/12 to 2014/15:

|  | 2011/12 | 2012/13 | 2013/14 | 2014/15 |
|---|---|---|---|---|
|  | £ | £ | £ | £ |
| Trading profit/(loss) | 7,290 | 42,600 | (79,000) | 14,725 |
| Building society interest | – | 6,100 | 3,800 | 2,130 |
| Chargeable gains/(loss) | 20,900 | 23,300 | (3,400) | 14,000 |

The chargeable gains are stated before taking account of loss relief and the annual exempt amount.

*Required*

(a) State the factors that will influence an individual's choice of loss relief claims. **(3 marks)**

(b) Calculate Samantha's taxable income and taxable gains for each of the tax years 2011/12, 2012/13, 2013/14 and 2014/15 on the assumption that she relieves the trading loss of £79,000 for the tax year 2013/14 on the most favourable basis.

You should assume that the tax rates and allowances for the tax year 2013/14 apply throughout. **(7 marks)**

**(Total = 10 marks)**

# 15 Michael and Sean (TX 06/12)

**27 mins**

(a) The UK Government uses tax policies to encourage certain types of activity.

*Required*

Briefly explain how the UK Government's tax policies encourage:
(i) Individuals to save; **(1 mark)**
(ii) Individuals to support charities; **(1 mark)**
(iii) Entrepreneurs to build their own businesses and to invest in plant and machinery. **(2 marks)**

(b) You are a trainee chartered certified accountant and your manager has asked for your help regarding two taxpayers who have both made trading losses.

**Michael**

Michael (born in 1988) commenced in self-employment on 1 July 2012, preparing accounts to 5 April. His results for the first two periods of trading were as follows:

|  |  | £ |
|---|---|---|
| Nine-month period ended 5 April 2013 | – Trading loss | (25,230) |
| Year ended 5 April 2014 | – Trading profit | 9,065 |

For the tax years 2008/09 to 2010/11 Michael had the following income from employment:

|  | £ |
|---|---|
| 2008/09 | 44,500 |
| 2009/10 | 18,765 |
| 2010/11 | 49,575 |

Michael did not have any income during the period 6 April 2011 to 30 June 2012.

**Sean**

Sean (born in 1976) has been in self-employment since 2003, but ceased trading on 31 December 2013. He has always prepared accounts to 31 December. His results for the final five years of trading were as follows:

|  |  | £ |
|---|---|---:|
| Year ended 31 December 2009 | – Trading profit | 21,300 |
| Year ended 31 December 2010 | – Trading profit | 14,400 |
| Year ended 31 December 2011 | – Trading profit | 18,900 |
| Year ended 31 December 2012 | – Trading profit | 3,700 |
| Year ended 31 December 2013 | – Trading loss | (23,100) |

For each of the tax years 2009/10 to 2013/14 Sean has property business profits of £9,765.

Sean has unused overlap profits brought forward of £3,600.

*Required*

For each of the two taxpayers Michael and Sean, identify the loss relief claims that are available to them, and explain which of the available claims would be the most beneficial.

*Notes*

1.  You should clearly state the amount of any reliefs claimed and the rates of income tax saved. However, you are not expected to calculate any income tax liabilities.

2.  You should assume that the tax rates and allowances for the tax year 2013/14 apply throughout.

3.  The following mark allocation is provided as guidance for this requirement:

    Michael, 5 marks
    Sean, 6 marks

**(11 marks)**

**(Total = 15 marks)**

# 16 Ae, Bee, Cae, and Eu (TX 12/08)    18 mins

(a)  Ae and Bee commenced in partnership on 1 July 2011 preparing accounts to 30 June. Cae joined as a partner on 1 July 2013. Profits have always been shared equally. The partnership's trading profits since the commencement of trading have been as follows:

|  | £ |
|---|---:|
| Year ended 30 June 2012 | 54,000 |
| Year ended 30 June 2013 | 66,000 |
| Year ended 30 June 2014 | 87,000 |

*Required*

Calculate the trading income assessments of Ae, Bee and Cae for each of the tax years 2011/12, 2012/13 and 2013/14. **(5 marks)**

(b)  Eu ceased trading on 30 September 2015, having been self-employed since 1 July 2005.

(1)  Eu's trading profits for the final three periods of trading were as follows:

|  | £ |
|---|---:|
| Year ended 30 June 2014 | 62,775 |
| Year ended 30 June 2015 | 57,600 |
| Three-month period ended 30 September 2015 | 14,400 |

These figures are before taking account of capital allowances.

(2)  The tax written-down value of the capital allowances main pool at 1 July 2013 was £8,750. On 15 September 2015 Eu purchased office furniture for £2,400. All of the items included in the main pool were sold for £5,175 on 30 September 2015.

(3)     Until the final period of trading Eu had always prepared accounts to 30 June. Her overlap profits for the period 1 July 2005 to 5 April 2006 were £19,800.

*Required*

Calculate the amount of trading profits that will have been assessed on Eu for each of the tax years 2014/15 and 2015/16. Assume that the rates of capital allowances in 2013/14 apply in future years.     **(5 marks)**

**(Total = 10 marks)**

# 17 Auy Man and Bim Men (TX 06/10)     54 mins

Auy Man and Bim Men have been in partnership since 6 April 2004 as management consultants. The following information is available for the tax year 2013/14.

### Personal information

Auy was born in 1981. During the tax year 2013/14 she spent 190 days in the United Kingdom.

Bim was born in 1957. During the tax year 2013/14 she spent 150 days in the United Kingdom during which time she lived in her home in the UK. Bim does not have a home outside the UK as she stays in hotels when she is not in the UK.

### Statement of profit or loss for the year ended 5 April 2014

The partnership's summarised statement of profit or loss for the year ended 5 April 2014 is as follows:

|                       | Note | £      | £        |
|-----------------------|------|--------|----------|
| Sales revenue         | 1    |        | 140,762  |
| Expenses              | 2    |        |          |
| Depreciation          |      | 3,400  |          |
| Motor expenses        | 3    | 4,100  |          |
| Other expenses        | 4    | 1,800  |          |
| Wages and salaries    | 5    | 50,900 |          |
|                       |      |        | (60,200) |
| Profit before taxation |     |        | 80,562   |

(1)     The sales figure of £140,762 is exclusive of output value added tax (VAT) of £25,600.

(2)     The expenses figures are exclusive of recoverable input VAT of:

Motor expenses £180

Other expenses £140

(3)     The figure of £4,100 for motor expenses includes £2,600 in respect of the partners' motor cars, with 30% of this amount being in respect of private journeys.

(4)     The figure of £1,800 for other expenses includes £720 for entertaining employees. The remaining expenses are all allowable.

(5)     The figure of £50,900 for wages and salaries includes the annual salary of £4,000 paid to Bim (see the profit sharing note below), and the annual salary of £15,000 paid to Auy's husband, who works part-time for the partnership. Another part-time employee doing the same job is paid a salary of £10,000 per annum.

### Plant and machinery

On 6 April 2013 the tax written down values of the partnership's plant and machinery were as follows:

|                | £      |
|----------------|--------|
| Main pool      | 3,100  |
| Motor car [1]  | 18,000 |
| Motor car [2]  | 14,000 |

The following transactions took place during the year ended 5 April 2014:

|  |  | Cost/(proceeds)<br>£ |
|---|---|---|
| 8 May 2013 | Sold motor car [2] | (13,100) |
| 8 May 2013 | Purchased motor car [3] | 11,600 |
| 21 November 2013 | Purchased motor car [4] | 14,200 |
| 14 January 2014 | Purchased motor car [5] | 10,875 |

Motor car [1] has a $CO_2$ emission rate of 185 grams per kilometre. It is used by Auy and 70% of the mileage is for business journeys.

Motor car [2] had a $CO_2$ emission rate of 115 grams per kilometre. It was used by Bim and 70% of the mileage was for business journeys.

Motor car [3] purchased on 8 May 2013 has a $CO_2$ emission rate of 90 grams per kilometre. It is used by Bim and 70% of the mileage is for business journeys.

Motor car [4] purchased on 21 November 2013 has a $CO_2$ emission rate of 105 grams per kilometre. Motor car [5] purchased on 14 January 2014 has a $CO_2$ emission rate of 200 grams per kilometre. These two motor cars are used by employees of the business.

### Profit sharing

Profits are shared 80% to Auy and 20% to Bim. This is after paying an annual salary of £4,000 to Bim, and interest at the rate of 5% on the partners' capital account balances. The capital account balances are:

|  | £ |
|---|---|
| Auy Man | 56,000 |
| Bim Men | 34,000 |

### VAT

The partnership has been registered for VAT since 6 April 2004. However, the partnership has recently started invoicing for its services on new payment terms, and the partners are concerned about output VAT being accounted for at the appropriate time.

*Required*

(a) Explain why both Auy Man and Bim Men will each be automatically treated for tax purposes as resident in the United Kingdom for tax purposes for the tax year 2013/14. **(2 marks)**

(b) Calculate the partnership's tax adjusted trading profit for the year ended 5 April 2014 and the trading income assessments of Auy Man and Bim Men for the tax year 2013/14.

*Note:* your computation should commence with the profit before taxation figure of £80,562, and should also list all of the items referred to in notes (2) to (5) indicating by the use of zero (0) any items that do not require adjustment. **(15 marks)**

(c) Calculate the Class 4 national insurance contributions payable by Auy Man and Bim Men for the tax year 2013/14. **(3 marks)**

(d) (i) Advise the partnership of the VAT rules that determine the tax point in respect of a supply of services. **(3 marks)**

   (ii) Calculate the amount of VAT paid by the partnership to HM Revenue & Customs throughout the year ended 5 April 2014.

   *Note:* you should ignore the output VAT scale charges due in respect of fuel for private journeys. **(2 marks)**

   (iii) Advise the partnership of the conditions that it must satisfy in order to join and continue to use the VAT flat rate scheme, and calculate the tax saving if the partnership had used the flat rate scheme to calculate the amount of VAT payable throughout the year ended 5 April 2014. The relevant flat rate scheme percentage for the partnership's trade is 14%. **(5 marks)**

**(Total = 30 marks)**

# 18 Flick Pick (TX 06/12)

On 6 April 2013 Flick Pick, born in 1990, commenced employment with 3D Ltd as a film critic. On 1 January 2014 she commenced in partnership with Art Reel running a small cinema, preparing accounts to 30 April. The following information is available for the tax year 2013/14:

## Employment

(1)     During the tax year 2013/14 Flick was paid a gross annual salary of £25,665.

(2)     Throughout the tax year 2013/14 3D Ltd provided Flick with living accommodation. The company had purchased the property in 2004 for £89,000, and it was valued at £144,000 on 6 April 2013. The annual value of the property is £4,600. The property was furnished by 3D Ltd during March 2013 at a cost of £9,400.

## Partnership

(1)     The partnership's tax adjusted trading profit for the four-month period ended 30 April 2014 is £29,700. This figure is before taking account of capital allowances.

(2)     The only item of plant and machinery owned by the partnership is a motor car that cost £18,750 on 1 February 2014. The motor car has a $CO_2$ emission rate of 190 grams per kilometre. It is used by Art, and 40% of the mileage is for private journeys.

(3)     Profits are shared 40% to Flick and 60% to Art. This is after paying an annual salary of £6,000 to Art.

## Property income

(1)     Flick owns a freehold house which is let out furnished. The property was let throughout the tax year 2013/14 at a monthly rent of £660.

(2)     During the tax year 2013/14 Flick paid council tax of £1,320 in respect of the property, and also spent £2,560 on replacing damaged furniture.

(3)     Flick claims the wear and tear allowance.

## Value added tax (VAT)

(1)     The partnership voluntarily registered for VAT on 1 January 2014, and immediately began using the flat rate scheme to calculate the amount of VAT payable. The relevant flat rate scheme percentage for the partnership's trade is 12%.

(2)     For the quarter ended 31 March 2014 the partnership had standard rated sales of £59,700, and these were all made to members of the general public. For the same period standard rated expenses amounted to £27,300. Both figures are stated inclusive of VAT.

(3)     The partnership has two private boxes in its cinema that can be booked on a special basis by privileged customers. Such customers can book the boxes up to two months in advance, at which time they have to pay a 25% deposit. An invoice is then given to the customer on the day of the screening of the film, with payment of the balance of 75% required within seven days. For VAT purposes, the renting out of the cinema boxes is a supply of services.

*Required*

(a)     Calculate Flick Pick's taxable income for the tax year 2013/14.                                                                                  **(12 marks)**

(b)     State what classes of national insurance contribution will be paid in respect of Flick Pick's income for the tax year 2013/14, and in each case who is responsible for paying them.

        *Note:* you are not required to calculate the actual national insurance contributions.                    **(4 marks)**

(c)     List the advantages and disadvantages for the partnership of choosing 30 April as its accounting date rather than 5 April.                                                                                                                        **(4 marks)**

(d) (i) Explain whether or not it was beneficial for the partnership to have used the VAT flat rate scheme for the quarter ended 31 March 2014.

*Notes*

1. Your answer should be supported by appropriate calculations.

2. You should ignore the 1% reduction from the flat rate that is available during the first year of VAT registration. **(3 marks)**

(ii) Explain whether or not it was financially beneficial for the partnership to have voluntarily registered for VAT from 1 January 2014.

*Note:* your answer should be supported by appropriate calculations. **(3 marks)**

(iii) Advise the partnership as to when it should account for output VAT on the renting out of its private boxes to privileged customers. **(4 marks)**

**(Total = 30 marks)**

# 19 Pi Casso (TX 06/08)                                          27 mins

Pi Casso has been a self-employed artist since 1994, making up her accounts to 30 June. Pi's tax liabilities for the tax years 2011/12, 2012/13 and 2013/14 are as follows:

|  | 2011/12 | 2012/13 | 2013/14 |
|---|---|---|---|
|  | £ | £ | £ |
| Income tax liability | 3,240 | 4,100 | 2,730 |
| Class 2 national insurance contributions | 130 | 138 | 140 |
| Class 4 national insurance contributions | 1,240 | 990 | 990 |
| Capital gains tax liability | – | 4,880 | – |

No income tax has been deducted at source.

*Required*

(a) Prepare a schedule showing the payments on account and balancing payments that Pi will have made or will have to make during the period from 1 July 2013 to 31 March 2015 if Pi makes any appropriate claims to reduce her payments on account, clearly identifying the relevant due date of each payment. **(8 marks)**

(b) State the implications if Pi had made a claim to reduce her payments on account for 2013/14 to nil.

**(2 marks)**

(c) Advise Pi of the latest submission date for her 2013/14 self-assessment tax return. **(2 marks)**

(d) State the date by which HMRC will have to notify Pi if they intend to make a compliance check enquiry into her self-assessment tax return for 2013/14 and the possible reasons why such an enquiry would be made.

**(3 marks)**

**(Total = 15 marks)**

# 20 Ernest Vader (TX 06/10)                                      27 mins

**You should assume that today's date is 30 June 2015.**

You are a trainee Chartered Certified Accountant and your firm is dealing with the tax affairs of Ernest Vader.

Ernest's self-assessment tax return for the tax year 2013/14 was submitted to HM Revenue & Customs (HMRC) on 15 May 2014 and Ernest paid the resulting income tax liability by the due date of 31 January 2015. However, you have just discovered that during the tax year 2013/14 Ernest disposed of a freehold property, the details of which were omitted from his self-assessment tax return. The capital gains tax liability in respect of this disposal is £18,000 and this amount has not been paid.

Ernest has suggested that since HMRC's right to make a compliance check enquiry into his self-assessment tax return for the tax year 2013/14 expired on 15 May 2015, no disclosure should be made to HMRC of the capital gain.

*Required*

(a) Briefly explain the difference between tax evasion and tax avoidance, and how HMRC would view the situation if Ernest Vader does not disclose his capital gain. **(3 marks)**

(b) Briefly explain from an ethical viewpoint how your firm should deal with the suggestion from Ernest Vader that no disclosure is made to HMRC of his capital gain. **(4 marks)**

(c) Explain why, even though the right to make a compliance check enquiry has expired, HMRC will still be entitled to raise an assessment should they discover that Ernest Vader has not disclosed his capital gain. **(2 marks)**

(d) Assuming that HMRC discover the capital gain and raise an assessment in respect of Ernest Vader's capital gains tax liability of £18,000 for the tax year 2013/14, and that this amount is then paid on 31 July 2015:

    (i) Calculate the amount of interest that will be payable.

       *Note:* you should assume that the rates for the tax year 2013/14 continue to apply. **(2 marks)**

    (ii) Advise Ernest Vader as to the amount of penalty that is likely to be charged as a result of the failure to notify HMRC and how this could have been reduced if the capital gain had been disclosed. **(4 marks)**

**(Total = 15 marks)**

CHARGEABLE GAINS FOR INDIVIDUALS

Questions 21 to 25 cover the taxation of chargeable gains for individuals, the subject of Part C of the BPP Study Text for Paper F6.

# 21 Aloi, Bon, Cherry and Dinah (TX 06/11)          27 mins

On 15 October 2013 Alphabet Ltd, an unquoted trading company, was taken over by XYZ plc. Prior to the takeover Alphabet Ltd's share capital consisted of 100,000 £1 ordinary shares, and under the terms of the takeover the shareholders received either cash of £6 per share or one £1 ordinary share in XYZ plc for each £1 ordinary share in Alphabet Ltd. The following information is available regarding the four shareholders of Alphabet Ltd:

### Aloi

Aloi has been the managing director of Alphabet Ltd since the company's incorporation on 1 January 2003, and she accepted XYZ plc's cash alternative of £6 per share in respect of her shareholding of 60,000 £1 ordinary shares in Alphabet Ltd. Aloi had originally subscribed for 50,000 shares in Alphabet Ltd on 1 January 2003 at their par value, and purchased a further 10,000 shares on 20 May 2004 for £18,600.

On 6 February 2014 Aloi sold an investment property, and this disposal resulted in a chargeable gain of £22,900.

For the tax year 2013/14 Aloi has taxable income of £60,000.

### Bon

Bon has been the sales director of Alphabet Ltd since 1 February 2013, having not previously been an employee of the company. She accepted XYZ plc's share alternative of one £1 ordinary share for each of her 25,000 £1 ordinary shares in Alphabet Ltd. Bon had purchased her shareholding on 1 February 2013 for £92,200.

On 4 March 2014 Bon made a gift of 10,000 of her £1 ordinary shares in XYZ plc to her brother. On that date the shares were quoted on the Stock Exchange at £7.10 – £7.18. There were no recorded bargains. Holdover relief is not available in respect of this disposal.

For the tax year 2013/14 Bon has taxable income of £55,000.

### Cherry

Cherry has never been an employee or a director of Alphabet Ltd. She accepted XYZ plc's cash alternative of £6 per share in respect of her shareholding of 12,000 £1 ordinary shares in Alphabet Ltd. Cherry had purchased her shareholding on 27 July 2006 for £23,900.

For the tax year 2013/14 Cherry has taxable income of £28,010, and during the year she contributed £3,400 (gross) into a personal pension scheme.

### Dinah

Dinah has been an employee of Alphabet Ltd since 1 May 2004. She accepted XYZ plc's share alternative of one £1 ordinary share for each of her 3,000 £1 ordinary shares in Alphabet Ltd. Dinah had purchased her shareholding on 20 June 2005 for £4,800.

On 13 November 2013 Dinah sold 1,000 of her £1 ordinary shares in XYZ plc for £6,600.

Dinah died on 5 April 2014, and her remaining 2,000 £1 ordinary shares in XYZ plc were inherited by her daughter. On that date these shares were valued at £15,600.

For the tax year 2013/14 Dinah had taxable income of £12,000.

*Required*

(a)     State why Bon, Cherry and Dinah did not meet the qualifying conditions for entrepreneurs' relief as regards their shareholdings in Alphabet Ltd.                                              **(3 marks)**

(b)     Calculate the capital gains tax liabilities of Aloi, Bon, Cherry and Dinah for the tax year 2013/14.

*Note:* in each case, the taxable income is stated after the deduction of the personal allowance.

**(12 marks)**

**(Total = 15 marks)**

# 22 Winston King (TX 06/12)                          27 mins

(a)     'Tax is charged when there is a chargeable disposal of a chargeable asset by a chargeable person.'

*Required*

(i)     State which individuals are subject to capital gains tax on the disposal of chargeable assets situated in the United Kingdom.                                                                                  **(1 mark)**

(ii)    State which companies are subject to corporation tax on the disposal of chargeable assets situated in the United Kingdom.                                                                                  **(1 mark)**

(b)     On 19 May 2013 Winston King disposed of a painting, and this resulted in a chargeable gain of £46,160. For the tax year 2013/14 Winston has taxable income of £19,410 after the deduction of the personal allowance.

Winston is considering the sale of a business that he has run as a sole trader since 1 July 2006. The business will be sold for £260,000, and this figure, along with the respective cost of each asset, is made up as follows:

|  | Sale proceeds £ | Cost £ |
|---|---|---|
| Freehold shop | 140,000 | 80,000 |
| Freehold warehouse | 88,000 | 102,000 |
| Net current assets | 32,000 | 32,000 |
|  | 260,000 |  |

The freehold warehouse has never been used by Winston for business purposes.

*Required*

(i)     Assuming that Winston King does not sell his sole trader business, calculate his capital gains tax liability for the tax year 2013/14.                                                                       **(3 marks)**

(ii)    Calculate Winston King's capital gains tax liability for the tax year 2013/14 if he sold his sole trader business on 25 March 2014.                                                                            **(4 marks)**

(c)     Wiki Ltd sold a freehold warehouse on 3 February 2014 for £312,000. The warehouse had been purchased on 12 November 2003 for £171,000. Wiki Ltd incurred legal fees of £2,200 in connection with the purchase of the warehouse, and legal fees of £3,400 in connection with the disposal. The relevant retail price indexes (RPIs) are as follows:

November 2003                                          182.7
February 2014                                          255.3

Wiki Ltd is unsure as to how to reinvest the proceeds from the sale of the warehouse. The company can either purchase a freehold factory for £166,000, or it can purchase a freehold office building for £296,000. The reinvestment will take place during July 2014.

All of the above buildings have been, or will be, used for business purposes by Wiki Ltd.

*Required*

(i)     Before taking account of any available rollover relief, calculate Wiki Ltd's chargeable gain in respect of the disposal of the warehouse.                                                                 **(3 marks)**

(ii) Advise Wiki Ltd of the rollover relief that will be available in respect of each of the two alternative reinvestments.

*Note:* your answer should include details of the base cost of the replacement asset for each alternative. **(3 marks)**

**(Total = 15 marks)**

# 23 Jorge Jung (TX 12/11)        27 mins

Jorge Jung disposed of the following assets during the tax year 2013/14:

(1) On 30 June 2013 Jorge sold a house for £308,000. The house had been purchased on 1 January 1996 for £98,000, and throughout the 210 months of ownership had been occupied by Jorge as follows:

| **Months** | |
|---|---|
| 16 | Occupied |
| 18 | Unoccupied – Travelling overseas |
| 24 | Unoccupied – Required to work overseas by his employer |
| 11 | Occupied |
| 30 | Unoccupied – Required to work elsewhere in the United Kingdom by his employer |
| 22 | Unoccupied – Travelling overseas |
| 26 | Unoccupied – Required to work elsewhere in the United Kingdom by his employer |
| 17 | Occupied |
| 12 | Unoccupied – Required to work overseas by his employer |
| 13 | Unoccupied – Travelling overseas |
| 21 | Unoccupied – Lived with sister |
| 210 | |

Jorge let the house out during all of the periods when he did not occupy it personally. Throughout the period 1 January 1996 to 30 June 2013 Jorge did not have any other main residence.

(2) On 30 September 2013 Jorge sold a copyright for £8,200. The copyright had been purchased on 1 October 2011 for £7,000 when it had an unexpired life of 10 years.

(3) On 6 October 2013 Jorge sold a painting for £5,400. The painting had been purchased on 18 May 2009 for £2,200.

(4) On 29 October 2013 Jorge sold a motor car for £10,700. The motor car had been purchased on 21 December 2011 for £14,600.

(5) On 3 December 2013 Jorge sold two acres of land for £92,000. Jorge's father-in-law had originally purchased three acres of land on 4 August 2001 for £19,500. The father-in-law died on 17 June 2008, and the land was inherited by Jorge's wife. On that date the three acres of land were valued at £28,600. Jorge's wife transferred the land to him on 14 November 2011. On that date the three acres of land were valued at £39,000. The market value of the unsold acre of land as at 3 December 2013 was £38,000.

(6) On 14 January 2014 Jorge sold 5,000 £1 ordinary shares in Futuristic Ltd, an unquoted trading company, to his sister for £40,000. The market value of the shares on that date was £64,800. The shares had been purchased on 21 March 2009 for £26,300. Jorge and his sister have elected to hold over the gain as a gift of a business asset.

*Required*

Calculate Jorge Jung's taxable gains for the tax year 2013/14. **(15 marks)**

# 24 Nim and Mae (TX 06/09)

**36 mins**

Nim and Mae Lom are a married couple. They disposed of the following assets during the tax year 2013/14:

## Nim Lom

(1) On 20 July 2013 Nim made a gift of 10,000 £1 ordinary shares in Kapook plc to his daughter. On that date the shares were quoted on the Stock Exchange at £3.70 – £3.90, with recorded bargains of £3.60, £3.75 and £3.80. Nim has made the following purchases of shares in Kapook plc:

| | |
|---|---|
| 19 February 2003 | 8,000 shares for £16,200 |
| 6 June 2008 | 6,000 shares for £14,600 |
| 24 July 2013 | 2,000 shares for £5,800 |

Nim's total shareholding was less than 5% of Kapook plc, and so holdover relief is not available.

(2) On 13 August 2013 Nim transferred his entire shareholding of 5,000 £1 ordinary shares in Jooba Ltd, an unquoted company, to his wife, Mae. On that date the shares were valued at £28,200. Nim's shareholding had been purchased on 11 January 2009 for £16,000.

(3) On 26 November 2013 Nim sold an antique table for £8,700. The antique table had been purchased for £5,200.

(4) On 2 April 2014 Nim sold UK Government securities (Gilts) for £12,400. The securities had been purchased for £10,100.

## Mae Lom

(1) On 28 August 2013 Mae sold 2,000 of the 5,000 £1 ordinary shares in Jooba Ltd that had been transferred to her from Nim (see (2) above). The sale proceeds were £30,700. Entrepreneurs' relief is not available in respect of this disposal.

(2) On 30 September 2013 Mae sold a house for £186,000. The house had been purchased on 1 October 2003 for £122,000. Throughout the period of ownership the house was occupied by Nim and Mae as their main residence, but one of the house's eight rooms was always used exclusively for business purposes by Mae. Entrepreneurs' relief is not available in respect of this disposal.

(3) On 30 November 2013 Mae sold a business that she had run as a sole trader since 1 December 2005. The sale resulted in the following capital gains:

| | £ |
|---|---|
| Goodwill | 80,000 |
| Freehold office building | 136,000 |
| Investment property | 34,000 |

The investment property has always been rented out.

Mae claimed entrepreneurs' relief in respect of this disposal. This is her first claim for entrepreneurs' relief.

(4) On 31 March 2014 Mae sold a copyright for £9,600. The copyright had been purchased on 1 April 2009 for £10,000 when it had an unexpired life of 20 years.

## Other information

Nim has unused capital losses of £15,900 brought forward from the tax year 2012/13.

Mae has unused capital losses of £8,500 brought forward from the tax year 2012/13.

Nim has taxable income of £10,000 in tax year 2013/14.

Mae has taxable income of £25,000 in tax year 2013/14.

*Required*

Compute Nim and Mae Lom's respective capital gains tax liabilities, if any, for the tax year 2013/14. In each case, the amount of unused capital losses carried forward to future tax years, if any, should be clearly identified.

**(20 marks)**

# 25 Andrea, Bo and Charles (parts (b), (c) TX 12/09)     27 mins

You are a trainee accountant and your manager has asked for your help regarding three taxpayers who have all disposed of assets during the tax year 2013/14.

(a)  **Andrea Saturn**

On 30 June 2013 Andrea sold her sole trader business, which she had run since 1 July 2006, to an unconnected buyer at market value for £300,000.

This figure, along with the respective cost of each asset, is made up as follows:

|  | Market value £ | Cost £ |
|---|---|---|
| Goodwill | 90,000 | Nil |
| Freehold shop | 165,000 | 180,000 |
| Net current assets | 45,000 | 45,000 |
|  | 300,000 |  |

Andrea also disposed of some quoted shares in the tax year 2013/14, realising a gain of £16,500. She had taxable income (after deducting the personal allowance) of £20,000 in the tax year 2013/14.

*Required*

Calculate Andrea Saturn's capital gains tax liability for the tax year 2013/14.     **(5 marks)**

(b)  **Bo Neptune**

On 31 July 2013 Bo made a gift of his entire holding of 50,000 £1 ordinary shares (a 100% holding) in Botune Ltd, an unquoted trading company, to his son. The market value of the shares on that date was £210,000. The shares had been purchased by Bo on 22 January 2007 for £94,000. Bo and his son have elected to hold over the gain as a gift of a business asset.

*Required*

(i)  Calculate Bo Neptune's chargeable gain, if any, for the tax year 2013/14, and the base cost of his son's 50,000 £1 ordinary shares in Botune Ltd.     **(3 marks)**

(ii)  Explain how your answer to (i) above would have differed if the shares in Botune Ltd had instead been sold to Bo Neptune's son for £160,000.     **(2 marks)**

*Note:* you should ignore entrepreneurs' relief.

(c)  **Charles Orion**

On 30 September 2013 Charles sold a house for £282,000. The house had been purchased on 1 October 2001 for £110,000.

He occupied the house as his main residence from the date of purchase until 31 March 2003. The house was then unoccupied between 1 April 2003 and 31 December 2011 when Charles went to live with his parents due to his father's illness. From 1 January 2012 until 30 September 2013 Charles again occupied the house as his main residence.

Throughout the period 1 October 2001 to 30 September 2013 Charles did not have any other main residence.

*Required*

Calculate Charles Orion's chargeable gain, if any, for the tax year 2013/14.     **(5 marks)**

**(Total = 15 marks)**

INHERITANCE TAX

Questions 26 to 30 cover inheritance tax, the subject of Part E of the BPP Study Text for Paper F6.

# 26 Naomi                                                                     27 mins

On 6 May each year, Naomi gave quoted shares worth £3,000 to her son Marcus.

She also made the following gifts in her lifetime:

| Date | Gift | Donee |
|---|---|---|
| 15 August 2004 | Cash of £313,000 | Trust |
| | | (Trustees paid the IHT due) |
| 12 September 2008 | 3,000 shares in BCD Ltd (see below) | Marcus |
| 14 February 2011 | House valued at £82,000 | Trust |
| | | (Naomi paid the IHT due) |

BCD Ltd was an investment company owned by Naomi and her brother and sister. Naomi had owned 5,000 shares in the company since its incorporation. These shares had a market value of £50,000 immediately before the gift to Marcus. At 12 September 2008, the 3,000 shares gifted had a market value of £18,000 and the remaining 2,000 shares retained by Naomi had a market value of £4,000. In April 2013, Naomi sold the remainder of her shares to an outside investor.

Naomi died on 12 October 2013. At her death, the value of the house gifted in 2011 was £110,000.

Naomi left a net estate of £550,000 at her death. In her Will, she left a legacy of £250,000 to her husband, Robert, and the residue of her estate to Marcus.

*Required*

(a)   Describe the inheritance tax implications of the gifts made during Naomi's lifetime whilst Naomi was still alive and calculate any inheritance due during Naomi's lifetime.                                  **(7 marks)**

   **Nil rate bands for previous years**
   | | |
   |---|---|
   | 2004/05 | £263,000 |
   | 2008/09 | £312,000 |
   | 2010/11 | £325,000 |

(b)   Describe the inheritance tax implications of Naomi's death on the gifts made during her lifetime. Calculate any inheritance tax due on these gifts as the result of her death.                                  **(6 marks)**

(c)   Describe the inheritance tax implications of the terms of Naomi's Will. Compute any inheritance tax due on the death estate.                                                                                  **(2 marks)**

(**Total = 15 marks**)

# 27 Ning Gao (TX 06/12)                                                       27 mins

**You should assume that today's date is 15 March 2014.**

Ning Gao, aged 71, owns the following assets:

(1)   Two properties respectively valued at £674,000 and £442,000. The first property has an outstanding repayment mortgage of £160,000, and the second property has an outstanding endowment mortgage of £92,000.

(2)   Vintage motor cars valued at £172,000.

(3)   Investments in individual savings accounts valued at £47,000, National Savings & Investments savings certificates valued at £36,000, and government stocks (gilts) valued at £69,000.

Ning owes £22,400 in respect of a personal loan from a bank, and she has also verbally promised to pay legal fees of £4,600 incurred by her nephew.

Under the terms of her will Ning has left all of her estate to her children.

Ning's husband died on 12 March 2004, and 70% of his inheritance tax nil rate band was not used.

On 14 August 2003 Ning had made a gift of £100,000 to her daughter, and on 7 November 2013 she made a gift of £220,000 to her son. Both these figures are after deducting all available exemptions.

The nil rate band for the tax year 2003/04 is £255,000.

*Required*

(a)     Advise Ning Gao as to how much nil rate band will be available when calculating the inheritance tax payable in respect of her estate were she to die on 20 March 2014.     **(4 marks)**

(b)     (i)     Calculate the inheritance tax that would be payable in respect of Ning Gao's estate were she to die on 20 March 2014, and state who will be responsible for paying the tax;     **(7 marks)**

        (ii)     Advise Ning Gao as to whether the inheritance tax payable in respect of her estate would alter if she were to live for either another six or another seven years after 20 March 2014, and if so by how much.

        *Note:* you should assume that both the value of Ning Gao's estate and the nil rate band will remain unchanged.     **(2 marks)**

(c)     State what conditions would have to be met if Ning Gao wanted to make gifts out of her income to her children so that these gifts are exempt from inheritance tax.     **(2 marks)**

**(Total = 15 marks)**

# 28 Artem                                                27 mins

Artem died on 15 December 2013. During his lifetime he made the following cash gifts:

| Date | Donee | £ |
|---|---|---|
| 10 December 2005 | Daughter | 65,000 |
| 17 January 2009 | Trust | 336,000 |
| | (Artem paid the IHT) | |
| 15 February 2010 | Nephew | 200 |
| 18 August 2010 | Sister | 49,000 |
| 17 June 2011 | Trust | 103,000 |
| | (Trustees paid the IHT) | |
| 1 August 2012 | Grandson on the occasion of his marriage | 66,000 |
| 5 September 2013 | Wife | 40,000 |

*Required*

(a)     Explain the inheritance tax implications of these gifts during Artem's lifetime and compute any lifetime inheritance tax payable.     **(9 marks)**

        **Nil rate bands**
        | | |
        |---|---|
        | 2005/06 | £275,000 |
        | 2008/09 | £312,000 |
        | 2009/10 onwards | £325,000 |

(b)     Explain the inheritance tax implications of these gifts as a result of Artem's death on 15 December 2013 and compute the resulting inheritance tax payable.     **(6 marks)**

**(Total = 15 marks)**

# 29 Jimmy (TX 06/11)

27 mins

Jimmy died on 14 February 2014. He had made the following gifts during his lifetime:

(1)     On 2 August 2012 Jimmy made a cash gift of £50,000 to his grandson as a wedding gift when he got married.

(2)     On 14 November 2012 Jimmy made a cash gift of £800,000 to a trust. Jimmy paid the inheritance tax arising from this gift.

At the date of his death Jimmy owned the following assets:

(1)     His main residence valued at £260,000.

(2)     Building society deposits of £515,600.

(3)     A life assurance policy on his own life. On 14 February 2014 the policy had an open market value of £182,000, and proceeds of £210,000 were received following Jimmy's death.

The cost of Jimmy's funeral amounted to £5,600.

Under the terms of his will Jimmy left £300,000 to his wife, with the residue of his estate to his daughter.

The nil rate band for the tax year 2012/13 was £325,000.

*Required:*

(a)     Explain why it is important to differentiate between potentially exempt transfers and chargeable lifetime transfers for inheritance tax purposes.                                                          **(2 marks)**

(b)     Calculate the inheritance tax that will be payable as a result of Jimmy's death.                **(12 marks)**

(c)     State by when the personal representatives must pay the inheritance tax due on Jimmy's estate.     **(1 mark)**

**(Total = 15 marks)**

# 30 IHT transfers

27 mins

Describe the inheritance tax effects of the following events:

(a)     Bilal gives his daughter £20,000 on her marriage in June 2013 (his first lifetime gift).     **(3 marks)**

(b)     Sammy gives her grandson and granddaughter £200 each in August 2013.     **(1 mark)**

(c)     Terry sells a vase to his friend Alan for £1,000 which both Terry and Alan believe to be the market value of the vase. The vase is valued by an antiques expert and it is, in fact, worth £20,000.     **(3 marks)**

(d)     Lucas gives 2,000 shares (a 20% holding) in A Ltd, an investment company, to a trust for his children in December 2013. Before the transfer, Lucas owned 8,000 shares in A Ltd (an 80% holding). The following values per share applied at the date of the transfer:

| % shareholding | Value per share |
|---|---|
| | £ |
| 80% | 37.50 |
| 60% | 18.75 |
| 20% | 7.50 |

The only other lifetime gift that Lucas has made is a gift of quoted shares worth £3,000 each year to his son on 30 April each year.     **(3 marks)**

(e)     Donald decides to give his grandson £1,000 each month to pay university living expenses for at least four years. Donald will use income surplus to his living requirements to make these payments.     **(2 marks)**

(f)     Jas wants to make a gift to his son in November 2013. He can either give the son £100,000 in cash or shares in a newly incorporated investment company worth £100,000. These are the only shares Jas owns in the company. Jas thinks that the shares in the company will be worth five times their current value in three years' time. Jas gives £3,000 to his sister in June each year. He made a lifetime chargeable transfer of £500,000 in July 2013.     **(3 marks)**

**(Total = 15 marks)**

**TAXATION OF COMPANIES**

Questions 31 to 48 cover corporate businesses, the subject of Part F of the BPP Study Text for Paper F6.

# 31 Molten-Metal plc (TX 06/11)                     45 mins

Molten-Metal plc is a manufacturer of machine tools. The following information is available for the year ended 31 March 2014:

**Trading profit**

The tax adjusted trading profit for the year ended 31 March 2014 is £2,470,144. This figure is before making any deductions required for:

(1)     Interest payable.
(2)     Capital allowances.
(3)     Any revenue expenditure that may have been debited to the company's capital expenditure account in error.

**Interest payable**

During the year ended 31 March 2014 Molten-Metal plc paid loan stock interest of £22,500. Loan stock interest of £3,700 was accrued at 31 March 2014, with the corresponding accrual at 1 April 2013 being £4,200. The loan is used for trading purposes.

The company also incurred a loan interest expense of £6,800 in respect of a loan that is used for non-trading purposes.

**Capital expenditure account**

The following items of expenditure have been debited to the capital expenditure account during the year ended 31 March 2014:

| | |
|---|---|
| 1 May 2013 | Purchase of a second-hand freehold office building for £428,000. This figure included £31,000 for a ventilation system and £42,000 for a lift. Both the ventilation system and the lift are integral to the office building. During May 2013 Molten-Metal plc spent a further £97,400 on repairs. The office building was not usable until these repairs were carried out, and this fact was represented by a reduced purchase price. |
| 26 June 2013 | Purchase of machinery for £236,600. During June 2013 a further £7,700 was spent on building alterations that were necessary for the installation of the machinery. |
| 8 August 2013 | A payment of £41,200 for the construction of a new decorative wall around the company's premises. |
| 27 August 2013 | Purchase of movable partition walls for £22,900. Molten-Metal plc uses these to divide up its open plan offices, and the partition walls are moved around on a regular basis. |
| 18 November 2013 | Purchase of a motor car costing £24,000. This motor car has a $CO_2$ emission rate of 145 grams per kilometre. This car is used only for business purposes. |
| 28 January 2014 | Purchase of a computer costing £2,500. This computer has an expected working life of 5 years. Any relevant election will be made in respect of this asset. |
| 11 March 2014 | Purchase of two motor cars each costing £17,300. Each motor car has a $CO_2$ emission rate of 110 grams per kilometre. One motor car is used by the factory manager, and 60% of the mileage is for private journeys. The other motor car is used as a pool car. |

**Written down value**

On 1 April 2013 the tax written down value of plant and machinery in Molten-Metal plc's main pool was £87,800.

## Property income

Since 1 February 2014 Molten-Metal plc has let out an unfurnished freehold office building that is surplus to requirements. On that date the tenant paid the company £78,800, consisting of a premium of £68,000 for the grant of a six-year lease, and the advance payment of three months' rent.

## Interest receivable

Molten-Metal plc made a loan for non-trading purposes on 1 August 2013. Loan interest of £9,800 was received on 31 January 2014, and £3,100 was accrued at 31 March 2014.

The company also received bank interest of £2,600 during the year ended 31 March 2014. The bank deposits are held for non-trading purposes.

## Disposal of office building

On 20 May 2013 Molten-Metal plc sold a freehold office building for £872,000. The office building had been purchased on 13 June 2005 for £396,200 (including legal fees). During June 2009 the office building was extended at a cost of £146,000, and during the same month the company spent £48,000 replacing part of the office building roof following a fire. Molten-Metal plc incurred legal fees of £28,400 in connection with the disposal. Indexation factors are as follows:

June 2005 to May 2013      0.300

June 2009 to May 2013      0.171

## Quarterly instalment payments

Molten-Metal plc makes quarterly instalment payments in respect of its corporation tax liability. The first three instalment payments for the year ended 31 March 2014 totalled £381,811.

*Required*

(a)    Calculate Molten-Metal plc's corporation tax liability for the year ended 31 March 2014.

*Note:* you should ignore any chargeable gain arising from the grant of the lease and also ignore rollover relief. **(23 marks)**

(b)    Calculate the final quarterly instalment payment that will have to be made by Molten-Metal plc for the year ended 31 March 2014, and state when this will be due. **(2 marks)**

**(Total = 25 marks)**

# 32 Scuba Ltd (Pilot paper)                                    54 mins

(a)    Scuba Ltd is a manufacturer of diving equipment. The following information is relevant for the year ended 31 March 2014:

### Operating profit

The operating profit is £132,348. The expenses that have been deducted in calculating this figure include the following:

|  | £ |
|---|---|
| Depreciation | 45,200 |
| Entertaining customers | 7,050 |
| Entertaining employees | 2,470 |
| Gifts to customers (diaries costing £25 each displaying Scuba Ltd's name) | 1,350 |
| Gifts to customers (food hampers costing £80 each) | 1,600 |

### Leasehold property

On 1 July 2013 Scuba Ltd acquired a leasehold office building that is used for business purposes. The company paid a premium of £80,000 for the grant of a twenty-year lease.

**Plant and machinery**

On 1 April 2013 the tax written down values of plant and machinery were as follows:

|  | £ |
|---|---|
| Main pool | 47,200 |
| Special rate pool | 22,400 |

The following transactions took place during the year ended 31 March 2014:

|  |  | Cost (Proceeds) £ |
|---|---|---|
| 3 July 2013 | Purchased machinery | 14,020 |
| 29 August 2013 | Purchased a computer | 1,100 |
| 4 October 2013 | Purchased a motor car $CO_2$ emissions 115g/km | 10,400 |
| 18 November 2013 | Purchased machinery | 7,300 |
| 15 February 2014 | Sold a lorry | (12,400) |

The motor car purchased on 4 October 2013 for £10,400 is used by the factory manager, and 40% of the mileage is for private journeys. The lorry sold on 15 February 2014 for £12,400 originally cost £19,800.

**Property income**

Scuba Ltd lets a retail shop that is surplus to requirements. The shop was let until 31 March 2013 but was then empty from 1 April 2013 to 31 July 2013. During this period Scuba Ltd spent £6,200 on decorating the shop, and £1,430 on advertising for new tenants. The shop was let from 1 August 2013 to 31 March 2014 at a quarterly rent of £7,200, payable in advance.

**Interest received**

Interest of £430 was received from HM Revenue & Customs on 28 February 2014 in respect of the overpayment of corporation tax for the year ended 31 March 2013.

**Disposal of warehouse**

Scuba Ltd disposed of a small warehouse on 31 January 2014. The proceeds of sale were £90,000. Scuba Ltd had bought the warehouse for £50,000 on 1 December 2010. Scuba Ltd bought another small warehouse on 1 April 2013 for £60,000.

The relevant retail price indexes (RPIs) are as follows:

| December 2010 | 228.4 |
|---|---|
| January 2014 | 253.4 |

**Qualifying charitable donation**

Scuba Ltd made a qualifying charitable donation of £1,500 on 30 November 2013.

**Other information**

Scuba Ltd has no associated companies, and the company has always had an accounting date of 31 March.

*Required*

(i) Compute Scuba Ltd's tax adjusted trading profit for the year ended 31 March 2014. You should ignore value added tax (VAT).

*Note:* your computation should start with operating profit for the period of £132,348 and should list all of the items in the statement of profit or loss indicating by the use of a zero (0) any items that do not require adjustment. **(11 marks)**

(ii) Compute Scuba Ltd's corporation tax liability for the year ended 31 March 2014. **(8 marks)**

(b) Scuba Ltd registered for value added tax (VAT) on 1 July 2011. The company's VAT returns have been submitted as follows:

| Quarter ended | VAT paid (refunded) £ | Submitted |
|---|---|---|
| 30 September 2011 | 18,600 | One month late |
| 31 December 2011 | 32,200 | One month late |
| 31 March 2012 | 8,800 | On time |
| 30 June 2012 | 3,400 | Two months late |
| 30 September 2012 | (6,500) | One month late |
| 31 December 2012 | 42,100 | On time |
| 31 March 2013 | (2,900) | On time |
| 30 June 2013 | 3,900 | On time |
| 30 September 2013 | 18,800 | On time |
| 31 December 2013 | 57,300 | Two months late |
| 31 March 2014 | 9,600 | On time |

Scuba Ltd always pays any VAT that is due at the same time that the related return is submitted.

During May 2014 Scuba Ltd discovered that a number of errors had been made when completing its VAT return for the quarter ended 31 March 2014. As a result of these errors the company will have to make an additional payment of VAT to HM Revenue & Customs.

*Required*

(i) State, giving appropriate reasons, the default surcharge consequences arising from Scuba Ltd's submission of its VAT returns for the quarter ended 30 September 2011 to the quarter ended 31 March 2014 inclusive. You may assume that Scuba Ltd is not a small business for the purposes of the default surcharge regime. **(8 marks)**

(ii) Explain how Scuba Ltd can voluntarily disclose the errors relating to the VAT return for the quarter ended 31 March 2014. You are not required to discuss penalties for errors. **(3 marks)**

**(Total = 30 marks)**

# 33 Mice Ltd (TX 06/10)                                   45 mins

(a) **You should assume that today's date is 28 March 2014.**

Mice Ltd commenced trading on 1 July 2010 as a manufacturer of computer peripherals. The company prepares accounts to 31 March, and its results for the first three periods of trading were as follows:

| | Period ended 31 March 2011 £ | Year ended 31 March 2012 £ | Year ended 31 March 2013 £ |
|---|---|---|---|
| Trading profit | 83,200 | 24,700 | 51,200 |
| Property business profit | 2,800 | 7,100 | 12,200 |
| Qualifying charitable donations | (1,000) | (1,500) | - |

The following information is available in respect of the year ended 31 March 2014:

**Trading loss**

Mice Ltd expects to make a trading loss of £180,000.

**Property business income**

Mice Ltd lets out three freehold office buildings that are surplus to requirements.

The first office building was let throughout the year ended 31 March 2014 at a quarterly rent of £3,200, payable in advance. Mice Ltd paid business rates of £2,200 and insurance of £460 in respect of this property for the year ended 31 March 2014. During June 2013 Mice Ltd repaired the existing car park for this property at a cost of £1,060 and then subsequently enlarged the car park at a cost of £2,640.

The second office building was let on 1 April 2013 to a tenant, with Mice Ltd receiving a premium of £18,000 for the grant of an eight-year lease. The company also received the annual rent of £6,000 which was payable in advance. Mice Ltd paid insurance of £310 in respect of this property for the year ended 31 March 2014.

The third office building was purchased by Mice Ltd on 1 January 2014 and it will be empty until 31 March 2014. The building is to be let from 1 April 2014 at a monthly rent of £640, and on 15 March 2014 Mice Ltd received three months rent in advance. On 1 January 2014 Mice Ltd paid insurance of £480 in respect of this property for the year ended 31 December 2014, and during February 2014 spent £680 on advertising for tenants. Mice Ltd paid loan interest of £1,800 in respect of the period 1 January 2014 to 31 March 2014 on a loan that was taken out to purchase this property.

**Loan interest received**

On 1 July 2013 Mice Ltd made a loan for non-trading purposes. Loan interest of £6,400 was received on 31 December 2013 and £3,200 will be accrued at 31 March 2014.

**Chargeable gain**

On 20 December 2013 Mice Ltd sold a piece of freehold land which it acquired in August 2010 at a cost of £28,000. The proceeds of sale were £34,474.

The relevant retail price indexes (RPIs) are as follows:

August 2010          224.5
December 2013        254.4

*Required*

(i)     Calculate Mice Ltd's property business profit for the year ended 31 March 2014.          **(8 marks)**

(ii)    Assuming that Mice Ltd claims relief for its trading loss as early as possible, calculate the company's taxable total profits for the nine-month period ended 31 March 2011, and each of the years ended 31 March 2012, 2013 and 2014.          **(7 marks)**

(b)     Mice Ltd has owned 100% of the ordinary share capital of Web-Cam Ltd since it began trading on 1 April 2013. For the three-month period ended 30 June 2013 Web-Cam Ltd made a trading profit of £28,000 and is expected to make a trading profit of £224,000 for the year ended 30 June 2014. Web-Cam Ltd has no other taxable profits or allowable losses.

*Required*

Assuming that Mice Ltd does not make any loss relief claim against its own profits, advise Web-Cam Ltd as to the maximum amount of group relief that can be claimed from Mice Ltd in respect of the trading loss of £180,000 for the year ended 31 March 2014.          **(3 marks)**

(c)     Mice Ltd has surplus funds of £350,000 which it is planning to spend before 31 March 2014. The company will either purchase new equipment for £350,000, or alternatively it will purchase a new ventilation system for £350,000, which will be installed as part of its factory.

*Required*

Explain the maximum amount of capital allowances that Mice Ltd will be able to claim for the year ended 31 March 2014 in respect of each of the two alternative purchases of assets.

*Note:* you are not expected to recalculate Mice Ltd's trading loss for the year ended 31 March 2014, or redo any of the calculations made in parts (a) and (b) above.          **(4 marks)**

(d)     Mice Ltd is planning to pay its managing director a bonus of £40,000 on 31 March 2014. The managing director has already been paid gross director's remuneration of £50,000 during the tax year 2013/14 and the bonus of £40,000 will be paid as additional director's remuneration. The managing director has no other income in 2013/14.

*Required*

Advise the managing director as to the additional amount of income tax and national insurance contributions (both employee's and employer's) that will be payable as a result of the payment of the additional director's remuneration of £40,000.

*Note:* you are not expected to recalculate Mice Ltd's trading loss for the year ended 31 March 2014, or redo any of the calculations made in parts (a) and (b) above. **(3 marks)**

**(Total = 25 marks)**

# 34 Do-Not-Panic Ltd (TX 06/08)    18 mins

Do-Not-Panic Ltd is a company that installs burglar alarms. The company commenced trading on 1 January 2013 and its results for the fifteen-month period ended 31 March 2014 are summarised as follows:

(1) The trading profit as adjusted for tax purposes is £285,000. This figure is before taking account of capital allowances.

(2) Do-Not-Panic Ltd purchased equipment for £5,000 on 20 February 2014.

(3) Do-Not-Panic Ltd bought some loan stock on 1 January 2014 as an investment. Interest of £7,500 was received on 31 March 2014 which was also the amount accrued to that date.

(4) On 21 December 2013 Do-Not-Panic Ltd disposed of some investments and this resulted in a capital loss of £4,250. On 28 March 2014 the company made a further disposal and this resulted in a chargeable gain of £39,000.

(5) Franked investment income of £25,000 was received on 22 February 2014.

Do-Not-Panic Ltd has no associated companies.

*Required*

Calculate Do-Not-Panic Ltd's corporation tax liabilities in respect of the fifteen-month period ended 31 March 2014 and advise the company by when these should be paid. **(10 marks)**

# 35 Quagmire plc (TX 06/10)    18 mins

For the year ended 31 March 2014 Quagmire plc had taxable total profits of £1,200,000 and franked investment income of £200,000. For the year ended 31 March 2013 the company had taxable total profits of £1,600,000 and franked investment income of £120,000.

Quagmire plc's profits accrue evenly throughout the year.

Quagmire plc has one associated company.

*Required*

(a) Explain why Quagmire plc will have been required to make quarterly instalment payments in respect of its corporation tax liability for the year ended 31 March 2014. **(3 marks)**

(b) Calculate Quagmire plc's corporation tax liability for the year ended 31 March 2014 and explain how and when this will have been paid. **(3 marks)**

(c) Explain how your answer to part (b) above would differ if Quagmire plc did not have an associated company. Your answer should include a calculation of the revised corporation tax liability for the year ended 31 March 2014. **(4 marks)**

**(Total = 10 marks)**

# 36 Heavy Ltd and Soft Ltd (TX 06/12)    45 mins

Heavy Ltd runs a music publishing business. On 1 September 2012 Heavy Ltd acquired 100% of the ordinary share capital of Soft Ltd, a company that runs a music recording studio. Neither company has any other associated companies.

Heavy Ltd has prepared accounts for the year ended 31 December 2013, whilst Soft Ltd has prepared accounts for the 16-month period ended 31 December 2013 so as to make its accounting date coterminous with that of Heavy Ltd. The following information is available:

## Heavy Ltd

(1) The operating profit for the year ended 31 December 2013 is £417,340. Depreciation of £12,880 and amortisation of leasehold property of £9,000 (see note (2) below) have been deducted in arriving at this figure.

(2) On 1 January 2013 Heavy Ltd acquired a leasehold office building, paying a premium of £90,000 for the grant of a ten-year lease. The office building was used for business purposes by Heavy Ltd throughout the year ended 31 December 2013.

(3) On 1 January 2013 the tax written down values of Heavy Ltd's plant and machinery were as follows:

|  | £ |
|---|---|
| Main pool | 900 |
| Special rate pool | 21,700 |
| Short life asset (acquired July 2012) | 3,200 |

The following purchases and disposals of plant and machinery took place during the year ended 31 December 2013:

|  |  | Cost/ (proceeds) £ |
|---|---|---|
| 23 March 2013 | Purchased office equipment | 22,400 |
| 15 June 2013 | Sold the short life asset | (4,600) |
| 28 July 2013 | Sold all the items included in the special rate pool | (9,950) |

(4) On 1 August 2013 Heavy Ltd acquired loan stock as an investment. Interest of £8,800 was received on 30 November 2013, and £1,500 was accrued at 31 December 2013.

(5) During the year ended 31 December 2013 Heavy Ltd received bank interest of £1,600, which was the amount accrued during the year. The bank deposits are held for non-trading purposes.

(6) On 31 March 2013 Heavy Ltd repaid a bank loan taken out for non-trading purposes. The final interest payment on that date amounted to £900 which was the amount accrued since 1 January 2013.

(7) On 18 October 2013 Heavy Ltd sold a freehold office building to Soft Ltd for £113,600. The indexed cost of the office building on that date was £102,800.

(8) During the year ended 31 December 2013 Heavy Ltd received the following dividends:

|  | £ |
|---|---|
| *Company paying the dividend* |  |
| An unconnected company | 27,000 |
| Soft Ltd | 6,300 |

## Soft Ltd

(1) The tax adjusted trading profit for the 16-month period ended 31 December 2013 is £120,200. This figure is before taking account of capital allowances.

(2) On 1 September 2012 the tax written down value of Soft Ltd's plant and machinery in the main pool was £24,000. On 15 December 2013 Soft Ltd sold an item of plant for £3,900. The plant had originally cost £5,200.

(3) On 4 August 2013 Soft Ltd disposed of some investments and this resulted in a chargeable gain of £16,170. On 3 September 2013 the company made a further disposal and this resulted in a capital loss of £2,900.

## Required

(a) Calculate Heavy Ltd's corporation tax liability for the year ended 31 December 2013. **(18 marks)**

(b) Calculate Soft Ltd's corporation tax liabilities in respect of the 16-month period ended 31 December 2013.
**(7 marks)**

1   The annual investment allowance has been £250,000 since 1 January 2013.
2   The rates of writing down allowances for Financial Year 2012 were the same as for Financial Year 2013.

**(Total = 25 marks)**

# 37 Thai Curry Ltd (BTX)                    47 mins

Thai Curry Ltd is a manufacturer of ready to cook food. The following information is available in respect of the year ended 31 March 2014:

## Trading loss

The trading loss is £55,036. This figure is before taking account of capital allowances.

## Plant and machinery

On 1 April 2013 the tax written down values of plant and machinery were as follows:

|  | £ |
| --- | --- |
| Main pool | 10,600 |
| Special rate pool | 16,400 |

The special rate pool consists of one motor car which has $CO_2$ emissions of 180 g/km and was acquired in July 2011.

The following transactions took place during the year ended 31 March 2014:

|  |  | Cost/ (Proceeds) £ |
| --- | --- | --- |
| 1 May 2013 | Sold equipment | (12,800) |
| 8 July 2013 | Purchased equipment | 9,460 |
| 14 July 2013 | Sold the special rate pool motor car | (9,700) |
| 26 August 2013 | Purchased motor car (1) $CO_2$ emissions 119g/km | 15,800 |
| 19 November 2013 | Purchased motor car (2) $CO_2$ emissions 93g/km | 9,700 |
| 20 March 2014 | Purchased a new freehold office building | 220,000 |

The equipment sold on 1 May 2013 for £12,800 originally cost £27,400.

The cost of the new freehold office building purchased on 20 March 2014 included £5,500 for the central heating system, £2,200 for sprinkler equipment and the fire alarm system and £5,050 for the ventilation system.

## Income from property

Thai Curry Ltd lets out two warehouses that are surplus to requirements.

The first warehouse was let from 1 April 2013 until 30 November 2013 at a monthly rent of £2,200. On that date the tenant left owing two months rent which Thai Curry Ltd was not able to recover. During February 2014 £8,800 was spent on painting the warehouse. The warehouse was not re-let until 1 April 2014.

The second warehouse was empty from 1 April 2013 until 31 July 2013, but was let from 1 August 2013. On that date Thai Curry Ltd received a premium of £60,000 for the grant of a four-year lease, and the annual rent of £18,000 which is payable in advance.

## Loan interest received

Loan interest of £8,000 was received on 30 September 2013 relating to the period from 1 April 2013 and £3,500 was accrued at 31 March 2014. The loan was made for non-trading purposes.

## Dividends received

During the year ended 31 March 2014 Thai Curry Ltd received dividends of £36,000 from African Spice plc, an unconnected company. This figure was the actual cash amount received.

## Profit on disposal of shares

On 28 July 2013 Thai Curry Ltd sold 10,000 £1 ordinary shares in investment company African Spice plc, making a capital gain of £152,300 on the disposal.

**Other information**

Thai Curry Ltd has three associated companies.

*Required*

(a) Calculate Thai Curry Ltd's tax adjusted trading loss for the year ended 31 March 2014. You should assume that the company claims the maximum available capital allowances. **(9 marks)**

(b) Assuming that Thai Curry Ltd claims relief for its trading loss against total profits, calculate the company's corporation tax liability for the year ended 31 March 2014. **(11 marks)**

(c) (i) State the date by which Thai Curry Ltd's self-assessment corporation tax return for the year ended 31 March 2014 should be submitted, and advise the company of the penalties that will be due if the return is not submitted until 30 November 2015. **(3 marks)**

   (ii) State the date by which Thai Curry Ltd's corporation tax liability for the year ended 31 March 2014 should be paid, and advise the company of the interest that will be due if the liability is not paid until 30 November 2015. **(3 marks)**

**(Total = 26 marks)**

# 38 Hawk Ltd (TX 12/08)　　　　　　　　　　　　　　36 mins

Hawk Ltd sold the following assets during the year ended 31 March 2014:

(1) On 30 April 2013 a freehold office building was sold for £275,000. The office building had been purchased on 2 July 2004 for £81,000, and had been extended at a cost of £43,000 during May 2006. Hawk Ltd incurred legal fees of £3,200 in connection with the purchase of the office building, and legal fees of £5,726 in connection with the disposal. The office building has always been used by Hawk Ltd for business purposes. The relevant retail prices indexes (RPIs) are as follows:

| | |
|---|---|
| July 2004 | 186.8 |
| May 2006 | 197.7 |
| April 2013 | 250.0 |

(2) On 29 August 2013 5,000 £1 ordinary shares in Albatross plc were sold for £42,500. Hawk Ltd had purchased 6,000 shares in Albatross plc on 1 August 2013 for £18,600, and purchased a further 2,000 shares on 17 August 2013 for £9,400.

(3) On 27 October 2013 10,000 £1 preference shares in Cuckoo plc were sold for £32,000. Hawk Ltd had originally purchased 5,000 £1 ordinary shares in Cuckoo plc on 2 October 2013 for £60,000. On 18 October 2013 Cuckoo plc had a reorganisation whereby each £1 ordinary share was exchanged for three new £1 ordinary shares and two £1 preference shares. Immediately after the reorganisation each new £1 ordinary share was quoted at £4.50 and each £1 preference share was quoted at £2.25.

(4) On 28 March 2014 two acres of land were sold for £120,000. Hawk Ltd had originally purchased three acres of land on 1 March 2014 for £203,500. The market value of the unsold acre of land as at 28 March 2014 was £65,000. The land has never been used by Hawk Ltd for business purposes.

Hawk Ltd's only other income for the year ended 31 March 2014 was a trading profit of £125,000. Hawk Ltd does not have any associated companies.

*Required*

(a) Calculate Hawk Ltd's corporation tax liability for the year ended 31 March 2014. **(16 marks)**

(b)   Advise Hawk Ltd of:

(i)    The minimum amount that will have to be reinvested in qualifying replacement business assets in order for the company to claim the maximum possible amount of rollover relief in respect of its chargeable gains for the year ended 31 March 2014.                                                                                    **(2 marks)**

(ii)   The period during which the reinvestment must take place.                                                       **(1 mark)**

(iii)  The amount of corporation tax that will be deferred if the maximum possible amount of rollover relief is claimed for the year ended 31 March 2014.                                                                                  **(1 mark)**

**(Total = 20 marks)**

# 39 Problematic Ltd (TX 06/10)                                                                                    36 mins

Problematic Ltd sold the following assets during the year ended 31 March 2014:

(1)   On 14 June 2013 16,000 £1 ordinary shares in Easy plc were sold for £54,400. Problematic Ltd had originally purchased 15,000 shares in Easy plc on 26 June 2005 for £12,600. On 28 September 2008 Easy plc made a 1 for 3 rights issue. Problematic Ltd took up its allocation under the rights issue in full, paying £2.20 for each new share issued. The relevant retail prices indexes (RPIs) are as follows:

| | |
|---|---|
| June 2005 | 192.2 |
| September 2008 | 218.4 |
| June 2013 | 249.3 |

(2)   On 1 October 2013 an office building owned by Problematic Ltd was damaged by a fire. The indexed cost of the office building on that date was £169,000. The company received insurance proceeds of £36,000 on 10 October 2013 and spent a total of £41,000 during October 2013 on restoring the office building. Problematic Ltd has made a claim to defer the gain arising from the receipt of the insurance proceeds. The office building has never been used for business purposes.

(3)   On 28 January 2014 a freehold factory was sold for £171,000. The indexed cost of the factory on that date was £127,000. Problematic Ltd has made a claim to holdover the gain on the factory against the cost of a replacement leasehold factory under the rollover relief (replacement of business assets) rules. The leasehold factory has a lease period of 20 years, and was purchased on 10 December 2013 for £154,800. The two factory buildings have always been used entirely for business purposes.

(4)   On 20 February 2014 an acre of land was sold for £130,000. Problematic Ltd had originally purchased four acres of land, and the indexed cost of the four acres on 20 February 2014 was £300,000. The market value of the unsold three acres of land as at 20 February 2014 was £350,000. Problematic Ltd incurred legal fees of £3,200 in connection with the disposal. The land has never been used for business purposes.

Problematic Ltd's only other income for the year ended 31 March 2014 is a tax adjusted trading profit of £106,970.

*Required*

(a)   Calculate Problematic Ltd's taxable total profits for the year ended 31 March 2014.                          **(16 marks)**

(b)   Advise Problematic Ltd of the carried forward indexed base costs for capital gains purposes of any assets included in (1) to (4) above that are still retained at 31 March 2014.                                                  **(4 marks)**

**(Total = 20 marks)**

# 40 Lim Lam (TX 12/10)

**27 mins**

Lim Lam is the controlling shareholder and managing director of Mal-Mil Ltd, an unquoted trading company that provides support services to the oil industry.

## Lim Lam

Lim disposed of the following assets during the tax year 2013/14:

(1)     On 8 July 2013 Lim sold five acres of land to Mal-Mil Ltd for £260,000, which was the market value of the land on that date. The land had been inherited by Lim upon the death of her mother on 17 January 2007, when the land was valued at £182,000. Lim's mother had originally purchased the land for £137,000.

(2)     On 13 August 2013 Lim made a gift of 5,000 £1 ordinary shares in Oily plc, a quoted trading company, to her sister. On that date the shares were quoted on the Stock Exchange at £7.40–£7.56, with recorded bargains of £7.36, £7.38 and £7.60. Lim had originally purchased her 5,000 shares in the company on 23 November 2007 for £15,925.

Entrepreneurs' relief and holdover relief are not available in respect of this disposal.

(3)     On 22 March 2014 Lim sold 40,000 £1 ordinary shares in Mal-Mil Ltd for £280,000. She had originally purchased 125,000 shares in the company on 8 June 2006 for £142,000, and had purchased a further 60,000 shares on 23 May 2008 for £117,000. Mal-Mil Ltd has a total share capital of 250,000 £1 ordinary shares.

Entrepreneurs' relief is available in respect of this disposal. Lim has made no previous disposals eligible for entrepreneurs' relief.

Lim had taxable income of £28,000 in 2013/14.

## Mal-Mil Ltd

On 20 December 2013 Mal-Mil Ltd sold two of the five acres of land that had been purchased from Lim on 8 July 2013. The sale proceeds were £162,000 and legal fees of £3,800 were incurred in connection with the disposal. The market value of the unsold three acres of land as at 20 December 2013 was £254,000. During July 2013 Mal-Mil Ltd had spent £31,200 levelling the five acres of land. The relevant retail price indexes (RPIs) are as follows:

July 2013          249.6
December 2013      254.4

Mal-Mil Ltd's only other income for the year ended 31 December 2013 was a trading profit of £163,000.

*Required*

(a)     Calculate Lim Lam's capital gains tax liability for the tax year 2013/14, and state by when this should be paid.

**(8 marks)**

(b)     Calculate Mal-Mil Ltd's corporation tax liability for the year ended 31 December 2013, and state by when this should be paid.

**(7 marks)**

**(Total = 15 marks)**

# 41 Starfish Ltd (TX 12/11)

**54 mins**

Starfish Ltd, a retailer of scuba diving equipment, was incorporated on 15 October 2009, and commenced trading on 1 December 2009. The company initially prepared accounts to 31 March, but changed its accounting date to 31 December by preparing accounts for the nine-month period ended 31 December 2013. Starfish Ltd ceased trading on 31 March 2014, and a resolution was subsequently passed to commence winding up procedures.

Starfish Ltd's results for each of its periods of account up to 31 December 2013 are as follows:

| | Tax adjusted trading profit/(loss) | Bank interest | Qualifying charitable donations |
|---|---|---|---|
| | £ | £ | £ |
| Four-month period ended 31 March 2010 | (12,600) | 600 | (800) |
| Year ended 31 March 2011 | 64,200 | 1,400 | (1,000) |
| Year ended 31 March 2012 | 53,900 | 1,700 | (900) |
| Year ended 31 March 2013 | 14,700 | 0 | (700) |
| Nine-month period ended 31 December 2013 | 49,900 | 0 | (600) |

The company's summarised statement of profit or loss for its final three-month period of trading ended 31 March 2014 is as follows:

| | Note | £ | £ |
|---|---|---|---|
| Gross profit | | | 16,100 |
| Expenses | | | |
| Depreciation | | 25,030 | |
| Donations | 1 | 1,650 | |
| Impairment loss | 2 | 2,000 | |
| Legal fees | 3 | 9,370 | |
| Other expenses | 4 | 168,050 | |
| | | | (206,100) |
| Loss before taxation | | | (190,000) |

*Note 1 – Donations*

Donations were made to the following:

| | £ |
|---|---|
| A political party | 300 |
| A charity (not qualifying charitable donation) | 600 |
| A national charity (qualifying charitable donation) | 750 |
| | 1,650 |

*Note 2 – Impairment loss*

On 31 March 2014 Starfish Ltd wrote off an impairment loss of £2,000 in respect of a trade debt.

*Note 3 – Legal fees*

Legal fees were in connection with the following:

| | £ |
|---|---|
| Defence of the company's internet domain name | 3,490 |
| Court action for a misleading advertisement | 2,020 |
| Issue of 6% loan notes that was subsequently cancelled | 3,860 |
| | 9,370 |

*Note 4 – Other expenses*

Other expenses are as follows:

| | £ |
|---|---|
| Entertaining customers | 3,600 |
| Entertaining employees | 1,840 |
| Counselling services provided to employees who were made redundant | 8,400 |
| Balance of expenditure (all allowable) | 154,210 |
| | 168,050 |

*Note 5 – Plant and machinery*

On 1 January 2014 the tax written down values of the company's plant and machinery were as follows:

|  | £ |
|---|---|
| Main pool | 23,600 |
| Special rate pool | 13,200 |

The special rate pool consists of a motor car that was purchased on 18 June 2010, and which has $CO_2$ emissions of 190 grams per kilometre.

On 10 January 2014 Starfish Ltd purchased a laptop computer for £3,120. This figure is inclusive of value added tax (VAT).

On 31 March 2014 the company sold all of the items included in the main pool for £31,200, the laptop computer for £1,800, and the motor car for £9,600. These figures are inclusive of VAT where applicable. None of the items included in the main pool was sold for more than its original cost, and all of the items were standard rated.

*Note 6 – Final VAT return*

Starfish Ltd deregistered from VAT on 31 March 2014. The following information relates to the company's final VAT return for the quarter ended 31 March 2014:

(i)   Cash sales revenue amounted to £41,160, of which £38,520 was in respect of standard rated sales and £2,640 was in respect of zero-rated sales.

(ii)  Sales invoices totalling £2,000 were issued in respect of credit sales revenue. This figure is exclusive of VAT, and the sales were all standard rated. Starfish Ltd offered all of its credit sale customers a 4% discount for payment within 14 days of the date of the sales invoice, and 60% of the customers paid within this period.

(iii) In addition to the above sales revenue, Starfish Ltd sold its remaining inventory of scuba diving equipment on 31 March 2014 for £28,800. The inventory had originally cost £32,400.

(iv)  There were no purchases of inventory during the period.

(v)   Standard rated expenses amounted to £69,960, of which £4,320 was in respect of entertaining UK customers.

(vi)  The impairment loss which Starfish Ltd wrote off on 31 March 2014 (as per note (2) above) was in respect of a sales invoice (exclusive of VAT) that was due for payment on 8 August 2013. Output VAT of £384 was originally paid in respect of this sale.

(vii) Purchases and sales of non-current assets during the period are as per note (5) above.

Unless otherwise stated, all of the above figures are inclusive of VAT where applicable.

Starfish Ltd did not use the cash accounting scheme for VAT.

*Required*

(a)   State when an accounting period starts and when an accounting period finishes for corporation tax purposes.                                                                                                                          **(4 marks)**

(b)   Calculate Starfish Ltd's tax adjusted trading loss for the three-month period ended 31 March 2014.

      *Notes:*

      1.   Your computation should commence with the loss before taxation figure of £190,000, and should also list all of the items referred to in notes (1) to (4) indicating by the use of zero (0) any items that do not require adjustment.

      2.   In answering this part of the question you are not expected to take account of any of the information provided in note (6) above regarding the final VAT return.                    **(12 marks)**

(c)   Assuming that Starfish Ltd claims relief for its trading losses on the most beneficial basis, calculate the company's taxable total profits for the four-month period ended 31 March 2010, the years ended 31 March 2011, 2012 and 2013 and the nine-month period ended 31 December 2013.                    **(5 marks)**

(d)   (i)   Calculate the amount of VAT payable by Starfish Ltd in respect of its final VAT return for the quarter ended 31 March 2014.

Notes:

1. In answering this part of the question you are not expected to take account of any of the information provided in notes (1), (3) or (4) above.

2. You should ignore the output VAT scale charge due in respect of fuel for private journeys.

(7 marks)

(ii) Explain, with supporting calculations, how your answer to part (d)(i) above would differ if Starfish Ltd had instead sold its entire business as a going concern to a single VAT registered purchaser.

(2 marks)

(Total = 30 marks)

# 42 Volatile Ltd (TX 12/09)                     18 mins

Volatile Ltd commenced trading on 1 July 2009. The company's results for its first five periods of trading are as follows:

|  | Period ended 31 December 2009 | Year ended 31 December 2010 | Year ended 31 December 2011 | Period ended 30 September 2012 | Year ended 30 September 2013 |
|---|---|---|---|---|---|
|  | £ | £ | £ | £ | £ |
| Trading profit/(loss) | 44,000 | (73,800) | 95,200 | 78,700 | (186,800) |
| Property business profit | 9,400 | 6,600 | 6,500 | – | – |
| Chargeable gains | 5,100 | – | – | 9,700 | – |
| Qualifying charitable donations | (800) | (1,000) | (1,200) | – | – |

Required

(a) State the factors that will influence a company's choice of loss relief claims.

Note: you are not expected to consider group relief.                     (3 marks)

(b) Assuming that Volatile Ltd claims relief for its trading losses as early as possible, calculate the company's taxable total profits for the six-month period ended 31 December 2009, each of the years ended 31 December 2010 and 2011 and the nine-month period ended 30 September 2012. Your answer should also clearly identify the amount of any unrelieved trading losses as at 30 September 2013.                     (7 marks)

(Total = 10 marks)

# 43 Jogger Ltd (TX 12/08)                     54 mins

(a) Jogger Ltd is a manufacturer of running shoes. The company's summarised statement of profit or loss for the year ended 31 March 2014 is as follows:

|  | Note | £ | £ |
|---|---|---|---|
| Operating profit | 1 |  | 143,482 |
| Income from investments |  |  |  |
| Bank interest | 3 | 8,460 |  |
| Loan interest | 4 | 24,600 |  |
| Income from property | 5 | 144,000 |  |
| Dividends | 6 | 45,000 |  |
|  |  |  | 222,060 |
| Profit from sale of non-current assets |  |  |  |
| Disposal of shares | 7 |  | 102,340 |
| Profit before taxation |  |  | 467,882 |

Note 1 – Operating profit

Depreciation of £58,840 has been deducted in arriving at the operating profit of £143,482.

*Note 2 – Plant and machinery*

On 1 April 2013 the tax written down values of plant and machinery were as follows:

|  | £ |
|---|---|
| Main pool | 26,600 |
| Special rate pool | 18,800 |

The following transactions took place during the year ended 31 March 2014:

|  |  | Cost/(proceeds)<br>£ |
|---|---|---|
| 20 July 2013 | Sold a special rate pool motor car | (11,700) |
| 31 July 2013 | Purchased motor car<br>$CO_2$ emissions 105g/km | 11,800 |
| 30 September 2013 | Purchased machinery | 250,000 |
| 15 December 2013 | Purchased computer system | 12,500 |
| 14 March 2014 | Sold a lorry | (8,600) |

The motor car sold on 20 July 2013 for £11,700 originally cost more than this amount. The computer system purchased on 15 December 2013 has a predicted working life of six years and any relevant election has been made. The lorry sold on 14 March 2014 for £8,600 originally cost £16,600.

*Note 3 – Bank interest received*

The bank interest was received on 31 March 2014. The bank deposits are held for non-trading purposes.

*Note 4 – Loan interest receivable*

The loan was made for non-trading purposes on 1 July 2013. Loan interest of £16,400 was received on 31 December 2013, and interest of £8,200 was accrued at 31 March 2014.

*Note 5 – Income from property*

Jogger Ltd lets out an unfurnished freehold office building that is surplus to requirements. The office building was let throughout the year ended 31 March 2014. On 1 April 2013 Jogger Ltd received a premium of £100,000 for the grant of a ten-year lease, and the annual rent of £44,000 which is payable in advance.

*Note 6 – Dividends received*

During the year ended 31 March 2014 Jogger Ltd received dividends of £45,000 from Sprinter plc, an unconnected company. This figure was the actual cash amount received.

*Note 7 – Profit on disposal of shares*

The profit on disposal of shares is in respect of a shareholding that was sold on 5 December 2013. The disposal resulted in a chargeable gain of £98,300. This figure is after taking account of indexation.

*Note 8 – Other information*

Jogger Ltd has two associated companies.

*Required*

Ignore VAT throughout part (a).

(i)    Calculate Jogger Ltd's tax adjusted trading loss for the year ended 31 March 2014.

*Notes:* (1)    Your computation should start with the operating profit of £143,482.
         (2)    You should assume that the company claims the maximum available capital allowances.

**(7 marks)**

(ii)   Assuming that Jogger Ltd claims relief for its trading loss against total profits, calculate the company's corporation tax liability for the year ended 31 March 2014.          **(8 marks)**

(iii)  State the date by which Jogger Ltd's self-assessment corporation tax return for the year ended 31 March 2014 should be submitted, and advise the company of the penalties that will be due if the return is submitted eight months late.

*Note:* you should assume that the company pays its corporation tax liability at the same time that the self-assessment tax return is submitted. **(4 marks)**

(b) *Note:* in answering this part of the question you are not expected to take account of any of the information provided in part (a) above.

Jogger Ltd has been registered for value added tax (VAT) since 1 April 2007. From that date until 30 June 2012 the company's VAT returns were all submitted on time. Since 1 July 2012 the company's VAT returns have been submitted as follows:

| Quarter ended | VAT paid | Submitted |
|---|---|---|
| | £ | |
| 30 September 2012 | 42,700 | One month late |
| 31 December 2012 | 41,200 | On time |
| 31 March 2013 | 38,900 | One month late |
| 30 June 2013 | 28,300 | On time |
| 30 September 2013 | 49,100 | On time |
| 31 December 2013 | 63,800 | On time |
| 31 March 2014 | 89,100 | Two months late |

Jogger Ltd always pays any VAT that is due at the same time as the related return is submitted.

*Required*

(i) State, giving appropriate reasons, the default surcharge consequences arising from Jogger Ltd's submission of its VAT returns for the quarter ended 30 September 2012 to the quarter ended 31 March 2014 inclusive, at the times stated. You may assume that Scuba Ltd is not a small business for the purposes of the default surcharge regime. **(6 marks)**

(ii) Advise Jogger Ltd why it might be beneficial to use the VAT annual accounting scheme, and state the conditions that it will have to satisfy before being permitted to do so. **(5 marks)**

**(Total = 30 marks)**

# 44 Black Ltd, Cherry Grey and Blu Reddy (parts (a),(c) TX 12/11) 27 mins

(a) Black Ltd owns 100% of the ordinary share capital of White Ltd. The results of Black Ltd and White Ltd for the year ended 31 March 2014 are as follows:

| | Black Ltd | White Ltd |
|---|---|---|
| | £ | £ |
| Trading profit/(loss) | 396,800 | (351,300) |
| Property business profit | 21,100 | 26,700 |
| Capital loss | – | (17,200) |
| Qualifying charitable donations | (4,400) | (5,600) |

As at 1 April 2013 Black Ltd had unused trading losses of £57,900, and unused capital losses of £12,600, whilst White Ltd had unused trading losses of £21,800.

*Required*

Advise Black Ltd as to the maximum amount of group relief that can be claimed from White Ltd in respect of its losses for the year ended 31 March 2014. Clearly identify any losses that cannot be surrendered by White Ltd as part of the group relief claim.

*Note:* you are not expected to calculate either company's corporation tax liability. **(5 marks)**

(b)     Cherry Grey was not resident in the United Kingdom in any tax year before 2013/14, but she spent 92 days in the UK in the tax year 2012/13.

Cherry married Rob (a UK resident) on 15 March 2013. On 6 April 2013, Cherry and Rob bought a house in the UK. Cherry spent 95 days in the UK during the tax year 2013/14, during which time she lived in the UK house. Cherry also has an overseas house. Cherry did not work in 2013/14.

*Required*

Explain why Cherry is UK resident for tax purposes for the tax year 2013/14.     **(4 marks)**

(c)     On 15 January 2014 Blu Reddy made a gift of 200,000 £1 ordinary shares in Purple Ltd, an unquoted investment company, to a trust. Blu paid the inheritance tax arising from this gift.

Before the transfer Blu owned 300,000 shares out of Purple Ltd's issued share capital of 500,000 £1 ordinary shares. On 15 January 2014 Purple Ltd's shares were worth £2 each for a holding of 20%, £3 each for a holding of 40%, and £4 each for a holding of 60%.

Blu has not made any previous gifts.

*Required*

Calculate the inheritance tax that will be payable as a result of Blu Reddy's gift to the trust, and the additional inheritance tax that would be payable if Blu were to die on 31 May 2018.

*Note:* you should ignore annual exemptions, and should assume that the nil rate band for the tax year 2013/14 remains unchanged.     **(6 marks)**

**(Total = 15 marks)**

# 45 A Ltd     18 mins

On 1 July 2013 **A Ltd**, a manufacturing company, acquired 100% of the share capital of B Ltd, also a manufacturing company.

B Ltd makes up accounts each year to 30 June. For its year ended 30 June 2014, it sustained a trading loss of £68,000 and had no other profits.

A Ltd produced the following information in relation to its nine-month period of accounts to 31 December 2013.

**Income**

|  | £ |
| --- | --- |
| Trading income | 342,000 |
| Property income | 10,000 |
| Loan interest receivable (received gross) (including £2,000 accrued at 31 December 2013) | 16,000 |
| Franked investment income (FII) (including tax credit; received August 2013) | 1,000 |

**Payments**

|  | |
| --- | --- |
| Qualifying charitable donation (paid September 2013) | 17,000 |

A Ltd wishes to claim maximum group relief in respect of B Ltd's trading loss.

*Required*

(a)     Compute the corporation tax payable by A Ltd for the nine-month period to 31 December 2013.     **(8 marks)**

(b)     State the due date for payment of the corporation tax payable by A Ltd for the nine-month period to 31 December 2013.     **(1 mark)**

(c)     State the date by which A Ltd must file the corporation tax return for the nine-month period to 31 December 2013.     **(1 mark)**

**(Total = 10 marks)**

# 46 Apple Ltd

27 mins

**You should assume that today's date is 30 November 2013.**

Apple Ltd has owned 80% of the ordinary share capital of Bramley Ltd and 85% of the ordinary share capital of Cox Ltd since these two companies were incorporated on 1 April 2011. Cox Ltd acquired 80% of the ordinary share capital of Delicious Ltd on 1 April 2012, the date of its incorporation.

The tax adjusted trading profits/(losses) of each company for the years 31 March 2012, 2013 and 2014 are as follows.

|  | Year ended 31 March | | |
|---|---|---|---|
|  | 2012 | 2013 | 2014 (forecast) |
|  | £ | £ | £ |
| Apple Ltd | 620,000 | 250,000 | 585,000 |
| Bramley Ltd | (64,000) | 52,000 | 70,000 |
| Cox Ltd | 83,000 | (58,000) | 40,000 |
| Delicious Ltd | n/a | 90,000 | (15,000) |

The following information is also available.

(1)   Apple Ltd sold a freehold office building on 10 March 2013 for £380,000, and this resulted in a capital gain of £120,000.

(2)   Apple Ltd sold a freehold warehouse on 5 October 2013 for £365,000, and this resulted in a capital gain of £80,000.

(3)   Cox Ltd purchased a freehold factory on 20 September 2013 for £360,000.

(4)   Delicious Ltd is planning to sell a leasehold factory building on 15 February 2014 for £180,000, and this will result in a capital loss of £44,000.

Because each of the subsidiary companies has minority shareholders, the managing director of Apple Ltd has proposed that:

(1)   Trading losses should initially be carried back and relieved against profits of the loss making company, with any unrelieved amount then being carried forward.

(2)   Chargeable gains and allowable losses should not be transferred between group companies, and rollover relief should only be claimed where reinvestment is made by the company that incurred the chargeable gain.

*Required*

(a)   Assuming that the managing director's proposals are followed, calculate the taxable total profits for each of the companies in the Apple Ltd group for the years ended 31 March 2012, 2013 and 2014 respectively.

**(5 marks)**

(b)   Advise the Apple Ltd group of the amount of corporation tax that could be saved for the years ended 31 March 2012, 2013 and 2014 if reliefs were instead claimed in the most beneficial manner.

**(10 marks)**

Assume that Financial Year 2013 rates apply throughout.

**(Total = 15 marks)**

# 47 Sofa Ltd (TX 12/07)                                    40 mins

(a)   Sofa Ltd is a manufacturer of furniture. The company's summarised statement of profit or loss for the year ended 31 March 2014 is as follows:

|  | £ | £ |
|---|---|---|
| Gross profit | | 257,298 |
| Operating expenses | | |
| Depreciation | 87,100 | |
| Professional fees (note 1) | 19,900 | |
| Repairs and renewals (note 2) | 22,800 | |
| Other expenses (note 3) | 363,000 | (492,800) |
| Operating loss | | (235,502) |
| Profit from sale of non-current assets | | |
| Disposal of shares (note 4) | | 3,300 |
| Income from investments | | |
| Bank interest (note 5) | | 8,400 |
| | | (223,802) |
| Interest payable (note 6) | | (31,200) |
| Loss before taxation | | (255,002) |

### Notes

1   *Professional fees*

Professional fees are as follows:

|  | £ |
|---|---|
| Accountancy and audit fee | 3,400 |
| | |
| Legal fees in connection with the issue of share capital | 7,800 |
| Legal fees in connection with the renewal of a ten year property lease | 2,900 |
| Legal fees in connection with the issue of loan stock (see note 6) | 5,800 |
| | 19,900 |

2   *Repairs and renewals*

The figure of £22,800 for repairs and renewals includes £9,700 for constructing a new wall around the company's premises and £3,900 for repairing the wall of an office building after it was damaged by a lorry. The remaining expenses are all fully allowable.

3   *Other expenses*

The figure of £363,000 for other expenses includes £1,360 for entertaining suppliers; £700 for entertaining employees; £370 for counselling services provided to an employee who was made redundant; and a fine of £420 for infringing health and safety regulations. The remaining expenses are all fully allowable.

4   *Profit on disposal of shares*

The profit on the disposal of shares of £3,300 is in respect of a shareholding that was sold on 29 October 2013.

5   *Bank interest received*

The bank interest was received on 31 March 2014. The bank deposits are held for non-trading purposes.

6   *Interest payable*

Sofa Ltd issued loan stock on 1 July 2013, and this was used for trading purposes. Interest of £20,800 was paid on 31 December 2013, and £10,400 was accrued at 31 March 2014.

7    *Plant and machinery*

On 1 April 2013 the tax written down values of plant and machinery were as follows:

|  | £ |
|---|---|
| Main pool | 27,800 |
| Special rate pool | 16,400 |

The following transactions took place during the year ended 31 March 2014:

|  |  | Cost/proceeds |
|---|---|---|
|  |  | £ |
| 12 May 2013 | Purchased equipment | 1,400 |
| 8 June 2013 | Sold motor car from the special rate pool | (17,800) |
| 8 June 2013 | Purchased motor car (1) $CO_2$ emissions 145g/km | 22,200 |
| 2 August 2013 | Purchased motor car (2) $CO_2$ emissions 125 g/km | 10,900 |
| 19 October 2013 | Purchased motor car (3) $CO_2$ emissions 90 g/km | 13,800 |
| 8 January 2014 | Sold a lorry | (7,600) |
| 18 January 2014 | Sold motor car (2) | (8,800) |
| 10 February 2014 | Purchased a second-hand freehold office building | 280,000 |

The motor car sold on 8 June 2013 for £17,800 originally cost £28,400. The lorry sold on 8 January 2014 for £7,600 originally cost £24,400.

The cost of the second-hand office building purchased on 10 February 2014 for £280,000 includes fixtures qualifying as plant and machinery (but not as integral features). These fixtures originally cost £11,200, and at the date of purchase had a market value of £6,200 and a written down value of £3,400. Sofa Ltd and the vendor of the office building have made a joint election regarding the sale price of the fixtures to enable Sofa Ltd to claim the maximum possible amount of capital allowances in respect of them.

*Required*

Calculate Sofa Ltd's tax adjusted trading loss for the year ended 31 March 2014. Your answer should commence with the loss before taxation figure of £255,002 and should list all of the items in the statement of profit or loss indicating by the use of a zero (0) any items that do not require adjustment. You should assume that the company claims the maximum available capital allowances.          **(17 marks)**

(b)    Sofa Ltd has three subsidiary companies:

**Settee Ltd**

Sofa Ltd owns 100% of the ordinary share capital of Settee Ltd. For the year ended 30 June 2013 Settee Ltd had taxable total profits of £240,000, and for the year ended 30 June 2014 will have taxable total profits of £90,000.

**Couch Ltd**

Sofa Ltd owns 60% of the ordinary share capital of Couch Ltd. For the year ended 31 March 2014 Couch Ltd had taxable total profits of £64,000.

**Futon Ltd**

Sofa Ltd owns 80% of the ordinary share capital of Futon Ltd. Futon Ltd commenced trading on 1 January 2014, and for the three-month period ended 31 March 2014 had taxable total profits of £60,000.

*Required*

Advise Sofa Ltd as to the maximum amount of group relief that can potentially be claimed by each of its three subsidiary companies in respect of its trading loss for the year ended 31 March 2014.

**(5 marks)**

**(Total = 22 marks)**

# 48 Gastron Ltd (TX 06/09)                                        54 mins

Gastron Ltd is a luxury food manufacturer. The company's summarised statement of profit or loss for the year ended 31 March 2014 is as follows:

|  | Note | £ | £ |
|---|---|---|---|
| Gross profit |  |  | 844,668 |
| Operating expenses |  |  |  |
| Depreciation |  | 85,660 |  |
| Amortisation of leasehold property | 1 | 6,000 |  |
| Gifts and donations | 2 | 2,700 |  |
| Professional fees | 3 | 18,800 |  |
| Other expenses | 4 | 220,400 |  |
|  |  |  | (333,560) |
| Operating profit |  |  | 511,108 |
| Income from investments |  |  |  |
| Income from property | 5 | 20,600 |  |
| Bank interest | 6 | 12,400 |  |
| Dividends | 7 | 54,000 |  |
|  |  |  | 87,000 |
| Profit from sale of non-current assets |  |  |  |
| Disposal of shares | 8 |  | 80,700 |
|  |  |  | 678,808 |
| Interest payable | 9 |  | (60,800) |
| Profit before taxation |  |  | 618,008 |

## Note 1 – Leasehold property

On 1 April 2013 Gastron Ltd acquired a leasehold office building, paying a premium of £60,000 for the grant of a new ten-year lease. The office building was used for business purposes by Gastron Ltd throughout the year ended 31 March 2014. No legal costs were incurred by Gastron Ltd in respect of this lease.

## Note 2 – Gifts and donations

Gifts and donations are as follows:

|  | £ |
|---|---|
| Gifts to customers (pens costing £60 each and displaying Gastron Ltd's name) | 1,200 |
| Gifts to customers (hampers of food costing £25 each) | 1,100 |
| Donation to local charity (Gastron Ltd received free advertising in the charity's magazine) | 400 |
|  | 2,700 |

## Note 3 – Professional fees

Professional fees are as follows:

|  | £ |
|---|---|
| Legal fees in connection with the renewal of a 45-year property lease in respect of a warehouse | 3,600 |
| Legal fees in connection with the issue of loan stock (see note 9) | 15,200 |
|  | 18,800 |

## Note 4 – Other expenses

The figure of £220,400 for other expenses includes £1,300 for entertaining suppliers and £900 for entertaining employees.

## Note 5 – Income from property

Gastron Ltd lets out the whole of an unfurnished freehold office building that is surplus to requirements. The office building was let from 1 April 2013 to 31 December 2013 at a monthly rent of £1,800, payable in advance. On 31 December 2013 the tenant left owing two months' rent which Gastron Ltd was unable to recover. During January 2014 the company spent £3,700 decorating the property. The office building was then re-let from 1 February 2014 at a monthly rent of £1,950, on which date the new tenant paid six months' rent in advance.

## Note 6 – Bank interest received

The bank interest was received on 31 March 2014. The bank deposits are held for non-trading purposes.

*Note 7 – Dividends received*

During the year ended 31 March 2014 Gastron Ltd received dividends of £36,000 from Tasteless plc, an unconnected company, and dividends of £18,000 from Culinary Ltd, a 100% subsidiary company (see note 11). Both figures are the actual cash amounts received.

*Note 8 – Profit on disposal of shares*

The profit on disposal of shares is in respect of a 1% shareholding that was sold on 14 October 2013. The disposal resulted in a chargeable gain of £74,800. This figure is after taking account of indexation.

*Note 9 – Interest payable*

The interest payable is in respect of the company's 5% loan stock that was issued on 1 April 2013. The proceeds of the issue were used to finance the company's trading activities. Interest of £30,400 was paid on 30 September 2013 and again on 31 March 2014.

*Note 10 – Plant and machinery*

On 1 April 2013 the tax written down values of plant and machinery were as follows:

| | £ |
|---|---|
| Main pool | 16,700 |
| Special rate pool | 18,400 |

The following transactions took place during the year ended 31 March 2014:

| | | Cost/(Proceeds) £ |
|---|---|---|
| 19 May 2013 | Purchased equipment | 1,600 |
| 12 July 2013 | Purchased motor car (1) | 9,800 |
| | $CO_2$ emissions 120 g/km | |
| 11 August 2013 | Purchased motor car (2) | 16,200 |
| | $CO_2$ emissions 94 g/km | |
| 5 October 2013 | Purchased a lorry | 17,200 |
| 5 March 2014 | Sold equipment | (3,300) |

The equipment sold on 5 March 2014 for £3,300 was originally purchased in 2009 for £8,900.

*Note 11 – Subsidiary company*

Gastron Ltd owns 100% of the ordinary share capital of Culinary Ltd. On 13 February 2014 Culinary Ltd sold a freehold factory and this resulted in a capital loss of £66,000. For the year ended 31 March 2014 Culinary Ltd made no other disposals and paid corporation tax at the small profits rate of 20%.

*Required*

(a)  Calculate Gastron Ltd's tax adjusted trading profit for the year ended 31 March 2014, after deducting capital allowances. Your computation should commence with the profit before taxation figure of £618,008, and should list all of the items referred to in notes (1) to (9) indicating by the use of zero (0) any items that do not require adjustment.

(15 marks)

(b)  Calculate Gastron Ltd's corporation tax liability for the year ended 31 March 2014, on the basis that no election is made between Gastron Ltd and Culinary Ltd in respect of capital gains.          (7 marks)

(c)  State the date by which Gastron Ltd's corporation tax liability for the year ended 31 March 2014 should be paid, and advise the company of the interest that will be due if the liability is not paid until 31 August 2014.

(3 marks)

(d)  Explain the group relationship that must exist in order for two or more companies to form a group for capital gains purposes.          (2 marks)

(e)  State the time limit for Gastron Ltd and Culinary Ltd to make a joint election to transfer the capital gain on Gastron Ltd's disposal of shares (see note 8) to Culinary Ltd, and explain why such an election will be beneficial.

(3 marks)

(Total = 30 marks)

**VAT**

Questions 49 to 53 cover the VAT rules for both corporate and unincorporated businesses, the subject of Part G of the BPP Study Text for Paper F6.

# 49 Lithograph Ltd (BTX)                                    18 mins

Lithograph Ltd runs a printing business, and is registered for VAT. Because its annual taxable turnover is only £250,000, the company uses the annual accounting scheme so that it only has to prepare one VAT return each year. The annual VAT period is the year ended 31 December.

**Year ended 31 December 2012**

The total amount of VAT payable by Lithograph Ltd for the year ended 31 December 2012 was £10,200.

**Year ended 31 December 2013**

The following information is available:

(1)    Sales invoices totalling £250,000 were issued to VAT registered customers, of which £160,000 were for standard rated sales and £90,000 were for zero-rated sales.

(2)    Purchase invoices totalling £45,000 were received from VAT registered suppliers, of which £38,000 were for standard rated purchases and £7,000 were for zero-rated purchases.

(3)    Standard rated expenses amounted to £28,000. This includes £3,600 for entertaining UK customers.

(4)    On 1 January 2013 Lithograph Ltd purchased a motor car costing £18,400 for the use of its managing director. The manager director is provided with free petrol for private mileage, and the cost of this is included in the standard rated expenses in note (3). Lithograph Ltd wishes to use the fuel scale charge: the relevant annual scale charge is £1,415. Both figures are inclusive of VAT.

(5)    During the year ended 31 December 2013 Lithograph Ltd purchased machinery for £24,000, and sold office equipment for £8,000. Input VAT had been claimed when the office equipment was originally purchased.

(6)    On 31 December 2013 Lithograph Ltd wrote off £4,800 due from a customer as an impairment loss. The debt was in respect of an invoice for a standard rated supply that was due for payment on 31 May 2013.

Unless stated otherwise all of the above figures are exclusive of VAT.

*Required*

(a)    Calculate the monthly payments on account of VAT that Lithograph Ltd will have made in respect of the year ended 31 December 2013, and state in which months these will have been paid.                    **(3 marks)**

(b)    (i)    Calculate the total amount of VAT payable by Lithograph Ltd for the year ended 31 December 2013.
                                                                                            **(5 marks)**

        (ii)    Based on your answer to part (i) above, calculate the balancing payment that would have been paid with the annual VAT return, and state the date by which this return was due for submission.
                                                                                            **(2 marks)**

                                                                                    **(Total = 10 marks)**

# 50 Aston Martyn (TX 06/11)   **27 mins**

Aston Martyn commenced self-employment on 1 August 2013 providing consultancy services to the motor industry.

His sales revenue has been as follows:

|      |           | Standard rated £ | Zero rated £ |
|------|-----------|-----------------:|-------------:|
| 2013 | August    | 4,300            | –            |
|      | September | 6,400            | –            |
|      | October   | 21,900           | 4,800        |
|      | November  | 11,700           | –            |
|      | December  | 17,100           | –            |
| 2014 | January   | 13,800           | 1,200        |
|      | February  | 4,200            | –            |
|      | March     | 31,500           | 3,300        |
|      | April     | 44,600           | 6,600        |

Where applicable, the above figures are stated exclusive of value added tax (VAT). Aston only supplies services and all of his supplies are to VAT registered businesses. He does not offer any discount for prompt payment.

The following is a sample of the new sales invoice that Aston is going to issue to his customers:

---

**SALES INVOICE**

**Aston Martyn**
111 Long Road
London W1 9MG
Telephone 0207 123 3456

**Customer:** Faster Motors plc
**Address:** 22 Short Lane
Manchester M1 8MB

**Invoice Date**  6 June 2014
**Tax Point**     6 June 2014

**Description of services**
Business advice

|                            | £         |
|----------------------------|----------:|
| Total price (excluding VAT) | 12,000.00 |
| Total price (including VAT) | 14,400.00 |

---

Aston sometimes receives supplies of standard rated services from VAT registered businesses situated elsewhere within the European Union. As business to business services these are treated as being supplied in the United Kingdom. Aston wants to know how he should account for these services for VAT purposes.

Because of the complexity of the VAT legislation, Aston is concerned that despite his best efforts he will incorrectly treat a standard rated supply as zero-rated, thus understating the amount of VAT payable. He wants to know if such an error will result in a penalty, and if so how much the penalty will be.

Aston understands that he is entitled to use the annual accounting scheme so that he would only have to submit one VAT return each year, but wants to know how using the scheme will otherwise affect him as regards the submission of VAT returns and the payment of VAT.

*Required*

(a)   Explain from what date Aston Martyn's business was required to be registered for VAT.   **(3 marks)**

(b)   State the FOUR additional pieces of information that Aston Martyn will have to show on his new sales invoices in order for them to be valid for VAT purposes.   **(2 marks)**

(c)   Explain when and how Aston Martyn should account for VAT in respect of the supplies of services he receives from VAT registered businesses situated elsewhere within the European Union.   **(2 marks)**

(d)   Assuming that Aston Martyn incorrectly treats a standard rated supply as zero-rated with the result that the amount of VAT payable is understated, advise him as to the maximum amount of penalty that is likely to be charged by HM Revenue and Customs, and by how much this penalty would be reduced as a result of a subsequent unprompted disclosure.   **(3 marks)**

(e)   (i)   If Aston Martyn does not use the annual accounting scheme, advise him as to how and when he will have to submit his quarterly VAT returns and pay the related VAT.   **(2 marks)**

(ii)   If Aston Martyn uses the annual accounting scheme, advise him as to when he will have to pay VAT and submit his annual VAT return.   **(3 marks)**

**(Total = 15 marks)**

# 51 Ram-Rom Ltd (BTX)                                                18 mins

Ram-Rom Ltd commenced trading as a manufacturer of computer equipment on 1 January 2013. The company registered for value added tax (VAT) on 1 September 2013. Its inputs for each of the months from January 2013 to August 2013 are as follows:

|  |  | Goods purchased £ | Services incurred £ | Non-current assets £ |
|---|---|---|---|---|
| 2013 | January | 12,300 | 1,400 | 42,000 |
|  | February | 11,200 | 5,100 | – |
|  | March | 12,300 | 7,400 | – |
|  | April | 16,400 | 6,300 | 14,400 |
|  | May | 14,500 | 8,500 | – |
|  | June | 18,800 | 9,000 | – |
|  | July | 18,500 | 9,200 | – |
|  | August | 23,400 | 8,200 | 66,600 |

During August 2013 Ram-Rom Ltd sold all of the non-current assets purchased during April 2013 for £12,000.

On 1 September 2013 £92,000 of the goods purchased were still in inventory.

The above figures are all exclusive of VAT. Ram-Rom Ltd's sales are all standard rated.

The following is a sample of the new sales invoice that Ram-Rom Ltd is going to issue to its customers:

---

**SALES INVOICE**

**Ram-Rom Ltd**                                   **Customer:** XYZ Computers plc
123 The High Street                               **Address:** 99 The Low Road
London WC1 2AB                                                 Glasgow G1 2CD
Telephone 0207 100 1234

Invoice Date and Tax Point: 1 September 2013

| Item Description | Quantity | Price £ |
|---|---|---|
| Hard Drives | 5 | 220.00 |
| Motherboards | 2 | 100.00 |
| Total Amount Payable (Including VAT) | | 320.00 |

Directors: Y Ram & Z Rom
Company Number: 1234567
Registered Office: 123 The High Street, London WC1 2AB

---

Ram-Rom Ltd pays for all of its inputs one month after receiving the purchase invoice. However, many customers are not paying Ram-Rom Ltd until four months after the date of the sales invoice. In addition, several customers have recently defaulted on the payment of their debts. In order to encourage more prompt payment, Ram-Rom Ltd is considering offering all of its customers a 5% discount if they pay within one month of the date of the sales invoice. No discount is currently offered.

*Required*

(a)   Explain why Ram-Rom Ltd was able to recover input VAT totalling £49,840 in respect of inputs incurred prior to registering for VAT on 1 September 2013.                                                    **(5 marks)**

(b)   State what alterations Ram-Rom Ltd will have to make to its new sales invoices in order for them to be valid for VAT purposes.                                                                                      **(3 marks)**

(c)   Explain the VAT implications of Ram-Rom Ltd offering all of its customers a 5% discount for prompt payment.                                                                                                        **(2 marks)**

**(Total = 10 marks)**

# 52 Sandy Brick (BTX)                                                                        18 mins

Sandy Brick has been a self-employed builder since 2006. He registered for value added tax (VAT) on 1 January 2014, and is in the process of completing his VAT return for the quarter ended 31 March 2014. The following information is relevant to the completion of this VAT return:

(1)   Sales invoices totalling £44,000 were issued to VAT registered customers in respect of standard rated sales. Sandy offers his VAT registered customers a 5% discount for prompt payment.

(2)   Sales invoices totalling £16,920 were issued to customers that were not registered for VAT. Of this figure, £5,170 was in respect of zero-rated sales with the balance being in respect of standard rated sales. Standard rated sales are inclusive of VAT.

(3)   On 10 January 2014 Sandy received a payment on account of £5,000 in respect of a contract that was completed on 28 April 2014. The total value of the contract is £10,000. Both of these figures are inclusive of VAT at the standard rate.

(4)   Standard rated materials amounted to £11,200, of which £800 were used in constructing Sandy's private residence.

(5)   Since February 2013 Sandy has paid £120 on the 15th of each month for the lease of office equipment. This expense is standard rated.

(6)   During the quarter ended 31 March 2014 £400 was spent on mobile telephone calls, of which 30% relates to private calls. This expense is standard rated.

(7)   On 20 February 2014 £920 was spent on repairs to a motor car. The motor car is used by Sandy in his business, although 20% of the mileage is for private journeys. This expense is standard rated.

(8)   On 15 March 2014 equipment was purchased for £6,000. The purchase was partly financed by a bank loan of £5,000. This purchase is standard rated.

Unless stated otherwise all of the above figures are exclusive of VAT.

*Required*

Calculate the amount of VAT payable by Sandy for the quarter ended 31 March 2014.                 **(10 marks)**

# 53 Anne Attire (TX 06/09)

**27 mins**

Anne Attire runs a retail clothing shop. She is registered for value added tax (VAT) and is in the process of completing her VAT return for the quarter ended 30 November 2013.

The following information is available (all figures are exclusive of VAT):

(1) Cash sales amounted to £42,000, of which £28,000 was in respect of standard rated sales and £14,000 was in respect of zero-rated sales.

(2) Sales invoices totalling £12,000 were issued in respect of credit sales. These sales were all standard rated. Anne offers all of her credit sale customers a 5% discount for payment within one month of the date of the sales invoice, and 90% of the customers pay within this period. The sales figure of £12,000 is stated before any deduction for the 5% discount.

(3) Purchase and expense invoices totalling £19,200 were received from VAT registered suppliers. This figure is made up as follows:

|  | £ |
|---|---|
| Standard rated purchases and expenses | 11,200 |
| Zero rated purchases | 6,000 |
| Exempt expenses | 2,000 |
|  | 19,200 |

Anne pays all of her purchase and expense invoices two months after receiving the invoice.

(4) On 30 November 2013 Anne wrote off two impairment losses that were in respect of standard rated credit sales. The first impairment loss was for £300, and was in respect of a sales invoice due for payment on 15 July 2013. The second impairment loss was for £800, and was in respect of a sales invoice due for payment on 10 April 2013.

Anne does not use the cash accounting scheme.

Anne will soon be 60 years old and is therefore considering retirement. On the cessation of trading Anne can either sell the non-current assets of her business on a piecemeal basis to individual VAT registered purchasers, or she can sell the entire business as a going concern to a single VAT registered purchaser.

*Required*

(a) Calculate the amount of VAT payable by Anne Attire for the quarter ended 30 November 2013 and state the date by which the VAT return for this period was due for submission. **(6 marks)**

(b) State the conditions that Anne Attire must satisfy before she will be permitted to use the cash accounting scheme and advise her of the implications of using the scheme. **(5 marks)**

(c) Advise Anne Attire as to what will happen to her VAT registration, and whether output VAT will be due in respect of the non-current assets, if she ceases trading and then:

    (i) Sells these assets on a piecemeal basis to individual VAT registered purchasers **(2 marks)**

    (ii) Sells her entire business as a going concern to a single VAT registered purchaser **(2 marks)**

**(Total = 15 marks)**

# Answers

# 1 Brad, Lauren, Tom, Sarah and Louise

**Text references.** All the topics in this question are covered in Chapters 2 and 3.

**Top tips.** Note that in parts (a) to (c), the requirement is for the tax liability of each individual and not the tax due – the tax liability is **before** deduction of any tax credits such as PAYE.

| | | **Marks** | |
|---|---|---|---|
| (a) | **Brad** | | |
| | Employment income | ½ | |
| | Building society interest | ½ | |
| | Personal allowance | 1 | |
| | Tax bands | 1 | |
| | Tax rates | 1 | |
| | **Lauren** | | |
| | Interest and treasury stock (gross) | ½ | |
| | ISA interest (exempt) | ½ | |
| | Dividends | ½ | |
| | Personal allowance | ½ | |
| | Gift Aid – increase basic rate limit | 1 | |
| | Tax bands | 1 | |
| | Tax rates | 1 | |
| | | | 9 |
| (b) | **Tom** | | |
| | Pensions | ½ | |
| | Building society interest | ½ | |
| | Gift Aid | 1 | |
| | Higher personal allowance | 1 | |
| | Tax bands | 1 | |
| | Tax rates | 1 | |
| | | | 5 |
| (c) | **Sarah** | | |
| | Trade profit | ½ | |
| | Bank interest | ½ | |
| | Dividend | ½ | |
| | Pension premiums | 1 | |
| | Tax bands | 1½ | |
| | Tax rates | 1 | |
| | | | 5 |
| (d) | **Louise** | | |
| | Adjusted net income | 1 | |
| | Excess over threshold | ½ | |
| | Divided by £100 | ½ | |
| | Child benefit income tax charge | 1 | |
| | | | 3 |
| | | | 22 |

(a) **Brad: Income tax computation 2013/14**

| | Non-savings £ | Savings £ | Total £ |
|---|---|---|---|
| Employment income | 104,500 | | |
| BSI (2,200 × 100/80) | | 2,750 | |
| Net income | 104,500 | 2,750 | 107,250 |
| Less personal allowance (W) | (5,815) | | (5,815) |
| Taxable income | 98,685 | 2,750 | 101,435 |

**Tax**

| | £ |
|---|---|
| *On Non-savings income* | |
| £32,010 @ 20% | 6,402 |
| £66,675 @ 40% | 26,670 |
| *On Savings income* | |
| £2,750 @ 40% | 1,100 |
| Income tax liability | 34,172 |

*Personal allowance*

| | £ | £ |
|---|---|---|
| Personal allowance born on or after 6 April 1948 | | 9,440 |
| Net income | 107,250 | |
| Less limit | (100,000) | |
| | 7,250 | |
| ÷ 2 | | (3,625) |
| PA | | 5,815 |

**Lauren: Income tax computation 2013/14**

| | Non-savings £ | Savings £ | Dividend £ | Total £ |
|---|---|---|---|---|
| Employment income | 45,975 | | | |
| BSI (2,200 × 100/80) | | 2,750 | | |
| Treasury stock | | 2,000 | | |
| ISA interest (exempt) | | 0 | | |
| Dividends (2,250 × 100/90) | | | 2,500 | |
| Net income | 45,975 | 4,750 | 2,500 | 53,225 |
| Less personal allowance | (9,440) | | | (9,440) |
| Taxable income | 36,535 | 4,750 | 2,500 | 43,785 |

**Tax**

| | £ |
|---|---|
| *On Non-savings Income* | |
| £33,260 @ 20% (N) | 6,652 |
| £3,275 @ 40% | 1,310 |
| *On Savings Income* | |
| £4,750 @ 40% | 1,900 |
| *On Dividend Income* | |
| £2,500 @ 32.5% | 812 |
| Income tax liability | 10,674 |

*Note:* the basic rate limit is increased by the gross amount of the Gift Aid payment. £32,010 + (1,000 × 100/80) = £33,260.

(b) **Tom: Income tax computation 2013/14**

| | Non-savings income | Savings income | Total |
|---|---|---|---|
| | £ | £ | £ |
| State pension | 4,926 | | |
| Employment pension | 7,890 | | |
| BSI (14,320 × 100/80) | | 17,900 | |
| Net income | 12,816 | 17,900 | 30,716 |
| Less higher personal allowance (W) | (10,192) | | (10,192) |
| Taxable income | 2,624 | 17,900 | 20,524 |

**Tax**

| | £ |
|---|---|
| *On Non-savings income* | |
| £2,624 @ 20% | 525 |
| *On Savings income* | |
| (£2,790 − £2,624) = £166 @ 10% | 17 |
| (£17,900 − £166) = £17,734 @ 20% | 3,547 |
| Income tax liability | 4,089 |

*Working*
*Higher personal allowance*

| | £ | £ |
|---|---|---|
| Higher personal allowance | | |
| born between 6 April 1938 and 5 April 1948 | | 10,500 |
| Net income | 30,716 | |
| Less Gift Aid £3,200 × 100/80 | (4,000) | |
| | 26,716 | |
| Less limit | (26,100) | |
| | 616 | |
| ÷ 2 | | (308) |
| Revised higher personal allowance | | 10,192 |

*Note:* the grossed up value of the Gift Aid payment is deducted from net income when calculating the higher personal allowance.

(c) **Sarah: Income tax computation 2013/14**

| | Non-savings | Savings | Dividend | Total |
|---|---|---|---|---|
| | £ | £ | £ | £ |
| Trading income | 164,000 | | | |
| BI (8,000 × 100/80) | | 10,000 | | |
| Dividends (4,950 × 100/90) | | | 5,500 | |
| Net/taxable income (no PA) | 164,000 | 10,000 | 5,500 | 179,500 |

**Tax**

| | £ |
|---|---|
| *On Non-savings income* | |
| £52,010 @ 20% (N) | 10,402 |
| £111,990 @ 40% | 44,796 |
| *On Savings income* | |
| £6,000 @ 40% | 2,400 |
| £4,000 @ 45% | 1,800 |
| *On Dividend income* | |
| £5,500 @ 37.5% | 2,062 |
| Income tax liability | 61,460 |

*Note:* the basic rate limit and the higher rate limit are increased by the gross amount of the personal pension payments to £32,010 + (16,000 × 100/80) = £52,010 and £150,000 + (16,000 × 100/80) = £170,000 respectively.

(d)  **Louise: Child benefit tax charge 2013/14**

|  | £ |
|---|---|
| Net income | 59,000 |
| Less: personal pension contributions £4,000 × 100/80 | (5,000) |
| Adjusted net income | 54,000 |
| Less: threshold | (50,000) |
| Excess | 4,000 |
|  |  |
| ÷ £100 | 40 |
|  |  |
| Child benefit income tax charge: 1% × £1,056 × 40 | 422 |

# 2 Domingo, Erigo and Fargo

**Text references.** Chapters 3 and 4 on employees, Chapter 5 on pensions, Chapter 7 on trading income, Chapter 8 on capital allowances and Chapter 17 on self assessment for individuals.

**Top tips.** Watch out for the starting rate band for savings income where there is little or no non-savings income.

**Easy marks.** The administrative aspects in parts (b) and (c) were easy marks.

**Examiner's comments.** In part (a) many candidates did not appreciate that donations to charity not made under gift aid are simply ignored, and some candidates missed the income limit for the age-related personal allowance. The expense claim in respect of the business mileage driven by the employed brother often caused problems. Either it was incorrectly calculated, or it was treated as a benefit. Part (b) was well answered. In part (c) few candidates appreciated that the period of retention differs between taxpayers in business and those not in business. However, virtually all candidates were aware of the £3,000 penalty.

## Marking scheme

|  |  |  |  | Marks |
|---|---|---|---|---|
| (a) | (i) | *Domingo Gomez* |  |  |
|  |  | Pensions | 1 |  |
|  |  | Building society interest | 1 |  |
|  |  | Interest from savings certificates | ½ |  |
|  |  | Donations | ½ |  |
|  |  | Personal allowance | 2 |  |
|  |  | Income tax | 1 |  |
|  |  |  |  | 6 |
|  | (ii) | *Erigo Gomez* |  |  |
|  |  | Salary | ½ |  |
|  |  | Pension contributions | 1 |  |
|  |  | Charitable payroll deductions | 1 |  |
|  |  | Relocation costs | 1 |  |
|  |  | Mileage allowance | 1½ |  |
|  |  | Personal allowance | ½ |  |
|  |  | Income tax | ½ |  |
|  |  |  |  | 6 |

|  | (iii) | *Fargo Gomez* | |
|---|---|---|---|
|  |  | Trading profit | ½ |
|  |  | Pre-trading expenditure | 1 |
|  |  | Capital allowances | 2 |
|  |  | Personal allowance | ½ |
|  |  | Increase of basic rate limit | 2 |
|  |  | Income tax | 1 |
|  |  |  | **7** |
| (b) | Paper returns | | 2 |
|  | Return filed online | | 1 |
|  |  |  | **3** |
| (c) | Domingo and Erigo | | 1 |
|  | Fargo | | 1 |
|  | Penalty for not keeping records | | 1 |
|  |  |  | **3** |
|  |  |  | **25** |

---

(a)  (i)  **Domingo Gomez – Income tax computation 2013/14**

|  | Non-savings income | Savings income | Total |
|---|---|---|---|
|  | £ | £ | £ |
| State pension | 4,500 |  |  |
| Private pension | 3,400 |  |  |
| BSI £15,520 × 100/80 |  | 19,400 |  |
| NS&I certificate interest - exempt |  |  |  |
| Net income | 7,900 | 19,400 | 27,300 |
| Less:  higher personal allowance | (7,900) | (2,000) | (9,900) |
| Taxable income | - | 17,400 | 17,400 |

*Income tax*
£
|  |  |
|---|---|
| 2,790 @ 10% | 279 |
| 14,610 @ 20% | 2,922 |
| 17,400 |  |
| Income tax liability | 3,201 |

*Note:* no tax relief is available in respect of the donations as they were not made under the Gift Aid scheme.

*Working*

|  | £ |
|---|---|
| Net income | 27,300 |
| Less income limit | (26,100) |
| Excess | 1,200 |
|  |  |
| Higher personal allowance born between 6 April 1938 and 5 April 1948 | 10,500 |
| Less half excess £1,200 × ½ | (600) |
| Revised higher personal allowance | 9,900 |

(ii)     **Erigo Gomez – Income tax computation 2013/14**

|  | Non-savings income £ |
|---|---:|
| Salary | 36,000 |
| Less:  pension contributions £36,000 × 6% | (2,160) |
| charitable payroll deductions £100 × 12 | (1,200) |
|  | 32,640 |
| Relocation costs (W1) | 3,400 |
|  | 36,040 |
| Less:  mileage allowance (W2) | (2,000) |
| Net income | 34,040 |
| Less:  personal allowance | (9,440) |
| Taxable income | 24,600 |

*Income tax*

|  | |
|---|---:|
| £24,600 @ 20%/ Income tax liability | 4,920 |

*Workings*

1     Only £8,000 of relocation costs are exempt, and so the taxable benefit is £3,400 (11,400 – 8,000).

2     The mileage allowance received will be tax-free, and Erigo can make the following expense claim:

|  | £ |
|---|---:|
| 10,000 miles @ 45p | 4,500 |
| 8,000 miles @ 25p | 2,000 |
|  | 6,500 |
| Mileage allowance 18,000 @ 25p | (4,500) |
|  | 2,000 |

(iii)    **Fargo Gomez – Income tax computation 2013/14**

|  | Non-savings income £ |
|---|---:|
| Trading profit £(64,775 – 2,600) (N) | 62,175 |
| Less:  capital allowances (W1) | (990) |
| Net income | 61,185 |
| Less:  personal allowance | (9,440) |
| Taxable income | 51,745 |

*Income tax*

|  | £ | |
|---|---|---:|
| 40,210 @ 20% (W2) |  | 8,042 |
| 11,535 @ 40% |  | 4,614 |
| 51,745 |  |  |
| Income tax liability |  | 12,656 |

*Note:* the advertising expenditure incurred during May 2013 is pre-trading, and is treated as incurred on 6 July 2013. An adjustment is therefore required.

*Workings*

1     Fargo's period of account is nine months' long so the capital allowances in respect of his motor car are £11,000 × 18% × 9/12 = 1,485 × 16,000/24,000 = £990.

2     Fargo's basic rate tax limit is increased by £5,200 in respect of the personal pension contribution and £2,400 × 100/80 = £3,000 in respect of the gift aid donations. The basic rate limit is therefore £32,010 + £(5,200 + 3,000) = £40,210.

(b)  (1)  Unless the return is issued late, the latest date that Domingo and Erigo can file paper self-assessment tax returns for 2013/14 is 31 October 2014.

(2)  If Domingo completes a paper tax return by 31 October 2014 then HM Revenue and Customs will prepare a self-assessment tax computation on his behalf.

(3)  Fargo has until 31 January 2015 to file his self-assessment tax return for 2013/14 online.

(c)  (1)  Domingo and Erigo were not in business during 2013/14, so their records must be retained until one year after 31 January following the tax year, which is 31 January 2016.

(2)  Fargo was in business during 2013/14, so all of his records (both business and non-business) must be retained until five years after 31 January following the tax year, which is 31 January 2020.

(3)  A failure to retain records for 2013/14 could result in a maximum penalty of £3,000.

# 3 The Wind Family

**Text references.** Chapter 2 deals with the computation of taxable income and the income tax liability. Chapters 3 and 4 cover employment income. The basis of assessment for trading income is dealt with in Chapter 9. National insurance contributions are covered in Chapter 12.

**Top tips.** You must deal with each member of the Wind family separately – one possible approach to this question might have been to deal with all the parts in relation to one member of the family (leaving an appropriate amount of space to insert the remaining parts of your answer), then go back to the second and then the third. Setting out your computations using the standard layouts would also have been helpful.

**Easy marks.** There were some easy marks here for basic income tax computations such as the restriction of the personal allowance, the increase in the basic rate limit, and the car and fuel benefits. The national insurance contributions were also straightforward.

**Examiner's comments.** Part (a) was very well answered, particularly for the second and third taxpayers. The only aspect which sometimes caused problems was the benefit calculations. For the fuel benefit, the contribution towards the cost of fuel was often incorrectly deducted. There were few problems in part (b) as regards the calculation of the national insurance contributions. Part (c) was the most difficult aspect on the paper, and it was pleasing to see several good attempts. For the second taxpayer most candidates appreciated that the basic rate tax band would be extended by the amount of the pension contribution, and several candidates realised that that the amount of contribution was the exact amount required so that the personal allowance was not restricted. For the third taxpayer several candidates stated that tax could be saved if the whole of the contributions were set against just the car benefit, and marks were awarded for this approach. However, the most beneficial basis was to allocate additional contributions towards the fuel benefit so as to cover the full cost of fuel for private journeys – and a few candidates did take this approach.

## Marking scheme

|  |  |  | | Marks |
|---|---|---|---|---|
| (a) | (i) | **Philip Wind** | | |
|  |  | Pensions | ½ | |
|  |  | Building society interest | ½ | |
|  |  | Personal allowance | 2 | |
|  |  | Income tax | 1 | |
|  |  | | | 4 |
|  | (ii) | **Charles Wind** | | |
|  |  | Trading profit | ½ | |
|  |  | Personal allowance | 2 | |
|  |  | Increase in basic rate limit | ½ | |
|  |  | Income tax | 1 | |
|  |  | | | 4 |

|  |  |  |  | Marks |
|---|---|---|---|---|
| (iii) | **William Wind** | | | |
| | Salary | ½ | | |
| | Pension contributions - employee | ½ | | |
| | Pension contributions - employer | ½ | | |
| | Car benefit - List price | ½ | | |
| | - Relevant percentage | 1 | | |
| | - Contribution | ½ | | |
| | - Calculation | ½ | | |
| | Fuel benefit | 1 | | |
| | Personal allowance | 1 | | |
| | Income tax | 1 | | |
| | | | 7 | |

| | | | | Marks |
|---|---|---|---|---|
| (b) | **Philip Wind** | | | |
| | No NICs | ½ | | |
| | **Charles Wind** | | | |
| | Class 2 NICs | ½ | | |
| | Class 4 NICs | 1½ | | |
| | **William Wind** | | | |
| | Class 1 NICs | 1½ | | |
| | | | 4 | |

| | | | | Marks |
|---|---|---|---|---|
| (c) | (i) | **Charles Wind** | | |
| | | Personal allowance | 1 | |
| | | Basic rate band | 1 | |
| | | Income tax liability | 1 | |
| | | | 3 | |
| | (ii) | **William Wind** | | |
| | | Allocation | 1 | |
| | | Contributions for use of motor car | 1 | |
| | | Income tax | 1 | |
| | | | 3 | |
| | | | 25 | |

(a) (i) **Philip Wind – Income tax computation 2013/14**

| | Non-savings income £ | Savings income £ | Total £ |
|---|---|---|---|
| Pensions | 13,140 | | |
| Building society interest £13,280 × 100/80 | | 16,600 | |
| Net income | 13,140 | 16,600 | 29,740 |
| Less: higher personal allowance (W) | (8,840) | | (8,840) |
| Taxable income | 4,300 | 16,600 | 20,900 |

*Working*

| | £ | £ |
|---|---|---|
| Higher personal allowance - born before 6 April 1938 | | 10,660 |
| Net income | 29,740 | |
| Less: income limit for age related allowances | (26,100) | |
| Excess income | 3,640 | |
| ÷ 2 | | (1,820) |
| Adjusted higher personal allowance | | 8,840 |

*Tax*

|  | £ |
|---|---|
| *On non-savings income* | |
| £4,300 @ 20% | 860 |
| *On savings income* | |
| £16,600 @ 20% | 3,320 |
| Income tax liability | 4,180 |

(ii)   **Charles Wind – Income tax computation 2013/14**

|  | *Non-savings Income* £ |
|---|---|
| Trading income/net income | 111,400 |
| Less: personal allowance (W) | (4,140) |
| Taxable income | 107,260 |

*Working*

|  | £ | £ |
|---|---|---|
| PA – born on or after 6 April 1948 | | 9,440 |
| Net income | 111,400 | |
| Less: gift aid donation | (800) | |
| Adjusted net income | 110,600 | |
| Less: income limit for standard personal allowance | (100,000) | |
| Excess income | 10,600 | |
| ÷ 2 | | (5,300) |
| Adjusted personal allowance | | 4,140 |

*Tax*

|  | £ |
|---|---|
| *On non-savings income* | |
| £32,810 (W) @ 20% | 6,562 |
| £(107,260 – 32,810) = 74,450 @ 40% | 29,780 |
| Income tax liability | 36,342 |

*Working*

|  | £ |
|---|---|
| Basic rate limit | 32,010 |
| Add: gift aid donation (gross) | 800 |
| Increased basic rate limit | 32,810 |

(iii)   **William Wind – Income tax computation 2013/14**

|  | *Non-savings income* £ |
|---|---|
| Employment income | |
| Salary | 181,335 |
| Less: pension contributions (employee) | (7,300) |
| | 174,035 |
| Pension contributions by Crown plc (exempt benefit) | 0 |
| Car benefit (W1) | 24,285 |
| Fuel benefit (W2) | 7,385 |
| Net income | 205,705 |
| Less: personal allowance (net income clearly exceeds £118,880) | (0) |
| Taxable income | 205,705 |

*Workings*

1    *Car benefit*

Amount by which $CO_2$ emissions exceed base level: (220 (rounded down) − 95) = 125 ÷ 5 = 25

Add to 11% = 36% − but maximum taxable % is 35%

| | £ |
|---|---:|
| £83,100 (list price) × 35% | 29,085 |
| Less: contribution for private use | (4,800) |
| Taxable benefit | 24,285 |

2    *Fuel benefit*

| | |
|---|---:|
| £21,100 × 35% | £7,385 |

*Tutorial note*

There is no reduction in the taxable benefit for part reimbursement of private fuel.

*Tax*

| | £ |
|---|---:|
| On non-savings income | |
| £32,010 @ 20% | 6,402 |
| £(150,000 − 32,010) = 117,990 @ 40% | 47,196 |
| £(205,705 − 150,000) = 55,705 @ 45% | 25,067 |
| Income tax liability | 78,665 |

(b)   **Philip Wind**

There are no national insurance contributions (NICs) suffered by Philip for 2013/14 as he has no income liable for these contributions.

**Charles Wind**

*Class 2 NICs*

| | |
|---|---:|
| £2.70 × 52 | £140 |

*Class 4 NICs*

| | £ |
|---|---:|
| £(41,450 − 7,755) = 33,695 × 9% | 3,033 |
| £(111,400 − 41,450) = 69,950 × 2% | 1,399 |
| | 4,432 |

**William Wind**

*Primary Class 1 NICs*

| | £ |
|---|---:|
| £(41,450 − 7,755) = 33,695 × 12% | 4,043 |
| £(181,335 − 41,450) = 139,885 × 2% | 2,798 |
| | 6,841 |

*Tutorial note*

Pension contributions are not deductible for Class 1 NICs and taxable benefits are subject to Class 1A NICs payable by Crown plc.

(c)   (i)   **Charles Wind**

If Charles Wind had contributed £10,600 (gross) into a personal pension scheme during the tax year 2013/14, his adjusted net income would have been £(110,600 − 10,600) = £100,000. This means that his personal allowance will not be restricted.

The personal pension contribution will also increase the basic rate limit by £10,600.

Charles' income tax liability would therefore have been reduced by £4,240 as follows:

|  | £ |
|---|---|
| Personal allowance £5,300 @ 40% | 2,120 |
| Income tax on income now in basic rate band instead of higher rate band | |
| £10,600 × (40 – 20)% | 2,120 |
| Reduction in income tax | 4,240 |

(ii)  **William Wind**

William and Crown plc should have allocated £4,400 of the contributions towards the fuel for private use, as there will then be no fuel benefit.

This will then reduce the contributions for the use of the motor car by £(4,400 – 3,200) = £1,200.

William's income tax liability would have been reduced by £2,935 as follows:

|  | £ |
|---|---|
| Fuel benefit no longer taxable £7,385 @ 45% | 3,323 |
| Less: increase in car benefit £1,200 @ 45% | (540) |
| Reduction in income tax | 2,783 |

# 4 Joe Jones

**Text references.** Chapters 3 and 4 deal with employment income, employment benefits and the PAYE system.

**Top tips.** Read the requirement of the question carefully. Did you remember to deduct the personal allowance from net income to compute Joe Jones' taxable income?

**Examiner's comments.** Part (a) of this question was reasonably well answered, but part (b) caused problems for virtually all candidates. In part (a) there were no areas that consistently caused difficulty, although a surprising number of candidates did not appreciate that a bonus would have been assessed in the previous tax year as the taxpayer was entitled to it in that year. When calculating the beneficial loan using the average method, many candidates used a nil figure rather than the balance at the date of repayment. Candidates should try not to repeat their answers. For example, exempt benefits were often shown as such in the computation of taxable income, but were then shown again in subsequent notes. There is no need to do this. It was surprising in part (b) that very few candidates knew anything about the PAYE tax code, and not much more about the PAYE forms. This just seems to be an area of the syllabus that was not revised. As regards the PAYE forms, a bit of common sense together with the knowledge that form P45 is given when employment ceases, form P60 is given at the end of the tax year, and form P11D is in respect of the benefits provided to a taxpayer, would have meant that most of the marks were easily obtainable.

**Marks**

(a)    Salary – Firstly plc     ½
Occupational pension scheme contributions     1
Bonus     ½
Salary – Secondly plc     ½
Personal pension contributions     ½
Beneficial loan    – Average method     1½
                – Strict method     1½
Workplace nursery     1
Gym membership     ½
Home entertainment system     – Use     1½
                                – Acquisition     1½
Living accommodation     2
Furniture     1½
Running costs     ½
Childcare vouchers     1
Company gym     ½
Mobile telephone     ½
Personal allowance     ½

                                                        17

(b)    (i)    Basic of calculation     1
            Deduction from salary     1

                                                           2

      (ii)    **Form P45**
            By Firstly plc when employment ceases     ½
            Details     1
            Date provided     ½
            **Form P60**
            By Secondly plc at end of tax year     ½
            Details     1½
            Date provided     ½
            **Form P11D**
            Both employers     ½
            Details     ½
            Date provided     ½

                                                         6
                                                         25

(a)  **Joe Jones – Taxable income 2013/14**

|  |  | £ |
|---|---|---:|
| Employment income |  |  |
| Salary – Firstly plc (6,360 × 9) |  | 57,240 |
| Pension contributions (57,240 × 6%) (N2) |  | (3,434) |
|  |  | 53,806 |
| Bonus (N1) |  | Nil |
| Salary – Secondly plc (6,565 × 3) |  | 19,695 |
| Beneficial loan (W1) |  | 2,367 |
| Workplace nursery (N3) |  | Nil |
| Gym membership |  | 1,650 |
| Home entertainment system | – Use (W2) | 660 |
|  | – Acquisition (W2) | 3,860 |
| Living accommodation (W3) |  | 6,750 |
| Furniture (W3) |  | 816 |
| Running costs |  | 1,900 |
| Childcare vouchers (W4) |  | 936 |
| Company gym (N3) |  | Nil |
| Mobile telephone (N3) |  | Nil |
| Net income |  | 92,440 |
| Less: personal allowance |  | (9,440) |
| Taxable income |  | 83,000 |

*Workings*

1    *Loan benefit*

The benefit of the beneficial loan using the average method is £2,533 ((120,000 + 70,000)/2 = 95,000 at 4% × 8/12).

Using the strict method the benefit is £2,367 ((120,000 at 4% × 3/12) + (70,000 at 4% × 5/12)).

Joe will therefore elect to have the taxable benefit calculated according to the strict method.

2    *Home entertainment system*

The benefit for the use of the home entertainment system is £660 (4,400 × 20% × 9/12).

The benefit for the acquisition of the home entertainment system is the market value of £3,860, as this is greater than £3,740 (4,400 – 660).

3    *Living accommodation and furniture*

The benefit for the living accommodation is the higher of the annual value of £2,600 (10,400 × 3/12) and the rent paid of £6,750 (2,250 × 3).

The benefit for the use of the furniture is £816 (16,320 × 20% × 3/12).

4    *Childcare vouchers*

The exemption for childcare vouchers is £28 per week since Joe is a higher rate employee. The benefit for the provision of the vouchers is therefore £936 ((100 – 28) = 72 × 13).

*Notes*

1    The bonus of £12,000 will have been treated as being received during 2012/13 as Joe became entitled to it during that tax year.

2    The personal pension contributions will increase Joe's basic rate tax limit, and are therefore irrelevant as regards the calculation of taxable income.

3    The provision of a place in a workplace nursery, the use of a company gym (sporting facility), and the provision of one mobile telephone do not give rise to taxable benefits.

(b)  (i)  **Joe's tax code**

Joe's tax code will have been calculated by starting with his personal allowance of £9,440, and then reducing it by the value of the taxable benefits.

An employee's tax code is used to adjust their salary when calculating the amount of income tax that has to be paid each week or month under the PAYE system.

(ii)  **Form P45**

Form P45 will be prepared by Firstly plc when Joe's employment ceases. It will show his taxable earnings and income tax deducted up to the date of leaving, together with his tax code at the date of leaving.

Firstly plc should have provided this form to Joe immediately following his cessation of employment with the company.

**Form P60**

Form P60 will be prepared by Secondly plc at the end of the tax year. It will show Joe's taxable earnings, income tax deducted, final tax code, national insurance contributions, and Secondly plc's name and address.

Secondly plc should have provided this form to Joe by 31 May 2014.

**Form P11D**

A separate form P11D will be prepared by both Firstly plc and Secondly plc, detailing the cash equivalents of the benefits provided to Joe.

Both companies should have provided a form to Joe by 6 July 2014.

# 5 Sam and Kim White

**Text references.** Chapter 2 includes individual savings accounts. Chapter 3 deals with employment income and Chapter 4 covers employment benefits. Chapter 7 is about the computation of trading income and Chapter 8 covers capital allowances.

**Top tips.** Allocate your time for each part of the question and ensure you attempt every part.

**Easy marks.** The adjustment to profit in part (a) and Kim's income tax computation in part (b) were easy marks.

**Examiner's comments.** This question was very well answered by the majority of candidates. In part (a) the adjustments for use of office, business use of a private telephone and own consumption caused the most problems, with a number of candidates being unsure as to whether adjustments should be added or subtracted in order to arrive at the tax adjusted trading profit. Part (b) was also well answered, with only the expense claim for the business mileage causing any difficulty. This was often treated as a benefit rather than as an expense. Part (c) was answered reasonably well, especially the transfer into the spouse's sole name. Many candidates correctly calculated the amount of income tax saving.

|  |  |  | Marks |
|---|---|---|---|
| (a) | Net profit | ½ | |
| | Depreciation | ½ | |
| | Motor expenses | 1½ | |
| | Patent royalties | 1 | |
| | Professional fees: breach of contract | ½ | |
| | Professional fees: professional fees | ½ | |
| | Gifts to customers | 1 | |
| | Own consumption | 1 | |
| | Use of office | 1 | |
| | Private telephone | 1 | |
| | Capital allowances – Main pool | 1 | |
| | – Motor car | 1½ | |
| | | | 11 |
| (b) | **Sam White** | | |
| | Trading profit | ½ | |
| | Building society interest | 1 | |
| | Personal allowance | ½ | |
| | Income tax | 1 | |
| | **Kim White** | | |
| | Salary | ½ | |
| | Beneficial loan | 1 | |
| | Expense claim | 2 | |
| | Building society interest | ½ | |
| | Loan interest | 1 | |
| | Personal allowance | ½ | |
| | Income tax | 1½ | |
| | | | 10 |
| (c) (i) | **Individual savings accounts** | | |
| | Limit | 1 | |
| | Tax saving | 1 | |
| | | | 2 |
| (ii) | **Transfer to Kim's sole name** | | |
| | Tax rates | 1 | |
| | Tax saving | 1 | |
| | | | 2 |
| | | | 25 |

**(a) Sam White – Trading profit for the year ended 5 April 2014**

|  |  | £ | £ |
|---|---|---:|---:|
| Net profit |  |  | 50,000 |
| Add back: | Depreciation | 6,123 |  |
|  | Motor expenses £8,800 × 20% (N1) | 1,760 |  |
|  | Patent royalties (N2) | 0 |  |
|  | Professional fees: breach of contract | 0 |  |
|  | Professional fees: accountancy personal CGT advice | 320 |  |
|  | Other expenses: gifts to customers £(560 + 420) (N3) | 980 |  |
|  | Goods for own consumption | 1,480 | 10,663 |
|  |  |  | 60,663 |
| Less: | Use of home £5,120 × 1/8 | 640 |  |
|  | Private telephone £1,600 × 25% | 400 |  |
|  | Capital allowances (W) | 4,623 | (5,663) |
| Trading profit |  |  | 55,000 |

*Working – Capital allowances*

|  | Main pool £ | Motor car £ | Allowances £ |
|---|---:|---:|---:|
| TWDV brought forward | 18,500 | 20,200 |  |
| WDA – 18% | (3,330) |  | 3,330 |
| WDA – 8% |  | (1,616) × 80% | 1,293 |
| WDV carried forward | 15,170 | 18,584 |  |
| Allowances |  |  | 4,623 |

*Notes*

1 Of the 25,000 miles driven by Sam during the year ended 5 April 2014, 20,000 (5,000 + 15,000 [(25,000 − 5,000 = 20,000) × 75%]) were for business journeys. The business proportion is therefore 80% (20,000/25,000 × 100).

2 Patent royalties are allowed as a deduction when calculating the trading profit, so no adjustment is required.

3 Gifts to customers are an allowable deduction if they cost less than £50 per recipient per year, are not of food, drink, tobacco or vouchers for exchangeable goods and carry a conspicuous advertisement for the business making the gift.

**(b) Sam White – Income tax computation 2013/14**

|  | Non-savings income £ | Savings income £ | Total £ |
|---|---:|---:|---:|
| Trading income (part (a)) | 55,000 |  |  |
| Building society interest |  |  |  |
| £1,200/2 × 100/80 = £1,500/2 |  | 750 |  |
| Net income | 55,000 | 750 | 55,750 |
| Less: personal allowance | (9,440) |  | (9,440) |
| Taxable income | 45,560 | 750 | 46,310 |

**Income tax**

|  | £ |
|---|---:|
| *Non-savings income* |  |
| £32,010 × 20% | 6,402 |
| £13,550 × 40% | 5,420 |
| *Savings income* |  |
| £750 × 40% | 300 |
| Income tax liability | 12,122 |

**Kim White – Income tax computation 2013/14**

| | £ | Non-savings income £ | Savings income £ | Total £ |
|---|---|---|---|---|
| Employment income | | | | |
| Salary | 23,730 | | | |
| Loans (W1) | 400 | | | |
| | 24,130 | | | |
| Less expense claim (W3) | (5,125) | 19,005 | | |
| BSI £1,200/2 × 100/80 = £1,500 ÷2 | | | 750 | |
| Total income | | 19,005 | 750 | 19,755 |
| Less deductible interest (W4) | | (140) | | (140) |
| Net income | | 18,865 | 750 | 19,615 |
| Less personal allowance | | (9,440) | | (9,440) |
| Taxable income | | 9,425 | 750 | 10,175 |

**Income tax**

| | £ |
|---|---|
| *Non-savings income* | |
| £9,425 × 20% | 1,885 |
| *Savings income* | |
| £750 × 20% | 150 |
| Income tax liability | 2,035 |

*Workings*

(1)  The taxable benefit from the beneficial loan is £12,000 at 4% × 10/12 = £400.

(2)  Ordinary commuting (travel between home and the permanent workplace) does not qualify for relief. The travel to a temporary workplace qualifies as it is for a period lasting less than 24 months.

(3)  Kim can therefore make an expense claim based on 12,500 (11,200 + 1,300) miles as follows:

| | £ |
|---|---|
| 10,000 miles at 45p | 4,500 |
| 2,500 miles at 25p | 625 |
| | 5,125 |

(4)  The loan interest paid of £140 is eligible for relief since the loan was used by Kim to finance expenditure for a relevant purpose.

(c)  (i)  **Individual savings accounts**

(1)  Both Sam and Kim can invest a maximum of £11,520 each tax year into an ISA of which up to £5,760 can be held as cash.

(2)  Interest received from ISAs is exempt from income tax, so Sam will save tax at the rate of 40% whilst Kim will save tax at the rate of 20%, each on gross interest of £346 (£1,500 × 5,760/25,000).

(ii)  **Transfer to Kim's sole name**

(1)  Sam pays income tax at the rate of 40%, whilst Kim's basic rate tax band is not fully utilised.

(2)  Transferring the building society deposit account into Kim's sole name would therefore save tax of £150 (£750 × 20% (40% – 20%)).

# 6 Sammi Smith

> **Text references.** Chapter 4 deals with employment benefits. National insurance contributions are covered in Chapter 12. Computing taxable total profits is in Chapter 19 and computing corporation tax in Chapter 20.
>
> **Top tips.** Use headings to show the examiner which of two options you are dealing with.
>
> **Easy marks.** There were easy marks for computing the car benefit and computing the national insurance contributions.
>
> **Examiner's comments.** This question was generally answered quite badly, with the main problem being that candidates simply did not spend enough time thinking and planning their answers, but just plunged straight in performing every calculation that they could think of. In part (a) the answer was in fact very straightforward, with a fairly simple car benefit calculation and then income tax and NIC calculations at the director's marginal rates of 45% and 2% respectively. Far too many candidates calculated a fuel benefit despite being told that fuel was not provided for private journeys. In part (b) many candidates stated that capital allowances would be available despite the motor car being leased. Candidates often stated that the company's corporation tax liability would be increased rather than reduced as a result of the additional expenditure, and very few candidates appreciated that NIC was a deductible expense. Part (c) was more difficult, although credit was given for any sensible approach such as comparing the tax liabilities under each alternative.

## Marking scheme

|  |  |  | Marks |
|---|---|---|---|
| (a) | **Company motor car** |  |  |
|  | Car benefit | 2 |  |
|  | Income tax | 1 |  |
|  | NIC implications | ½ |  |
|  | **Additional director's remuneration** |  |  |
|  | Income tax | ½ |  |
|  | Class 1 NIC | 1 |  |
|  |  |  | 5 |
| (b) | **Company motor car** |  |  |
|  | Class 1A NIC | 1 |  |
|  | Allowable leasing costs | 1 |  |
|  | Corporation tax saving | 1 |  |
|  | **Additional director's remuneration** |  |  |
|  | Class 1 NIC | 1 |  |
|  | Corporation tax saving | 1 |  |
|  |  |  | 5 |
| (c) | **Sammi** |  |  |
|  | Director's remuneration   - Net of tax income | 1 |  |
|  |                            - Overall result | 1 |  |
|  | Conclusion | 1 |  |
|  | **Smark Ltd** |  |  |
|  | Director's remuneration | 1 |  |
|  | Conclusion | 1 |  |
|  |  |  | 5 |
|  |  |  | 15 |

(a) **Sammi Smith – Company motor car**

The list price used in the car benefit calculation is £80,000. The relevant percentage is restricted to a maximum of 35% (11% + 41% (300 − 95 = 205/5) = 52%).

Sammi will therefore be taxed on a car benefit of £28,000 (80,000 x 35%).

Sammi's marginal rate of income tax is 45%, so her additional income tax liability for 2013/14 will be £12,600 (28,000 at 45%).

There are no national insurance contribution implications for Sammi.

*Tutorial note*

There is no fuel benefit as fuel is not provided for private journeys.

### Sammi Smith – Additional director's remuneration

Sammi's additional income tax liability for 2013/14 will be £11,700 (26,000 at 45%).

The additional employee's Class 1 NIC liability will be £520 (26,000 at 2%).

*Tutorial note*

Sammi's director's remuneration exceeds the upper earnings limit of £41,450, so her additional class 1 NIC liability is at the rate of 2%.

(b) **Smark Ltd – Company motor car**

The employer's Class 1A NIC liability in respect of the car benefit will be £3,864 (28,000 at 13.8%).

The motor car has a $CO_2$ emission rate in excess of 130 grams per kilometre, so only £22,423 (26,380 less 15%) of the leasing costs are allowed for corporation tax purposes.

Smark Ltd's corporation tax liability will be reduced by £6,046 (22,423 + 3,864 = 26,287 at 23%).

### Smark Ltd – Additional director's remuneration

The employer's Class 1 NIC liability in respect of the additional director's remuneration will be £3,588 (26,000 at 13.8%).

Smark Ltd's corporation tax liability will be reduced by £6,805 (26,000 + 3,588 = 29,588 at 23%).

(c) **More beneficial alternative for Sammi Smith**

Under the director's remuneration alternative, Sammi will receive additional net of tax income of £13,780 (26,000 – 11,700 – 520).

However, she will have to lease the motor car at a cost of £26,380, so the overall result is additional expenditure of £12,600 (26,380 – 13,780).

If Sammi is provided with a company motor car then she will have an additional tax liability of £12,600, so she is in exactly the same financial position.

### Most beneficial alternative for Smark Ltd

The net of tax cost of paying additional director's remuneration is £22,783 (26,000 + 3,588 – 6,805).

This is more beneficial than the alternative of providing a company motor car since this has a net of tax cost of £24,198 (26,380 + 3,864 – 6,046).

# 7 Edmond Brick

**Text references.** Chapter 6 deals with property income.

**Top tips.** Remember that property income is pooled to give a single profit or loss. However, if someone has furnished holiday lettings and other lettings, two sets of accounts have to be drawn up as if there were two separate UK property businesses. This is so that profits and losses treated as trade profits and losses can be identified. The examiner has helpfully structured this question so that you were required to make such separate calculations.

**Easy marks.** Deduction of expenses such as council tax, insurance and advertising were easy marks.

**Examiner's comments.** This was a very well answered question. In part (a) some candidates discussed the qualifying conditions for a furnished holiday letting rather than the advantages of a property being so treated. Parts (b) and (c) presented few problems. The only aspects that consistently caused difficulty were the capital allowances for the furnished holiday letting (candidates either claimed wear and tear allowance or deducted the full cost of the capital expenditure) and the furnished room (candidates did not appreciate that rent-a-room relief could be claimed).

|  |  | | Marks |
|---|---|---|---|
| (a) | Availability of capital allowances | 1 | |
| | Capital gains tax business reliefs | 1 | |
| | Relevant earnings for pension purposes | 1 | |
| | | | 3 |
| (b) | Rent receivable | ½ | |
| | Repairs | 1 | |
| | Other expenses | ½ | |
| | Capital allowances | 1 | |
| | | | 3 |
| (c) | **Property two** | | |
| | Rent receivable | ½ | |
| | Council tax | ½ | |
| | Insurance | ½ | |
| | Wear and tear allowance | 1 | |
| | **Property three** | | |
| | Rent receivable | ½ | |
| | Insurance | ½ | |
| | Advertising | ½ | |
| | Impairment loss | ½ | |
| | Loan interest | ½ | |
| | **Property four** | | |
| | Lease premium | 1 | |
| | Rent receivable | ½ | |
| | Insurance | ½ | |
| | Rent paid | ½ | |
| | **Room** | | |
| | Rent received | ½ | |
| | Rent a room relief | 1 | |
| | | | 9 |
| | | | 15 |

(a) The tax advantages of property one being treated as a trade under the furnished holiday letting rules are:

(i) Capital allowances are available on furniture instead of the 10% wear and tear allowance.

(ii) Capital gains tax reliefs which apply to businesses, apply here ie entrepreneurs' relief, rollover relief, gift relief.

(iii) The income qualifies as relevant earnings for pension relief purposes.

(b) **Property one**

| | £ |
|---|---|
| Rent receivable £370 × 18 | 6,660 |
| Less: repairs | (7,400) |
| other allowable expenditure | (2,710) |
| capital allowances | |
| £5,700 (covered by AIA) | (5,700) |
| Loss | (9,150) |

(c)  **Property two**

|  |  | £ | £ |
|---|---|---:|---:|
| Rent receivable £575 × 12 | | 6,900 | |
| Less: | council tax | (1,200) | |
| | insurance | (340) | |
| | wear and tear allowance | | |
| | 10% × £(6,900 − 1,200) | (570) | |
| Profit | | | 4,790 |

**Property three**

|  |  | £ | £ |
|---|---|---:|---:|
| Rent receivable £710 × 7 | | 4,970 | |
| Less: | insurance | (290) | |
| | advertising | (670) | |
| | impairment loss £710 × 3 | (2,130) | |
| | loan interest | (6,700) | |
| Loss | | | (4,820) |

**Property four**

|  |  | £ | £ |
|---|---|---:|---:|
| Premium taxable as property business income (W) | | 13,800 | |
| Rent receivable | | 4,600 | |
| | | 18,400 | |
| Less: | insurance | (360) | |
| | rent payable | (6,800) | |
| | | | 11,240 |

Furnished Room

|  | £ | £ |
|---|---:|---:|
| Rent receivable | 5,040 | |
| Less: rent a room relief (note) | (4,250) | |
| Profit | | 790 |
| | | |
| Property business profit | | 12,000 |

*Working*

|  | £ |
|---|---:|
| Premium paid | 15,000 |
| Less: 2% × (5 − 1) × £15,000 | (1,200) |
| Taxable as property business income | 13,800 |

*Note:* claiming rent a room relief in respect of the furnished room £(5,040 − 4,250) = £790 is more beneficial than the normal basis of assessment £(5,040 − 1,140) = £3,900.

# 8 Peter Chic

**Text reference.** Employment income and benefits are covered in Chapters 3 and 4. Property income is dealt with in Chapter 6. The computation of taxable income and the income tax liability is covered in Chapter 2. National insurance contributions are dealt with in Chapter 12.

**Top tips.** Set out the computation of taxable income in the standard three column layout. Use workings to show the details rather than putting them directly into the computation.

**Easy marks.** The calculation of national insurance contributions should have been easy marks.

**Examiner's comments.** In part (a) a few candidates did not appreciate that both bonuses were to be treated as earnings, whilst the basis of assessing the second mobile telephone was not always known. Some candidates deducted the gift aid donation rather than extending the basic rate tax band. In part (b) the most common mistake was to include taxable benefits when calculating Class 1 national insurance contributions.

| | | | Marks |
|---|---|---|---|
| (a) | Salary | | ½ |
| | Bonus payments | | 1 |
| | Car benefit | – relevant percentage | 1 |
| | | – capital contribution | ½ |
| | | – calculation | ½ |
| | Fuel benefit | | 1 |
| | Living accommodation | – annual value | 1 |
| | | – additional benefit | 2 |
| | Mobile telephone | | 1 |
| | Health club membership | | ½ |
| | Overseas allowance | | ½ |
| | Property business profit | – rent receivable | 1 |
| | | – irrecoverable rent | ½ |
| | | – repairs | ½ |
| | | – advertising | ½ |
| | | – loan interest | 1 |
| | | – insurance | 1 |
| | | – wear and tear allowance | 1 |
| | Building society interest | | ½ |
| | Dividends | | ½ |
| | Premium bond prize (exempt) | | ½ |
| | Personal allowance | | ½ |
| | Increase in basic rate limit | | 1 |
| | Income tax | | 1½ |
| | Tax suffered at source | | 1½ |
| | | | 21 |
| | | | |
| (b) | Employee Class 1 NIC | | 1½ |
| | Employer Class 1 NIC | | 1½ |
| | Employer Class 1A NIC | | 1 |
| | | | 4 |
| | | | 25 |

**(a)    Income tax computation 2013/14**

|  | Non-savings income £ | Savings income £ | Dividend income £ | Total £ |
|---|---|---|---|---|
| Employment income (W1) | 79,425 | | | |
| Property income (W5) | 3,660 | | | |
| BSI £1,760 × 100/80 | | 2,200 | | |
| Dividends £720 × 100/90 | | | 800 | |
| Premium bond prize (exempt) | | 0 | | |
| Net income | 83,085 | 2,200 | 800 | 86,085 |
| Less: personal allowance | (9,440) | | | |
| Taxable income | 73,645 | 2,200 | 800 | 76,645 |

|  | £ | £ |
|---|---|---|
| *Tax* | | |
| £35,010 (W6) × 20% | | 7,002 |
| £38,635 × 40% | | 15,454 |
| £2,200 × 40% | | 880 |
| £800 × 32½% | | 260 |
| Tax liability | | 23,596 |
| Less:  tax deducted at source | | |
| PAYE | 14,270 | |
| BSI £2,200 × 20% | 440 | |
| Dividend £800 × 10% | 80 | (14,790) |
| Tax payable | | 8,806 |

*Workings*

1    *Employment income*

|  | £ | £ |
|---|---|---|
| Salary | 44,260 | |
| Bonus received 10.4.13 | 4,300 | |
| Bonus received 25.3.14 | 3,600 | 52,160 |
| | | |
| Car benefit (W2) | 7,175 | |
| Fuel benefit (W2) | 7,385 | |
| Living accommodation (W3) | 12,145 | |
| Mobile phone (W4) | 50 | |
| Health club membership | 510 | |
| Overseas allowance – exempt up to £10 per night for overseas expenses | nil | 27,265 |
| Employment income | | 79,425 |

2    *Car benefit*

$$\frac{205 - 95}{5} = 22 + 11 + 3 \text{ (diesel)} = 36\%$$

Maximum % is 35.

|  | £ |
|---|---|
| List price | 22,500 |
| Less: contribution | (2,000) |
| | 20,500 |
| | |
| × 35% | 7,175 |

*Fuel benefit*

| | £ |
|---|---|
| £21,100 × 35% | 7,385 |

3    *Living accommodation*

|  | £ | £ |
|---|---|---|
| Annual benefit | | 8,225 |
| Additional benefit | | |
| Cost of property | 160,000 | |
| Improvements before start of tax year | 13,000 | |
| | 173,000 | |
| Less: *de minimis* | (75,000) | |
| | 98,000 | |
| Benefit @ 4% | | 3,920 |
| Total accommodation benefit | | 12,145 |

4    *Mobile phone*

| | |
|---|---|
| One mobile phone is exempt | |
| Second mobile phone is calculated on private use of asset basis ie £250 × 20% | £50 |

5    *Property income*

|  | £ | £ |
|---|---|---|
| Property one – rent receivable £500 × 5 | | 2,500 |
| Property two – rent receivable £820 × 8 | | 6,560 |
| | | 9,060 |
| Irrecoverable rent £500 × 2 | 1,000 | |
| Repairs to roof | 600 | |
| Advertising | 875 | |
| Loan interest | 1,800 | |
| Insurance £(660 × 3/12 + 1,080 × 9/12) | 975 | |
| Wear and tear £(2,500 – 1,000) × 10% (N) | 150 | (5,400) |
| Property income | | 3,660 |

*Note:* it is arguable that the wear and tear allowance should be calculated as 10% of the gross rents receivable as this is more beneficial than 10% of the rents receivable. Credit would be given for either approach in the exam.

6    Basic rate limit increased by gross Gift Aid donations
     £32,010 + £(2,400 × 100/80)                                      £35,010

(b)   **National insurance contributions 2013/14**

*Primary Class 1 (paid by Peter)*

| | £ |
|---|---|
| £(41,450 – 7,755) = 33,695 × 12% | 4,043 |
| £(52,160 – 41,450) = 10,710 × 2% | 214 |
| | 4,257 |

*Secondary Class 1 (paid by Haute-Couture Ltd)*

| | |
|---|---|
| £(52,160 – 7,696) = 44,464 × 13.8% | 6,136 |

*Class 1A (paid by Haute-Couture Ltd )*

| | |
|---|---|
| £27,265 × 13.8% | 3,763 |

# 9 Leticia Stone

## Marking scheme

|   |   |   | Marks |
|---|---|---|---|
| (a) | **Furnished holiday letting loss** | | |
| | Rent receivable | ½ | |
| | Loan interest | 1 | |
| | Repairs | 1 | |
| | Mileage allowance | 1½ | |
| | Other expenses | ½ | |
| | Capital allowances | 1 | |
| | **Property business loss** | | |
| | Lease premium received | 1 | |
| | Rent receivable – Property 2 | 1 | |
| | – Property 3 | 1 | |
| | – Security deposit | ½ | |
| | Rent payable | 1 | |
| | Impairment loss | 1 | |
| | Loan interest | ½ | |
| | Other expenses | ½ | |
| | Furnished room | 1 | |
| | | | 13 |
| (b) | Furnished holiday letting loss | 1 | |
| | Property business loss | 1 | |
| | | | 2 |
| | | | 15 |

(a) **Leticia Stone – Furnished holiday letting loss 2013/14**

|  | £ | £ |
|---|---|---|
| **Income** | | |
| Rent receivable £425 × 22 | | 9,350 |
| **Expenses** | | |
| Loan interest | 12,700 | |
| Repairs not covered by insurance £(12,200 − 10,900) | 1,300 | |
| Mileage allowance (N1) (880 + 130) = 1,010 × 45p | 455 | |
| Other expenses | 3,770 | |
| Capital allowances (N2) | 4,600 | |
| | | (22,825) |
| Furnished holiday letting loss | | (13,475) |

*Tutorial notes*

1　The mileage that Leticia drove in respect of the property purchase is a capital expense and so not deductible.

2　Capital allowances on furniture are available for furnished holiday lettings. The expenditure is covered by the annual investment allowance.

**Leticia Stone – Property business loss 2013/14**

|  | £ | £ |
|---|---|---|
| **Income** | | |
| Premium received for sublease – Property 2 | 45,000 | |
| Less: £45,000 × (5 − 1) × 2% | (3,600) | |
| | | 41,400 |
| Rent receivable　– Property 2 £(2,160 × 4) = 8,640 × 11/12 | | 7,920 |
| 　　　　　　　– Property 3 £580 ×10 | | 5,800 |
| 　　　　　　　– Property 3 Security deposit (N1) | | 0 |
| 　　　　　　　– Room in own residence (N2) | | 3,170 |
| | | 58,290 |
| **Expenses** | | |
| Rent payable　– Property 2 £1,360 × 11 | 14,960 | |
| Impairment loss　– Property 3 | 580 | |
| Loan interest　– Property 3 | 9,100 | |
| Other expenses　– Properties 2 and 3 | 36,240 | |
| Other expenses　– Room in own residence | 4,840 | |
| | | (65,720) |
| Property business loss | | (7,430) |

*Tutorial notes*

1　The security deposit received on 1 March 2014, even if it was treated as rental income, relates to a letting commencing in 2014/15 and is therefore not relevant for 2013/14.

2　Leticia should claim to ignore the rent a room exemption since this allows a loss to be generated.

(b) The furnished holiday letting loss is relieved by carrying it forward and deducting from the first available future profits of the same furnished holiday letting business.

The general property business loss is relieved by carrying it forward and deducting from the first available future profits of the general property business.

# 10 Peach, Plum and Pear

## Marking scheme

|  | | Marks |
|---|---|---|
| **Ann Peach** | | |
| Taxable income | ½ | |
| Increase in basic rate limit | 1 | |
| Income tax | ½ | |
| Amount qualifying for tax relief | 1 | |
|  | | 3 |
| **Basil Plum** | | |
| Taxable income | ½ | |
| Increase in basic rate limit | ½ | |
| Increase in higher rate limit | ½ | |
| Income tax | 1½ | |
| Excess contribution charge | 1 | |
| Amount qualifying for tax relief | 1 | |
|  | | 5 |
| **Chloe Pear** | | |
| Taxable income | ½ | |
| Income tax | ½ | |
| Amount qualifying for tax relief | 1 | 2 |
|  | | 10 |

**Ann Peach**

|  | Non-savings income |
|---|---|
|  | £ |
| Trading income | 46,065 |
| Less: personal allowance | (9,440) |
| Taxable income | 36,625 |

Maximum personal pension contribution is higher of (1) £3,600 and (2) Relevant earnings £46,065 ie £46,065. The remaining £2,935 is not given tax relief.

| Basic rate limit £(32,010 + 46,065) | £78,075 |
|---|---|
| Tax £36,625 × 20% | £7,325 |

**Basil Plum**

Basil can make a maximum personal pension contribution of £330,000. Therefore his contribution of £60,000 will be given tax relief. However, the excess charge applies to the contribution over the annual allowance of £50,000 so some of the tax relief given will be clawed back.

|  | Non-savings income £ |
|---|---|
| Employment income | 330,000 |
| Excess pension contribution over annual allowance £(60,000 – 50,000) | 10,000 |
| Taxable income (no PA as adjusted net income exceeds £118,880) | 340,000 |

The excess contribution is treated as extra non-savings income.

| | |
|---|---|
| Basic rate limit £(32,010 + 60,000) | 92,010 |
| Higher rate limit £(150,000 + 60,000) | 210,000 |

Tax is therefore calculated as follows:

| | |
|---|---|
| £92,010 × 20% | 18,402 |
| £(210,000 – 92,010) = £117,990 × 40% | 47,196 |
| £(340,000 – 210,000) = £130,000 × 45% | 58,500 |
| Tax | 124,098 |

**Chloe Pear**

|  | Non-savings income £ |
|---|---|
| Property income | 26,630 |
| Less: personal allowance | (9,440) |
| Taxable income | 17,190 |

Maximum personal pension contribution is £3,600 since Chloe has no relevant earnings. This will have been given tax relief at source by Chloe paying £3,600 × 80% = £2,880. The remaining £4,600 contribution is not given tax relief.

| | |
|---|---|
| Tax is therefore £17,190 × 20% | 3,438 |

# 11 Na Style

> **Text references.** Assessment of trading profits is covered in Chapter 9. Adjustment of trading profit is in Chapter 7. The income tax computation is dealt with in Chapter 2 and administration aspects in Chapter 17.
>
> **Top tips.** As you deal with each adjustment to profit, tick it off in the question – this method should ensure that you do not miss out any item and thus lose marks.
>
> **Easy marks.** The administration aspects in part (d) should have been 3 easy marks.
>
> **Examiner's comments.** This question was very well answered, and there were many high scoring answers. In part (a) some candidates lost marks because they did not show the relevant tax years in which profits were assessable. There were few problems as regards the calculation of the trading profit or the income tax payable, although many candidates did not appreciate that interest from government stocks is received gross and is taxable. As regards the balancing payment and payments on account, candidates were often not aware of the relevant dates. In part (d) many candidates did not appreciate that a 5% penalty would be imposed in addition to the interest charge.

|     |      |                                                 | Marks |     |
|-----|------|-------------------------------------------------|-------|-----|
| (a) |      | First tax year trading profits                  | 1     |     |
|     |      | Second tax year trading profits                 | 1½    |     |
|     |      | Third tax year trading profits                  | ½     |     |
|     |      | Overlap profits                                 | 2     |     |
|     |      |                                                 |       | 5   |
| (b) |      | Net profit                                      | ½     |     |
|     |      | Depreciation                                    | ½     |     |
|     |      | Motor expenses                                  | 1     |     |
|     |      | Accountancy                                     | ½     |     |
|     |      | Legal fees                                      | ½     |     |
|     |      | Property expenses                               | 1     |     |
|     |      | Own consumption                                 | 1     |     |
|     |      | Fine                                            | ½     |     |
|     |      | Donation to political party                     | ½     |     |
|     |      | Trade subscription                              | ½     |     |
|     |      | Private telephone                               | 1     |     |
|     |      | Capital allowances                              | ½     |     |
|     |      |                                                 |       | 8   |
| (c) | (i)  | *Income tax computation*                        |       |     |
|     |      | Trading profit                                  | ½     |     |
|     |      | Building society interest                       | ½     |     |
|     |      | Individual savings account interest (exempt)    | ½     |     |
|     |      | Interest from NS&I certificates (exempt)        | ½     |     |
|     |      | Interest from government stocks                 | 1     |     |
|     |      | Dividends                                       | ½     |     |
|     |      | Personal allowance                              | ½     |     |
|     |      | Income tax liability                            | 1     |     |
|     |      | Income tax suffered at source                   | 1     |     |
|     |      |                                                 |       | 6   |
|     | (ii) | *Income tax payments*                           |       |     |
|     |      | Balancing payment                               | 1½    |     |
|     |      | Payments on account                             | 1½    |     |
|     |      |                                                 |       | 3   |
| (d) |      | Interest                                        | 1     |     |
|     |      | Calculation                                     | 1     |     |
|     |      | Penalty                                         | 1     |     |
|     |      |                                                 |       | 3   |
|     |      |                                                 |       | 25  |

(a) **Na Style trading profits 2010/11, 2011/12 and 2012/13**

| Year | Basis period | Working | Taxable Profits £ |
|------|-------------|---------|-------------------|
| 2010/11 | 1.1.11 – 5.4.11 | £25,200 × 3/6 | 12,600 |
| 2011/12 | 1.1.11 – 31.12.11 (N) | £25,200 + £21,600 × 6/12 | 36,000 |
| 2012/13 | 1.7.11 – 30.6.12 |  | 21,600 |

*Note:* because the accounting period ending in the second tax year is less than twelve months, the basis period for that year is the first twelve months of trading.

**Overlap profits**

| Overlap period | Working | Overlap profits £ |
|---|---|---|
| 1.1.11 – 5.4.11 | £25,200 × 3/6 | 12,600 |
| 1.7.11 – 31.12.11 | £21,600 × 6/12 | 10,800 |

(b) **Na Style tax adjusted trading profit for year ended 30 June 2013**

| | | £ | £ |
|---|---|---|---|
| Net profit | | | 23,000 |
| Add: | depreciation | 2,635 | |
| | motor expenses – private use | | |
| | 7,000/8,000 × £2,200 | 1,925 | |
| | professional fees – accountancy | 0 | |
| | professional fees – lease (N) | 1,260 | |
| | property expenses – private use | | |
| | 1/3 × £12,900 | 4,300 | |
| | purchases – goods taken for own use (selling price) | 450 | |
| | other expenses – fine | 400 | |
| | other expenses – political party donation | 80 | |
| | other expenses – trade subscription | 0 | |
| | | | 11,050 |
| | | | 34,050 |
| Less: | telephone – business use 20% × £1,200 | 240 | |
| | capital allowances | 810 | (1,050) |
| Tax adjusted trading profit | | | 33,000 |

*Note:* legal expenses relating to the *grant* of a short lease are not allowable.

(c) (i) **Na Style tax payable for 2013/14**

| | Non-savings income £ | Savings income £ | Dividend income £ | Total £ |
|---|---|---|---|---|
| Trading income (part (b)) | 33,000 | | | |
| BSI £560 × 100/80 | | 700 | | |
| ISA interest (exempt) | | 0 | | |
| NS&I interest (exempt) | | 0 | | |
| Interest from stocks (gross) | | 1,440 | | |
| UK dividends £1,080 × 100/90 | | | 1,200 | |
| Net income | 33,000 | 2,140 | 1,200 | 36,340 |
| Less: personal allowance | (9,440) | | | |
| Taxable income | 23,560 | 2,140 | 1,200 | 26,900 |

| | £ | £ |
|---|---|---|
| Income tax | | |
| Non-savings income | | |
| £23,560 × 20% | | 4,712 |
| Savings income | | |
| £2,140 × 20% | | 428 |
| Dividend income | | |
| £1,200 × 10% | | 120 |
| Tax liability | | 5,260 |

|  | £ | £ |
|---|---|---|
| Less: tax suffered | | |
| Tax credit on dividend income £1,200 × 10% | 120 | |
| Tax on building society interest £700 × 20% | 140 | |
| | | (260) |
| Tax payable | | 5,000 |

(ii) **Na Style balancing payment for 2013/14**

|  | £ |
|---|---|
| Tax payable (part (i)) | 5,000 |
| Less: payments on account | (3,200) |
| Balancing payment due 31 January 2015 | 1,800 |
| | |
| *First payment on account 2014/15* | |
| ½ × £5,000 due 31 January 2015 | 2,500 |
| *Second payment on account 2014/15* | |
| ½ × £5,000 due 31 July 2015 | 2,500 |

(d) **Consequences of not making balancing payment until 31 May 2015**

Interest is charged where a balancing payment is paid late. This will run from 1 February 2015 to 31 May 2015.

The interest charge will be £1,800 × 3% × 4/12 = £18.

In addition, a penalty of £1,800 @ 5% = £90 will be imposed as the balancing payment is made after the penalty date (30 days after the due date) but not more than five months after the penalty date.

# 12 Simon House

**Text references.** The badges of trade are discussed in Chapter 7 which also deals with the computation of trading profit. Chapter 2 deals with income tax computation. Chapter 13 covers computation of chargeable gains for individuals.

**Top tips.** Think carefully about what costs are allowable as part of trading expenses in part (b) and, alternatively, as part of the cost of the asset in part (c). Not all the expenses are allowable in both cases.

**Easy marks.** The examiner gave you the badges of trade in part (a) so it should have been easy marks to comment on them.

**Examiner's comments.** This question was very well answered, and often helped marginal candidates to achieve a pass mark. In part (a) a number of candidates failed to score any marks because they did not state what did or did not indicate trading. For example, stating that the 'length of ownership' means how long an item has owned did not score any marks. It was necessary to explain that the sale of property within a short time of its acquisition is an indication of trading. Part (b) presented no problems for most candidates. In this type of question it is always best to produce full computations for each option. This will maximise marks if any mistakes are made. It was pleasing to see that many candidates correctly restricted the Class 2 NIC to 19 weeks' contributions.

|  |  |  | Marks |
|---|---|---|---|
| (a) | Subject matter | ½ | |
| | Length of ownership | ½ | |
| | Frequency of transactions | ½ | |
| | Work done | ½ | |
| | Circumstances of realisation | ½ | |
| | Profit motive | ½ | |
| | | | 3 |
| (b) | Income | ½ | |
| | Acquisition of house | ½ | |
| | Legal fees on acquisition | ½ | |
| | Renovation costs | ½ | |
| | Legal fees on sale | ½ | |
| | Loan interest | 1 | |
| | Personal allowance | ½ | |
| | Income tax liability | 1 | |
| | Class 4 NICs | 1½ | |
| | Class 2 NICs | 1½ | |
| | | | 8 |
| (c) | Sale proceeds | ½ | |
| | Legal fees on sale | ½ | |
| | Cost of house | ½ | |
| | Legal fees on acquisition | ½ | |
| | Enhancement expenditure | ½ | |
| | Loan interest – not allowable | ½ | |
| | Annual exempt amount | ½ | |
| | Capital gains tax liability | ½ | |
| | | | 4 |
| | | | 15 |

(a) **Badges of trade**

*Subject matter*

Some assets are commonly held as investments for their intrinsic value, for example an individual may buy shares for dividend income produced by them or may buy a painting to enjoy it as a work of art. A subsequent disposal of an investment asset usually produces a capital gain. Where the subject matter of a transaction is not an investment asset, any profit on resale is usually a trading profit.

*Length of ownership*

If items purchased are sold soon afterwards, this indicates trading transactions.

*Frequency of transactions*

Transactions which may, in isolation, be of a capital nature will be interpreted as trading transactions where their frequency indicates the carrying on of a trade.

*Work done*

When work is done to make an asset more marketable, or steps are taken to find purchasers, this is likely to be indicative of trading.

*Circumstances of realisation*

A forced sale, for example to realise funds for an emergency, is not likely to be treated as trading.

*Motive*

The absence of a profit motive will not necessarily preclude a tax charge as trading income, but its presence is a strong indication that a person is trading.

(b) **Simon House income tax and NICs for 2013/14 if trading**

|  | £ | £ |
|---|---:|---:|
| Income |  | 260,000 |
| Less: *costs incurred* |  |  |
| house | 127,000 |  |
| legal fees on acquisition | 1,800 |  |
| renovation | 50,600 |  |
| legal fees on sale | 2,600 |  |
| loan interest |  |  |
| £150,000 × 6% × 4/12 | 3,000 |  |
|  |  | (185,000) |
| Trading income/Net income |  | 75,000 |
| Less: personal allowance |  | (9,440) |
| Taxable income |  | 65,560 |
|  |  |  |
| *Income tax* |  |  |
| £32,010 @ 20% |  | 6,402 |
| £33,550 @ 40% |  | 13,420 |
| Income tax liability |  | 19,822 |
|  |  |  |
| *Class 4 NICs* |  |  |
| £(41,450 – 7,755) = £33,695 @ 9% |  | 3,033 |
| £(75,000 – 41,450) = £33,550 @ 2% |  | 671 |
| Total Class 4 NICs |  | 3,704 |
|  |  |  |
| *Class 2 NICs* |  |  |
| £2.70 × 19 weeks (N) |  | 51 |

*Note:* marks were awarded for any reasonable attempt at calculating the number of weeks. ½ mark was deducted if 52 weeks were used.

(c) **Simon House capital gains tax 2013/14 if not trading**

|  | £ | £ |
|---|---:|---:|
| Sale proceeds |  | 260,000 |
| Less: legal fees on sale |  | (2,600) |
| Net proceeds of sale |  | 257,400 |
| Less: cost of house | 127,000 |  |
| legal fees on acquisition | 1,800 |  |
| Renovation | 50,600 |  |
| loan interest (N) | 0 |  |
|  |  | (179,400) |
| Chargeable gain |  | 78,000 |
| Less: annual exempt amount |  | (10,900) |
| Taxable gain |  | 67,100 |
|  |  |  |
| *Capital gains tax* |  |  |
| £32,010 @ 18% |  | 5,762 |
| £(67,100 – 32,010) = 35,090 @ 28% |  | 9,825 |
| Capital gains tax liability |  | 15,587 |

*Note:* the loan interest is a revenue expense and so is not allowable in computing the chargeable gain.

# 13 Bayle Defender

## Marking scheme

|  |  |  |  | Marks |
|---|---|---|---|---|
| (a) | (i) | Impairment loss | ½ | |
|  |  | Gifts to customers | 1 | |
|  |  | Donations to political parties | ½ | |
|  |  | Lease of motor car | 1 | |
|  |  | Personal tax advice | ½ | |
|  |  | Property expenses | 1 | |
|  |  | Parking fines | ½ | |
|  |  | Professional subscription | ½ | |
|  |  | Golf membership fee | ½ | |
|  |  |  |  | 6 |
|  | (ii) | Trading profits | ½ | |
|  |  | Director's remuneration | ½ | |
|  |  | Bonus payments | 1 | |
|  |  | Interest from savings certificates | ½ | |
|  |  | Interest from government stocks | ½ | |
|  |  | Dividends | ½ | |
|  |  | Personal allowance | 1 | |
|  |  | Income tax | 2 | |
|  |  | Tax suffered at source | 1½ | |
|  |  |  |  | 8 |

(iii) **Tax payments**

| | | |
|---|---|---|
| Balancing payment | 1 | |
| Payments on account | 1 | |
| **Interest and penalties** | | |
| Interest | 1½ | |
| Penalties | 1½ | |
| | | 5 |

(b) (i) Monthly earnings period thresholds    1

| | | |
|---|---|---|
| Employee Class 1 NIC | 1½ | |
| Employer Class 1 NIC | 1½ | |
| | | 4 |

(ii) **Trading income assessments**

| | | |
|---|---|---|
| 2013/14 | 1½ | |
| 2014/15 | 2½ | |
| | | 4 |

**NIC**

| | | |
|---|---|---|
| Class 2 NIC | 1½ | |
| Class 4 NIC | 1 | |
| Bayle | ½ | |
| | | 3 |
| | | 30 |

---

(a) (i) **Bayle Defender – Trading profit for the year ended 30 September 2013**

| | £ |
|---|---|
| Net profit | 173,302 |
| Add: Impairment loss | 0 |
| Gifts to customers  - Clocks | 3,300 |
|                   - Bottles of champagne | 2,480 |
| Donations to political parties | 2,900 |
| Lease of motor car £4,345 × 15% | 652 |
| Personal tax advice | 600 |
| Property expenses £46,240 × 2/5 | 18,496 |
| Parking fines | 520 |
| Professional subscriptions | 0 |
| Golf club membership fee | 960 |
| Taxable trading profit | 203,210 |

*Tutorial notes*

(1) The recovered impairments loss will have been allowed as a deduction when originally written off, so the recovery is now taxable. Therefore no adjustment is required.

(2) Gifts to customers are only an allowable deduction if they cost less than £50 per recipient per tax year, are not of food, drink, tobacco or vouchers for exchangeable goods and carry a conspicuous advertisement for the trader making the gift.

(3) The motor car has a $CO_2$ emission rate in excess of 130 grams per kilometre, so 15% of the leasing costs are not allowed.

(ii)     **Bayle Defender – Income tax computation 2013/14**

| | Non-savings income £ | Savings income £ | Dividend income £ | Total £ |
|---|---|---|---|---|
| Trading profit (from a(i) above) | 203,210 | | | |
| Employment income £(42,000 + 6,000) | 48,000 | | | |
| Interest from savings certificates (exempt) | | 0 | | |
| Interest from gilts (gross) | | 3,600 | | |
| Dividends (£9,900 × 100/90) | | | 11,000 | |
| Net income | 251,210 | 3,600 | 11,000 | 265,810 |
| Less: PA | (0) | (0) | (0) | (0) |
| Taxable income | 251,210 | 3,600 | 11,000 | 265,810 |

| Tax | £ | £ |
|---|---|---|
| £32,010 @ 20% | | 6,402 |
| £(150,000 – 32,010) = 117,990 @ 40% | | 47,196 |
| £(251,210 – 150,000 + 3,600) = 104,810 @ 45% | | 47,164 |
| £11,000 @ 37.5% | | 4,125 |
| Income tax liability | | 104,887 |
| Tax suffered at source | | |
| PAYE £48,000 @ 45% | 21,600 | |
| Dividends £11,000 @ 10% | 1,100 | (22,700) |
| Income tax payable | | 82,187 |

*Tutorial notes*

(1)     The bonus payment of £6,000 that Bayle became entitled to on 10 March 2013 will have been treated as being received during 2012/13.

(2)     Interest received on maturity of savings certificates issued by National Savings and Investments is exempt.

(3)     No personal allowance is available as Bayle's net income of £265,810 exceeds £118,880.

(iii)   **Tax payments**

Bayle's balancing payment for 2013/14 will be £31,580 (82,187 – 50,607).

In addition, she will have to make the first payment on account for 2014/15 of £41,093 (82,187 × 50%), so the total amount payable on 31 January 2015 will be £72,673 (31,580 + 41,093).

**Interest and penalties**

Interest is charged where payments are made late. This will run from the end of the due date of 31 January 2015 to 31 August 2015.

The interest charge will be £1,272 (72,673 × 3% × 7/12).

Two penalties each of £1,579 (31,580 at 5%) will be imposed on the balancing payment, one when it is thirty days late and the other when it is a further five months late.

(b)    (i)    The monthly primary earnings threshold is £646 (7,755/12) and the monthly secondary earnings threshold is £641 (7,696/12).

Fyle will pay employee Class 1 NIC for 2013/14 of £1,274 (£(3,300 – 646) = 2,654 @ 12% × 4).

Bayle will pay employer's Class 1 NIC for 2013/14 of £1,468 (£(3,300 – 641) = 2,659 @ 13.8% × 4).

*Tutorial note*

The alternative approach using the annual earnings threshold and then taking 4/12ths of an annual NIC figure is acceptable.

(ii)    (1)    **Trading income assessments**

Fyle's trading income assessment for 2013/14 is £14,400 calculated as follows:

|  | £ |
|---|---|
| Basis period: 1 December 2013 to 5 April 2014 | |
| £216,000 × 4/12 | 72,000 |
| | |
| Profit share £72,000 × 20% | 14,400 |

The assessment for 2014/15 is £44,000 calculated as follows:

|  | £ |
|---|---|
| Basis period: 1 December 2013 to 30 November 2014 | |
| £216,000 × 10/12 | 180,000 |
| £240,000 × 2/12 | 40,000 |
| | 220,000 |
| | |
| Profit share £220,000 × 20% | 44,000 |

*Tutorial notes*

(1)    The commencement rules apply to Fyle for 2013/14 since he will join as a partner on 1 December 2013.

(2)    The assessment for 2014/15 is for the 12 months from when Fyle joins the partnership.

(2)    NIC

Fyle will pay Class 2 NIC for 2013/14 of £(2.70 × 18) = £49.

He will pay Class 4 NIC for 2013/14 of £(14,400 − 7,755) = 6,645 @ 9% = £598.

There are no NIC implications for Bayle.

# 14 Samantha Fabrique

**Text references.** Chapter 10 deals with trading losses.

**Top tips.** You should use the standard layout for losses: set up the columns and lines required and then slot in the numbers. A loss memorandum is also useful as a double check that you have used the losses correctly.

**Easy marks.** There were easy marks for setting out the trading income and gains stated in the question and using the personal allowance and annual exempt amount.

**Examiner's comments.** In part (a) many candidates explained the loss reliefs that were available rather than the factors that must be taken into account when deciding which loss reliefs to actually claim. In part (b) many candidates claimed loss relief against the total income for the year of the loss despite this income clearly being covered by the personal allowance. Very few candidates, even if they showed the capital gains separately, claimed loss relief against capital gains.

|  |  | Marks |  |
|---|---|---|---|
| (a) | Rate of tax | 1 |  |
|  | Timing of relief | 1 |  |
|  | Waste of personal allowance/annual exempt amount | 1 |  |
|  |  |  | 3 |
| (b) | Trading income | ½ |  |
|  | Trading loss relief carried forward | 1 |  |
|  | Building society interest | ½ |  |
|  | Trading loss relief against general income | 1 |  |
|  | Personal allowance | ½ |  |
|  | Gains | ½ |  |
|  | Capital loss relief carried forward | 1 |  |
|  | Trading loss relief against gains | 1 |  |
|  | Annual exempt amount | 1 | 7 |
|  |  |  | 10 |

(a) Factors that will influence an individual's choice of loss relief claim are:

(i) The rate of income tax or capital gains tax at which relief will be obtained, with preference being given to income charged at the additional rate of 45%, then the higher rate of 40%.

(ii) The timing of the relief obtained, with a claim against general income/capital gains of the current year or preceding year resulting in earlier relief than a carry forward claim against future trading profits.

(iii) The extent to which the income tax personal allowance and the capital gains tax annual exempt amount will be wasted by using a claim against general income/capital gains.

(b) **Samantha Fabrique – taxable income**

|  | 2011/12 £ | 2012/13 £ | 2013/14 £ | 2014/15 £ |
|---|---|---|---|---|
| Trading income | 7,290 | 42,600 | 0 | 14,725 |
| Less: trading loss relief carried forward | (0) | (0) | (0) | (7,000) |
|  | 7,290 | 42,600 | 0 | 7,725 |
| Building society interest | 0 | 6,100 | 3,800 | 2,130 |
|  | 7,290 | 48,700 | 3,800 | 9,855 |
| Less: trading loss relief against general income (N) | (0) | (48,700) | (0) | (0) |
| Net income | 7,290 | 0 | 3,800 | 9,855 |
| Less: personal allowance | (7,290) | (0) | (3,800) | (9,440) |
| Taxable income | 0 | 0 | 0 | 415 |

**Samantha Fabrique – taxable gains**

|  | 2011/12 £ | 2012/13 £ | 2013/14 £ | 2014/15 £ |
|---|---|---|---|---|
| Gains | 20,900 | 23,300 | 0 | 14,000 |
| Less: trading loss relief against gains (note) | (0) | (23,300) | (0) | (0) |
|  | 20,900 | 0 | 0 | 14,000 |
| Less: capital loss carried forward | (0) | (0) | (0) | (3,400) |
|  | 20,900 | 0 | 0 | 10,600 |
| Less: annual exempt amount | (10,900) | (0) | (0) | (10,900) |
| Taxable gains | 10,000 | 0 | 0 | 0 |

*Note.* Loss relief has been claimed against general income and gains for 2012/13 since this gives relief at the earliest date and at the highest rates of tax. No claim should be made to set the loss against general income in 2013/14 since this is already covered by the personal allowance for that year.

*Trading loss memorandum*

| | £ |
|---|---|
| Loss 2013/14 | 79,000 |
| Less: used 2012/13 (income) | (48,700) |
| used 2012/13 (gains) | (23,300) |
| Available for c/f | 7,000 |
| Less: used 2014/15 | (7,000) |
| Loss unused | 0 |

# 15 Michael and Sean

**Text references.** Chapter 1 covers the overall function and purpose of taxation in a modern economy. Chapter 10 deals with trading losses.

**Top tips.** Remember that if a taxpayer claims loss relief against general income, the benefit of the personal allowance may be lost.

**Easy marks.** A few minutes thought should have enabled you to identify the points required for part (a). One mark usually indicates one point needs to be made so don't write more than one or two sentences for each part.

**Examiner's comments.** Part (a) was generally well answered, although candidates should note that where just one or two marks are available for a requirement then just a short sentence is required – not a detailed explanation. Not surprisingly, it was part (b) that caused the most problems in the exam paper. For Michael, the claims should have been fairly straightforward given that he only had one source of income for each year. However, some candidates were not even aware that a claim could be made against total income. For Sean, a few candidates suggested that the loss be carried forward despite the trade ceasing. In both cases, it was generally not appreciated that the most advantageous choice of loss relief claims would generally preserve the benefit of personal allowances.

**Marking scheme**

| | | | | | Marks |
|---|---|---|---|---|---|
| (a) | (i) | Saving | | | 1 |
| | (ii) | Charitable support | | | 1 |
| | (iii) | Capital gains reliefs | | 1 | |
| | | Plant and machinery | | 1 | |
| | | | | | 2 |
| (b) | **Michael** | | | | |
| | Relief against total income | | | 1 | |
| | Claims | | | 1 | |
| | Rate of tax saved | – 2009/10 | | 1 | |
| | | – 2010/11 | | 1 | |
| | Carry forward | | | 1 | |
| | **Sean** | | | | |
| | Available loss | | | 1 | |
| | Terminal loss relief | | | 1 | |
| | Claims | | | 1 | |
| | Rates of tax saved | | | 1½ | |
| | Relief against total income | | | 1½ | |
| | | | | | 11 |
| | | | | | 15 |

(a) (i) Saving is encouraged by offering individuals tax incentives such as income tax and capital gains tax exemptions on individual savings accounts and income tax relief on pension contributions.

(ii) Charitable support is encouraged by giving individuals income tax relief on donations made through the gift aid scheme or by payroll deduction.

(iii) Entrepreneurs are encouraged to build their own businesses through various capital gains tax reliefs such as entrepreneurs' relief.

Investment in plant and machinery is encouraged through capital allowances.

(b) **Michael**

The loss of £25,230 for 2012/13 can be claimed against general income for the three preceding years, under early years loss relief, earliest year first, since it is incurred in the first four years of trading.

The loss relief claim will therefore be £18,765 in 2009/10 and £(25,230 – 18,765) = £6,465 in 2010/11.

For 2009/10 this will waste Michael's personal allowance, with the balance of the claim of £(18,765 – 9,440) = £9,325 saving income tax at the basic rate of 20%.

For 2010/11 Michael has income of £(49,575 – 9,440 – 32,010) = £8,125 subject to income tax at the higher rate of 40%, so the claim of £6,465 will save tax at the higher rate.

Alternatively, Michael could have carried the trading loss forward against future trading profits, but the trading profit of £9,065 for 2013/14 is covered by the personal allowance, and there is no information regarding future trading profits.

*Tutorial note*

A claim for loss relief against general income for 2012/13 and/or 2011/12 is not possible since Michael does not have any income for either of these years.

**Sean**

The unused overlap profits brought forward are added to the loss for the year ended 31 December 2013, so the total loss for 2013/14 is £(23,100 + 3,600) = £26,700.

The whole of the loss can be claimed as a terminal since it is for the final 12 months of trading. The claim is against trading income for the year of the loss (2013/14 – nil) and the three preceding years, latest first.

The terminal loss claim will therefore be £3,700 in 2012/13, £18,900 in 2011/12 and £(26,700 – 3,700 – 18,900) = £4,100 in 2010/11.

The property business profits are sufficient to utilise Sean's personal allowance for each year, so the loss relief claims will save income tax at the basic rate of 20%.

Alternatively, Sean could have initially claimed loss relief against his general income for 2013/14 and/or 2012/13, but this would have wasted his personal allowance for either or both of those years.

# 16 Ae, Bee, Cae, and Eu

**Text references.** Partnerships are covered in Chapter 11. Assessable trading income is dealt with in Chapter 9 and capital allowances are covered in Chapter 8.

**Top tips.** Remember that there is no annual investment allowance nor writing down allowance in the final period of account.

**Easy marks.** Obtaining relief for overlap profits in part (b) was an easy mark.

**Examiner's comments.** This question was extremely well answered by the majority of candidates, many of whom scored maximum marks. One of the main problems in the answers of poorer candidates was not showing the appropriate tax years, thus losing a lot of marks throughout.

|  |  |  |  | Marks |
|---|---|---|---|---|
| (a) | 2011/12 |  | 1½ |  |
|  | 2012/13 |  | 1 |  |
|  | 2013/14 | – Ae and Bee | 1 |  |
|  |  | – Cae | 1½ |  |
|  |  |  |  | 5 |
| (b) | 2014/15 | – Assessment | 1 |  |
|  |  | – Capital allowances | ½ |  |
|  | 2015/16 | – Assessment | 1 |  |
|  |  | – Capital allowances | 1½ |  |
|  |  | – Relief for overlap profits | 1 |  |
|  |  |  |  | 5 |
|  |  |  |  | 10 |

(a) **Division of partnership profits for A, B and C**

|  | Total £ | A £ | B £ | C £ |
|---|---|---|---|---|
| y/e 30.6.12 | 54,000 | 27,000 | 27,000 | – |
| y/e 30.6.13 | 66,000 | 33,000 | 33,000 | – |
| y/e 30.6.14 | 87,000 | 29,000 | 29,000 | 29,000 |

Then allocate to tax years:
*2011/12*
A and B – First year
Actual basis 1.7.11 – 5.4.12

|  |  | A | B | C |
|---|---|---|---|---|
| 9/12 x £27,000 |  | 20,250 | 20,250 | – |

*2012/13*
A and B – Second year
First 12 months y/e 30.6.12

|  |  | A | B | C |
|---|---|---|---|---|
|  |  | 27,000 | 27,000 | – |

*2013/14*
A and B – Third year
CYB y/e 30.6.13

|  |  | A | B |
|---|---|---|---|
|  |  | 33,000 | 33,000 |

C – First year
Actual basis 1.7.13 – 5.4.14

|  |  | C |
|---|---|---|
| 9/12 × £29,000 |  | 21,750 |

(b)     **Cessation for E**

|  | £ | £ |
|---|---|---|
| *2014/15* | | |
| CYB y/e 30.6.14 Trading income | 62,775 | |
| Less: CAs (W) | (1,575) | 61,200 |
| | | |
| *2015/16* | | |
| Cessation y/e 30.6.15 and p/e 30.9.15 | 72,000 | |
| Trading income £(57,600 + 14,400) | | |
| Less: CAs  £(1,292 + 3,108)(W) | (4,400) | |
| Overlap profits | (19,800) | 47,800 |

Working

|  | Main pool | Allowances |
|---|---|---|
| | £ | £ |
| *y/e 30.6.14* | | |
| TWDV b/f | 8,750 | |
| WDA @ 18% | (1,575) | 1,575 |
| TWDV c/f | 7,175 | |
| *y/e 30.6.15* | | |
| WDA @ 18% | (1,292) | 1,292 |
| TWDV c/f | 5,883 | |
| *p/e 30.9.15* | | |
| Addition | 2,400 | |
| Disposal | (5,175) | |
| BA | 3,108 | 3,108 |

# 17 Auy Man and Bim Men

**Text references.** Residence is dealt with in Chapter 2. Adjustment of profit is covered in Chapter 7 and capital allowances in Chapter 8. Assessable trading income is dealt with in Chapter 9 and partnerships in Chapter 11. National insurance contributions are the subject of Chapter 12. VAT is covered in Chapters 26 and 27.

**Top tips.** You need to look carefully at the $CO_2$ emissions of the motor cars to determine the capital allowances treatment. Remember that the detail on this is in the tax tables available in the exam.

**Easy marks.** There were easy marks for the adjustment of profit in part (b) if you followed the instructions to start with the profit before taxation figure and indicated with a zero any items which did not require adjustment.

**Examiner's comments.** This question was well answered, especially parts (b) and (c). In part (a) several candidates simply repeated the information contained within the question [rather than explaining the relevant rules]. There were generally no problems with part (b) although a number of candidates did not appreciate that they had to deduct the salary and interest on capital before allocating the balance of profits. Most candidates scored maximum marks for part (c). In part (d) the tax point was explained reasonably well, although some candidates wasted time by also giving details for the supply of goods. Some students struggled with the VAT calculation, assuming this to be much more complicated than it actually was. For 2 marks, all that was required was to select the output VAT of £25,600 and input VAT of £140 and £180 from the text, and then calculate the amount payable of £25,280. It was not necessary to calculate any VAT. The main problem as regards the VAT calculation using the flat rate scheme was that candidates incorrectly deducted input VAT.

| | | | | Marks |
|---|---|---|---|---|
| (a) | Auy Man | | 1 | |
| | Bim Men | | 1 | |
| | | | | 2 |
| (b) | **Trading profit** | | | |
| | Depreciation | | ½ | |
| | Input VAT | | ½ | |
| | Motor expenses | | 1 | |
| | Entertaining employees | | ½ | |
| | Appropriation of profit | | ½ | |
| | Excessive salary | | ½ | |
| | Deduction of capital allowances | | ½ | |
| | Capital allowances | - Main pool | 2 | |
| | | - Motor car [1] | 1½ | |
| | | - Motor car [2] | 2 | |
| | | - Special rate pool | 1½ | |
| | | - First year allowance | 1½ | |
| | **Trading income assessments** | | | |
| | Salary | | ½ | |
| | Interest on capital | | 1 | |
| | Balance of profits | | 1 | |
| | | | | 15 |
| (c) | Auy Man | | 2 | |
| | Bim Men | | 1 | |
| | | | | 3 |
| (d) | (i) | **Tax point** | | |
| | | Basic tax point | 1 | |
| | | Payment received or invoice issued | 1 | |
| | | Issue of invoice within 14 days | 1 | |
| | | | | 3 |
| | (ii) | **VAT paid** | | |
| | | Output VAT and input VAT | 1 | |
| | | Calculation | 1 | |
| | | | | 2 |
| | (iii) | **Flat rate scheme** | | |
| | | Joining the scheme | 1 | |
| | | Continuing to use the scheme | 1½ | |
| | | VAT payable | 2 | |
| | | VAT saving | ½ | |
| | | | | 5 |
| | | | | 30 |

## (a) Residence status

Auy will automatically be treated as resident in the United Kingdom for 2013/14 as she spent 183 days or more in the United Kingdom in this tax year.

Bim will automatically be treated as resident in the United Kingdom for 2013/14 as she had a home in the United Kingdom and no home overseas in this tax year.

## (b) Adjusted trading profit for y/e 5 April 2014

|  | £ | £ |
|---|---|---|
| Profit before taxation |  | 80,562 |
| Add: depreciation | 3,400 |  |
| input VAT | 0 |  |
| motor expenses £2,600 × 30% | 780 |  |
| entertaining employees | 0 |  |
| appropriation of profit: salary for Bim | 4,000 |  |
| appropriation of profit: excessive salary for Auy's husband £(15,000 – 10,000) | 5,000 |  |
|  |  | 13,180 |
|  |  | 93,742 |
| Less: capital allowances (W) |  | (13,742) |
| Tax adjusted trading profit |  | 80,000 |

*Working*

Capital allowances y/e 5 April 2014

|  | £ | Main pool £ | Motor car [1] £ | Motor car [2] £ | Special rate pool £ | Allowances £ |
|---|---|---|---|---|---|---|
| TWDV b/f |  | 3,100 | 18,000 | 14,000 |  |  |
| *Additions* |  |  |  |  |  |  |
| Motor car [4] |  | 14,200 |  |  |  |  |
| Motor car [5] |  |  |  |  | 10,875 |  |
|  |  | 17,300 |  |  |  |  |
| *Disposal* |  |  |  |  |  |  |
| Motor car [2] |  |  |  | (13,100) |  |  |
| BA |  |  |  | (900) × 70% |  | 630 |
| WDA @ 18% |  | (3,114) |  |  |  | 3,114 |
| WDA @ 8% |  |  | (1,440) × 70% |  | (870) | 1,878 |
| *Addition* |  |  |  |  |  |  |
| Motor car [3] | 11,600 |  |  |  |  |  |
| FYA @ 100% | (11,600) × 70% |  |  |  |  | 8,120 |
|  | 0 |  |  |  |  |  |
| TWDV c/f |  | 14,186 | 16,560 |  | 10,005 |  |
| Allowances |  |  |  |  |  | 13,742 |

*Tutorial notes*

Motor car [1] and Motor car [5] have $CO_2$ emissions over 130 grams per kilometre and therefore qualify for writing down allowances at the rate of 8%. Motor car [1] is in a single asset pool because of private use by a partner. Motor car [5] is in the special rate pool because it is not used privately by either partner.

Motor car [3] has $CO_2$ emissions of less than 95 grams per kilometre and therefore qualifies for the 100% first year allowance.

Motor car [4] has $CO_2$ emissions between 96 and 130 grams per kilometre, and therefore qualifies for writing down allowances at the rate of 18% as part of the main pool.

### Trading income assessments 2013/14

|  | Total £ | Auy Man £ | Bim Men £ |
|---|---|---|---|
| Salary | 4,000 | 0 | 4,000 |
| Interest £56,000/34,000 @ 5% | 4,500 | 2,800 | 1,700 |
| Balance (80:20) | 71,500 | 57,200 | 14,300 |
|  | 80,000 | 60,000 | 20,000 |

(c)     **Auy Man and Bim Men – national insurance contributions 2013/14**

*Auy Man*

|  | £ |
|---|---|
| Main rate: £(41,450 – 7,755) = 33,695 @ 9% | 3,033 |
| Additional rate: £(60,000 – 41,450) = 18,550 @ 2% | 371 |
|  | 3,404 |

*Bim Men*

| Main rate only: £ (20,000 – 7,755) = 12,245 @ 9% | £1,102 |
|---|---|

(d)     (i)     **Tax point**

The basic tax point is the date when services are completed.

If an invoice is issued or payment received before the basic tax point, then this becomes the actual tax point.

If an invoice is issued within 14 days of the basic tax point, the invoice date will usually be the actual tax point.

(ii)    **VAT paid for the year ended 5 April 2014**

The partnership's output VAT is £25,600 and its total input VAT is £(180 + 140) = £320.

Therefore VAT of £25,280 (25,600 – 320) will have been paid to HM Revenue & Customs during the year ended 5 April 2014.

(iii)   **Flat rate scheme**

The partnership can join the flat rate scheme if its expected taxable turnover (excluding VAT) for the next 12 months does not exceed £150,000.

The partnership can continue to use the scheme until its total turnover (including VAT, but excluding sales of capital assets) for the previous year exceeds £230,000.

If the partnership had used the flat rate scheme throughout the year ended 5 April 2014 then it would have paid VAT of £(140,762 + 25,600) = £166,362 @ 14% = £23,291.

This is a saving of £(25,280 – 23,291) = £1,989 for the year.

# 18 Flick Pick

**Text references.** Employment income is covered in Chapter 3 and taxable benefits in Chapter 4. Taxable income is covered in Chapter 2. Partnerships are the subject of Chapter 11. Property income is dealt with in Chapter 6. National insurance contributions are in Chapter 12. Choice of accounting date is covered in Chapter 9, which also contains the rules on basis periods. VAT will be found in Chapters 26 and 27.

**Top tips.** In a multiple part question such as this, it is really important to attempt all the parts.

**Easy marks.** The living accommodation benefit should have been familiar and the property income computation was straightforward. A quick look at the tax tables would have given the classes of national insurance contributions required for part (b). Part (d)(iii) might have looked a little unusual but was really a basic question on the tax point.

**Examiner's comments.** There were many very good answers to part (a). The aspects that caused problems were not appreciating that:

*   When calculating Flick's share of the partnership profits, the capital allowances had to be deducted before allocating the profit.

*   When calculating the property business profit, no deduction is given for the cost of replacement furniture but the wear and tear allowance can be claimed.

There were many very good answers to part (b), but some candidates missed some very easy marks by explaining NIC in detail, but not actually answering the requirements of the question.

In part (c), quite a few candidates appreciated that an accounting date of 30 April would result in overlap profits and that the basis period rules would be more complicated. Very few knew that the interval between earning profits and paying the related tax liability would be longer or that it would be easier to implement tax planning. In part (d), although it was disappointing to see a number of candidates deduct inputs when calculating VAT using the flat rate basis, the first requirement was otherwise generally answered very well. The second requirement caused a lot of confusion, with quite a few candidates discussing VAT registration – the correct answer was simply that voluntary VAT registration reduced the partnership's profits by the amount of VAT payable calculated in the first requirement. For the final requirement, quite a few candidates just explained the time of supply rules, without relating them to the information given in the question. It was clearly stated that an invoice was issued on the date of a film being screened – so the 14-day rule for issuing an invoice was irrelevant.

## Marking scheme

| | | | Marks | |
|---|---|---|---|---|
| (a) | Salary | | ½ | |
| | Living accommodation | – Annual value | ½ | |
| | | – Additional benefit | 2 | |
| | | – Furniture | 1 | |
| | Trading profit | – Profit share | 2 | |
| | | – Assessment | 1 | |
| | | – Capital allowances | 2 | |
| | Property business profit | – Rent receivable | ½ | |
| | | – Council tax | ½ | |
| | | – Wear and tear allowance | 1 | |
| | | – Furniture | ½ | |
| | Personal allowance | | ½ | |
| | | | | 12 |
| (b) | Class 1 NIC | | 1 | |
| | Class 1A NIC | | 1 | |
| | Class 2 NIC | | 1 | |
| | Class 4 NIC | | 1 | |
| | | | | 4 |
| (c) | Interval | | 1 | |
| | Tax planning | | 1 | |
| | Basis period rules more complicated | | 1 | |
| | Profit assessed in the year of cessation | | 1 | |
| | | | | 4 |
| (d) | (i) | Flat rate scheme | 1 | |
| | | Normal basis | 1 | |
| | | Conclusion | 1 | |
| | | | | 3 |
| | (ii) | No recovery of VAT by customers | 1 | |
| | | Possible need to absorb VAT | 1 | |
| | | Conclusion | 1 | |
| | | | | 3 |
| | (iii) | VAT period | 1 | |
| | | Basic tax point | 1 | |
| | | Deposit | 1 | |
| | | Balance | 1 | |
| | | | | 4 |
| | | | | 30 |

## (a) Flick Pick – Taxable income 2013/14

|  |  |  | Non-savings income £ |
|---|---|---|---:|
| Employment income |  |  |  |
| Salary |  |  | 25,665 |
| Living accommodation | – Annual value |  | 4,600 |
|  | – Additional benefit (W1) |  | 2,760 |
|  | – Furniture £9,400 × 20% |  | 1,880 |
|  |  |  | 34,905 |
| Trading profit (W2) |  |  | 8,220 |
| Property income (W3) |  |  | 5,940 |
| Net income |  |  | 49,065 |
| Less personal allowance |  |  | (9,440) |
| Taxable income |  |  | 39,625 |

*Workings*

### 1 Living accommodation additional benefit

|  | £ |
|---|---:|
| Market value | 144,000 |
| Less limit | (75,000) |
|  | 69,000 |
|  |  |
| Additional benefit £69,000 × 4% | 2,760 |

*Tutorial note*

Since the property was acquired more than 6 years before being provided to Flick, the market value at the date it was provided to her is used as the cost of providing the benefit, instead of the original cost.

### 2 Trading profit

First work out the capital allowances for the partnership.

|  | Motor car £ | Allowances @ 60% £ |
|---|---:|---:|
| Purchase | 18,750 |  |
| WDA @ 8% × 4/12 | (500) | 300 |
| TWDV c/f | 18,250 |  |

*Tutorial note*

The partnership's motor car has $CO_2$ emissions over 130 g/km and therefore qualifies for writing down allowance at the rate of 8%.

Flick's share of the partnership's trading profit for the period ended 30 April 2014 is then calculated as follows.

|  | £ |
|---|---:|
| Trading profit | 29,700 |
| Less capital allowances | (300) |
|  | 29,400 |
| Less salary paid to Art £6,000 × 4/12 | (2,000) |
| Profits available for profit sharing | 27,400 |
|  |  |
| Profit share for Flick £27,400 × 40% | 10,960 |
|  |  |
| Flick's trading income for 2013/14 £10,960 × 3/4 | 8,220 |

*Tutorial note*

Flick's basis period for 2013/14 is 1 January 2014 to 5 April 2014 since this is her first year of trading.

3    *Property business profit*

|  | £ | £ |
|---|---|---|
| Rent receivable £660 × 12 | | 7,920 |
| Less   council tax | 1,320 | |
| wear and tear allowance £(7,920 – 1,320) × 10% | 660 | |
| Furniture | 0 | |
| | | (1,980) |
| | | 5,940 |

*Tutorial note*

No deduction is available for replacement furniture. Instead the wear and tear allowance is claimed.

(b)    3D Ltd will be responsible for paying class 1 NIC (both primary and secondary contributions) in respect of Flick's salary.

3D Ltd will be responsible for paying class 1A NIC in respect of Flick's taxable benefits.

Flick will be responsible for paying class 2 NIC in respect of her trading income.

Flick will be responsible for paying class 4 NIC in respect of her trading income.

(c)    **Advantages**

The interval between earning profits and paying the related tax liability will be 11 months longer. This can be particularly beneficial where profits are rising.

It will be possible to calculate taxable profits well in advance of the end of the tax year, making it much easier to implement tax planning and make pension contributions.

**Disadvantages**

The application of the basis period rules is more complicated.

The amount of profit assessed in the year of cessation could potentially be quite high as the basis period will be up to 23 months in length. Although overlap profits are deductible, these might be insignificant if the opening years' profits are low.

(d)    (i)    Using the flat rate scheme to calculate its VAT liability the partnership will have paid VAT of £(59,700 × 12%) = £7,164 for the quarter ended 31 March 2014.

If the partnership had used the normal basis it would have paid VAT of £(59,700 – 27,300 = 32,400 × 20/120) = £5,400.

It was therefore not beneficial to use the flat rate scheme as the additional cost of £(7,164 – 5,400) = £1,764 for the quarter would appear to outweigh the advantage of simplified VAT administration.

(ii)    The partnership's sales are all to members of the general public, who cannot recover the input VAT.

It may not therefore be possible to pass the output VAT on to customers in the prices charged. To the extent this is not possible the partnership would have had to absorb all or some of this amount itself as a cost.

It was therefore not beneficial for the partnership to have voluntarily registered for VAT from 1 January 2014. For the quarter ended 31 March 2014 voluntary registration reduced the partnership's profits by a maximum of £7,164 (£5,400 if the normal basis had been used).

(iii)    Output VAT must be accounted for according to the VAT period in which the supply is treated as being made. This is determined by the tax point.

The basic tax point is the date when the service is completed, which will be the date that a film is screened.

Where payment is received before the basic tax point, then this date becomes the actual tax point. The tax point for each 25% deposit is therefore the date that it is received.

Invoices are issued on the same day as the basic tax point, so this is the tax point for the balance of 75%.

# 19 Pi Casso

**Text references.** Chapter 17 covers self assessment and payment by individuals.

**Top tips.** Take care to start with the correct tax year. You need to realise that if you are paying tax for 2013/14 that the payments on account will be based on the previous year 2012/13. Take care when stating payment dates. Take the time to start correctly and then be methodical.

**Easy marks.** Parts (c) and (d) required you to write out the rules for filing returns and compliance check enquiries.

**Examiner's comments.** Part (a) caused the most problems, with the vast majority of candidates not being able to demonstrate how payments are calculated and paid under the self-assessment system. Class 2 national insurance contributions were often incorrectly included, whilst few candidates appreciated that a claim to reduce payments on account was possible. In part (b) most candidates appreciated that interest would be due, but very few mentioned the potential penalty that could be charged. It was disappointing that the self-assessment tax return submission dates were often not know in part (c). The same comment applies to part (d). Candidates often gave a long list of reasons why HMRC could make a compliance check enquiry on a return, but failed to mention that an enquiry might be on a completely random basis.

## Marking scheme

| | | Marks | |
|---|---|---|---|
| (a) | Second payment on account for 2012/13 | 2 | |
| | Balancing payment for 2012/13 | 2 | |
| | Claim to reduce payments on account | 1 | |
| | Payments on account for 2013/14 | 1 | |
| | Balancing payment for 2013/14 | 1 | |
| | First payment on account for 2014/15 | 1 | |
| | | | 8 |
| (b) | Interest | 1 | |
| | Penalty | 1 | |
| | | | 2 |
| (c) | Paper based return | 1 | |
| | Return filed online | 1 | |
| | | | 2 |
| (d) | Notification date | 1 | |
| | Random bases | 1 | |
| | Income/Deductions | 1 | |
| | | | 3 |
| | | | 15 |

(a)

| Due date | Tax year | Payment | £ |
|---|---|---|---|
| 31 July 2013 | 2012/13 | Second payment on account (N1) | 2,240 |
| 31 January 2014 | 2012/13 | Balancing payment (N2) | 5,490 |
| 31 January 2014 | 2013/14 | First payment on account (N3) | 1,860 |
| 31 July 2014 | 2013/14 | Second payment on account | 1,860 |
| 31 January 2015 | 2013/14 | Balancing payment (N4) | Nil |
| 31 January 2015 | 2014/15 | First payment on account (N5) | 1,860 |

*Notes*

(1)  The second payment on account for 2012/13 is based on Pi's income tax and Class 4 NIC liability for 2011/12. It is therefore £2,240 ((3,240 + 1,240 = 4,480) × 50%).

(2)  The balancing payment for 2012/13 is £5,490 (4,100 + 990 + 4,880) = £9,970 less the payments on account of £4,480 (£2,240 × 2)).

(3)  Pi will make a claim to reduce her total payments on account for 2013/14 to £3,720 (2,730 + 990), so each payment will be £1,860 (3,720 × 50%).

(4)  The balancing payment for 2013/14 is £Nil (3,720 less the payments on account of 3,720 (1,860 × 2)).

(5)  The first payment on account for 2014/15 is based on Pi's income tax and Class 4 NIC liability for 2013/14. It is therefore £1,860 ((2,730 + 990 = 3,720) × 50%).

(b)  (1)  If Pi's payments on account for 2013/14 were reduced to nil, then she would be charged interest on the payments due of £1,860 from the relevant due date to the date of payment.

(2)  A penalty of the difference between the reduced payment on account and the correct payment on account may be charged if the claim to reduce the payments on account to nil was made fraudulently or negligently.

(c)  (1)  Unless the return is issued after 31 July 2014, the latest date that Pi can submit a paper based self-assessment tax return for 2013/14 is 31 October 2014.

(2)  Alternatively, Pi has until 31 January 2015 to file her self-assessment tax return for 2013/14 online.

(d)  (1)  If HMRC intend to make a compliance check enquiry on Pi's 2013/14 tax return they will have to notify her within twelve months of the actual filing date if the return was delivered on or before the due date.

(2)  HMRC have the right to make a compliance check enquiry into the completeness and accuracy of any return and such an enquiry may be made on a completely random basis.

(3)  However, compliance check enquiries are generally made because of a suspicion that income has been undeclared or because deductions have been incorrectly claimed.

# 20 Ernest Vader

**Text references.** Self assessment for individuals is covered in Chapter 17. Ethics are covered in Chapter 1.

**Top tips.** The number of marks for each part gives an indication of the scope of the answer required. Part (c) was only awarded 2 marks so should have been answered by a couple of sentences.

**Easy marks.** The calculation of interest in part (d) required very little technical knowledge – 2 easy marks.

**Examiner's comments.** This question was not well answered, with many candidates attempting it as their final question or omitting it altogether. In part (a) most candidates knew the difference between tax evasion and tax avoidance, but many failed to score an easy mark by not stating that the taxpayer's actions would be viewed as tax evasion. Part (b) caused problems for most candidates but a common sense approach would have gained most of the available marks. Unfortunately, far too many candidates instead just incorrectly explained that it would be necessary to inform HMRC themselves. The time limits in part (c) were often not known and most candidates were unaware of the use of a discovery assessment despite being given help in the wording of the requirement. There was little excuse for getting the interest calculation wrong in part (d) as candidates were given the tax liability, the due date, the payment date and the rate of interest.

| | | | Marks |
|---|---|---|---|
| (a) | Tax evasion | 1 | |
| | Tax avoidance | 1 | |
| | Non-disclosure of disposal | 1 | |
| | | | 3 |
| (b) | Professional judgement: standard of conduct | 1 | |
| | Advise disclosure | 1 | |
| | Obligation to report for money laundering | 1 | |
| | Cease to act and inform HMRC | 1 | |
| | | | 4 |
| (c) | Lack of sufficient information | 1 | |
| | Time limits | 1 | |
| | | | 2 |
| (d) | (i) Interest period | 1 | |
| | Calculation | 1 | |
| | | | 2 |
| | (ii) Maximum penalty | 1 | |
| | Link to behaviour | 1 | |
| | Actual penalty | 1 | |
| | Disclosure | 1 | |
| | | | 4 |
| | | | 15 |

## (a) Tax evasion and tax avoidance

Tax evasion is illegal and involves the reduction of tax liabilities by not providing information to which HMRC is entitled or providing HMRC with deliberately false information.

In contrast, tax avoidance involves the minimisation of tax liabilities by the use of any lawful means, although certain tax avoidance schemes must be disclosed to HMRC.

If Ernest makes no disclosure of the capital gain then this will be viewed as tax evasion as his tax liability for 2013/14 will be understated by £18,000.

## (b) Ethics

The matter is one of professional judgement. Your firm would be expected to act honestly and with integrity.

Ernest should therefore be advised to disclose details of the capital gain to HMRC.

If such disclosure is not made your firm would be obliged to report under the money laundering regulations and your firm should also consider ceasing to act for Ernest. In these circumstances your firm would be advised to notify HMRC that it no longer acts for him although your firm would not need to provide any reason for this.

## (c) Discovery assessment

A discovery assessment can be raised because Ernest's self-assessment tax return did not contain sufficient information to make HMRC aware of the capital gain.

The normal time limit for making a discovery assessment is 4 years after the end of the tax year, but this is extended to 6 years if there has been careless understatement and 20 years if there has been deliberate understatement.

(d) (i) **Interest**

Interest will run from the due date of 31 January 2015 to the day before the payment date of 31 July 2015.

The interest charge will therefore be £18,000 × 3.0% × 6/12 = £270.

(ii) **Penalties**

The amount of penalty is based on the tax due but unpaid as a result of the failure to notify and the maximum penalty is 100% of that tax due.

However, the actual penalty will be linked to Ernest's behaviour.

Since Ernest would appear to have deliberately failed to notify HMRC of his capital gain, the actual penalty is likely to be 70% of the tax unpaid which is £18,000 × 70% = £12,600. This assumes that there is no attempt at concealment.

The penalty would have been substantially reduced if Ernest had disclosed the capital gain, especially if the disclosure had been unprompted by HMRC prior to discovery. The maximum reduction would be to 20% of the tax unpaid.

# 21 Aloi, Bon, Cherry and Dinah

**Text references.** Entrepreneurs' relief is dealt with in Chapter 15. Shares are covered in Chapter 16. Computing chargeable gains and the calculation of capital gains tax is the subject of Chapter 13.

**Top tips.** Par value means the face value of the shares. Aloi therefore had a cost of £50,000 for her first 50,000 £1 shares in Alphabet Ltd.

**Easy marks.** Make sure that you remember to deduct the annual exempt amount before computing the capital gains tax liability.

**Examiner's comments.** Answers to this question either tended to be very good or quite poor, with many candidates making the calculations far more complicated than they actually were. In part (a) many candidates simply reproduced the qualifying conditions for entrepreneurs' relief, without relating them to the information given for each of the three shareholders. In part (b) a number of candidates included taxable income as part of their calculations, and the annual exempt amount was often omitted. For the fourth shareholder, it should have been obvious that with sales proceeds of just £6,600 there would be no capital gains tax liability, yet the vast majority of candidates wasted time attempting to calculate a liability. Similarly, there was little awareness that the transfer on death was an exempt disposal.

## Marking scheme

|  |  |  | Marks |
|---|---|---|---|
| (a) | Bon | 1 | |
| | Cherry | 1 | |
| | Dinah | 1 | |
| | | | 3 |
| (b) | **Aloi** | | |
| | Alphabet Ltd - Disposal proceeds | ½ | |
| | - Cost | 1 | |
| | Investment property | ½ | |
| | Annual exempt amount | 1 | |
| | Capital gains tax | 1 | |

**Bon**

| | |
|---|---|
| Deemed proceeds | 1 |
| Cost | 1 |
| Annual exempt amount | ½ |
| Capital gains tax | ½ |

**Cherry**

| | |
|---|---|
| Disposal proceeds | ½ |
| Cost | ½ |
| Annual exempt amount | ½ |
| Capital gains tax | 2 |

**Dinah**

| | |
|---|---|
| Sale of shares | 1 |
| Exempt disposal on death | ½ |

$$\underline{\underline{\frac{\underline{12}}{15}}}$$

(a) Bon only acquired her shareholding and became a director on 1 February 2013, so the qualifying conditions were not met for one year prior to the date of disposal.

Cherry was not an officer or an employee of Alphabet Ltd.

Dinah's shareholding of 3% (3,000/100,000 × 100) is less than the minimum required holding of 5%.

(b) **Aloi – Capital gains tax (CGT) liability 2013/14**

*Summary*

| | Gains £ | CGT £ |
|---|---|---|
| *Gain qualifying for entrepreneurs' relief* | | |
| Ordinary shares in Alphabet Ltd | | |
| Proceeds of sale (60,000 × £6) | 360,000 | |
| Less costs (50,000 + 18,600) | (68,600) | |
| Gain | 291,400 | |
| CGT @ 10% on £291,400 | | 29,140 |
| *Gain not qualifying for entrepreneurs' relief* | | |
| Investment property | 22,900 | |
| Less: annual exempt amount (best use as saves tax @ 28%) | (10,900) | |
| Taxable gain | 12,000 | |
| CGT @ 28% on £12,000 | | 3,360 |
| Total CGT due | | 32,500 |

**Bon – Capital gains tax (CGT) liability 2013/14**

| | £ |
|---|---|
| Ordinary shares in XYZ plc | |
| Deemed proceeds of sale (10,000 × £7.12 (W1)) | 71,200 |
| Less cost (W2) | (36,880) |
| Gain | 34,320 |
| Less: annual exempt amount | (10,900) |
| Taxable gain | 23,420 |
| | |
| CGT @ 28% on £23,420 | 6,558 |

*Workings*

1 The shares in XYZ plc are valued at 710 + ¼ × (718 − 710) = 712p. There are no recorded bargains on the date of the gift so the average bargain basis does not apply.

2    Following the takeover, Bon received 25,000 shares in XYZ plc. The cost of the original shareholding is passed on to the new shareholding so the cost attributable to the 10,000 shares sold is £36,880 (92,200 × 10,000/25,000).

### Cherry – Capital gains tax (CGT) liability 2013/14

|  | £ |
|---|---|
| Ordinary shares in Alphabet Ltd |  |
| Disposal proceeds | 72,000 |
| Less cost | (23,900) |
| Gain | 48,100 |
| Less: annual exempt amount | (10,900) |
| Taxable gain | 37,200 |
|  |  |
| CGT @ 18% on £7,400 (W) | 1,332 |
| CGT @ 28% on £29,800 | 8,344 |
| Total CGT liability | 9,676 |

*Working*

Cherry's basic rate band limit is increased to £(32,010 + 3,400) = £35,410, of which £(35,410 – 28,010) = £7,400 is unused.

### Dinah

There is no CGT liability on the sale of the XYZ plc shares as the gain of £5,000 (6,600 – (4,800 × 1,000/3,000)) is less than the annual exempt amount.

The transfer of the XYZ plc shares on Dinah's death is an exempt disposal.

# 22 Winston King

**Text references.** Chapter 13 covers chargeability to capital gains tax, computing chargeable gains and CGT liability. Chapter 15 includes entrepreneurs' relief. Chapter 19 deals with chargeability to corporation tax and Chapter 21 covers chargeable gains for companies.

**Top tips.** Losses on assets not qualifying for entrepreneurs' relief and the annual exempt amount should be deducted to produce the lowest CGT liability. This means that they should be deducted from gains taxed at 18% or 28%, in priority to gains taxed at the 10% entrepreneurs' rate.

**Easy marks.** The calculation of capital gains tax in part (b)(i) was straightforward. The calculation of the chargeable gain for a company should have yielded an easy 3 marks.

**Examiner's comments.** There were many correct answers to part (a). However, candidates should appreciate that for just two marks a detailed explanation of the residence rules was not required. Part (b) was very well answered, with many candidates achieving maximum marks. However, it was sometimes not appreciated that the disposal of the business would fully utilise the available basic rate band – resulting in the painting being charged at the higher rate of 28%. In part (c), the first requirement was very well answered, although the incidental costs of acquisition were often omitted from the indexation allowance calculation. The final requirement was the only aspect of this question that was consistently not well answered. A number of candidates stated that the amount of proceeds not reinvested would be the chargeable gain, despite this figure being higher than the gain calculated in the initial requirement.

|  |  |  | Marks |
|---|---|---|---|
| (a) | (i) | Resident in the UK | 1 |
|  | (ii) | Resident in the UK | 1 |
| (b) | (i) | Annual exempt amount | 1 |
|  |  | Unused basic rate band | ½ |
|  |  | Capital gains tax | 1½ |
|  |  |  | 3 |
|  | (ii) | Freehold shop | ½ |
|  |  | Painting | ½ |
|  |  | Capital loss | 1 |
|  |  | Annual exempt amount | ½ |
|  |  | Capital gains tax | 1½ |
|  |  |  | 4 |
| (c) | (i) | Proceeds | ½ |
|  |  | Costs of disposal | ½ |
|  |  | Cost | ½ |
|  |  | Costs of acquisition | ½ |
|  |  | Indexation allowance | 1 |
|  |  |  | 3 |
|  | (ii) | Freehold factory | 1½ |
|  |  | Freehold office building | 1½ |
|  |  |  | 3 |
|  |  |  | 15 |

(a) (i) Individuals are subject to capital gains tax (CGT) on the disposal of chargeable assets during any tax year in which they are resident in the UK.

(ii) Companies are subject to corporation tax on gains from the disposal of chargeable assets if they are resident in the UK.

(b) (i) **Winston King – CGT liability 2013/14**

|  | £ |
|---|---|
| Chargeable gain on painting | 46,160 |
| Less annual exempt amount | (10,900) |
| Taxable gain | 35,260 |

| CGT liability: £(32,010 – 19,410) = 12,600 @ 18% | 2,268 |
|---|---|
| £(35,260 – 12,600) = 22,660 @ 28% | 6,345 |
|  | 8,613 |

(ii) **Winston King – Revised CGT liability 2013/14**

|  | £ |
|---|---|
| *Gain qualifying for entrepreneurs' relief* |  |
| Gain on freehold shop £(140,000 – 80,000) | 60,000 |
|  |  |
| *Gain not qualifying for entrepreneurs' relief* |  |
| Painting | 46,160 |
| Less allowable loss on warehouse £(102,000 – 88,000) | (14,000) |
| Net gain | 32,160 |
| Less annual exempt amount | (10,900) |
| Taxable gain | 21,260 |

|  |  | £ |
|---|---|---|
| CGT liability: | £60,000 @ 10% | 6,000 |
|  | £21,260 @ 28% | 5,953 |
|  |  | 11,953 |

*Tutorial notes*

(1)   The capital loss on the sale of the freehold warehouse and the annual exempt amount are set against the chargeable gain from the sale of the painting as this saves CGT at the higher rate of 28%. Although the warehouse is being sold with the business, it was never actually used in the business, and so this aspect of the sale does not qualify for entrepreneurs' relief. If it had been used in the business, the loss of £14,000 would have been deducted from the gain on the shop to give a net gain on sale of the business of £46,000. CGT would then be charged on £46,000 at 10%.

(2)   The unused basic rate tax band of £12,600 is set against the gain qualifying for entrepreneurs' relief of £60,000 even though this has no effect on the 10% tax rate.

(c)   (i)   **Wiki Ltd – Chargeable gain on disposal of warehouse**

|  | £ | £ |
|---|---|---|
| Disposal proceeds |  | 312,000 |
| Less   incidental costs of disposal |  | (3,400) |
|  |  | 308,600 |
| Less   cost | 171,000 |  |
|      incidental costs of acquisition | 2,200 |  |
|  |  | (173,200) |
|  |  | 135,400 |
| Less   indexation allowance |  |  |
| $\frac{255.3 - 182.7}{182.7}$ (= 0.397) × £173,200 |  | (68,760) |
| Chargeable gain |  | 66,640 |

(ii)   Freehold factory

No rollover relief is available as the amount not reinvested of £(308,600 – 166,000) = £142,600 exceeds the chargeable gain.

The base cost of the factory will be £166,000.

**Freehold office building**

The net sale proceeds are not fully reinvested, and so £(308,600 – 296,000) = £12,600 of the chargeable gain cannot be rolled over.

The base cost of the office building will be £296,000 – £(66,640 – 12,600) = £241,960.

*Tutorial note*

Equivalent marks were awarded if the gross proceeds of £312,000 were used instead of the net proceeds of £308,600.

# 23 Jorge Jung

**Text references.** Chapter 13 deals with the basic computation of chargeable gains, including the annual exempt amount. Chapter 14 covers wasting assets, chattels, and the principal private residence exemption. Chapter 15 deals with business reliefs including gift relief.

**Top tips.** Remember that deemed periods of occupation for principal private residence relief must usually be preceded by a period of actual occupation and followed by a period of actual occupation.

**Easy marks.** The painting and the motor car were easy half marks. Don't forget to deduct the annual exempt amount for another easy half mark.

## Marking scheme

| | Marks |
|---|---|
| **House** | |
| Proceeds | ½ |
| Cost | ½ |
| Period of exemption | 3 |
| Principal private residence exemption | 1 |
| Letting exemption | 1 |
| **Copyright** | |
| Proceeds | ½ |
| Cost | 1½ |
| **Painting** | ½ |
| **Motor car** | ½ |
| **Land** | |
| Proceeds | ½ |
| Cost – probate value taken over on transfer from spouse | 1 |
| Apportionment of cost | 1 |
| **Shares** | |
| Deemed proceeds | 1 |
| Cost | ½ |
| Gift relief | 1½ |
| **Annual exempt amount** | ½ |
| | 15 |

**Jorge Jung – Taxable gains computation 2013/14**

| | £ |
|---|---|
| House (W1) | 0 |
| Copyright (W4) | 2,600 |
| Painting (W5) – exempt as proceeds and cost £6,000 or less | 0 |
| Motor car (W6) – exempt asset so loss not allowable | 0 |
| Land (W7) | 71,760 |
| Ordinary shares in Futuristic Ltd (W8) | 13,700 |
| Chargeable gains | 88,060 |
| Less: annual exempt amount | (10,900) |
| Taxable gains | 77,160 |

*Workings*

1    *House*

| | £ |
|---|---:|
| Proceeds | 308,000 |
| Less: cost | (98,000) |
| Gain | 210,000 |
| Less:   principal private residence exemption (W2) | (188,000) |
|        letting exemption (W3) | (22,000) |
| Gain after exemptions | 0 |

2    *Principal private residence exemption*

| | Exempt months | Chargeable months | Total months |
|---|---:|---:|---:|
| Actual occupation | 16 | | 16 |
| Deemed occupation – up to 3 years any reason | 18 | | 18 |
| Deemed occupation – any time employed overseas | 24 | | 24 |
| Actual occupation | 11 | | 11 |
| Deemed occupation – up to 4 years working elsewhere in UK | 30 | | 30 |
| Deemed occupation – up to 3 years any reason balance (36 – 18) = 18, (22 – 18) = 4 chargeable | 18 | 4 | 22 |
| Deemed occupation – up to 4 years working elsewhere in UK balance (48 – 30) = 18, (26 – 18) = 8 chargeable | 18 | 8 | 26 |
| Actual occupation | 17 | | 17 |
| Working overseas (12 – [36 – 21 – 13] = 10 chargeable | | 10 | 10 |
| Last 36 months – always treated as period of occupation | 36 | — | 36 |
| Totals | 188 | 22 | 210 |

Principal private residence exemption £210,000 × 188/210        **£188,000**

*Tutorial note*

In calculating the principal private residence exemption, any periods of absence while working overseas, a maximum of four years absence while working elsewhere in the UK, and a maximum of three years absence for any reason are treated as deemed occupation, usually provided that they are preceded and followed by a period of actual occupation. The second period working overseas is therefore not a period of deemed occupation as it was not followed by a period of actual occupation.

*Alternative approach*

An alternative approach, suggested as the easiest by the examiner, is to calculate the chargeable months as follows:

| | |
|---|---:|
| Total period of ownership | 210 |
| Less:  Actual occupation (16 + 11 + 17) | (44) |
|         Deemed occupation  - any reason up to 3 years | (36) |
|                     - employed overseas without limit | (24) |
|                     - working in UK up to 4 years | (48) |
|         Last 36 months - always treated as period of occupation | (36) |
| Chargeable months | 22 |

3    *Letting exemption*

Lowest of:

| | | |
|---|---|---|
| (i) | Gain in letting period £210,000 × 22/210 | £22,000 |
| (ii) | Gain exempt under PPR (W2) | £188,000 |
| (iii) | Maximum exemption | £40,000 |

Therefore letting exemption is                                          £22,000

4    *Copyright*

| | £ |
|---|---|
| Proceeds | 8,200 |
| Less cost: £7,000 × 8/10 (N) | (5,600) |
| Gain | 2,600 |

*Tutorial note*

The copyright is a wasting asset. The cost of £7,000 must therefore be depreciated based on an unexpired life of ten years at the date of acquisition and an unexpired life of eight years at the date of disposal.

5    *Painting*

Non-wasting chattel. Gain is exempt as gross sale proceeds are £6,000 or less.

6    *Motor car*

Exempt asset for capital gains tax so loss of £(14,600 − 10,700) = £3,900 is not allowable.

7    *Land*

| | £ |
|---|---|
| Proceeds | 92,000 |
| Less: cost £28,600 (N) × $\dfrac{92,000}{92,000+38,000}$ | (20,240) |
| Gain | 71,760 |

*Tutorial note*

The cost of the land is £28,600 which is the value when Jorge's father-in-law died. Jorge would have taken over this cost when his wife transferred the land to him.

8    *Ordinary shares in Futuristic Ltd*

| | £ |
|---|---|
| Deemed proceeds – market value (N) | 64,800 |
| Less: cost | (26,300) |
| Gain | 38,500 |
| Less: gift relief – balancing figure £(38,500 − 13,700) | (24,800) |
| Gain chargeable – excess of actual proceeds over cost £(40,000 − 26,300) | 13,700 |

*Tutorial note*

Jorge and his sister are connected persons and therefore the market value of the ordinary shares in Futuristic Ltd is used.

# 24 Nim and Mae

## Marking scheme

|  |  | Marks |
|---|---|---|
| **Nim Lom** |  |  |
| Kapook plc | Deemed proceeds | 2 |
|  | Cost | 1 |
|  | Share pool | 2 |
| Jooba Ltd |  | 1 |
| Antique table |  | 1½ |
| UK Government securities |  | ½ |
| Capital losses brought forward |  | 1 |
| Annual exempt amount |  | ½ |
| Capital losses carried forward |  | ½ |
| **Mae Lom** |  |  |
| Jooba Ltd | Proceeds | ½ |
|  | Cost | 1 |
| House | Proceeds | ½ |
|  | Cost | ½ |
|  | Exemption | 1 |
| Business | Goodwill | ½ |
|  | Office building | ½ |
|  | Investment property | ½ |
| Copyright | Proceeds | ½ |
|  | Cost | 1½ |
| Capital losses brought forward |  | ½ |
| Annual exempt amount |  | ½ |
| Capital gains tax |  | 2 |
|  |  | 20 |

**Nim Lom – CGT liability 2013/14**

|  | £ | £ |
|---|---|---|
| *Ordinary shares in Kapook plc* | | |
| Deemed proceeds (10,000 × £3.70) (W1) | 37,000 | |
| Less: cost (W2) | (23,400) | |
| | | 13,600 |
| Ordinary shares in Jooba Ltd (no gain, no loss transfer between spouses) | | – |
| Antique table (W3) | | 3,500 |
| UK Government securities (exempt) | | – |
| Chargeable gains | | 17,100 |
| Less: losses b/f (W4) | | (6,200) |
| Net chargeable gains | | 10,900 |
| Less: annual exempt amount | | (10,900) |
| Taxable gains | | Nil |

Nim therefore has a nil liability to capital gains tax in 2013/14 and capital losses carried forward of £(15,900 – 6,200) = £9,700.

*Workings*

1    The shares in Kapook plc are valued at the lower of:

(a)    $370 + ¼ \times (390 - 370) = 375$;

(b)    $\dfrac{360 + 380}{2} = 370$

ie 370.

2    The disposal is first matched against the purchase on 24 July 2013 (this is within the following 30 days) and then against the shares in the share pool. The cost of the shares disposed of is, therefore, £23,400 (5,800 + 17,600).

| *Share pool* | *No. of shares* | *Cost* |
|---|---|---|
| | £ | £ |
| Purchase 19 February 2003 | 8,000 | 16,200 |
| Purchase 6 June 2008 | 6,000 | 14,600 |
| | 14,000 | 30,800 |
| Disposal 20 July 2013 £30,800 × 8,000/14,000 | (8,000) | (17,600) |
| Balance c/f | 6,000 | 13,200 |

3    The antique table is a non-wasting chattel.

| | £ |
|---|---|
| Proceeds | 8,700 |
| Less cost | (5,200) |
| Gain | 3,500 |

The maximum gain is 5/3 × £(8,700 – 6,000) = £4,500. The chargeable gain is the lower of £3,500 and £4,500, so it is £3,500.

4    The set off of the brought forward capital losses is restricted to £6,200 (17,100 – 10,900) so that chargeable gains are reduced to the amount of the annual exempt amount.

**Mae Lom – CGT liability 2013/14**

| | £ | Gains qualifying for entrepreneurs' relief £ | Gains not qualifying for entrepreneurs' relief £ |
|---|---|---|---|
| *Ordinary shares in Jooba Ltd* | | | |
| Disposal proceeds | 30,700 | | |
| Less: cost £16,000 × 2,000/5,000 (N1) | (6,400) | | |
| | | | 24,300 |
| *House* | | | |
| Disposal proceeds | 186,000 | | |
| Less: cost | (122,000) | | |
| | 64,000 | | |
| Less: principal private residence exemption (W) | (56,000) | | |
| | | | 8,000 |
| *Business* | | | |
| Goodwill | 80,000 | | |
| Freehold office building | 136,000 | | |
| | | 216,000 | |
| Investment property (N2) | | ———— | 34,000 |
| *Copyright* | | | |
| Disposal proceeds | 9,600 | | |
| Less: cost £10,000 × 15/20 (N3) | (7,500) | | |
| | | | 2,100 |
| Chargeable gains | | | 68,400 |
| Less: losses b/f (best use) | | | (8,500) |
| Net chargeable gains | | | 59,900 |
| Less: annual exempt amount (best use) | | ———— | (10,900) |
| Taxable gains | | 216,000 | 49,000 |
| Capital gains tax @ 10%/28% (N4) | | 21,600 | 13,720 |
| Capital gains tax liability 2013/14 £(21,600 + 13,720) | | | 35,320 |

*Working*

One of the eight rooms in Mae's house was always used exclusively for business purposes, so the principal private residence exemption is restricted to £(64,000 × 7/8) = £56,000.

*Notes*

1 Nim's original cost is used in calculating the capital gain on the disposal of the shares in Jooba Ltd because the transfer between the spouses was on a no gain/no loss basis.

2 The investment property does not qualify for entrepreneurs' relief because it was never used for business purposes.

3 The copyright is a wasting asset. The cost of £10,000 must therefore be depreciated based on an unexpired life of 20 years at the date of acquisition and an unexpired life of 15 years at the date of disposal.

4 Mae's taxable income plus the gains qualifying for entrepreneurs' relief use up her basic rate band, so the gains not qualifying for entrepreneurs' relief are taxable at 28%.

# 25 Andrea, Bo and Charles

## Marking scheme

| | | | Marks |
|---|---|---|---|
| (a) | Goodwill gain | 1 | |
| | Freehold shop loss | 1 | |
| | Net gain @ 10% | 1 | |
| | Annual exempt amount set against gain on shares | 1 | |
| | Taxable gain @ 28% | 1 | |
| | | | 5 |
| (b) (i) | Gain | 1 | |
| | Gift relief | 1 | |
| | Base cost of shares | 1 | |
| | | | 3 |
| (ii) | Gain chargeable | 1 | |
| | Base cost of shares | 1 | |
| | | | 2 |
| (c) | Gain | 1 | |
| | Period of exemption | 3 | |
| | PPR relief | 1 | |
| | | | 5 |
| | | | 15 |

(a) **Andrea Saturn: capital gains tax 2013/14**

| | £ | £ | CGT £ |
|---|---|---|---|
| Proceeds of goodwill | 90,000 | | |
| Less: cost | (nil) | 90,000 | |
| | | | |
| Proceeds of shop | 165,000 | | |
| Less: cost | (180,000) | (15,000) | |
| Net taxable gain on assets qualifying for entrepreneurs' relief | | 75,000 | |
| CGT @ 10% on net taxable gain (entrepreneurs' relief rate) | | | 7,500 |
| | | | |
| Gain on quoted shares | | 16,500 | |
| Less: annual exempt amount (best use) | | (10,900) | |
| Taxable gain | | 5,600 | |
| CGT @ 28% on taxable gain | | | 1,568 |
| CGT liability 2013/14 | | | 9,068 |

*Tutorial notes:*

1   Where there is a material disposal of business assets which results in both gains and losses, losses are netted off against gains to give a single chargeable gain on the disposal of the business assets.

2   The gain qualifying for entrepreneurs' relief is treated as the lowest part of the gains. Therefore the basic rate band is completely used up by the taxable income and the gain qualifying for entrepreneurs' relief.

(b)   (i)   **Bo Neptune: full gift relief**

| | £ |
|---|---|
| MV of shares | 210,000 |
| Less: cost | (94,000) |
| Gain | 116,000 |

Gift relief will apply to the whole of the gain because the shares are qualifying business assets (unquoted trading company shares) and there is no consideration paid for the disposal.

Therefore Bo will not have a chargeable gain in 2013/14.

The base cost of the shares for Bo's son will be £(210,000 – 116,000) = £94,000.

(ii)   **Bo Neptune: partial gift relief**

If Bo's son paid £160,000 for the shares, this is a sale at an undervalue and partial gift relief will be available. The part of the gain equal to the excess of actual consideration over actual cost is chargeable immediately and only the balance of the gain is deferred.

Bo's chargeable gain in 2013/14 will therefore be £(160,000 – 94,000) = £66,000. The remainder of the gain of £(116,000 – 66,000) = £50,000 will be deferred by gift relief.

The base cost of the shares for Bo's son will be £(210,000 – 50,000) = £160,000.

(c)   **Charles Orion: principal private residence relief**

| | £ |
|---|---|
| Sale proceeds | 282,000 |
| Less: cost | (110,000) |
| Gain | 172,000 |
| Less: PPR relief (W) | |
| $\dfrac{90}{144} \times £172,000$ | (107,500) |
| Chargeable gain | 64,500 |

*Working*

| Period | Total months | Exempt months | Chargeable months |
|---|---|---|---|
| 1.10.01 – 31.3.03 (occupied) | 18 | 18 | 0 |
| 1.4.03 – 31.3.06 (see below) | 36 | 36 | 0 |
| 1.4.06 – 30.9.10 (absent) | 54 | 0 | 54 |
| 1.10.10 – 30.9.13 (last 36 months) | 36 | 36 | 0 |
| | 144 | 90 | 54 |

During the period 1.4.03 and 31.3.06 (three years' absence for any reason), Charles is deemed to be resident in the property because he actually occupies the property both before and after the period of absence.

# 26 Naomi

**Text references.** Chapter 18 covers the inheritance tax examinable in F6.

**Top tips.** Deal with each transfer of value in date order. The question helpfully sets out how you should examine the transfers ie looking at the IHT implications during the donor's lifetime and then re-examining the effect of the donor's death.

**Easy marks.** There were easy marks for explaining the annual exemption and the spouse exemption.

## Marking scheme

| | | Marks | |
|---|---|---|---|
| (a) | *6 May each year* | | |
| | Annual exemptions | 1 | |
| | *15 August 2004* | | |
| | Transfer of value | ½ | |
| | Chargeable lifetime transfer | ½ | |
| | Nil rate band available | ½ | |
| | IHT on balance @ 20% | ½ | |
| | *12 September 2008* | | |
| | Transfer of value | 1 | |
| | Potentially exempt transfer | ½ | |
| | *14 February 2011* | | |
| | Transfer of value | ½ | |
| | Chargeable lifetime transfer | ½ | |
| | Nil rate band available | ½ | |
| | IHT on balance @ 20/80 | ½ | |
| | Gross transfer | ½ | |
| | | | 7 |
| (b) | *6 May each year* | | |
| | Remains exempt | ½ | |
| | *15 August 2004* | | |
| | Death more than 7 years of transfer - no additional tax chargeable | ½ | |
| | No repayment of lifetime IHT | ½ | |
| | *12 September 2008* | | |
| | Transfer of value at date of gift | ½ | |
| | Potentially exempt transfer becomes chargeable | ½ | |
| | Nil rate band available | ½ | |
| | IHT on balance @ 40% | ½ | |
| | Taper relief | ½ | |
| | *14 February 2011* | | |
| | Transfer of value at date of gift | ½ | |
| | Nil rate band available | ½ | |
| | IHT on balance @ 40% | ½ | |
| | Deduct lifetime tax | ½ | |
| | | | 6 |
| (c) | Spouse exemption | ½ | |
| | Residue chargeable | ½ | |
| | Nil rate band available | ½ | |
| | IHT @ 40% | ½ | |
| | | | 2 |
| | | | 15 |

(a) **IHT implications of lifetime gifts by Naomi**

*6 May each year*

The gift of quoted shares worth £3,000 on 6 May each year will use the annual exemption for the tax year starting on 6 April in that year.

*15 August 2004*

There is a transfer of value for inheritance tax of £313,000 as a gift is a gratuitous disposition which results in a diminution in the value of the donor's estate of this amount.

This is a chargeable lifetime transfer because it is not an exempt transfer and not a transfer to another individual.

The nil rate band available is £263,000 because the donor did not make any chargeable transfers in the seven years before 15 August 2004 (transfers after 15 August 1997).

The inheritance tax payable on this transfer is calculated as follows:

|  |  |  |  | £ |
|---|---|---|---|---|
| Gross transfer of value |  |  |  | 313,000 |
|  |  |  |  |  |
| IHT | £263,000 | × 0% = |  | Nil |
|  | £ 50,000 | × 20% = |  | 10,000 |
|  | £313,000 |  |  | 10,000 |

*12 September 2008*

There is a transfer of value for inheritance tax as a gift is a gratuitous disposition which results in a diminution in the value of the donor's estate. This diminution is:

|  | £ |
|---|---|
| Value of shares held before gift | 50,000 |
| Value of shares held after gift | (4,000) |
| Transfer of value | 46,000 |

This is potentially exempt transfer because it is not an exempt transfer but it is a transfer to another individual. A potentially exempt transfer is exempt during the lifetime of the donor so there is no lifetime tax payable.

*14 February 2011*

There is a transfer of value for inheritance tax as a gift is a gratuitous disposition which results in a diminution in the value of the donor's estate. The diminution in value is the value of the house plus the lifetime inheritance tax that Naomi agrees to pay.

This is a chargeable lifetime transfer because it is not an exempt transfer and not a transfer to another individual.

There was a lifetime transfer of value of £313,000 in seven years before 14 February 2011 (transfers after 14 February 2004) so the nil rate band available was £(325,000 – 313,000) = £12,000.

The inheritance tax payable on this transfer is calculated as follows:

|  |  |  |  | £ |
|---|---|---|---|---|
| Net transfer of value |  |  |  | 82,000 |
|  |  |  |  |  |
| IHT | £12,000 | × 0% = |  | Nil |
|  | £ 70,000 | × 20/80 = |  | 17,500 |
|  | £82,000 |  |  | 17,500 |

The gross transfer is £(82,000 + 17,500) = £99,500.

*Check*

|  |  |  |  | £ |
|---|---|---|---|---|
| IHT | £12,000 | × 0% = |  | Nil |
|  | £ 87,500 | × 20% = |  | 17,500 |
|  | £99,500 |  |  | 17,500 |

(b) **IHT implications of Naomi's death on lifetime gifts**

*6 May each year*

These transfers remain exempt and there are no implications of Naomi's death on them.

*15 August 2004*

There is no additional tax charge on this transfer because the donor died more than seven years from making it.

There is no repayment of lifetime inheritance tax.

*12 September 2008*

This potentially exempt transfer becomes chargeable because of the donor's death within seven years of making it.

The transfer of value is £46,000 which was the diminution in value of the donor's estate at the date of the transfer. The subsequent sale does not affect this value.

There was a lifetime transfer of value of £313,000 in seven years before 12 September 2008 (transfers after 12 September 2001) so the nil rate band available is £(325,000 – 313,000) = £12,000.

The inheritance tax payable on this transfer is calculated as follows:

|  | | £ |
|---|---|---|
| Gross transfer of value | | 46,000 |

| IHT | £12,000 | × 0% = | Nil |
|---|---|---|---|
|  | £ 34,000 | × 40% = | 13,600 |
|  | £46,000 | | 13,600 |
|  | Less taper relief @ 60% (death between 5 and 6 years after transfer) | | (8,160) |
| IHT payable | | | 5,440 |

*14 February 2011*

Additional tax is payable on this chargeable lifetime transfer because the donor died within seven years of making it.

The gross transfer of value is £99,500. The increase in value of the house at the date of the donor's death is not subject to inheritance tax.

There were lifetime transfers of value of £313,000 and £46,000 in seven years before 14 February 2011 (transfers after 14 February 2004) so the nil rate band of £325,000 is completely used up.

The inheritance tax payable on this transfer is calculated as follows:

|  | | £ |
|---|---|---|
| Gross transfer of value | | 99,500 |

| IHT | £99,500 × 40% = | 39,800 |
|---|---|---|
|  | Less: lifetime tax paid | (17,500) |
| Additional death tax | | 22,300 |

There is no taper relief because the donor died within three years of making the transfer.

(c) **Inheritance tax implications of the terms of Naomi's Will**

There is no inheritance tax on legacy of £250,000 given to Robert under Naomi's Will because of the spouse exemption.

The residue of the estate is chargeable to IHT as it a transfer of value to another individual.

There were lifetime transfers of value of £46,000 and £99,500 in seven years before 12 October 2013 (transfers after 12 October 2006) so the nil rate band available is £(325,000 – 46,000 – 99,500) = £179,500.

The inheritance tax payable on this transfer is calculated as follows:

|  |  |  |  | £ |
| --- | --- | --- | --- | ---: |
| Gross transfer of value £(550,000 − 250,000) |  |  |  | 300,000 |
| IHT | £179,500 | × 0% = |  | Nil |
|  | £120,500 | × 40% = |  | 48,200 |
|  | £300,000 |  |  | 48,200 |

# 27 Ning Gao

**Text references.** Inheritance tax is covered in Chapter 18.

**Top tips.** In part (b) (ii) it was important to deal with the situation if Ning Gao lived for another six years and also if she lived for another seven years. You should have spotted that the gift to her son was a potentially exempt transfer which would become fully exempt once she survived seven years.

**Easy marks.** The death estate was quite straightforward as long as you did not confuse the exemptions for income tax and capital gains tax on certain investments with the inheritance tax position.

**Examiner's comments.** Part (a) was well answered, with candidates being given credit for their treatment of the PETs even if this was included in part (b). Part (b) was also well answered, although a number of candidates deducted the endowment mortgage (it would have been repaid upon death by the life assurance element of the mortgage) and the promise to pay a nephew's legal fee (not deductible being purely gratuitous). Somewhat surprisingly, there was often little knowledge of who was responsible for paying the tax – many candidates stated that it was the beneficiaries (or even the deceased!), rather than the personal representatives. The effect of living for another six years or another seven years was often not understood – the difference being that after seven years all the PETs would become exempt, thus increasing the available nil rate band. Too many candidates discussed taper relief despite this having no impact on the tax payable in respect of the estate.

### Marking scheme

|  |  |  |  | Marks |
| --- | --- | --- | ---: | ---: |
| (a) |  | Husband's nil rate band | 1 |  |
|  |  | Total nil rate band | 1 |  |
|  |  | PET on 7 November 2013 | 1 |  |
|  |  | PET on 14 August 2003 | 1 |  |
|  |  |  |  | 4 |
| (b) | (i) | Property one | ½ |  |
|  |  | Repayment mortgage | ½ |  |
|  |  | Property two | ½ |  |
|  |  | Endowment mortgage | ½ |  |
|  |  | Motor cars | ½ |  |
|  |  | Investments | 1 |  |
|  |  | Bank loan | ½ |  |
|  |  | Legal fees | 1 |  |
|  |  | IHT liability | 1 |  |
|  |  | Payment responsibility | 1 |  |
|  |  |  |  | 7 |
|  | (ii) | Live for more than six years | 1 |  |
|  |  | Live for more than seven years | 1 |  |
|  |  |  |  | 2 |
| (c) |  | Exemption | 1 |  |
|  |  | Normal expenditure | ½ |  |
|  |  | Standard of living unaffected | ½ |  |
|  |  |  |  | 2 |
|  |  |  |  | 15 |

(a) Ning's personal representatives could claim her deceased husband's unused nil rate band of £325,000 × 70% = £227,500.

The total amount of nil rate band is therefore £(325,000 + 227,500) = £552,500.

The potentially exempt transfer on 7 November 2013 will utilise £220,000 of the nil rate band, so only £(552,500 − 220,000) = £332,500 is available against the death estate.

The potentially exempt transfer on 14 August 2003 is exempt from inheritance tax as it was made more than seven years before 20 March 2014.

(b) (i) **Ning Gao – Inheritance tax (IHT) on death estate 20 March 2014**

|  | £ | £ |
|---|---|---|
| Property one | 674,000 | |
| Less repayment mortgage | (160,000) | |
| | | 514,000 |
| Property two | | 442,000 |
| Motor cars | | 172,000 |
| Investments £(47,000 + 36,000 + 69,000) | | 152,000 |
| Gross estate | | 1,280,000 |
| Less bank loan | 22,400 | |
| nephew's legal fees | 0 | |
| | | (22,400) |
| Net estate | | 1,257,600 |
| | | |
| £332,500 @ 0% | | 0 |
| £925,100 @ 40% | | 370,040 |
| Inheritance tax liability | | 370,040 |

The personal representatives of Ning Gao's estate will be responsible for paying the inheritance tax.

*Tutorial notes*

1    There is no deduction in respect of the endowment mortgage as this will be repaid upon death by the life assurance element of the mortgage.

2    The promise to pay the nephew's legal fee is not deductible as it is purely gratuitous (not made for valuable consideration).

(ii) If Ning were to live for another six years until 20 March 2020 then the inheritance tax payable in respect of her estate would not alter, as the potentially exempt transfer on 7 November 2013 will still be made within the previous seven years.

If Ning were to live for another seven years until 20 March 2021 then the potentially exempt transfer will become exempt, and the inheritance tax payable in respect of her estate would therefore decrease by £220,000 @ 40% = £88,000.

(c) A lifetime transfer of value made out of income may be exempt under the normal expenditure out of income exemption.

The transfer of value must be part of the normal expenditure of the donor (regular payments, rather than a single gift).

The transfer must leave the donor with sufficient income to maintain her usual standard of living.

# 28 Artem

**Text references.** Chapter 18 covers the inheritance tax examinable in F6.

**Top tips.** Remember that potentially exempt transfers are treated as exempt during the donor's lifetime and will be exempt if the donor survives 7 years from making the gift.

**Easy marks.** There were easy marks for spotting various exemptions

**Marks**

(a)  *10 December 2005*

Annual exemptions x 2                                              ½
Potentially exempt transfer                                       ½

*17 January 2009*

Annual exemptions x 2                                              ½
Chargeable lifetime transfer                                      ½
Nil rate band available                                           ½
IHT on balance @ 20/80                                            ½
Gross transfer                                                    ½

*15 February 2010*

Small gift exemption                                              ½

*18 August 2010*

Annual exemption                                                  ½
Potentially exempt transfer                                       ½

*17 June 2011*

Annual exemption                                                  ½
Chargeable lifetime transfer                                      ½
Nil rate band available                                           ½
IHT on balance @ 20%                                              ½

*1 August 2012*

Marriage exemption                                               ½
Annual exemption                                                  ½
Potentially exempt transfer                                       ½

*5 September 2013*

Spouse exemption                                                 $\underline{½}$

                                                                            9

(b)  *10 December 2005*

Exempt as more than 7 years before death                          ½

*17 January 2009*

Within nil rate band at death                                     ½

*18 August 2010*

Potentially exempt transfer now chargeable                        ½
Nil rate band available                                           ½
IHT on balance @ 40%                                              ½
Taper relief                                                      ½

*17 June 2011*

Nil rate band exceeded                                            ½
IHT @ 40%                                                         ½
Lifetime tax deducted                                             ½

*1 August 2012*

Potentially exempt transfer now chargeable                        ½
Nil rate band exceeded                                            ½
IHT @ 40%                                                         ½

                                                                     $\underline{6}$
                                                                     $\underline{\underline{15}}$

(a)  **Lifetime inheritance tax implications**

*10 December 2005*

The first £6,000 of this transfer is an exempt transfer because of the annual exemptions for 2005/06 and 2004/05.

The remaining £(65,000 – 6,000) = £59,000 is a potentially exempt transfer as it is a gift to an individual. This is treated as an exempt transfer during Artem's life.

*17 January 2009*

The first £6,000 of this transfer is an exempt transfer because of the annual exemptions for 2008/09 and 2007/08.

The remaining £(323,000 – 6,000) = £317,000 is a chargeable lifetime transfer because it is not a transfer to another individual.

This is the first chargeable transfer that Artem makes and so the nil rate band is available in full.

|  | £ |
|---|---|
| The inheritance tax on this transfer is: | 317,000 |

Net transfer of value (Artem pays IHT)

| IHT | £312,000 | × 0% = | Nil |
|---|---|---|---|
|  | £ 5,000 | × 20/80 = | 1,250 |
|  | £317,000 |  | 1,250 |

The gross transfer of value for accumulation is £(317,000 + 1,250) = £318,250.

*Check*

| IHT | £312,000 | × 0% = | Nil |
|---|---|---|---|
|  | £ 6,250 | × 20% = | 1,250 |
|  | £ 318,250 |  | 1,250 |

*15 February 2010*

The gift to the nephew is exempt as a small gift.

*18 August 2010*

The first £6,000 of this transfer is an exempt transfer because of the annual exemptions for 2010/11 and 2009/10.

The remaining £(49,000 – 6,000) = £43,000 is a potentially exempt transfer as it is a gift to an individual. This is treated as an exempt transfer during Artem's life.

*17 June 2011*

The first £3,000 of this transfer is an exempt transfer because of the annual exemption for 2011/12.

The remaining £(103,000 – 3,000) = £100,000 is a chargeable lifetime transfer because it is not a transfer to another individual.

There was a lifetime transfer of value of £318,250 in seven years before 17 June 2011 (transfers after 17 June 2004) so the nil rate band available was £(325,000 – 318,250) = £6,750.

|  | £ |
|---|---|
| The inheritance tax on this transfer is: | 100,000 |

Gross transfer of value (Trustees pay tax)

| IHT | £6,750 | × 0% = | Nil |
|---|---|---|---|
|  | £ 93,250 | × 20% = | 18,650 |
|  | £100,000 |  | 18,650 |

*1 August 2012*

The first £2,500 of this gift is exempt under the marriage exemption as a transfer from a remoter ancestor. The next £3,000 of this transfer is an exempt transfer because of the annual exemption for 2012/13.

The remaining £(66,000 – 2,500 – 3,000) = £60,500 is a potentially exempt transfer as it is a gift to an individual. This is treated as an exempt transfer during Artem's life.

*5 September 2013*

The gift to Artem's wife is an exempt transfer under the spouse exemption.

(b) **Death inheritance tax implications**

*10 December 2005*

The potentially exempt transfer of £59,000 is exempt because Artem died more than 7 years after making it.

*17 January 2009*

The gross chargeable lifetime transfer of £318,250 was made within 7 years before Artem's death and so additional inheritance tax might be payable.

However, the transfer is now covered by the nil rate band at the date of Artem's death of £325,000.

*18 August 2010*

The potentially exempt transfer of £43,000 is chargeable transfer because it was made within the 7 years before Artem's death.

There was a lifetime transfer of value of £318,250 in seven years before 18 August 2010 (transfers after 18 August 2003) so the nil rate band available is £(325,000 – 318,250) = £6,750.

The inheritance tax on this transfer is:

|  | | | £ |
|---|---|---|---|
| Gross transfer of value | | | 43,000 |
| | | | |
| IHT | £6,750 | × 0% = | Nil |
| | £36,250 | × 40% = | 14,500 |
| | £43,000 | | 14,500 |
| Less: taper relief (3 to 4 years) @ 20% | | | (2,900) |
| Death tax payable | | | 11,600 |

*17 June 2011*

The chargeable transfer of £100,000 was made within 7 years before Artem's death and so additional inheritance tax might be payable.

Lifetime transfers of value of £318,250 and £43,000 were made in seven years before 17 June 2011 (transfers after 17 June 2004) which exceed the nil rate band on death of £325,000.

The inheritance tax on this transfer is:

|  | | £ |
|---|---|---|
| Gross transfer of value | | 100,000 |
| | | |
| IHT | £100,000 × 40% = | 40,000 |
| Less: lifetime IHT paid | | (18,650) |
| Death tax payable | | 21,350 |

There is no taper relief as Artem died within 3 years of making this transfer.

*1 August 2012*

The potentially exempt transfer of £60,500 is chargeable transfer because it was made within the 7 years before Artem's death.

Lifetime transfers of value of £318,250, £43,000 and £100,000 were made in seven years before 1 August 2012 (transfers after 1 August 2005). These exceed the nil rate band on death of £325,000.

The inheritance tax on this transfer is:

|  | | £ |
|---|---|---|
| Gross transfer of value | | 60,500 |
| | | |
| IHT | £60,500 × 40% = | 24,200 |

There is no taper relief as Artem died within 3 years of making this transfer.

# 29 Jimmy

## Marking scheme

|  |  |  |  | Marks |
|---|---|---|---:|---:|
| (a) | PET | | 1 | |
| | CLT | | 1 | |
| | | | | 2 |
| (b) | **Lifetime transfers** | | | |
| | PET | – Recognition as PET | ½ | |
| | | – Marriage exemption | 1 | |
| | | – Annual exemption | 1 | |
| | CLT | – Recognition as CLT | ½ | |
| | | – IHT liability | 2 | |
| | **Additional liability arising on death** | | | |
| | PET | | 1 | |
| | CLT | – IHT liability | 1 | |
| | | – IHT already paid | ½ | |
| | **Death estate** | | | |
| | Property | | ½ | |
| | Building society deposits | | ½ | |
| | Life assurance policy | | 1 | |
| | Funeral expenses | | 1 | |
| | Spouse exemption | | 1 | |
| | IHT liability | | ½ | |
| | | | | 12 |
| (c) | Due date | | | 1 |
| | | | | 15 |

(a) A potentially exempt transfer only becomes chargeable to inheritance tax (IHT) if the donor dies within seven years of making the gift.

In contrast, a chargeable lifetime transfer is immediately charged to IHT. An additional IHT liability may then arise if the donor dies within seven years of making the gift.

(b) **Jimmy – inheritance tax computation**

**Lifetime transfers**

*2 August 2012*

|  | £ |
|---|---|
| Transfer of value | 50,000 |
| Less: marriage exemption | (2,500) |
| annual exemption 2012/13 | (3,000) |
| annual exemption 2011/12 b/f | (3,000) |
| Potentially exempt transfer (no lifetime tax) | 41,500 |

*14 November 2012*

|  | £ |
|---|---|
| Net transfer of value (Jimmy pays IHT) | 800,000 |

| IHT | £325,000 | × 0% = | Nil |
|---|---|---|---|
|  | £475,000 | × 20/80 = | 118,750 |
|  | £800,000 |  | 118,750 |

The gross transfer of value for accumulation is £(800,000 + 118,750) = £918,750.

*Tutorial note*

Check IHT using 20% rate on gross transfers

| IHT | £325,000 | × 0% = | Nil |
|---|---|---|---|
|  | £593,750 | × 20% = | 118,750 |
|  | £ 918,750 |  | 118,750 |

**Additional liabilities arising on death**

*2 August 2012*

|  | £ |
|---|---|
| Potentially exempt transfer (within nil band at death, no tax to pay) | 41,500 |

*14 November 2012*

There was a lifetime transfer of value of £41,500 in seven years before 14 November 2012 (transfers after 14 November 2005) so the nil rate band available is £(325,000 – 41,500) = £283,500. There is no taper relief as death occurred within three years of the transfer.

|  |  |  | £ |
|---|---|---|---|
| Gross transfer of value |  |  | 918,750 |
| IHT | £283,500 | × 0% = | Nil |
|  | £635,250 | × 40% = | 254,100 |
|  | £918,750 |  | 254,100 |
| Less: lifetime tax paid |  |  | (118,750) |
| Death tax payable |  |  | 135,350 |

**Death estate**

*14 February 2014*

There were transfers of £(41,500 + 918,750) = £960,250 in seven years before 14 February 2014 (transfers after 14 February 2007) so there is no nil rate band available to be set against the death estate.

| | £ |
|---|---|
| Property | 260,000 |
| Building society deposits | 515,600 |
| Proceeds of life assurance policy | 210,000 |
| | 985,600 |
| Less: funeral expenses | (5,600) |
| Value of estate | 980,000 |
| Less: spouse exemption | (300,000) |
| Chargeable death estate | 680,000 |
| £680,000 × 40% = | 272,000 |

(c) The due date on which the IHT liability of £272,000 will be payable by the personal representatives of Jimmy's estate is the earlier of 31 August 2014 or the date when they deliver their account to HMRC.

# 30 IHT transfers

**Text references.** Chapter 18 covers the inheritance tax examinable in F6.

**Top tips.** Where a question is divided into discrete parts such as this one, it is important to attempt ALL of the parts of the question to achieve a reasonable mark.

**Easy marks.** There were easy marks for explaining common exemptions such as the annual exemption, the marriage exemption and the small gifts exemption.

**Marking scheme**

| | | | Marks |
|---|---|---|---|
| (a) | Gift is transfer of value | ½ | |
| | Annual exemptions | 1 | |
| | Marriage exemption | ½ | |
| | Potentially exempt transfer | 1 | |
| | | | 3 |
| (b) | Small gifts exemption | | 1 |
| (c) | Sale at undervalue so diminution in estate | 1 | |
| | Transfer of value definition | 1 | |
| | No gratuitous intent so not transfer of value | 1 | |
| | | | 3 |
| (d) | Diminution in estate | 1 | |
| | Chargeable lifetime transfer | ½ | |
| | Nil rate band | ½ | |
| | Cumulation for seven years | 1 | |
| | | | 3 |
| (e) | Transfer of value but exempt | ½ | |
| | Out of income | ½ | |
| | Habitual | ½ | |
| | Maintains usual standard of living | ½ | |
| | | | 2 |

|  |  | Marks |
|---|---|---|
| (f) | Potentially exempt transfer | 1 |
|  | Chargeable on death within 7 years | ½ |
|  | Value of transfer | ½ |
|  | Better to give shares than cash | ½ |
|  | Taper relief | ½ |
|  |  | $\underline{3}$ |
|  |  | $\underline{15}$ |

(a) **Bilal**

The gift of £20,000 is a transfer of value for inheritance tax.

Bilal can use his £3,000 annual exemptions for 2013/14 and 2012/13 and also the marriage exemption which is £5,000 for a gift to the donor's child.

The remaining transfer of value is £(20,000 – 3,000 – 3,000 – 5,000) = £9,000. This is a potentially exempt transfer as it is a transfer to another individual. It will become a chargeable transfer if Bilal dies within seven years of making it but will be covered by his nil rate band.

(b) **Sammy**

Gifts up to £250 per person in any one tax year are exempt under the small gifts exemption.

(c) **Terry**

There has been a sale at an undervalue and Terry's estate has been reduced in value by £(20,000 – 1,000) = £19,000.

However, a transfer of value for IHT requires the diminution to be as a result of a gratuitous disposition. Since Terry thought that he was obtaining a market value for the value, his bad business deal is not a transfer of value as he had no gratuitous intent.

(d) **Lucas**

There is a transfer of value as the gift is a gratuitous disposition which results in a diminution in the value of the donor's estate. This diminution is:

|  | £ |
|---|---|
| Value of shares held before gift (8,000 × £37.50) | 300,000 |
| Value of shares held after gift (6,000 × £18.75) | (112,500) |
| Transfer of value | 187,500 |

This is chargeable lifetime transfer as it is a transfer to trustees. However there is no lifetime tax payable because the transfer is within the available nil rate band of £325,000.

The transfer will be cumulated with any further transfers in the next seven years, including the death estate, if Lucas dies within this time.

(e) **Donald**

There is a transfer of value of £1,000 each month. The transfers will be exempt under the normal expenditure out of income exemption because the transfer is:

- made out of income; and
- part of the normal expenditure of the donor (habitual); and
- leaves the donor with sufficient income to maintain his usual standard of living.

(f) **Jas**

If either cash or shares are given, the transfer of value will be a potentially exempt transfer so the transfer will be treated as exempt while Jas is alive.

If Jas dies within seven years of making the transfer it will become a chargeable transfer and will be subject to death rates at the date of death. However, in either case, the transfer of value will be £100,000 as any increase in value of the shares is not be subject to inheritance tax. On purely IHT terms, Jas should therefore make a gift of the shares rather than cash.

If Jas dies between three and seven years of making the transfer, taper relief will reduce the death tax.

# 31 Molten-Metal plc

**Text references.** Computing taxable total profits is covered in Chapter 19 and computing the corporation tax liability in Chapter 20. Chargeable gains for companies is the subject of Chapter 21. Capital allowances are covered in Chapter 8 and property income in Chapter 6. Computing trading income (including the point about the repairs to the office building) is dealt with in Chapter 7. Payment of tax by companies is covered in Chapter 24.

**Top tips.** This question has a lot to information for you to deal with. Study the layout of the suggested solution, in particular note how detailed calculations are contained in Workings. Try to adopt this layout in your answers.

**Easy marks.** Part (b) stating the balancing payment and its due date should have been easy marks.

**Examiner's comments.** This question was generally well answered, and there were many very good answers. In part (a) there was no need to have separate computations for the trading profit and for taxable total profits, since it was quite straightforward to combine everything into one computation. The accruals for the interest payable and interest income often caused problems, and many candidates did not appreciate that no adjustment to the trading profit was necessary in respect of any of the items debited to the capital expenditure account. The writing down allowance for a motor car with private use was often restricted, despite such an adjustment only being relevant for an unincorporated business. The calculations for the property business profit and the chargeable gain were often made much more difficult than they actually were. Although most candidates correctly calculated the final quarterly instalment in part (b), the due date was generally not known.

## Marking scheme

|  |  |  | Marks |
|---|---|---|---|
| (a) | Trading profit | | ½ |
| | Loan stock interest payable | | 1½ |
| | Repairs to office building | | 1 |
| | P&M | - Office building | ½ |
| | | - Ventilation system and lift | 1 |
| | | - AIA | 1 |
| | | - Machinery | ½ |
| | | - Building alterations | ½ |
| | | - Wall | ½ |
| | | - Partition walls | 1 |
| | | - AIA | 1 |
| | | - Main pool | 2 |
| | | - Special rate pool | 1½ |
| | | - Short life asset | 1 |
| | Property business profit | - Premium received | 1½ |
| | | - Rent | 1 |
| | Interest income | | 2 |
| | Chargeable gain | - Disposal proceeds | ½ |
| | | - Costs of disposal | ½ |
| | | - Cost | ½ |
| | | - Enhancement expenditure | 1½ |
| | | - Indexation allowance | 1½ |
| | Corporation tax | | ½ |
| | | | **23** |
| (b) | Instalment payment | | 1 |
| | Due date | | 1 |
| | | | **2** |
| | | | **25** |

(a)  **Molten-Metal plc – Corporation tax computation for the year ended 31 March 2014**

|  | £ | £ |
|---|---|---|
| Trading profit | | 2,470,144 |
| Less: Loan stock interest payable £(22,500 + 3,700 – 4,200) | 22,000 | |
| Repairs to office building | 0 | |
| Capital allowances    P&M (W1) | 290,638 | |
| | | (312,638) |
| | | 2,157,506 |
| Property business profit (W2) | | 68,400 |
| Interest income (W3) | | 8,700 |
| Chargeable gain (W4) | | 157,574 |
| Taxable total profits | | 2,392,180 |
| | | |
| Corporation tax £2,392,180 @ 23% | | 550,201 |

*Tutorial notes*

(1)   Interest paid in respect of a loan used for trading purposes is deductible in calculating the trading profit.

(2)   The repairs to the office building are not deductible, being capital in nature, as the building was not in a useable state when purchased and this fact was reflected in the reduced purchased price.

*Workings*

1   *Capital allowances*

| | AIA | Main pool | Special rate pool | Short life asset | Allowances |
|---|---|---|---|---|---|
| | £ | £ | £ | £ | £ |
| TWDVs c/f | | 87,800 | | | |
| *Additions on which AIA claimed* | | | | | |
| Office building | 0 | | | | |
| Ventilation system | 31,000 | | | | |
| Lift | 42,000 | | | | |
| | 73,000 | | | | |
| AIA – 100% | (73,000) | | | | 73,000 |
| Transfer balance to special rate pool | 0 | | | 0 | |
| | | | | | |
| Machinery | 236,600 | | | | |
| Building alterations | 7,700 | | | | |
| Wall | 0 | | | | |
| Partition walls | 22,900 | | | | |
| | 267,200 | | | | |
| AIA | (177,000) | | | | 177,000 |
| Transfer balance to main pool | 90,200 | 90,200 | | | |
| *Addition on which AIA not claimed* | | | | | |
| Computer | | | | 2,500 | |
| *Additions not qualifying for AIA* | | | | | |
| Motor car | | | 24,000 | | |
| Motor cars £17,300 × 2 | | 34,600 | | | |
| | | 212,600 | | | |
| WDA @ 18% | | (38,268) | | (450) | 38,718 |
| WDA @ 8% | | | (1,920) | | 1,920 |
| TWDVs c/f | | 174,332 | 22,080 | 2,050 | |
| Allowances | | | | | 290,638 |

*Tutorial notes*

(1) The ventilation system and lift are both integral to a building and so are special rate pool expenditure. It is beneficial to claim the annual investment allowance of £250,000 initially against this expenditure, as it would otherwise only qualify for writing down allowance at the rate of 8%.

(2) The building alterations were necessary for the installation of the machinery, and therefore qualify for capital allowances. Walls are specifically excluded, with the exception of partition walls which are movable and intended to be so moved.

(3) The computer will be depooled by making the election and treated as a short life asset. The annual investment allowance should not be claimed against this asset as this will effectively disapply the depooling election.

(4) The motor car acquired in November 2013 has $CO_2$ emissions over 130 grams per kilometre, and therefore qualifies for writing down allowances at the rate of 8% as part of the special rate pool.

(5) The motor cars acquired in March 2014 have $CO_2$ emissions between 96 and 130 grams per kilometre, and therefore qualify for writing down allowances at the rate of 18% as part of the main pool. The private use of a motor car is irrelevant, since such usage will be assessed on the employee as a benefit.

2 *Property Business Profit*

| | £ |
|---|---:|
| Premium received | 68,000 |
| Less: £68,000 × 2% × (6 – 1) | (6,800) |
| | 61,200 |
| Rent receivable £((78,800 – 68,000) = 10,800) × 2/3 | 7,200 |
| Property business profit | 68,400 |

3 *Interest income*

| | £ |
|---|---:|
| Loan interest receivable £(9,800 + 3,100) | 12,900 |
| Bank interest receivable | 2,600 |
| | 15,500 |
| Less: interest payable | (6,800) |
| Net interest income | 8,700 |

4 *Chargeable gain*

| | £ | £ |
|---|---:|---:|
| Disposal proceeds | | 872,000 |
| Less: costs of disposal | | (28,400) |
| Net proceeds of disposal | | 843,600 |
| Cost | 396,200 | |
| Enhancement expenditure   - Extension | 146,000 | |
|           - Roof | 0 | |
| | | (542,200) |
| | | 301,400 |
| Indexation allowance | | |
| Cost £396,200 × 0.300 | 118,860 | |
| Enhancement expenditure £146,000 × 0.171 | 24,966 | |
| | | (143,826) |
| Chargeable gain | | 157,574 |

*Tutorial note*

The cost of replacing part of the roof is not enhancement expenditure as the office building is simply being restored to its original state prior to the fire.

(b) The fourth and final quarterly instalment payment will be for £(550,201 – 381,811) = £168,390.

This is due on 14 July 2014.

# 32 Scuba Ltd

**Text references.** Calculation of taxable profits, taxable total profits and corporation tax in Chapters 19 and 20. Chapter 8 for capital allowances. Administration in Chapter 24. VAT in Chapters 25 and 26.

**Top tips.** When dealing with an adjustment to profits, make a brief note to the examiner about why you have treated an item in a particular way. Ensure that you comment on every item in the question to obtain maximum marks.

Most of the calculations are fairly straightforward with perhaps the lease premium being the most challenging and only possible if you have studied this topic.

The most likely trap is not reading the question carefully and missing some information. It is good to mark the question in some way when you have dealt with each item (eg tick off or highlight each item dealt with).

**Easy marks.** The adjustment to profit was straightforward, as was the calculation of corporation tax.

Once again using a proforma for

- Adjustments of profit
- Capital allowances
- Calculation of taxable total profits

would have helped gain marks. You can slot the appropriate item into the proformas as you read through the question in many cases.

## Marking scheme

|  |  |  |  | Marks |
|---|---|---|---|---|
| (a) | (i) | Trading profit | | |
| | | Operating profit | ½ | |
| | | Depreciation | ½ | |
| | | Entertaining (½ each) | 1 | |
| | | Gifts to customers (½ each) | 1 | |
| | | Lease premium – assessable amount | 1½ | |
| | | – deduction | 1½ | |
| | | P&M – main pool | 2½ | |
| | | – special rate pool | 1½ | |
| | | – AIA | 1 | |
| | | | | 11 |
| | (ii) | Corporation tax computation | | |
| | | Trading profit | ½ | |
| | | Property business profit – rent receivable | 1 | |
| | | – expenses | 1 | |
| | | Interest | ½ | |
| | | Chargeable gain | 2 | |
| | | Rollover relief | 1 | |
| | | Qualifying charitable donation | 1 | |
| | | Corporation tax | 1 | |
| | | | | 8 |

| | | | | Marks |
|---|---|---|---|---|
| (b) | (i) | Default surcharge | | |
| | | Quarter ended 30 September 2011 | 1 | |
| | | Quarter ended 31 December 2011 | 1 | |
| | | Quarter ended 30 June 2012 | 2 | |
| | | Quarter ended 30 September 2012 | 1 | |
| | | Extension of surcharge period | 1 | |
| | | Four consecutive VAT returns on time | 1 | |
| | | Quarter ended 31 December 2013 | 1 | |
| | | | | 8 |
| | (ii) | Errors on VAT return | | |
| | | Limits | 2 | |
| | | Notify in writing | 1 | |
| | | | | 3 |
| | | | | 30 |

---

(a) (i) **Scuba Ltd – tax adjusted trading profit year ended 31 March 2014**

| | £ | £ |
|---|---|---|
| Profit before tax | | 132,348 |
| Add depreciation | 45,200 | |
| customer entertaining (N1) | 7,050 | |
| employee entertaining (N1) | 0 | |
| gifts to customers: diaries (N2) | 0 | |
| gifts to customers: food hampers (N2) | 1,600 | |
| | | 53,850 |
| Less lease premium (W1) | | (1,860) |
| Adjusted profits | | 184,338 |
| Capital allowances (W2) | | (32,348) |
| Taxable trading profit | | 151,990 |

*Notes*

(1) Customer entertaining is never an allowable expense. Staff entertaining is allowable.

(2) Expenditure on gifts to customers is only allowable if the gift (i) costs less than £50 per item, (ii) is not food, tobacco, alcohol or vouchers, and (iii) clearly advertises the business's name.

(ii) **CT liability year ended 31 March 2014**

| | £ |
|---|---|
| Taxable trading profit (above) | 151,990 |
| Property income (W3) | 11,570 |
| Interest (W4) | 430 |
| Chargeable gain (W5) | 30,000 |
| Total profits | 193,990 |
| Less qualifying charitable donation | (1,500) |
| Taxable total profits/augmented profits | 192,490 |

Small profits rate applies (augmented profits < £300,000)

| *FY 2013* | £192,490 × 20% | 38,498 |
|---|---|---|

*Workings*

1   *Lease premium*

|  |  | £ |
|---|---|---|
| Premium (P) |  | 80,000 |
| Less 2% × (n − 1) × P |  |  |
| 2% × (20 − 1) × 80,000 |  | (30,400) |
| Taxable as Landlord's income |  | 49,600 |

This amount is deductible for the company over the life of the lease:

$$\frac{£49,600}{20} = £2,480$$

Allowable on an accruals basis ie 1 July 2013 to 31 March 2014 = 9/12 × £2,480 = £1,860

2   *Capital allowances*

|  | AIA £ | Main Pool £ | Special rate pool £ | Allowances £ |
|---|---|---|---|---|
| TWDV b/f |  | 47,200 | 22,400 |  |
| Additions qualifying for AIA |  |  |  |  |
| 3.7.13 Machinery | 14,020 |  |  |  |
| 29.8.13 Computer | 1,100 |  |  |  |
| 18.11.13 Machinery | 7,300 |  |  |  |
|  | 22,420 |  |  |  |
| AIA | (22,420) |  |  | 22,420 |
| Additions not qualifying for AIA |  |  |  |  |
| 4.10.13 Car |  | 10,400 |  |  |
| Disposals |  |  |  |  |
| 15.2.14 Lorry |  | (12,400) |  |  |
|  |  | 45,200 |  |  |
| WDA @ 18% |  | (8,136) |  | 8,136 |
| WDA @ 8% |  |  | (1,792) | 1,792 |
| TWDV c/f |  | 37,064 | 20,608 |  |
| Allowances |  |  |  | 32,348 |

3   *Property income*

1 August 2013 to 31 March 2014 = 8m

|  | £ |
|---|---|
| £7,200 × 4 = £28,800 × 8/12 | 19,200 |
| Less   expenses: |  |
| Decorating | (6,200) |
| Advertising | (1,430) |
| Property income | 11,570 |

4   *Interest*

Non-trading loan relationship therefore £430 is taxable as non-trading interest receivable.

5    *Chargeable gain*

|  | £ |
|---|---|
| Disposal proceeds | 90,000 |
| Less: cost | (50,000) |
|  | 40,000 |
| Less: indexation allowance £50,000 × $\frac{253.4 - 228.4}{228.4}$ (= 0.109) | (5,450) |
| Gain | 34,550 |
| Less: gain rolled over into new warehouse (balance) | (4,550) |
| Gain left in charge - amount not reinvested £(90,000 – 60,000) | 30,000 |

(b)   (i)   **Default surcharge**

|  | Quarter ended | Circumstance | Default surcharge consequence |
|---|---|---|---|
| 1 | 30 September 2011 | Late return and payment | Surcharge liability notice (SLN) issued, ending 30 September 2012. As this is the first default there is no surcharge |
| 2 | 31 December 2011 | Late return and payment | SLN extended to 31 December 2012 Surcharge @ 2% = £644 |
| 3 | 31 March 2012 | On time | SLN remains in place until 31 December 2012 |
| 4 | 30 June 2012 | Late return and payment | SLN extended to 30 June 2013 Surcharge @ 5% = £170 Not collected as < £400 |
| 5 | 30 September 2012 | Late return but no VAT due | SLN extended to 30 September 2013 No surcharge as no VAT due |
| 6 | 31 December 2012 to 30 September 2013 | On time | As returns and payments have been on time until the end of the SLN period, the SLN record is wiped clean |
| 7 | 31 December 2013 | Late return and payment | New SLN issued to 31 December 2014 As this is the first default there is no surcharge |
| 8 | 31 March 2014 | On time | SLN remains in place until 31 December 2014 |

(ii)   Errors can be connected on the next VAT return if they do not exceed the greater of:

- £10,000 (under-declaration minus over-declaration)
- 1% of VAT turnover for the return period (maximum £50,000)

Other errors must be notified to HMRC in writing (eg by letter).

# 33 Mice Ltd

**Text references.** Property business income is dealt with in Chapters 6 and 19. Losses for companies are in Chapter 22 and group relief in Chapter 23. Capital allowances are covered in Chapter 8. Calculation of income tax is in Chapter 2 and national insurance contributions in Chapter 12.

**Top tips.** You should use the loss relief pro-forma in part (a)(ii).

**Easy marks.** The calculation of property business profit in part (a) was straightforward and should have been easy marks.

**Examiner's comments.** This question was generally very well answered, especially the calculation of the property business profit in part (a) where most candidates scored virtually maximum marks. In part (b) several candidates explained whether or not group relief would be available rather than calculating the amount of relief. In part (c) most candidates were aware of what capital allowances were available. Many candidates complicated part (d) by performing long calculations, making this much more time consuming than necessary for 3 marks. However, they should have appreciated that this was additional remuneration so the calculations were simply £40,000 × 40%, £40,000 × 2% and £40,000 × 13.8% for the 3 marks.

**Marks**

| | | | | | |
|---|---|---|---|---|---|
| (a) | (i) | Lease premium received | | 1½ | |
| | | Rent receivable | - Property 1 | 1 | |
| | | | - Property 2 | ½ | |
| | | | - Property 3 | ½ | |
| | | Business rates | | ½ | |
| | | Repairs | | 1 | |
| | | Advertising | | ½ | |
| | | Insurance | | 1½ | |
| | | Loan interest | | 1 | |
| | | | | | 8 |
| | (ii) | **Year ended 31 March 2014** | | | |
| | | Property business profit | | ½ | |
| | | Loan interest | | 1½ | |
| | | Chargeable gain | | 1½ | |
| | | Loss relief | | 1 | |
| | | **Other periods** | | | |
| | | Trading profit | | ½ | |
| | | Property business profit | | ½ | |
| | | Loss relief | | 1 | |
| | | Qualifying charitable donations | | ½ | |
| | | | | | 7 |
| (b) | | Period ending 30 June 2013 | | 1½ | |
| | | Year ended 30 June 2014 | | 1½ | |
| | | | | | 3 |
| (c) | | Equipment | | 2 | |
| | | Ventilation system | | 2 | |
| | | | | | 4 |
| (d) | | Income tax | | 1 | |
| | | Employee's NIC | | 1 | |
| | | Employer's NIC | | 1 | |
| | | | | | 3 |
| | | | | | 25 |

(a)  (i)  **Mice Ltd – property business profit y/e 31 March 2014**

| | £ | £ |
|---|---|---|
| Premium received for lease | 18,000 | |
| Less: £18,000 × 2% × (8 – 1) | (2,520) | |
| Amount taxable as property business income | | 15,480 |
| Property 1 rent accrued £3,200 × 4 | | 12,800 |
| Property 2 rent accrued | | 6,000 |
| Property 3 rent accrued | | 0 |
| Gross income accrued | | 34,280 |
| | | |
| Less: expenses accrued | | |
| business rates | 2,200 | |
| repairs (N1) | 1,060 | |
| Advertising | 680 | |
| insurance £(460 + 310 + (480 × 3/12)) | 890 | |
| loan interest (N2) | 0 | |
| | | (4,830) |
| Property business profit | | 29,450 |

*Notes*

1　The enlargement of the car park is capital expenditure which cannot be deducted when calculating the property business profit.

2　Interest paid in respect of a loan to purchase property is set off under the loan relationship rules.

(ii)　**Mice Ltd – taxable total profits y/e 31 March 2014**

| | £ | £ |
|---|---:|---:|
| Property business profit | | 29,450 |
| Loan interest | | |
| Received 31 December 2013 | 6,400 | |
| Accrued 31 March 2014 | 3,200 | |
| Paid on property 3 loan – 1 January 2014 to 31 March 2014 | (1,800) | |
| | | 7,800 |
| Chargeable gain (W) | | 2,750 |
| Total profits | | 40,000 |
| Less:  current period loss relief | | (40,000) |
| Taxable total profits | | 0 |

*Working*

| | £ |
|---|---:|
| Disposal proceeds | 34,474 |
| Less: cost | (28,000) |
| | 6,474 |
| Less: indexation allowance £28,000 × $\frac{254.4 - 224.5}{224.5}$ (= 0.133) | (3,724) |
| Gain | 2,750 |

**Mice Ltd – total taxable profits for periods ending 31 March 2011, 2012 and 2013**

| | p/e 31.3.11 | y/e 31.3.12 | y/e 31.3.13 |
|---|---:|---:|---:|
| | £ | £ | £ |
| Trading profit | 83,200 | 24,700 | 51,200 |
| Property business profit | 2,800 | 7,100 | 12,200 |
| Total profits | 86,000 | 31,800 | 63,400 |
| Less:  carry back loss relief | (0) | (0) | (63,400) |
| | 86,000 | 31,800 | 0 |
| Less:  qualifying charitable donation | (1,000) | (1,500) | (0) |
| Taxable total profits | 85,000 | 30,300 | 0 |

There is no loss relief in the period to 31 March 2011 or the year ended 31 March 2012 because loss relief for a continuing business is restricted to 12 months before the loss making period.

(b)　**Mice Ltd and Web-Cam Ltd – group relief**

For the three-month period ended 30 June 2013 group relief is restricted to the profit of £28,000, as this is lower than the loss of £180,000 x 3/12 = £45,000 for the corresponding period.

For the year ended 30 June 2014, group relief is restricted to the loss of £180,000 × 9/12 = £135,000 for the corresponding period, as this is lower than the corresponding profit of £224,000 × 9/12 = £168,000.

(c) **Mice Ltd – capital allowance**

*Equipment*

The first £250,000 of expenditure will qualify for the annual investment allowance at the rate of 100%. The remainder of the expenditure will be added to the main pool and therefore will be eligible for writing down allowance at the rate of 18%.

Capital allowances for the year ended 31 March 2014 will therefore be £250,000 + (£100,000 × 18%) = £268,000.

*Ventilation system*

The annual investment allowance will be available as above. The ventilation system will be integral to the factory, and so the balance of expenditure will only qualify for writing down allowances at the rate of 8%.

Capital allowances for the year ended 31 March 2014 will therefore be £250,000 + (£100,000 × 8%) = £258,000.

(d) **Director's income tax and national insurance contributions**

The managing director's additional income tax liability for 2013/14 will be £40,000 @ 40% = £16,000.

The additional employee's Class 1 NIC will be £40,000 @ 2% = £800.

The additional employer's Class 1 NIC will be £40,000 @ 13.8% = £5,520.

# 34 Do-Not-Panic Ltd

## Marking scheme

| | | Marks |
|---|---|---|
| Trading profit | | 1 |
| Capital allowances | – period ended 31 March 2014 | 1 |
| Interest income | – period ended 31 March 2014 | 1 |
| Capital gains | | 1 |
| Franked investment income | | 1 |
| Corporation tax | – year ended 31 December 2013 | 2 |
| | – period ended 31 March 2014 | 2 |
| Due dates | | 1 |
| | | 10 |

**Do-Not-Panic Ltd – Corporation tax liabilities for the fifteen-month period ended 31 March 2014**

| | Year ended 31 December 2013 £ | Period ended 31 March 2014 £ |
|---|---|---|
| Trading profit (12:3) | 228,000 | 57,000 |
| Capital allowances (W) | – | (5,000) |
| | 228,000 | 52,000 |
| Interest income (accruals basis) | – | 7,500 |
| Capital gains (39,000 – 4,250) | – | 34,750 |
| Taxable total profits | 228,000 | 94,250 |
| Franked investment income | – | 25,000 |
| Augmented profits | 228,000 | 119,250 |

| | FY 2012/FY 2013 | FY 2013 |
|---|---|---|
| *y/e 31.12.13* | | |
| Limits for FY 2012 and FY 2013 are same so can be dealt with together | £ | |
| Taxable total profits/augmented profits | 228,000 | |
| Lower limit £300,000 | | |
| Small profits rate applies in both financial years at 20% so can be dealt with together | | |
| *FY 2012/FY 2013* | | |
| £228,000 × 20%/CT for y/e 31.12.13 | 45,600 | |

*p/e 31.3.14*
*FY 2013*
Lower limit
    £300,000 × 3/12 = £75,000
Upper limit
    £1,500,000 × 3/12 = £375,000
Marginal relief applies

| | | £ |
|---|---|---|
| £94,250 × 23% | | 21,677 |
| Less: $\dfrac{3}{400} \times £(375,000 - 119,250) \times \dfrac{94,250}{119,250}$ | | (1,516) |
| CT for p/e 31.3.14 | | 20,161 |
| Due dates | 1 October 2014 | 1 January 2015 |

*Working*

**Period ended 31 March 2014**

| | AIA £ | Main pool £ | Allowances £ |
|---|---|---|---|
| Equipment | 5,000 | | |
| AIA £250,000 × 3/12 = £62,500 maximum | (5,000) | | 5,000 |

# 35 Quagmire plc

## Marking scheme

| | | | Marks |
|---|---|---|---|
| (a) | Large company | 1 | |
| | Associated company | 1 | |
| | No exception | 1 | |
| | | | 3 |
| (b) | Corporation tax liability | 1 | |
| | Instalments | 1 | |
| | Due dates | 1 | |
| | | | 3 |
| (c) | Augmented profit | 1 | |
| | No longer a large company | ½ | |
| | Due date | ½ | |
| | Corporation tax | 2 | |
| | | | 4 |
| | | | 10 |

(a)    **Quagmire plc – payment of corporation tax**

Large companies have to make quarterly instalment payments in respect of their corporation tax liability. A large company is one paying corporation tax at the main rate.

Quagmire plc has one associated company, so the upper limit is reduced to £750,000 (1,500,000/2). Corporation tax will therefore be at the main rate for the year ended 31 March 2014.

There is an exception for the first year that a company is large, provided augmented profits do not exceed £10 million. No exception applies because Quagmire plc was also a large company for the year ended 31 March 2013.

(b)    **Quagmire plc – corporation tax liability**

Quagmire plc's corporation tax liability for the year ended 31 March 2014 is £(1,200,000 × 23%) = £276,000.

The company will have paid this in four quarterly instalments of £276,000/4 = £69,000.

The instalments will have been due on 14 October 2013, 14 January 2014, 14 April 2014 and 14 July 2014.

**Effect of no associated company**

Quagmire plc's augmented profits for the year ended 31 March 2014 are £1,200,000 plus franked investment income of £200,000 = £1,400,000.

Quagmire plc is no longer a large company since its augmented profits are below the upper limit of £1,500,000. The corporation tax liability will therefore be due in one amount on 1 January 2015.

The corporation tax liability will be calculated as follows:

|  | £ |
|---|---|
| £1,200,000 × 23% | 276,000 |
| Less   marginal relief |  |
| £(1,500,000 − 1,400,000) × (1,200,000/1,400,000) × $\dfrac{3}{400}$ | (643) |
| Corporation tax liability | 275,357 |

# 36 Heavy Ltd and Soft Ltd

**Text references.** Chapter 19 covers the computation of taxable total profits and Chapter 20 deals with the computation of the corporation tax liability. Details of capital allowances are to be found in Chapter 8.

**Top tips.** A chargeable period of account for corporation tax cannot exceed 12 months in length. A long period of account must therefore be divided into two chargeable accounting periods – the first period is always 12 months and the second period is the balance.

**Easy marks.** There was an easy mark in this question for adding back depreciation and amortisation. The main capital allowances should also have yielded easy marks, even if you missed the more unusual small pool write-off and the restriction for the short accounting period.

**Examiner's comments.** There were many very good answers to part (a). The aspects that caused problems were not appreciating that:

- There was no chargeable gain on a disposal of an office building to Soft Ltd because of the 75% group relationship.

- As the accounting period spanned 31 March 2013 it was necessary to apportion the taxable total profits of Heavy Ltd between the financial years 2012 and 2013.

- The balance on main capital allowances pool could be fully written off as it was less than £1,000.

- There was no balancing allowance on the special rate pool despite all the items included therein having been sold.

Part (b) was often not well answered, with the main problem being that candidates simply did not know the long period of account rules. This lack of a basic piece of knowledge cost many candidates several very easy marks. Even those candidates who knew the rules often deducted the capital loss in the second period, when it should have simply been carried forward.

**Marks**

(a) Operating profit — ½
Depreciation — ½
Amortisation — ½
Lease premium — Assessable amount — 1½
— Deduction — 1
Capital allowances — AIA — 1
— Main pool — 1
— Short life asset — 1½
— Special rate pool — 1½
Interest income — 2
Chargeable gain — 1
Franked investment income — 2
Corporation tax — Upper limit — ½
— Apportionment to tax years — ½
— Main rates — 1
— Marginal reliefs — 2

18

(b) Trading profits — 1
Capital allowances — Year ended 31 August 2013 — 1
— Period ended 31 December 2013 — 1½
Chargeable gain/allowable loss — 1½
Corporation tax — Year ended 31 August 2013 — 1
— Period ended 31 December 2013 — 1

7

25

---

(a) **Heavy Ltd – Corporation tax computation for the year ended 31 December 2013**

| | £ |
|---|---:|
| Operating profit | 417,340 |
| Depreciation | 12,880 |
| Amortisation | 9,000 |
| Deduction for lease premium (W1) | (7,380) |
| Capital allowances (W2) | (22,840) |
| Trading profit | 409,000 |
| Interest income (W3) | 11,000 |
| Chargeable gain | 0 |
| Taxable total profits | 420,000 |
| Add: franked investment income (W4) | 30,000 |
| Augmented profits | 450,000 |

*Y/e 31.12.13 FY 2012 and FY 2013*
Upper limit £1,500,000/2 = £750,000
Lower limit £300,000/2 = £150,000
Marginal relief applies in both financial years

|  | £ |
| --- | --- |
| *FY 2012 (1 January 2013 – 31 March 2013)* | |
| £420,000 × 3/12 × 24% | 25,200 |
| Less marginal relief £(750,000 – 450,000) $\times \dfrac{420,000}{450,000} \times 3/12 \times 1/100$ | (700) |
| *FY 2013 (1 April 2013 – 31 December 2013)* | |
| £420,000 × 9/12 × 23% | 72,450 |
| Less marginal relief £(750,000 – 450,000) $\times \dfrac{420,000}{450,000} \times 9/12 \times 3/400$ | (1,575) |
| Corporation tax liability for the year ended 31 December 2013 | 95,375 |

*Tutorial notes*

1    The sale of the office building does not give rise to a chargeable gain as this is a no gain, no loss disposal since Heavy Ltd and Soft Ltd are members of a 75% capital gains group.

2    Heavy Ltd has one associated company (Soft Ltd) and so the upper limit and the lower limit are divided by two. A company which has only been associated for part of an accounting period is deemed to have been associated for the whole period for the purpose of determining the profit limits.

3    The taxable total profits must be apportioned between the Financial Years 2012 and 2013 because of the change in the main rate of corporation tax.

*Workings*

1    *Deduction for lease premium*

|  | £ |
| --- | --- |
| Premium received | 90,000 |
| Less £90,000 × 2% × (10 -1) | (16,200) |
| Amount assessable on landlord as property business income | 73,800 |
| | |
| Deductible for year ended 31 December 2013 £73,800/10 | 7,380 |

*Tutorial note*

The office building has been used for business purposes and so the proportion of the lease premium assessed as property business income on the landlord can be deducted, spread over the life of the lease.

2    *Capital allowances*

|  | AIA | Main pool | Special rate pool | Short life asset | Allowances |
| --- | --- | --- | --- | --- | --- |
|  | £ | £ | £ | £ | £ |
| TWDVs b/f | | 900 | 21,700 | 3,200 | |
| *Addition qualifying for AIA* | | | | | |
| Office equipment | 22,400 | | | | |
| AIA | (22,400) | | | | 22,400 |
| *Disposal* | | | | | |
| Special rate pool | | | (9,950) | | |
| | | | 11,750 | | |
| Short life asset | | | | (4,600) | |
| Balancing charge | | | | 1,400 | (1,400) |
| WDA – small pool | | (900) | | | 900 |
| WDA @ 8% | | | (940) | | 940 |
| TWDV c/f | | 0 | 10,810 | | |
| Allowances | | | | | 22,840 |

*Tutorial notes*

1    The balance on the main pool is less than £1,000 so a writing down allowance equal to the unrelieved expenditure can be claimed.

2    Although all the items included in the special rate pool have been sold, there is no balancing allowance as the business has not ceased. Compare this to the short life asset which is held in a single asset pool and does have a balancing adjustment when the business is continuing.

3    *Interest income*

|  | £ |
|---|---:|
| Loan interest receivable £(8,800 + 1,500) | 10,300 |
| Bank interest receivable | 1,600 |
|  | 11,900 |
| Less loan interest payable | (900) |
| Net interest income | 11,000 |

4    *Franked investment income*

|  | £ |
|---|---:|
| Unconnected company | 27,000 |
| Soft Limited (group dividend) | 0 |
| Total dividends | 27,000 |
|  |  |
| Franked investment income £27,000 × 100/90 | 30,000 |

(b)    **Soft Ltd – Corporation tax liabilities for the 16-month period ended 31 December 2013**

|  | Y/e 31.8.13 | P/e 31.12.13 |
|---|---:|---:|
|  | £ | £ |
| Trading profit 12:4 | 90,150 | 30,050 |
| Less    capital allowances (W) | (4,320) | (947) |
|  | 85,830 | 29,103 |
| Chargeable gain | 16,170 | 0 |
| Taxable total profits | 102,000 | 29,103 |

*Y/e 31.8.13 FY 2012 and FY 2013*
Lower limit £300,000/2 = £150,000
*P/e 31.12.13 FY 2013*
Lower limit £300,000/2 × 4/12 = £50,000
Small profits rate applies in both financial years
FY 2012 and FY 2013

|  | | |
|---|---:|---:|
| £102,000 × 20% | 20,400 | |
| £29,103 × 20% | | 5,821 |

*Tutorial notes*

1    Trading profits are allocated on a time basis between the two chargeable accounting periods. However, capital allowances are calculated separately for each chargeable accounting period.

2    The capital loss for £2,900 for the period ended 31 December 2013 is carried forward. It cannot be carried back against the gain in the year ended 31 August 2013.

3    Soft Ltd has one associated company (Heavy Ltd) and so the lower limit is divided by two. For the short period of 4 months ended 31 December 2013, the limit must also be reduced proportionately.

*Working*

|  | Main pool | Allowances |
|---|---|---|
| *Year ended 31 August 2013* | £ | £ |
| TWDV b/f | 24,000 | |
| WDA @ 18% | (4,320) | 4,320 |
| | 19,680 | |
| *Period ended 31 December 2013* | | |
| Disposal | (3,900) | |
| | 15,780 | |
| WDA @ 18% × 4/12 | (947) | 947 |
| TWDV c/f | 14,833 | |

# 37 Thai Curry Ltd

**Text references.** Chapters 19 and 20 for calculation of augmented profits and taxable total profits. Chapter 8 covers capital allowances. Chapter 24 for corporation tax administration.

**Top tips.** It is essential to set out your capital allowances proforma in the correct layout to achieve maximum marks. Ensure that you state all of your assumptions so that you do not miss out on any method marks.

You cannot avoid administration questions in the exam so make sure you know due dates for returns and tax payments.

| | | | Marks |
|---|---|---|---|
| (a) | Capital allowances | | |
| | TWDV b/f | ½ | |
| | AIA | 2 | |
| | Disposals | 2 | |
| | WDA @ 18% | 1 | |
| | WDA @ 8% | 1 | |
| | FYA @ 100% | 1 | |
| | Trading loss | ½ | |
| | Deduct allowances | 1 | |
| | | | 9 |
| (b) | Trading profit nil | ½ | |
| | Property income | | |
| | Property 1 – rent | 1 | |
| | – expense | ½ | |
| | – bad debt | 1 | |
| | Property 2 – rent | ½ | |
| | – lease premium | 1½ | |
| | Interest | 1 | |
| | Chargeable gain | ½ | |
| | Deduct CY loss | 1 | |
| | FII | ½ | |
| | CT limits | 1 | |
| | CT @ 23% | ½ | |
| | Marginal relief | 1½ | |
| | | | 11 |
| (c) (i) | Return deadline | 1 | |
| | Fixed penalty | 1 | |
| | Tax geared penalty | 1 | |
| | | | 3 |

| (ii) | 9 months 1 day | 1 |
|---|---|---|
| | Late payment interest | 1 |
| | Interest calculation | 1 |
| | | $\frac{3}{26}$ |

(a) **Thai Curry Ltd's adjusted trading loss y/e 31 March 2014**

| | £ |
|---|---|
| Trading loss | (55,036) |
| Less: Capital allowances (W) | (34,894) |
| Allowable trading loss | (89,930) |

*Working*

*Capital allowances*

| | AIA £ | FYA @ 100% £ | Main pool £ | Special rate pool £ | Allowances £ |
|---|---|---|---|---|---|
| TWDV b/f | | | 10,600 | 16,400 | |
| *Additions qualifying for AIA* | | | | | |
| 8.7.13 Equipment | 9,460 | | | | |
| 20.3.14 Office (N1) | 12,750 | | | | |
| | 22,210 | | | | |
| AIA | (22,210) | | | | 22,210 |
| *Additions not qualifying for AIA* | | | | | |
| 26.8.13 Car | | | 15,800 | | |
| *Disposals* | | | | | |
| 1.5.13 Equipment | | | (12,800) | | |
| | | | 13,600 | | |
| WDA @ 18% | | | (2,448) | | 2,448 |
| 14.7.13 Car | | | | (9,700) | |
| | | | | 6,700 | |
| WDA @ 8% | | | | (536) | 536 |
| *Addition qualifying for FYA* | | | | | |
| 19.11.13 Car | | 9,700 | | | |
| 100% FYA | | (9,700) | | | 9,700 |
| TWDV c/f | | | 11,152 | 6,164 | |
| Allowances | | | | | 34,894 |

*Notes*

The items included within the cost of the office building purchased on 20 March 2014 will qualify for plant and machinery capital allowances. All of the expenditure is covered by the AIA so it is not necessary to distinguish between main pool and special rate pool expenditure. The disposal of the car from the special rate pool does not result in a balancing allowance as the business is continuing. The balance of the expenditure will continue to be written down at 8%.

(b) **Corporation tax liability y/e 31 March 2014**

| | £ |
|---|---:|
| Trading profit | Nil |
| Property income (W1) | 72,800 |
| Interest (W3) | 11,500 |
| Chargeable gain | 152,300 |
| Total profits | 236,600 |
| Less: current year loss relief | (89,930) |
| Taxable total profits | 146,670 |
| Add: gross dividends: £36,000 × 100/90 | 40,000 |
| Augmented profits | 186,670 |

| CT liability (W4) | £ |
|---|---:|
| FY 2013: £146,670 × 23% | 33,734 |
| Less 3/400 (375,000 − 186,670) × (146,670/186,670) | (1,110) |
| CT liability | 32,624 |

*Workings*

1   *Property income*

Property 1

| | £ | £ |
|---|---:|---:|
| 8m × £2,200 | 17,600 | |
| Less: redecoration costs | (8,800) | |
| Less: rent not recoverable: 2m × £2,200 | (4,400) | |
| Property income | | 4,400 |

Property 2

| | £ | £ |
|---|---:|---:|
| 8/12 × £18,000 | 12,000 | |
| Premium taxable as income (W2) | 56,400 | |
| Property income | | 68,400 |
| Total property income | | 72,800 |

2   *Lease premium*

| | £ |
|---|---:|
| Premium (P) | 60,000 |
| Less: 2% × (n-1) × P | |
| 2% × (4-1) × 60,000 | (3,600) |
| Taxable as income | 56,400 |

3   *Loan interest*

| | £ |
|---|---:|
| Received at 30.9.13 | 8,000 |
| Accrued at 31.3.14 | 3,500 |
| Total amount (accruals basis) | 11,500 |

4

| | *FY 2013* *12 months to 31.3.14* |
|---|---:|
| Taxable total profits | 146,670 |
| Augmented profits | 186,670 |
| Lower limit | |
| £300,000/4 | 75,000 |
| Upper limit | |
| £1,500,000/4 | 375,000 |

Therefore marginal relief applies.

(c) (i) **Date for return submission and penalties**

The CT return must be submitted one year after the end of the period of account ie by 31 March 2015.

If the return is not submitted until 30 November 2015 it will be 8 months late. If the return is up to 3 months late there is a fixed penalty of £100. If it more than 3 months late, as it is here, the fixed penalty increases to £200.

As the return is more than 6 months late there is also a tax geared penalty if the tax is unpaid six months after the return is due. The penalty is 10% × unpaid tax, ie 10% × £32,624 = £3,262.

(ii) **Date for CT payment & interest**

As the company is not large it must pay its corporation tax by 9 months and 1 day after the accounting period, ie by 1 January 2015.

If the tax is not paid until 30 November 2015 it will be 11 months late and interest will be charged from the due date. (In practice, interest is calculated on a daily basis.)

The rate of interest on unpaid tax is 3% and therefore the amount that will be charged is:

3% × 11/12 × £32,624 = £897.

# 38 Hawk Ltd

**Text reference.** Chargeable gains for companies are covered in Chapter 21.

**Top tips.** Work out each of the gains separately and then bring them together in a summary. Even if you are unsure about how to deal with one of the gains, make sure that you attempt the calculation of tax.

**Easy marks.** The calculation of corporation tax was an easy mark.

**Marking scheme**

|  |  | Marks |
|---|---|---|
| (a) | **Office building** | |
| | Disposal proceeds | ½ |
| | Costs of disposal | ½ |
| | Cost | ½ |
| | Costs of acquisition | ½ |
| | Enhancement expenditure | ½ |
| | Indexation – Cost | 1 |
| | – Enhancement | 1 |
| | **Albatross plc** | |
| | Proceeds | ½ |
| | Cost | 2 |
| | **Cuckoo plc** | |
| | Proceeds | ½ |
| | Value of shares – Ordinary shares | 1 |
| | – Preference shares | 1 |
| | Cost | 1½ |
| | **Land** | |
| | Proceeds | ½ |
| | Costs | 2 |
| | **Corporation tax liability** | |
| | Net chargeable gains | 1 |
| | Calculation | 1½ |
| | | 16 |

|  |  |  | Marks |
|---|---|---|---|
| (b) | (i) | Qualifying disposal | 1 |  |
|  |  | Amount of reinvestment | 1 | 2 |
|  | (ii) | Period of reinvestment |  | 1 |
|  | (iii) | Corporation tax savings |  | 1 |
|  |  |  |  | 20 |

## (a) Corporation tax liability y/e 31 March 2014

|  | £ |
|---|---|
| Trading income | 125,000 |
| Net chargeable gains (W5) | 132,219 |
| Taxable total profits | 257,219 |

Hawk Ltd is a small profit company

| £257,219 × 20% | 51,444 |
|---|---|

*Workings*

### 1 Office building

|  | £ |
|---|---|
| Proceeds | 275,000 |
| Less: disposal costs | (5,726) |
| Net proceeds of sale | 269,274 |
| Less: original costs £(81,000 + 3,200) | (84,200) |
| enhancement expenditure | (43,000) |
| Unindexed gain | 142,074 |
| Less: indexation allowance on original cost |  |
| $\dfrac{(250.0 - 186.8)}{186.8}(0.338) \times £84,200$ | (28,460) |
| on enhancement |  |
| $\dfrac{(250.0 - 197.7)}{197.7}(0.265) \times £43,000$ | (11,395) |
| Indexed gain | 102,219 |

### 2 Albatross plc shares

FA 1985 pool

|  | No. of shares | Cost |
|---|---|---|
|  |  | £ |
| 1.8.13 Acquisition | 6,000 | 18,600 |
| 17.8.13 Acquisition | 2,000 | 9,400 |
|  | 8,000 | 28,000 |
| 29.8.13 Disposal | (5,000) | (17,500) |
| c/f | 3,000 | 10,500 |

|  | £ |
|---|---|
| Proceeds | 42,500 |
| Less: cost | (17,500) |
| Gain (no indexation allowance) | 25,000 |

### 3 Cuckoo plc preference shares
Reorganisation

|  | MV | Cost |
|---|---|---|
|  | £ | £ |
| 15,000 Ordinary shares (5,000 × 3) × £4.50 | 67,500 | 45,000 |
| 10,000 Preference shares (5,000 × 2) × £2.25 | 22,500 | 15,000 |
|  | 90,000 | 60,000 |

|  | £ |
|---|---|
| Proceeds | 32,000 |
| Less: cost | (15,000) |
| Gain (no indexation allowance) | 17,000 |

4   *Land*

|  | £ |
|---|---|
| Proceeds | 120,000 |

Less: costs £203,500 × $\dfrac{120,000}{120,000 + 65,000}$     (132,000)

| Loss | (12,000) |
|---|---|

5   *Net chargeable gains*

|  | £ |
|---|---|
| Office building (W1) | 102,219 |
| Albatross plc Shares (W2) | 25,000 |
| Cuckoo plc preference shares (W3) | 17,000 |
| Land (W4) | (12,000) |
| Net chargeable gains | 132,219 |

(b)   (i)   The only disposal that qualifies for rollover relief is the sale of the freehold office building. Shares do not qualify and the land has not been used for business purposes.

The office building was sold for £275,000, and this is therefore the amount that Hawk Ltd will have to reinvest in order to claim the maximum possible amount of rollover relief.

*Tutorial note.* It would also have been acceptable to state that the net disposal proceeds (£269,274) had to be reinvested to claim the maximum possible of rollover relief.

(ii)   The reinvestment will have to take place between 1 May 2012 and 30 April 2016, which is the period starting one year before and ending three years after the date of disposal.

(iii)   Corporation tax of £20,444 (£102,219 × 20%) will be saved if the maximum possible amount of rollover relief is claimed.

# 39 Problematic Ltd

**Text references.** Chargeable gains for companies are covered in Chapter 21. Taxable total profits are defined in Chapter 20.

**Top tips.** Make sure you use the three column pro-forma for the FA 1985 pool.

**Easy marks.** The calculations of taxable total profits simply required the gains calculated to be added together with the figure for trading profit.

**Examiner's comments.** It was pleasing to see that this question was well answered. On an overall note, it does not create a very good impression when candidates deduct the annual exempt amount when dealing with a company. The only aspect that consistently caused problems in part (a) was the restoration of the asset. Despite the question telling candidates that a claim to defer the gain had been made, many insisted that such a claim was not possible and instead calculated a capital loss. Many candidates did not even attempt part (b) despite the fact that this section generally just required them to provide figures already calculated in part (a).

|  |  | Marks |
|---|---|---|
| (a) | **Easy plc** | |
|  | FA 1985 pool - Purchase | ½ |
|  |            - Rights issue | 1½ |
|  |            - Indexation | 2 |
|  |            - Disposal | 1 |
|  | Chargeable gain | 1½ |
|  | **Office building** | |
|  | Proceeds fully reinvested | 1 |
|  | No disposal on receipt of proceeds | 1 |
|  | **Freehold factory** | |
|  | Disposal proceeds | ½ |
|  | Indexed cost | ½ |
|  | Rollover relief | 2 |
|  | **Land** | |
|  | Proceeds | ½ |
|  | Incidental costs of disposal | 1 |
|  | Cost | 2 |
|  | **Taxable total profits** | |
|  | Chargeable gains | ½ |
|  | Calculation | ½ |
|  |  | 16 |
| (b) | Ordinary shares in Easy plc | ½ |
|  | Office building | 1½ |
|  | Leasehold factory | 1 |
|  | Land | 1 |
|  |  | 4 |
|  |  | 20 |

(a) **Problematic plc – taxable total profits for y/e 31 March 2014**

|  | £ |
|---|---|
| Easy plc shares (W1) | 31,280 |
| Office building (W2) | 0 |
| Freehold factory (W3) | 16,200 |
| Land (W4) | 45,550 |
| Trading profit | 106,970 |
| Taxable total profits | 200,000 |

*Workings*

(1) *Easy plc shares*

FA85 pool

|  | No. of shares | Cost £ | Indexed cost £ |
|---|---|---|---|
| Purchase 26.6.05 | 15,000 | 12,600 | 12,600 |
| Index to September 2008 | | | |
| $\dfrac{(218.4 - 192.2)}{192.2} \times £12,600$ | | | 1,718 |
| Rights issue 1 for 3 @ £2.20 | 5,000 | 11,000 | 11,000 |
| c/f | 20,000 | 23,600 | 25,318 |

|  | No. of shares | Cost £ | Indexed cost £ |
|---|---|---|---|
| b/f | 20,000 | 23,600 | 25,318 |
| Index to June 2013 | | | |
| $\dfrac{(249.3 - 218.4)}{218.4} \times £25,318$ | | | 3,582 |
| | | | 28,900 |
| Sale | (16,000) | (18,880) | (23,120) |
| C/f | 4,000 | 4,720 | 5,780 |

| Gain | £ |
|---|---|
| Proceeds | 54,400 |
| Less: cost | (18,880) |
| | 35,520 |
| Less: indexation £ (23,120 – 18,880) | (4,240) |
| Chargeable gain | 31,280 |

(2)   *Office building*

The insurance proceeds of £36,000 received by Problematic Ltd have been fully applied in restoring the office building.

There is therefore no disposal on the receipt of the insurance proceeds.

(3)   *Freehold factory*

| | £ |
|---|---|
| Proceeds | 171,000 |
| Less: indexed cost | (127,000) |
| | 44,000 |
| Less: gain deferred on purchase of leasehold factory £(44,000 – 16,200) | (27,800) |
| Chargeable gain (amount not reinvested £(171,000 – 154,800)) | 16,200 |

(4)   *Land*

| | £ |
|---|---|
| Proceeds | 130,000 |
| Less: disposal costs | (3,200) |
| Net disposal proceeds | 126,800 |
| Less: indexed cost | |
| $\dfrac{130,000}{130,000 + 350,000} \times £300,000$ | (81,250) |
| Chargeable gain | 45,550 |

(b)   **Carried forward indexed base costs**

The 4,000 £1 ordinary shares in Easy plc have an indexed base cost of £5,780

The indexed base cost of the office building is £(169,000 – 36,000 + 41,000) = £174,000.

The leasehold factory is a depreciating asset, so there is no adjustment to the base cost of £154,800.

The indexed base cost of the remaining three acres of land is £(300,000 – 81,250) = £218,750.

*Tutorial note.* When a replacement asset is a depreciating asset then the gain is not rolled over by reducing the cost of the replacement asset. Instead, the gain is deferred until it crystallises on the earliest of:

–   The disposal of the replacement asset.

–   The date the replacement asset is no longer used in the business.

–   Ten years after the acquisition of the replacement asset which in this case is 10 December 2023.

# 40 Lim Lam

**Marking scheme**

|  |  |  |  | Marks |
|---|---|---|---|---|
| (a) | Land | – Proceeds | ½ | |
| | | – Cost | ½ | |
| | Oily plc | – Deemed proceeds | 2 | |
| | | – Cost | 1 | |
| | Mal-Mil Ltd | – Proceeds | ½ | |
| | | – Cost | 1 | |
| | Annual exempt amount | – Use first against gains not qualifying for ER | 1 | |
| | Capital gains tax @ 28% | | ½ | |
| | Capital gains tax @ 10% | | ½ | |
| | Due date | | ½ | |
| | | | | 8 |
| (b) | **Chargeable gain** | | | |
| | Proceeds | | ½ | |
| | Incidental costs of disposal | | ½ | |
| | Cost | | 1½ | |
| | Enhancement expenditure | | 1 | |
| | Indexation | | 1½ | |
| | **Corporation tax liability** | | | |
| | Calculation | | 1½ | |
| | Due date | | ½ | |
| | | | | 7 |
| | | | | 15 |

(a) **Lim Lam – Capital gains tax liability 2013/14**

*Summary*

|  | £ | Gains not qualifying for entrepreneurs' relief £ | Gains qualifying for entrepreneurs' relief £ |
|---|---|---|---|
| Land |  |  |  |
| Disposal proceeds | 260,000 |  |  |
| Less: cost | (182,000) |  |  |
|  |  | 78,000 |  |
| Ordinary shares in Oily plc |  |  |  |
| Deemed proceeds | 37,200 |  |  |
| (5,000 × £7.44) (W1) |  |  |  |
| Less: cost | (15,925) |  |  |
|  |  | 21,275 |  |
| Ordinary shares in Mal-Mil Ltd |  |  |  |
| Disposal proceeds | 280,000 |  |  |
| Less: cost (W2) | (56,000) |  |  |
|  |  |  | 224,000 |
| Chargeable gains |  | 99,275 | 224,000 |
| Less: annual exempt amount (N1) |  | (10,900) |  |
| Taxable gains |  | 88,375 | 224,000 |
|  |  |  |  |
| Capital gains tax on 88,375 @ 28% (N2) |  | 24,745 |  |
| Capital gains tax on 224,000 @ 10% |  |  | 22,400 |
|  |  |  |  |
| Capital gains tax liability 2013/14 |  | £47,145 |  |

Lim's capital gains tax liability should be paid by 31 January 2015.

*Workings*

1   The shares in Oily plc are valued at £7.44 (£7.40 + ¼(£7.56 – £7.40)) as this is lower than £7.48 ((£7.36 + £7.60)/2).

2   Share pool

|  | Number | Cost £ |
|---|---|---|
| Purchase 8 June 2006 | 125,000 | 142,000 |
| Purchase 23 May 2008 | 60,000 | 117,000 |
|  | 185,000 | 259,000 |
| Disposal 22 March 2014 (259,000 × 40,000/185,000) | (40,000) | (56,000) |
| Balance carried forward | 145,000 | 203,000 |

*Tutorial notes*

1   The annual exempt amount is set against the gains not qualifying for entrepreneurs' relief as this gives the best use of the annual exempt amount as it reduces tax at 28%.

2   The gains qualifying for entrepreneurs' relief are the lowest part of the gains and therefore use up the remaining basic rate band of £4,010 (32,010 – 28,000). This means that the gains not qualifying for entrepreneurs' relief are all taxed at 28%.

(b)     **Mal-Mil Ltd – Chargeable gain on the disposal of the land**

|  | £ | £ |
|---|---|---|
| Disposal proceeds | | 162,000 |
| Incidental costs of disposal | | (3,800) |
| | | 158,200 |
| Less: cost (W1) | 101,250 | |
| Enhancement expenditure (W2) | 12,150 | |
| | | (113,400) |
| Less: indexation allowance £113,400 × 0.019 (W3) | | (2,155) |
| Chargeable gain | | 42,645 |

*Workings*

1    Cost of land

The cost relating to the two acres of land sold is £101,250 (260,000 × 162,000/416,000 (162,000 + 254,000)).

2    Enhancement expenditure

The levelling of the land is enhancement expenditure. The cost relating to the two acres of land sold is £12,150 (31,200 × 162,000/416,000).

3    Indexation factor

Both the cost and the enhancement expenditure were incurred during July 2013. The relevant indexation factor is therefore $\frac{(254.4 - 249.6)}{249.6} = 0.019$.

**Corporation tax liability**

Mal-Mil Ltd's taxable total profits for the year ended 31 December 2013 are £(163,000 + 42,645) = £205,645.

Mal-Mil Ltd's corporation tax liability for the year ended 31 December 2013 is £41,129 (£205,645 × 20% – FYs 2012 & 2013 same rate for small profits). This is due on 1 October 2014.

# 41 Starfish Ltd

**Text references.** Computing taxable total profits is covered in Chapter 19. Corporation tax losses are dealt with in Chapter 22. Chapters 25 and 26 cover value added tax.

**Top tips.** Make sure that you set out the computation of taxable total profits in part (c) using the standard layout, leaving space for losses carried forward against trading profits and losses carried back against total profits.

**Easy marks.** The adjustment of profit computation was reasonably straightforward.

**Examiner's comments.** Part (a) surprisingly caused quite a few problems, with a number of candidates discussing long periods of account or, even worse, the basis period rules for unincorporated businesses. Some candidates just stated that an accounting period starts when trading commences, and ends when trading ceases – which would imply that all companies have just one long accounting period. Part (b) was very well answered, with many very good answers. The only aspect consistently answered incorrectly was the treatment of a purchased asset. In the final capital allowances computation no allowances are given, so the addition should simply have been added to the main pool. In part (c) many candidates overlooked the trading loss for the final period of trading. The VAT calculation in part (d) was generally well answered, although few candidates appreciated that output VAT would not be due on the sale of inventory and non-current assets if the business was sold as a going concern. Many candidates simply stated that no VAT would be due, which was too vague to score marks.

|  |  |  |  | Marks |
|---|---|---|---|---|
| (a) | Start of accounting period | | 2 | |
| | Finish of accounting period | | 2 | |
| | | | | 4 |
| (b) | Depreciation | | ½ | |
| | Donations | | 1½ | |
| | Impairment loss | | 1 | |
| | Legal fees | | 1½ | |
| | Entertaining customers | | ½ | |
| | Entertaining employees | | ½ | |
| | Counselling services | | ½ | |
| | Plant and machinery | – WDV brought forward | 1 | |
| | | – Addition | 1½ | |
| | | – Main pool proceeds | 2 | |
| | | – Motor car proceeds | 1 | |
| | | – Balancing adjustments | ½ | |
| | | | | 12 |
| (c) | Trading profit | | ½ | |
| | Relief for 2010 loss | – Period ended 31 March 2010 | ½ | |
| | | – Carry forward | ½ | |
| | Bank interest | | ½ | |
| | Relief for 2013 loss | – Year ended 31 March 2011 | 1 | |
| | | – Other periods | 1 | |
| | Qualifying charitable donations | | 1 | |
| | | | | 5 |
| (d) | (i) | Output VAT | – Cash sales revenue | 1½ | |
| | | | – Credit sales revenue | 1½ | |
| | | | – Inventory | 1 | |
| | | | – Sale of non-current assets | ½ | |
| | | Input VAT | – Expenses | 1 | |
| | | | – Impairment loss | 1 | |
| | | | – Purchase of non-current asset | ½ | |
| | | | | | 7 |
| | (ii) | Output VAT not due on TOGC | | 1 | |
| | | VAT refund | | 1 | |
| | | | | | 2 |
| | | | | | 30 |

(a) **Start and finish of accounting periods**

An accounting period will normally start immediately after the end of the preceding accounting period.

An accounting period will also start when a company starts to trade, or otherwise becomes liable to corporation tax.

An accounting period will normally finish 12 months after the beginning of the accounting period or at the end of a company's period of account (if less than 12 months).

An accounting period will also finish when a company ceases to trade, when it ceases to otherwise be liable to corporation tax, when it ceases to be resident in the UK, or on the commencement of winding up procedures.

**(b)** **Starfish Ltd – Trading loss for the period ended 31 March 2014**

|  |  | £ | £ |
|---|---|---:|---:|
| Loss before taxation |  |  | (190,000) |
| Add: | Depreciation | 25,030 |  |
|  | Donation to political party | 300 |  |
|  | Donation (not qualifying charitable donation) | 600 |  |
|  | Donation paid (qualifying charitable donation) | 750 |  |
|  | Impairment loss | 0 |  |
|  | Legal fees – Internet domain name | 0 |  |
|  | – Misleading advertisement | 2,020 |  |
|  | – Issue of loan notes (N1) | 0 |  |
|  | Entertaining customers (N2) | 3,600 |  |
|  | Entertaining employees (N2) | 0 |  |
|  | Counselling services (N3) | 0 |  |
|  |  |  | 32,300 |
|  |  |  | (157,700) |
| Less: Capital allowances (W1) |  |  | (2,300) |
| Adjusted trading loss |  |  | (160,000) |

*Workings*

1   *Capital allowances*

|  | Main pool | Special rate pool | Allowances |
|---|---:|---:|---:|
|  | £ | £ | £ |
| TWDVs b/f | 23,600 | 13,200 |  |
| Addition – computer (W2) (N4) | 2,600 |  |  |
|  | 26,200 |  |  |
| Disposals (W3) | (27,500) | (9,600) |  |
| Balancing charge | (1,300) |  |  |
|  |  |  | (1,300) |
| Balancing allowance |  | 3,600 | 3,600 |
| Total allowances |  |  | 2,300 |

2   *Computer*

The input VAT on the computer is recoverable and so only the cost net of VAT is eligible expenditure which is £3,120 × 100/120 = £2,600.

3   *Disposal proceeds*

The output VAT charged on the disposals is not part of the proceeds for capital allowance purposes. The main pool proceeds are therefore £([31,200 + 1,800] × 100/120) = £27,500. There is no VAT charged on the sale of the car, as none was recovered on purchase (owing to private usage).

*Tutorial notes*

1   The cost of obtaining loan finance, even if abortive, is allowable as a trading loan relationship debit.

2   The only exception to the non-deductibility of entertainment expenditure is when it is in respect of employees.

3   The costs of counselling services for redundant employees are deductible if they qualify for exemption from the employment income charge on employees.

4   The annual investment allowance and writing down allowances are not given for the period in which a trade ceases. Therefore the addition is simply added into the main pool.

(c) **Starfish Ltd – Taxable total profits**

| | P/e 31.3.10 | Y/e 31.3.11 | Y/e 31.3.12 | Y/e 31.3.13 | P/e 31.12.13 |
|---|---|---|---|---|---|
| | £ | £ | £ | £ | £ |
| Trading profit | 0 | 64,200 | 53,900 | 14,700 | 49,900 |
| Less: c/f loss relief (N1) | 0 | (12,600) | 0 | 0 | 0 |
| | 0 | 51,600 | 53,900 | 14,700 | 49,900 |
| Bank interest | 600 | 1,400 | 1,700 | 0 | 0 |
| | 600 | 53,000 | 55,600 | 14,700 | 49,900 |
| Less: c/b loss relief (N2) | (0) | (13,250) | (55,600) | (14,700) | (49,900) |
| | 600 | 39,750 | 0 | 0 | 0 |
| Less: qualifying charitable donations (N3) | (600) | (1,000) | (0) | (0) | (0) |
| Taxable total profits | 0 | 38,750 | 0 | 0 | 0 |

*Tutorial notes*

1   Starfish Ltd would not have made a loss relief claim against total profits for the period ended 31 March 2010 as this would have wasted the £600 of relieved qualifying charitable donations for that period.

2   The trading loss for the period ended 31 March 2014 can be relieved against total profits for the 3 years immediately preceding the start of the loss making period since it is a terminal loss. The 3 year period is between 1 January 2011 and 31 December 2013. Relief is as follows:

| | £ |
|---|---|
| Loss of 3 month p/e 31.3.14 | 160,000 |
| Less: used in p/e 31.12.13 | (49,900) |
| | 110,100 |
| Less: used in y/e 31.3.13 | (14,700) |
| | 95,400 |
| Less: used in y/e 31.3.12 | (55,600) |
| | 39,800 |
| Less: used in y/e 31.3.11 | |
| (restricted to 3/12 × £53,000) | (13,250) |
| Balance unrelieved | 26,550 |

3   The qualifying charitable donations in the period ending 31 March 2014, and earlier years, are also unrelieved.

(d) (i)  **Starfish Ltd – VAT return for the quarter ended 31 March 2014**

| | £ | £ |
|---|---|---|
| **Output VAT** | | |
| Cash sales revenue £38,520 × 20/120 | | 6,420 |
| Credit sales revenue £2,000 × (100 – 4)% × 20% | | 384 |
| Sale of inventory on cessation £28,800 × 20/120 | | 4,800 |
| Sale of non-current assets £([31,200 + 1,800] × 20/120) | | 5,500 |
| **Input VAT** | | |
| Expenses £([69,960 – 4,320] = £65,640) × 20/120 | 10,940 | |
| Impairment loss | 384 | |
| Purchase of non-current asset (computer) | 520 | |
| | | (11,844) |
| VAT payable | | 5,260 |

*Tutorial notes*

1   The calculation of output VAT on the credit sales revenue takes into account the discount for prompt payment, even for the 40% of customers that did not take it.

2   Input VAT on business entertainment for UK customers is not recoverable.

3    Relief for the impairment loss is available because the claim is made more than six months from the time that payment was due, and the debt has been written off in the company's books.

(ii)    A sale of a business as a going concern is outside the scope of VAT, and therefore output VAT would not have been due on the sale of the inventory or the sale of the non-current assets.

Instead of VAT being payable, Starfish Ltd would have been due a refund of £5,040 (5,260 – 4,800 – 5,500).

# 42 Volatile Ltd

**Text references.** Corporation tax losses are covered in Chapter 22.

**Top tips.** Don't forget to set up a loss memorandum for each loss so that you can see how the loss is utilised.

**Easy marks.** You should have been able to state at least 2 of the principles of claiming loss relief in part (a).

**Examiner's comments.** This question was not particularly well answered. In part (a) far too many candidates explained the loss reliefs available rather than the factors influencing the choice of claims. In part (b) many candidates approached this on a year by year basis, rather than one computation with a column for each of the four periods. This not only wasted time in having to write out four computations, but also made it very difficult to calculate the correct loss relief claims. Other common mistakes included treating the chargeable gains separately (rather than as part of the taxable total profits), and deducting qualifying charitable donations from trading profits rather than total profits after loss relief.

## Marking scheme

|  |  |  | Marks |
|---|---|---|---|
| (a) | Rate of tax | 1 | |
| | Timing of relief | 1 | |
| | Qualifying charitable donations not relieved | 1 | |
| | | | 3 |
| (b) | Trading income | ½ | |
| | Property business income | ½ | |
| | Chargeable gains | ½ | |
| | Loss relief – y/e 31 December 2010 | 2 | |
| | Loss relief – y/e 30 September 2013 | 2½ | |
| | Qualifying charitable donations | ½ | |
| | Unrelieved losses | ½ | |
| | | | 7 |
| | | | 10 |

(a)    **Choice of loss relief**

The three factors that will influence a company's choice of loss relief claims are:

- The rate at which relief will be obtained:

    - 23.75% if marginal relief applies (best use)
    - 23% at the main rate (second best use)
    - 20% at the small profits rate (third best use)

- How quickly relief will be obtained: loss relief against total profits is quicker than carry forward loss relief.

- The extent to which relief for qualifying charitable donations might be lost.

(b)  **Volatile Ltd**

|  | P/e 31.12.09 £ | Y/e 31.12.10 £ | Y/e 31.12.11 £ | P/e 30.09.12 £ |
|---|---|---|---|---|
| Trading income | 44,000 | 0 | 95,200 | 78,700 |
| Less: carry forward loss relief | (0) | (0) | (8,700) | (0) |
|  | 44,000 | 0 | 86,500 | 78,700 |
| Property business income | 9,400 | 6,600 | 6,500 | 0 |
| Chargeable gains | 5,100 | 0 | 0 | 9,700 |
| Total profits | 58,500 | 6,600 | 93,000 | 88,400 |
| Less: current period loss relief | (0) | (6,600) | (0) | (0) |
| Less: carry back loss relief | (58,500) | | (23,250) | (88,400) |
|  | 0 | 0 | 69,750 | 0 |
| Less: qualifying charitable donations | (0) | (0) | (1,200) | (0) |
| Taxable total profits | 0 | 0 | 68,550 | 0 |

*Loss memorandum*

|  | £ |
|---|---|
| Loss in y/e 31.12.10 | 73,800 |
| Less:  used y/e 31.12.10 | (6,600) |
| Less:  used p/e 31.12.09 | (58,500) |
| Less:  used y/e 31.12.11 | (8,700) |
| Loss remaining unrelieved | 0 |

|  | £ |
|---|---|
| Loss in y/e 30.9.13 | 186,800 |
| Less:  used p/e 30.9.12 | (88,400) |
| Less:  used y/e 31.12.11 | |
| 3 months to 31.12.11 | |
| £93,000 × 3/12 | (23,250) |
| Loss remaining unrelieved | 75,150 |

The loss of y/e 30.9.13 can be carried back against total profits of the previous 12 months ie against the 9 month period ending 30.9.12 and 3 months of the y/e 31.12.11.

# 43 Jogger Ltd

## Marking scheme

|     |       |                                |        | Marks |
|-----|-------|--------------------------------|--------|-------|
| (a) | (i)   | Operating loss                 | ½      |       |
|     |       | Depreciation                   | ½      |       |
|     |       | P&M   – AIA                    | 1½     |       |
|     |       | – Main pool                    | 1½     |       |
|     |       | – Special rate pool            | 1½     |       |
|     |       | – Short life asset             | 1½     |       |
|     |       |                                |        | 7     |
|     | (ii)  | Property business profit       | 2      |       |
|     |       | Bank interest                  | ½      |       |
|     |       | Loan interest                  | 1      |       |
|     |       | Chargeable gain                | ½      |       |
|     |       | Loss relief                    | 1      |       |
|     |       | Franked investment income      | 1      |       |
|     |       | Corporation tax                | 2      |       |
|     |       |                                |        | 8     |
|     | (iii) | Due date                       | 1      |       |
|     |       | Fixed penalty                  | 1½     |       |
|     |       | Corporation tax related penalty| 1½     |       |
|     |       |                                |        | 4     |
| (b) | (i)   | Quarter ended 30 September 2012| 2      |       |
|     |       | Quarter ended 31 March 2013    | 2      |       |
|     |       | Quarter ended 31 March 2014    | 2      |       |
|     |       |                                |        | 6     |
|     | (ii)  | One VAT return                 | 1½     |       |
|     |       | Payments on account            | 1½     |       |
|     |       | Limit                          | 1      |       |
|     |       | VAT returns                    | 1      |       |
|     |       |                                |        | 5     |
|     |       |                                |        | 30    |

(a) (i) **Trading loss y/e 31.3.14**

|                              | £         |
|------------------------------|-----------|
| Operating profit             | 143,482   |
| Add:   depreciation          | 58,840    |
|                              | 202,322   |
| Less:  capital allowances (W)| (258,182) |
| Adjusted trading loss        | (55,860)  |

*Working*

*Plant and machinery*

| | AIA | Main pool | Special rate pool | SLA | Allowances |
|---|---|---|---|---|---|
| | £ | £ | £ | £ | £ |
| TWDV b/f | | 26,600 | 18,800 | | |
| *Additions qualifying for AIA* | | | | | |
| 30.9.13 Machinery | 250,000 | | | | |
| AIA | (250,000) | | | | 250,000 |
| *Additions qualifying for AIA but not claimed* | | | | | |
| 15.12.13 Computer | | | | 12,500 | |
| *Additions not qualifying for AIA* | | | | | |
| 31.7.13 Car | | 11,800 | | | |
| *Disposals* | | | | | |
| 20.7.13 Car | | | (11,700) | | |
| BC | | | 7,100 | | |
| 14.3.14 Lorry | | (8,600) | | | |
| | | 29,800 | | | |
| WDA @ 18% | | (5,364) | | (2,250) | 7,614 |
| WDA @ 8% | | | (568) | | 568 |
| TWDV c/f | | 24,436 | 6,532 | 10,250 | |
| Allowances | | | | | 258,182 |

(ii) **Jogger Ltd – corporation tax computation y/e 31.3.14**

| | £ |
|---|---|
| Interest income (W1) | 33,060 |
| Property income (W2) | 126,000 |
| Chargeable gain | 98,300 |
| Total profits | 257,360 |
| Less: loss relief | (55,860) |
| Taxable total profits | 201,500 |
| Add: FII £45,000 × 100/90 | 50,000 |
| Augmented profits | 251,500 |

*Corporation tax*

| | £ |
|---|---|
| Upper limit £1,500,000 / 3 associated companies | 500,000 |
| Lower limit £300,000 / 3 associated companies | 100,000 |

| | £ |
|---|---|
| Marginal relief applies | |
| £201,500 × 23% | 46,345 |
| Less: 3/400 × £(500,000 – 251,500) × 201,500/251,500 | (1,493) |
| Corporation tax payable | 44,852 |

*Workings*

1    *Interest income*

| | £ |
|---|---|
| Bank interest receivable | 8,460 |
| Loan interest – received 31.12.13 | 16,400 |
|            – accrued 31.3.14 | 8,200 |
| | 33,060 |

2    *Property income*

|                                              | £         |
| -------------------------------------------- | --------- |
| Premium received                             | 100,000   |
| Less: 2% × (10 − 1) × £100,000               | (18,000)  |
| Taxable as property income                   | 82,000    |
| Add: rental income accrued                   | 44,000    |
|                                              | 126,000   |

(iii)   Jogger Ltd's self-assessment tax return for the year ended 31 March 2014 must be submitted by 31 March 2015.

If the company submits its self-assessment tax return eight months late, then there will be an automatic fixed penalty of £200, since the return is more than three months late.

There will also be an additional corporation tax geared penalty of £4,485 (£44,852 × 10%) which is 10% of the tax unpaid six months after the return was due as the total delay is less than 12 months.

*Tutorial note*

The question states that the corporation tax liability is paid at the same time the self-assessment tax return is submitted which is eight months late.

(b)    (i)    The late submission of the VAT return for the quarter ended 30 September 2012 will have resulted in HM Revenue and Customs (HMRC) issuing a surcharge liability notice specifying a surcharge period running to 30 September 2013.

The late payment of VAT for the quarter ended 31 March 2013 will have resulted in a surcharge of £778 (£38,900 × 2%) because this is the first default in the surcharge period. The surcharge period will also have been extended to 31 March 2014.

The late payment of VAT for the quarter ended 31 March 2014 will therefore have resulted in a surcharge of £4,455 (£89,100 × 5%) because this is the second default in the surcharge period. The surcharge period will also have been extended to 31 March 2015.

(ii)   **Annual accounting scheme**

The reduced administration from only having to submit one VAT return each year should mean that default surcharges are avoided in respect of the late submission of VAT returns.

In addition, making payments on account based on the previous year's VAT liability will improve both budgeting and possibly cash flow if Jogger Ltd's business is expanding.

Jogger Ltd can apply to use the annual accounting scheme if its expected taxable turnover for the next 12 months does not exceed £1,350,000 exclusive of VAT.

However, the company must be up to date with its VAT returns before it is allowed to use the scheme.

# 44 Black Ltd, Cherry Grey and Blu Reddy

> **Text references.** Group relief is covered in Chapter 23. Residence of individuals is dealt with in Chapter 2. Inheritance tax is the subject of Chapter 18.
>
> **Top tips.** It is very important that you read the questions carefully and comply with any detailed instructions. For example, in parts (a) and (c) of this question, you were given notes about your answer such as to set out your answer in a particular way or to ignore exemptions.
>
> **Easy marks.** The inheritance tax part of this question was probably the easiest on which to obtain marks. The loss to the donor principle is an important aspect of inheritance tax and quite straightforward to deal with.

## Marking scheme

|  |  |  | Marks |
|---|---|---|---|
| (a) | *Maximum potential claim by Black Ltd* | | |
| | After losses brought forward used | 1 | |
| | Qualifying charitable donations | ½ | |
| | Maximum claim | ½ | |
| | *Maximum surrender by White Ltd* | | |
| | Trading loss – current period only/maximum claim | 1 | |
| | Qualifying charitable donations | 1 | |
| | Capital losses | ½ | |
| | *Maximum group relief claim that can be made* | ½ | |
| | | | 5 |
| (b) | Automatic overseas test | 1 | |
| | Automatic UK test | 1 | |
| | Sufficient ties test | 2 | |
| | | | 4 |
| (c) | *Lifetime transfer* | | |
| | Value transferred | 2 | |
| | IHT liability | 1½ | |
| | *Additional tax on death* | | |
| | Gross chargeable transfer | ½ | |
| | IHT liability | ½ | |
| | Taper relief | 1 | |
| | IHT already paid | ½ | |
| | | | 6 |
| | | | 15 |

(a) **Black Ltd – Group relief claim for year ended 31 March 2014**

*Maximum potential claim by Black Ltd*

Black Ltd uses its own losses brought forward in working out the taxable total profits against which it may claim group relief.

Furthermore, group relief is against taxable total profits after all other reliefs for the current period (for example qualifying charitable donations).

The maximum potential claim by Black Ltd is therefore £(396,800 – 57,900 + 21,100 – 4,400) = £355,600.

*Maximum potential surrender by White Ltd*

White Ltd may surrender its current period trading losses of £351,300. Only current period losses are available for group relief so White Ltd's loss of £21,800 brought forward cannot be group relieved.

White Ltd may also surrender excess qualifying charitable donations (ie to the extent that they exceed total profits before taking account of any losses). Since the qualifying charitable donations of £5,600 do not exceed the total profits of £26,700, there is no excess.

It is not possible to surrender capital losses as part of a group relief claim.

The maximum potential surrender by White Ltd is therefore £351,300.

*Maximum group relief claim*

The maximum group relief claim is the lower of the claim that can be made by Black Ltd and the surrender that can be made by White Ltd ie £351,300.

(b) **Cherry Grey – UK residence**

Cherry has not been resident in the UK for any of the previous three tax years. She does not satisfy any of the automatic overseas tests in the tax year 2013/14 since she spends 46 days or more in the UK and does not work full-time overseas.

Cherry does not satisfy any of the automatic UK tests in the tax year 2013/14 as she spent less than 183 days in the UK, has an overseas home, and does not work full-time in the UK.

The 'sufficient ties' test is therefore relevant. Cherry spends between 91 and 120 days in the UK during the tax year 2013/14. As she was not previously resident in the UK, Cherry would need three UK ties to be UK resident for this tax year. Cherry has three such ties in the tax year 2013/14:

- UK resident close family (spouse)
- Available UK accommodation which Cherry used during the tax year
- More than 90 days spent in the UK in the previous tax year

Cherry is therefore UK resident for tax purposes for the tax year 2013/14.

(c) **Blu Reddy – Inheritance tax on transfer of Purple Ltd shares**

| | £ |
|---|---:|
| *Lifetime transfer 15 January 2014* | |
| Value of shares held before the transfer | 1,200,000 |
| 300,000 × £4 | |
| Value of shares held after the transfer | |
| 100,000 × £2 | (200,000) |
| Net chargeable transfer | 1,000,000 |
| IHT liability | |
| £325,000 × 0% | 0 |
| £675,000 × 20/80 | 168,750 |
| Lifetime IHT payable | 168,750 |
| | |
| Gross chargeable transfer £(1,000,000 + 168,750) | 1,168,750 |
| | |
| *Additional IHT arising death 31 May 2018* | |
| Gross transfer of value | 1,168,750 |
| IHT liability | |
| £325,000 × 0% | 0 |
| £843,750 × 40% | 337,500 |
| | 337,500 |
| Less: taper relief (4 to 5 years @ 40%) | (135,000) |
| Death tax | 202,500 |
| Less: lifetime tax paid | (168,750) |
| Additional IHT payable | 33,750 |

# 45 A Ltd

> **Text references.** Chapters 19, 20, 23 and 24 are required reading for this question.
>
> **Top tips.** B Ltd's loss could be set only against the available profits of the corresponding accounting period.

|     |                               | Marks |     |
| --- | ----------------------------- | ----- | --- |
| (a) | Trading income                | ½     |     |
|     | Property business income      | ½     |     |
|     | Interest income               | ½     |     |
|     | Qualifying charitable donation | 1     |     |
|     | Group relief                  | 3     |     |
|     | FII                           | ½     |     |
|     | CT calculation                | 2     |     |
|     |                               |       | 8   |
| (b) | Payment date                  |       | 1   |
| (c) | Filing date                   |       | 1   |
|     |                               |       | 10  |

(a)    **Corporation Tax computation 9 m/e 31 December 2013**

|                                      | £ | £        |
| ------------------------------------ | - | -------- |
| Trading income                       |   | 342,000  |
| Property income                      |   | 10,000   |
| Interest income                      |   | 16,000   |
| Total profits                        |   | 368,000  |
| Less: qualifying charitable donation |   | (17,000) |
|                                      |   | 351,000  |
| Less: group relief (W1)              |   | (34,000) |
| Taxable total profits                |   | 317,000  |
| Add: Franked Investment Income       |   | 1,000    |
| Augmented profits                    |   | 318,000  |

|                   | £ |
| ----------------- | - |
| Corporation tax   |   |
| *FY 2013*         |   |
| £317,000 × 23%    | 72,910 |
| Less marginal relief |   |

$$3/400 \ (£562,500 - 318,000) \times \frac{317,000}{318,000}$$    (1,828)

| Corporation tax payable | 71,082 |
| ----------------------- | ------ |

*Note:* it is assumed that the loan interest arose on a non-trading loan and is therefore taxable as interest income.

*Workings*

1    B Ltd joined the group with A Ltd on 1 July 2013 so for A Ltd's profit making accounting period to 31 December 2013 there are 6 months in common with B Ltd's loss making period.

A Ltd   6/9 × £351,000  = £234,000
B Ltd   6/12 × (£68,000)  = £34,000

Maximum group relief available is lower of two, ie £34,000.

2    The 9 months to 31 December 2013 falls into FY 2013.

Augmented profits are between the upper and lower limits of £1,500,000 × 9/12 ÷ 2 = £562,500 and £300,000 × 9/12 ÷ 2 = £112,500, so marginal relief applies.

(b)   The corporation tax of £71,082 for the nine-month period ended 31 December 2013 must be paid by <u>1 October 2014</u>.

(c)   The corporation tax return for the nine-month period ended 31 December 2013 must be filed by <u>31 December 2014</u>.

# 46 Apple Ltd

**Text references.** Corporation tax computations are covered in Chapter 20. Chargeable gains for companies are dealt with in Chapters 21. Group relief is covered in Chapter 23.

**Top tips.** When using losses, consider the marginal rates of tax of each company.

Marking scheme

|  |  | Marks |  |
|---|---|---|---|
| (a) | *Taxable total profits* |  |  |
|  | Apple  – Trading profits | 1 |  |
|  |          – Capital gains | 1 |  |
|  | Bramley Ltd's Loss | 1 |  |
|  | Cox Ltd's loss | 1 |  |
|  | Delicious Ltd's loss | 1 |  |
|  |  |  | 5 |
| (b) | *Corporation tax saving* |  |  |
|  | Capital loss – use in Apple Ltd | 2 |  |
|  | Rollover relief | 1 |  |
|  | Proceeds not reinvested still chargeable | 1 |  |
|  | Corporation tax saving | 1 |  |
|  | Use of Bramley Ltd's loss | 2 |  |
|  | Use of Cox Ltd's loss | 2 |  |
|  | Delicious Ltd's loss – not advantageous to transfer | 1 |  |
|  |  |  | 10 |
|  |  |  | 15 |

(a)   **Apple Ltd**

|  | *Years ended 31 March* | | |
|---|---|---|---|
|  | *2012* | *2013* | *2014* |
|  | £ | £ | £ |
| Trading profits | 620,000 | 250,000 | 585,000 |
| Capital gain | – | 120,000 | 80,000 |
| Taxable total profits | 620,000 | 370,000 | 665,000 |

**Bramley Ltd**

|  | *Years ended 31 March* | | |
|---|---|---|---|
|  | *2012* | *2013* | *2014* |
|  | £ | £ | £ |
| Trading profits/total profits | – | 52,000 | 70,000 |
| Less: carry forward loss relief | – | (52,000) | (12,000) |
| Taxable total profits | – | – | 58,000 |

**Cox Ltd**

| | *Years ended 31 March* | | |
|---|---|---|---|
| | *2012* | *2013* | *2014* |
| | £ | £ | £ |
| Trading profits/total profits | 83,000 | – | 40,000 |
| Less: carry back loss relief | (58,000) | – | – |
| Taxable total profits | 25,000 | – | 40,000 |

**Delicious Ltd**

| | *Years ended 31 March* | | |
|---|---|---|---|
| | *2012* | *2013* | *2014* |
| | £ | £ | £ |
| Trading profits/total profits | – | 90,000 | – |
| Less: carry back loss relief | – | (15,000) | – |
| Taxable total profits | – | 75,000 | – |

(b)   **Apple Ltd**

| | *Years ended 31 March* | | |
|---|---|---|---|
| | *2012* | *2013* | *2014* |
| | £ | £ | £ |
| Trading profits | 620,000 | 250,000 | 585,000 |
| Chargeable gain | – | 20,000 | 36,000 |
| Total profits | 620,000 | 270,000 | 621,000 |
| Less group relief | (64,000) | (58,000) | (0) |
| Taxable total profits | 556,000 | 212,000 | 621,000 |

In the year to 31 March 2012 group relief has been claimed for Bramley Ltd's loss. This saves Apple Ltd corporation tax of £14,720 (£64,000 × 23%). If the loss had been carried forward as shown above it would have saved Bramley Ltd tax of £12,800 (20% × £64,000). The overall tax saving to the group arising as a result of the group relief claim is £1,920.

Rollover relief has been claimed to defer £100,000 of the chargeable gain arising in the year to 31 March 2013. The £20,000 gain remaining chargeable is equal to the amount of proceeds not reinvested by Cox Ltd in the freehold factory. The lower limit for the year to 31 March 2013 is £75,000 so the rollover relief saves Apple Ltd corporation tax of £23,750 (£100,000 × 23.75%).

It is assumed that Delicious Ltd and Apple Ltd will make an election to transfer the loss on the leasehold factory to Apple Ltd. If this occurs, Apple Ltd will be able to relieve the £44,000 loss by setting it against its chargeable gain for the year, saving tax of £10,120 (£44,000 × 23%).

In the year to 31 March 2013 group relief has been claimed for Cox Ltd's loss. This saves corporation tax of £13,775 (£58,000 × 23.75%). If the loss had been carried back as shown above, it would have saved Cox Ltd corporation tax of £11,600 (£58,000 × 20%). The overall tax saving to the group of a group relief claim is therefore £2,175 (£13,775 – £11,600).

Delicious Ltd could surrender its loss of £15,000 in the year to 31 March 2014 to Cox Ltd. This would not be beneficial as the tax saving would be at 20% whereas the tax saving will be at 23.75% if the carry back relief claim shown in (a) above is made.

# 47 Sofa Ltd

## Marking scheme

|  |  |  | Marks |
|---|---|---|---|
| (a) | *Adjustment to profit* |  |  |
|  | Loss before taxation |  | ½ |
|  | Depreciation |  | ½ |
|  | Accountancy fees |  | ½ |
|  | Legal fees – share capital |  | ½ |
|  | Legal fees – renewal of short lease |  | ½ |
|  | Legal fees – loan relationship |  | ½ |
|  | New wall |  | ½ |
|  | Repair to existing wall |  | ½ |
|  | Business entertaining |  | ½ |
|  | Staff entertaining |  | ½ |
|  | Redundancy counselling |  | ½ |
|  | Health and safety fine |  | ½ |
|  | Profit on sale of shares |  | ½ |
|  | Bank interest receivable |  | ½ |
|  | Loan stock interest payable |  | 1 |
|  | *Capital allowances on P&M* |  |  |
|  | TWDVs b/f |  | ½ |
|  | Additions qualifying for AIA: | equipment | ½ |
|  |  | Fixtures | ½ |
|  | AIA |  | 1 |
|  | Main pool |  | 1 |
|  | Special rate pool |  | 1 |
|  | Disposals |  | 1 |
|  | WDAs |  | 1 |
|  | Additions qualifying for FYA: | low emission car | ½ |
|  | FYA @ 100% |  | ½ |
|  | TWDVs c/f |  | ½ |
|  | Allowances |  | 1 |
|  |  |  | 17 |

(b)   *Settee Ltd*

| | |
|---|---|
| Availability of group relief | ½ |
| Corresponding period 1 | 1 |
| Corresponding period 2 | 1 |
| *Couch Ltd* | |
| No group relief – not in 75% group | 1 |
| *Futon Ltd* | |
| Availability of group relief | ½ |
| Corresponding period | 1 |

$$\frac{5}{22}$$

---

(a)   **Sofa Ltd – tax adjusted trading loss**

| | £ | £ |
|---|---|---|
| Loss before taxation | | (255,002) |
| Add:  depreciation | 87,100 | |
| professional fees: accountancy and audit | 0 | |
| professional fees (N1): share capital | 7,800 | |
| professional fees (N1): renewal of short lease | 0 | |
| professional fees (N1): issue of loan stock | 0 | |
| repairs and renewals (N2): new wall | 9,700 | |
| repairs and renewals (N2): repair to existing wall | 0 | |
| other expenses (N3): entertaining suppliers | 1,360 | |
| other expenses (N3): entertaining employees | 0 | |
| other expenses (N3): counselling on redundancy | 0 | |
| other expenses (N3): fine | 420 | |
| interest payable (N1) | 0 | 106,380 |
| | | (148,622) |
| Less:  profit on sale of shares | 3,300 | |
| bank interest – taxed as interest income | 8,400 | |
| CAs on plant and machinery (W) | 32,078 | (43,778) |
| Tax adjusted trading loss | | (192,400) |

*Notes*

1   The legal fees related to the renewal of a short lease (less than 50 years) are allowable. The cost of obtaining loan finance is allowable as a trading expense under the loan relationship rules as the loan was used for trading purposes. The loan stock interest payable is also allowable for the same reason. The cost of legal fees relating to the issue of share capital is not allowable as it is a capital expense.

2   The cost of the new wall is not allowable because it is a capital expense. The repair to the existing wall is allowable as a revenue expense.

3   Business entertaining is not allowable. Staff entertaining is allowable. Counselling on redundancy is specifically allowable. The health and safety fine is not allowable.

*Working: Capital allowances on plant and machinery*

| | FYA £ | AIA £ | Main pool £ | Special rate pool £ | Allowances £ |
|---|---|---|---|---|---|
| TWDV b/f | | | 27,800 | 16,400 | |
| *Additions qualifying for AIA* | | | | | |
| 12.5.13 Equipment | | 1,400 | | | |
| 10.2.14 Fixtures (N) | | 11,200 | | | |
| | | 12,600 | | | |
| AIA | | (12,600) | | | 12,600 |
| *Additions not qualifying for AIA* | | | | | |
| 8.6.13 Car | | | | 22,200 | |
| 2.8.13 Car | | | 10,900 | | |
| *Disposals* | | | | | |
| 8.6.13 Car | | | | (17,800) | |
| | | | | 20,800 | |
| 8.1.14 Lorry | | | (7,600) | | |
| 18.1.14 Car | | | (8,800) | | |
| | | | 22,300 | | |
| WDA @ 18% | | | (4,014) | | 4,014 |
| WDA @ 8% | | | | (1,664) | 1,664 |
| *Addition qualifying for FYA* | | | | | |
| 19.10.13 Car | 13,800 | | | | |
| FYA @ 100% | (13,800) | | | | 13,800 |
| TWDV c/f | | | 18,286 | 19,136 | |
| Allowances | | | | | 32,078 |

*Note*

The sale price put on the fixtures can be an amount up to their original cost. Since it has been agreed that Sofa Ltd is to obtain maximum capital allowances on the fixtures, the election must have been the maximum amount possible.

(b) **Settee Ltd**

Group relief is available between Sofa Ltd and Settee Ltd because they are part of a 75% group.

Group relief applies to corresponding accounting periods.

*Corresponding period 1 (1 April 2013 to 30 June 2013)*
Loss of Sofa Ltd
3/12 × £192,400                                                    £48,100

Profit of Settee Ltd
3/12 × £240,000                                                   £60,000

Maximum group relief is lower of these two figures ie      £48,100

*Corresponding period 2 (1 July 2013 to 31 March 2014)*
Loss of Sofa Ltd
9/12 × £192,400                                                  £144,300

Profit of Settee Ltd
9/12 × £90,000                                                    £67,500

Maximum group relief is lower of these two figures ie      £67,500

**Couch Ltd**

There is no group relief available between Sofa Ltd and Couch Ltd because they are not members of a 75% group as Couch Ltd is only a 60% subsidiary.

**Futon Ltd**

Group relief is available between Sofa Ltd and Futon Ltd because they are part of a 75% group.

*Corresponding period (1 January 2014 to 31 March 2014)*

| | |
|---|---|
| Loss of Sofa Ltd 3/12 × £192,400 | £48,100 |
| Profit of Futon Ltd | £60,000 |
| Maximum group relief is lower of these two figures ie | £48,100 |

# 48 Gastron Ltd

**Text references.** Chapter 19 deals with adjustment of profit for companies. Chapter 23 covers groups.

**Top tips.** Make sure that you attempt all parts of a multi-part question such as this.

**Easy marks.** Once again, the administration aspects of this question should have yielded easy marks.

**Examiner's comments.** This question was very well answered, with only part (e) consistently causing problems. In part (a) candidates were instructed to list all of the items referred to in the notes, and to indicate by the use of zero any items that did not require adjustment. Candidates are advised that this will be a standard approach in future and they should ensure they follow this instruction to be able to score full marks. Despite the instruction some candidates did not list those items not requiring any adjustment. Parts (a) and (b) were kept separate for a very good reason – namely to help candidates. Therefore those candidates who attempted to combine both parts into one calculation not surprisingly often had problems. It was pleasing to see many candidates correctly calculate the correct figure for capital allowances. Although I can applaud candidate's attempts to save paper, it is not good examination technique to try and squeeze a capital allowances computation of this size into 5 or 6 lines at the end of a page. In part (c) a disappointing number of candidates gave 31 January as the payment date. Only a few candidates appreciated that interest would be due, and fewer still correctly calculated the actual amount payable. In part (d) most candidates appreciated that a 75% shareholding was necessary, but were then often unsure where the 50% limit fitted in. The holding company must have an effective interest of over 50%. In part (e) many candidates simply stated that losses could be set against profits, without making any attempt to use the information given in the question.

**Marking scheme**

|  | | | Marks |
|---|---|---|---|
| (a) | Profit before taxation | | ½ |
| | Depreciation | | ½ |
| | Amortisation of leasehold property | | ½ |
| | Gifts of pens to customers | | ½ |
| | Gifts of hampers to customers | | ½ |
| | Donation | | ½ |
| | Legal fees re renewal of lease | | ½ |
| | Legal fees re issue of loan stock | | ½ |
| | Entertaining suppliers | | ½ |
| | Entertaining employees | | ½ |
| | Lease premium | – Assessable amount | 1½ |
| | | – Deduction | 1 |
| | Income from investments | | 1 |
| | Disposal of shares | | ½ |
| | Interest payable | | ½ |
| | P & M | – Main pool with WDA | 1½ |
| | | – AIA | 1½ |
| | | – Special rate pool with WDA | 1½ |
| | | – FYA @ 100% | 1 |
| | | | 15 |

|   | | Marks |
|---|---|---|
| **(b)** | Trading profit | ½ |
| | Property business profit | 2 |
| | Bank interest | ½ |
| | Chargeable gain | ½ |
| | Franked investment income | 1 |
| | Group dividends | ½ |
| | Corporation tax | 2 |
| | | 7 |
| **(c)** | Due date | 1 |
| | Interest | 2 |
| | | 3 |
| **(d)** | 75% shareholding | 1 |
| | Over 50% effective interest | 1 |
| | | 2 |
| **(e)** | Time limit | 1 |
| | Set off of capital losses | 1 |
| | Tax rate | 1 |
| | | 3 |
| | | 30 |

**(a)** **Gastron Ltd – Trading profit for the year ended 31 March 2014**

| | £ | £ |
|---|---|---|
| Profit before taxation | | 618,008 |
| *Add* | | |
| Depreciation | 85,660 | |
| Amortisation of leasehold property | 6,000 | |
| Gifts of pens to customers (N1) | 1,200 | |
| Gifts of hampers to customers (N1) | 1,100 | |
| Donation to local charity | 0 | |
| Legal fees re renewal of lease (N2) | 0 | |
| Legal fees re issue of loan stock (N2) | 0 | |
| Entertaining suppliers (N3) | 1,300 | |
| Entertaining employees (N3) | 0 | |
| | | 95,260 |
| *Deduct* | | |
| Lease premium (W1) | 4,920 | |
| Income from property | 20,600 | |
| Bank interest | 12,400 | |
| Dividends | 54,000 | |
| Profit on disposal of shares | 80,700 | |
| Interest payable (N4) | 0 | |
| Capital allowances (W2) | 40,648 | |
| | | (213,268) |
| Trading profit | | 500,000 |

*Notes*

1    Gifts to customers are only an allowable deduction if they cost less than £50 per recipient per year, are not of food, drink, tobacco, or vouchers for exchangeable goods, and carry a conspicuous advertisement for the company making the gift.

2    The costs of renewing a short-lease (less than 50 years) and of obtaining loan finance are allowable.

3    The only exception to the non-deductibility of entertainment expenditure is when it is in respect of employees.

4   Interest on a loan used for trading purposes is deductible in calculating the trading loss on an accruals basis.

*Workings*

1   The office building has been used for business purposes, and so the proportion of the lease premium assessed on the landlord can be deducted, spread over the life of the lease.

The amount assessed on the landlord is £49,200 calculated as follows:

|  | £ |
|---|---|
| Premium received | 60,000 |
| Less: £60,000 × 2% × (10 – 1) | (10,800) |
|  | 49,200 |

This is deductible over the life of the lease, so the deduction for the year ended 31 March 2014 is £(49,200/10) = £4,920.

2   *Plant and machinery*

|  | FYA @ 100% £ | AIA £ | Main pool £ | Special rate pool £ | Allowances £ |
|---|---|---|---|---|---|
| TWDV b/f |  |  | 16,700 | 18,400 |  |
| *Additions qualifying for AIA* |  |  |  |  |  |
| Equipment |  | 1,600 |  |  |  |
| Lorry |  | 17,200 |  |  |  |
|  |  | 18,800 |  |  |  |
| AIA |  | (18,800) |  |  | 18,800 |
| *Addition not qualifying for AIA* |  |  |  |  |  |
| Motor car |  |  | 9,800 |  |  |
|  |  |  | 26,500 |  |  |
| *Disposal* |  |  |  |  |  |
| Equipment (N) |  |  | (3,300) |  |  |
|  |  |  | 23,200 |  |  |
| WDA @ 18% |  |  | (4,176) |  | 4,176 |
| WDA @ 8% |  |  |  | (1,472) | 1,472 |
| *Addition qualifying for 100% FYA* |  |  |  |  |  |
| Motor car | 16,200 |  |  |  |  |
| FYA @ 100% | (16,200) |  |  |  | 16,200 |
| TWDV c/f |  |  | 19,024 | 16,928 |  |
| Total allowances |  |  |  |  | 40,648 |

*Note:* the cost of the equipment sold will have originally been added to the pool, so the disposal proceeds of £3,300 are deducted from the pool.

(b)   **Gastron Ltd – Corporation tax computation for the year ended 31 March 2014**

|  | £ |
|---|---|
| Trading profit | 500,000 |
| Property business profit (W1) | 12,800 |
| Bank interest | 12,400 |
| Chargeable gain | 74,800 |
| Taxable total profits | 600,000 |
| Franked investment income £36,000 × 100/90 (N) | 40,000 |
| Augmented profits | 640,000 |
|  |  |
| Corporation tax £600,000 @ 23% | 138,000 |
| Marginal relief 3/400 (750,000 – 640,000) × 600,000/640,000 (W2) | (773) |
|  | 137,227 |

*Note*

Group dividends are not included as franked investment income.

*Workings*

1   The property business profit is £12,800 calculated as follows:

|  |  | £ | £ |
|---|---|---|---|
| Rent receivable – First tenant £1,800 × 9 |  |  | 16,200 |
| – Second tenant £1,950 × 2 |  |  | 3,900 |
|  |  |  | 20,100 |
| Impairment loss £1,800 × 2 |  | 3,600 |  |
| Decorating |  | 3,700 |  |
|  |  |  | (7,300) |
|  |  |  | 12,800 |

2   Gastron Ltd has one associated company, so the upper limit is reduced to £750,000 (£1,500,000/2).

(c)   (1)   Gastron Ltd's corporation tax liability for the year ended 31 March 2014 must be paid by 1 January 2015.

(2)   If the company does not pay its corporation tax until 31 August 2015, then interest of £137,227 @ 3% × 8/12 = £2,745 will be charged by HM Revenue and Customs for the period between 1 January 2015 and 31 August 2015.

(d)   (1)   Companies form a capital gains group if at each level in the group structure there is a 75% shareholding.

(2)   However, the parent company must also have an effective interest of over 50% in each group company.

(e)   (1)   Gastron Ltd and Culinary Ltd must make the election by 31 March 2016 (within two years of the end of the accounting period in the gain arose).

(2)   The election will enable the capital gain of £74,800 to be set off against capital loss of £66,000.

(3)   It is also beneficial for the balance of the chargeable gain of £(74,800 – 66,000) = £8,800 to arise in Culinary Ltd as it will only be taxed at the rate of 20%, instead of at the marginal rate (23.75%) in Gastron Ltd.

# 49 Lithograph Ltd

**Text references.** Chapters 25 and 26 deal with VAT.

**Top tips.** Read the question carefully to determine whether the figures you have been given include the VAT or not.

Marking scheme

|  |  |  | **Marks** |
|---|---|---|---|
| (a) | Monthly payments |  | ½ |
|  | Based on prior year |  | ½ |
|  | 10% |  | ½ |
|  | Months 4 to 12 |  | ½ |
|  | Calculation |  | 1 |
|  |  |  | 3 |

| | | | Marks |
|---|---|---|---|
| (b) | (i) | Sales @ 20% | ½ |
| | | Office equipment sale @ 20% | ½ |
| | | Fuel scale charge @ 1/6 | 1 |
| | | Purchases | ½ |
| | | Expenses | ½ |
| | | Machinery | ½ |
| | | Bad debt | 1 |
| | | Output VAT less input VAT @ 20% | ½ |
| | | | 5 |
| | (ii) | Balancing payment | 1 |
| | | Due date | 1 |
| | | | 2 |
| | | | 10 |

---

(a) **Monthly payments on account**

As Lithograph Ltd uses the annual accounting scheme it will be paying monthly payments on account based on its previous year's liability.

It will make payments in months 4 to 12 of its VAT accounting period, each payment being 10% of the previous year's liability.

Lithograph Ltd will therefore have made payments of 10% × £10,200 = £1,020 from April 2013 to December 2013.

(b) (i) **VAT for y/e 31 December 2013**

| | £ | | £ |
|---|---|---|---|
| Output VAT | | | |
| Sales | 160,000 | @ 20% | 32,000 |
| Office equipment sale | 8,000 | @ 20% | 1,600 |
| Fuel scale charge (N1) | 1,415 | @¹/₆ | 236 |
| | | | 33,836 |
| Less: Input VAT | | | |
| Purchases | 38,000 | | |
| Expenses | | | |
| 28,000 − 3,600 (N2) | 24,400 | | |
| Machinery purchase | 24,000 | | |
| Impairment loss (N3) | 4,800 | | |
| | 91,200 | @ 20% | (18,240) |
| VAT due | | | 15,596 |

*Notes*

1   Fuel scale charge

As the whole of the fuel VAT expense, including private fuel, has been deducted (included in the expenses) we need to charge output tax, in this case using the fuel scale charge.

As this is a VAT inclusive figure we need to adjust by multiplying by $^1/_6$.

2   Expenses

Customer entertaining is never allowable for VAT purposes.

3   Impairment loss

As the liability is over 6 months old and has been written off in the company's books, it is possible to claim relief.

(ii) **Balancing payment and due date**

The balancing payment due would be:

|                                    | £       |
|------------------------------------|---------|
| VAT due                            | 15,596  |
| Less: paid on account (9 payments) | (9,180) |
| Due by 28 February 2014            | 6,416   |

# 50 Aston Martyn

> **Text references.** Value added tax is covered in Chapters 25 and 26.
>
> **Top tips.** This question is broken down into six parts, each with a specific number of marks. These indicate how detailed your answer should be – for example, in part (c) there are two marks which required two points to be made.
>
> **Easy marks.** There were easy marks for dealing with the registration of Aston Martyn, and the filing of the return and payment of VAT.
>
> **Examiner's comments.** With the exception of part (b), this question was generally answered quite poorly. In part (a) most candidates did not appreciate that the zero-rated supplies had to be included when calculating taxable supplies for registration purposes. Part (b) was well answered, although many candidates wasted time by stating more than four additional pieces of information. For example, common sense should mean that the business could not possibly state the VAT registration number of the customer. Many candidates simply ignored part (c), but marks were awarded for any sensible answer such as input VAT and output VAT would contra out. In part (d) too many candidates simply reproduced the penalty table without relating it to the facts given. Again, marks were awarded for any sensible conclusion. There was little knowledge of the online filing requirement for quarterly returns in part (e), although the annual accounting scheme aspects were answered much better.

## Marking scheme

|     |      |                                 |      | Marks |
|-----|------|---------------------------------|------|-------|
| (a) |      | Registration limit              | 1    |       |
|     |      | 31 January 2014                 | 1    |       |
|     |      | Date of registration            | 1    |       |
|     |      |                                 |      | 3     |
| (b) |      | Aston's VAT registration number | ½    |       |
|     |      | An identifying invoice number   | ½    |       |
|     |      | The rate of VAT for supply      | ½    |       |
|     |      | The amount of VAT payable       | ½    |       |
|     |      |                                 |      | 2     |
| (c) |      | Date of acquisition             | 1    |       |
|     |      | Entries on VAT return           | 1    |       |
|     |      |                                 |      | 2     |
| (d) |      | No penalty if reasonable care   | 1    |       |
|     |      | Treated as careless             | 1    |       |
|     |      | Amount of penalty               | 1    |       |
|     |      |                                 |      | 3     |
| (e) | (i)  | Online filing                   | ½    |       |
|     |      | Electronic payment              | ½    |       |
|     |      | Deadline                        | 1    |       |
|     |      |                                 |      | 2     |

| (ii) | Payments on account | 1 |
| | Amount of each payment | 1 |
| | Deadline | 1 |

$$\frac{3}{15}$$

(a) Aston would have been liable to compulsory value added tax (VAT) registration when his taxable supplies during any 12-month period (or the period from commencement of trade, if less) exceeded £79,000.

This happened on 31 January 2014 when taxable supplies amounted to £81,200 (4,300 + 6,400 + 21,900 + 4,800 + 11,700 + 17,100 + 13,800 + 1,200).

Registration is required from the end of the month following the month in which the limit is exceeded, so Aston will have been registered from 1 March 2014 or from an agreed earlier date.

(b) The following information is required:

- Aston's VAT registration number
- An identifying number (invoice number)
- The rate of VAT for each supply
- The amount of VAT payable

(c) VAT will have to be accounted for according to the date of acquisition. This is the earlier of the date that the service is completed or the date it is paid for.

The VAT charged at the UK VAT rate should be declared on Aston's VAT return as output VAT, but will then be reclaimed as input VAT on the same VAT return.

(d) HM Revenue and Customs will not charge a penalty if Aston has taken reasonable care, provided he informs them of any errors upon subsequent discovery.

However, applying the incorrect rate of VAT is more likely to be treated as careless, since Aston would be expected to check the VAT classification of his supplies.

The maximum amount of penalty will therefore be 30% of the VAT underpaid, but this penalty could be reduced to nil as a result of a subsequent unprompted disclosure to HM Revenue and Customs.

(e) (i) Aston will have to file his VAT returns online and pay the VAT that is due electronically. The deadline for doing this is one month and seven days after the end of each quarter. For example, for the quarter ended 31 May 2014 Aston will have until 7 July 2014 to file his VAT return and pay the VAT that is due.

(ii) Aston will have to make nine payments on account of VAT commencing in month four of the annual VAT return period. These will be due electronically.

Each payment on account will be 10% of the VAT payable for the previous year, although for the first year an estimated figure will be used.

The annual VAT return, along with the balancing payment, will be due two months after the end of the annual VAT period. The VAT return will have to be filed online.

# 51 Ram-Rom Ltd

> **Text references.** VAT is dealt with in Chapters 25 and 26.
>
> **Top tips.** In part (a) you are given the input VAT recoverable so you must make sure that your answer reconciles with this figure. For part (b), make a rough list of the contents of the VAT invoice and then see which items are missing from the sample invoice given.
>
> **Easy marks.** There were plenty of easy marks in this question. You should have been able to work out the items for part (a) since the examiner gave the amount of input tax recovered. Discounts are often examined, so you should ensure that you are very familiar with them.
>
> **Examiner's comments.** Candidates often failed to show their workings of how they calculated pre-registration input VAT.

## Marking scheme

|  |  |  | Marks |
|---|---|---|---|
| (a) | Goods – explanation | 1 | |
| | – inventory | ½ | |
| | – non-current assets | 1½ | |
| | Services – explanation | ½ | |
| | – calculation | 1½ | 5 |
| (b) | Registration number | ½ | |
| | Invoice number | ½ | |
| | Rate of VAT | ½ | |
| | VAT exclusive amount | ½ | |
| | Total VAT exclusive price | ½ | |
| | Total VAT | ½ | 3 |
| (c) | Charge to VAT | 1 | |
| | No change if not taken up | 1 | 2 |
| | | | 10 |

(a) Input VAT recovery – pre registration inputs

Input VAT is recoverable on goods if they are:

- Acquired within 4 years prior to registration
- For business purposes
- Not supplied onwards or consumed prior to registration

| | | £ |
|---|---|---|
| Non-current assets | – January 2013 acquisition £42,000 × 20% | 8,400 |
| | – August 2013 acquisition £66,600 × 20% | 13,320 |
| Inventory still held £92,000 × 20% | | 18,400 |
| Input VAT on goods recoverable | | 40,120 |

Input VAT is recoverable on services if they are:

- Supplied within six months prior to registration
- For purposes of business

|  |  | £ |
|---|---|---:|
| March 2013 | | 7,400 |
| April 2013 | | 6,300 |
| May 2013 | | 8,500 |
| June 2013 | | 9,000 |
| July 2013 | | 9,200 |
| August 2013 | | 8,200 |
| | | 48,600 |

£48,600 × 20% = £9,720

Total VAT recoverable £(40,120 + 9,720) = £49,840

(b)   Alterations to invoice – must include

- Registration number
- Invoice number
- Rate of VAT for each supply of goods
- VAT exclusive amount for each supply of goods
- Total invoice price excluding VAT
- The total amount of VAT

(c)   Where a discount is offered for prompt payment, VAT is chargeable on the net amount, regardless of whether the discount is taken up.

# 52 Sandy Brick

**Text references.** Chapters 25 and 26 for VAT.

**Top tips.** As with any question which requires a calculation, setting out the figures in a proforma will help both you and the examiner marking your paper.

**Easy marks.** The calculation of VAT on most items should have been easy marks.

**Examiner's comments.** Well answered but some candidates were penalised for not clearly showing which of their calculations were output VAT and which were input VAT.

**Marking scheme**

| | Marks |
|---|---:|
| Sales – VAT registered customers | 1½ |
| – Non-VAT registered customers | 1½ |
| Advance payment | 1 |
| Materials | 1 |
| Office equipment | 2 |
| Telephone | 1 |
| Motor repairs | 1 |
| Equipment | 1 |
| | 10 |

**VAT return**

| | £ | £ |
|---|---:|---:|
| *Output VAT* | | |
| Sales to VAT registered customers | | |
| (£(44,000 × 95%) = £41,800) × 20% | | 8,360 |
| Sales to non-VAT registered customers | | |
| (£(16,920 – 5,170) = £11,750) × 1/6 | | 1,958 |
| Payment on account | | |
| £5,000 × 1/6 | | 833 |
| Total output VAT c/f | | 11,151 |
| *Input VAT* | | |
| Materials (£(11,200 – 800) = £10,400) × 20% | 2,080 | |
| Office equipment £120 × 9 × 20% (N1) | 216 | |
| Telephone (£(400 × 70%) = 280) × 20% | 56 | |
| Motor repairs £920 × 20% (N2) | 184 | |
| Equipment £6,000 × 20% | 1,200 | (3,736) |
| Net VAT payable | | 7,415 |

*Notes*

(1)   Pre-registration VAT can be recovered on services for six months before the registration date. Therefore nine months of input tax can be recovered.

(2)   If a car is used for business purposes, then any VAT charged on repairs and maintenance costs can be treated as input tax. No apportionment has to be made for private use.

# 53 Anne Attire

**Text references.** Chapters 25 and 26 for VAT.

**Top tips.** Make sure that you read all the information given in the question – you are given this information by the examiner for a reason so you must make use of it when answering the question.

**Easy marks.** The due date for payment of VAT was an easy mark.

**Examiner's comments.** In part (a) candidates often did not appreciate that the calculation of output VAT on credit sales had to take account of the discount for prompt payment even if it was not taken by customers. In part (b) the answers of many candidates lacked sufficient depth to gain full marks. For example, the turnover limit of £1,350,000 was usually known, but only a minority of candidates correctly stated that it applied for the following 12-month period. The same comment applies to part (c). For example, candidates generally appreciated that the taxpayer's VAT registration would be cancelled, but few stated that the reason for the cancellation was the cessation of making taxable supplies. Many candidates stated that on a sale of the business as a going concern the VAT registration could be taken over by the purchaser despite the question clearly stating that the purchaser was already registered for VAT.

**Marking scheme**

| | | | **Marks** |
|---|---|---:|---:|
| (a) | Output VAT – Cash sales | 1 | |
| | – Credit sales | 1½ | |
| | Input VAT – Purchases and expenses | 1 | |
| | – Impairment loss | 1½ | |
| | Due date | 1 | |
| | | | 6 |

| | | | Marks |
|---|---|---|---:|
| (b) | Limit | 1 | |
| | VAT returns and VAT payments | 1 | |
| | Output VAT | 1 | |
| | Input VAT | 1 | |
| | Impairment loss relief | 1 | |
| | | | 5 |
| (c) | (i) *Sale of assets on a piecemeal basis* | | |
| | Cancellation of VAT registration | 1 | |
| | Output VAT | 1 | |
| | | | 2 |
| | (ii) *Sale of business as a going concern* | | |
| | Cancellation of VAT registration | 1 | |
| | Output VAT not due | 1 | |
| | | | 2 |
| | | | 15 |

## (a) VAT return – Quarter ended 30 November 2013

| | £ | £ |
|---|---:|---:|
| *Output VAT* | | |
| Cash sales £28,000 × 20% | | 5,600 |
| Credit sales £12,000 × 95% × 20% (N1) | | 2,280 |
| *Input VAT* | | |
| Purchases and expenses £11,200 × 20% | 2,240 | |
| Impairment loss £800 × 95% × 20% (N2) | 152 | |
| | | (2,392) |
| VAT payable | | 5,488 |

The VAT return for the quarter ended 30 November 2013 should have been submitted by 7 January 2014.

*Notes*

(1) The calculation of output VAT on the credit sales takes into account the discount for prompt payment, even for those 10% of customers that did not take it.

(2) Relief for an impairment loss is not given until six months from the time that payment is due. Therefore relief can only be claimed in respect of the invoice due for payment on 10 April 2013. Relief is based on the amount of output VAT that would originally have been paid, taking into account the discount for prompt payment.

(b) Anne can use the cash accounting scheme if her expected taxable turnover for the next 12 months does not exceed £1,350,000. Anne must also be up-to-date with her VAT returns and VAT payments.

Output VAT on most credit sales will be accounted for up to one month later than at present since the scheme will result in the tax point becoming the date that payment is received from customers. However, the recovery of input VAT will be delayed by two months.

The scheme will provide automatic impairment loss relief should a credit sale customer default on the payment of a debt.

(c) (i) **Sale of assets on a piecemeal basis**

On the cessation of trading Anne will cease to make taxable supplies, so her VAT registration will be cancelled on the date of cessation or an agreed later date.

Output VAT will be due in respect of the value of the non-current assets at the date of deregistration on which VAT has been claimed (although output VAT is not due if it is less than £1,000).

## (ii) Sale of business as a going concern

Since the purchaser is already registered for VAT, Anne's VAT registration will be cancelled as above.

A sale of a business as a going concern (TOGC) is outside the scope of VAT and therefore output VAT will not be due.

# Mock exams

# ACCA

# Paper F6

# Taxation (United Kingdom)

# Mock Examination 1

| Question Paper | |
|---|---|
| Time allowed | |
| Reading and Planning | 15 minutes |
| Writing | 3 hours |
| ALL FIVE questions are compulsory and MUST be attempted. | |

During reading and planning time only the question paper may be annotated.

**DO NOT OPEN THIS PAPER UNTIL YOU ARE READY TO START UNDER EXAMINATION CONDITIONS**

# ALL FIVE questions are compulsory and MUST be attempted

# 1 Josie Jones (TX 12/12)

On 30 June 2013 Josie Jones, born in 1972, ceased self-employment as a graphic designer. On 1 August 2013 she commenced employment with Typo plc as a creative director. The following information is available for the tax year 2013/14:

### Self-employment

(1)   Josie's trading profits for the final two periods of trading were as follows:

|  | £ |
|---|---|
| Year ended 30 April 2013 | 95,560 |
| Two-month period ended 30 June 2013 | 10,440 |

Both these figures are before taking account of capital allowances.

(2)   There were no capital allowances for the year ended 30 April 2013 and the tax written down value of the capital allowances main pool at 1 May 2013 was nil. On 21 May 2013 Josie purchased computer equipment for £2,000. This was sold for £1,700 on 30 June 2013.

(3)   Josie has unused overlap profits brought forward of £41,700.

### Employment

(1)   Josie is paid a salary of £15,100 per month by Typo plc. The salary is paid on the last day of each calendar month.

(2)   During August 2013 Typo plc paid £11,600 towards Josie's removal expenses when she permanently moved to take up her new employment with the company as she did not live within a reasonable commuting distance. The £11,600 covered both her removal expenses and the legal costs of acquiring a new main residence.

(3)   On 1 September 2013 Typo plc provided Josie with an interest free loan of £33,000 that she used to renovate her new main residence. This loan was still outstanding at 5 April 2014.

(4)   During the period from 1 August 2013 to 5 April 2014, Josie was provided with free meals in Typo plc's staff canteen. The total cost of these meals to the company was £1,340. The canteen is available to all of the company's employees.

(5)   During the period from 1 October 2013 to 5 April 2014, Typo plc provided Josie with a diesel powered motor car with an official $CO_2$ emission rate of 139 grams per kilometre. The motor car, which has a list price of £14,400, cost Typo plc £13,900. Typo plc does not provide Josie with any fuel for private journeys.

(6)   For the tax year 2013/14 Typo plc deducted a total of £41,577 in PAYE from Josie's earnings.

### Other information

(1)   Josie owns two properties, which are let out. Property one qualifies as a trade under the furnished holiday letting rules, whilst property two is let out unfurnished. The income and allowable expenditure for the two properties for the tax year 2013/14 are as follows:

|  | Property one<br>£ | Property two<br>£ |
|---|---|---|
| Income | 6,600 | 7,200 |
| Allowable expenditure | 9,700 | 2,100 |

(2)   During the tax year 2013/14 Josie received building society interest of £8,000, interest of £1,200 from a holding of £24,000 5% Treasury Stock 2025, and dividends of £6,480. These were the actual cash amounts received.

(3)   On 2 October 2013 Josie received a premium bond prize of £100.

(4)   During the tax year 2013/14 Josie made gift aid donations totalling £4,400 (net) to national charities.

(5)   Josie's payments on account of income tax in respect of the tax year 2013/14 totalled £34,400.

*Required*

(a) Calculate the income tax payable by Josie Jones for the tax year 2013/14.

*Note:*

You should indicate by the use of zero any items that are non-taxable/exempt from tax. **(20 marks)**

(b) (i) Calculate Josie Jones' balancing payment or repayment for the tax year 2013/14 and her payments on account for the tax year 2014/15. You should state the relevant due dates.

*Notes:*

1. You should assume that no claim is made to reduce the payments on account.
2. You should ignore value added tax (VAT) and national insurance contributions (NIC).
**(3 marks)**

(ii) Assuming that Josie Jones expects to remain employed throughout the tax year 2014/15, explain why she will probably be able to make a claim to reduce her payments on account for the tax year 2014/15. **(2 marks)**

**(Total = 25 marks)**

# 2 Clueless Ltd (TX 12/12)

(a) You are a trainee accountant and your manager has asked you to correct a corporation tax computation that has been prepared by the managing director of Clueless Ltd, a company which manufactures children's board games. The corporation tax computation is for the year ended 31 March 2014 and contains a significant number of errors:

**Clueless Ltd – Corporation tax computation for the year ended 31 March 2014**

|  | £ |
|---|---|
| Trading profit (working 1) | 413,438 |
| Loan interest received (working 2) | 32,100 |
|  | 445,538 |
| Dividends received (working 3) | 29,462 |
|  | 475,000 |
|  |  |
| Corporation tax (£475,000 at 23%) | 109,250 |

**Working 1 – Trading profit**

|  | £ |
|---|---|
| Profit before taxation | 345,966 |
| Depreciation | 15,740 |
| Donations to political parties | 400 |
| Qualifying charitable donations | 900 |
| Accountancy | 2,300 |
| Legal fees in connection with the issue of loan stock (the finance was used for a trading purpose) | 5,700 |
| Repairs to warehouse following a flood | 13,200 |
| Entertaining suppliers | 3,600 |
| Entertaining employees | 1,700 |
| Gifts to customers (pens costing £40 each and displaying Clueless Ltd's name) | 920 |
| Gifts to customers (food hampers costing £45 each and displaying Clueless Ltd's name) | 1,650 |
| Capital allowances (working 4) | 21,362 |
|  | 413,438 |

### Working 2 – Loan interest received

| | £ |
|---|---:|
| Loan interest receivable | 32,800 |
| Accrued at 1 April 2013 | 10,600 |
| Accrued at 31 March 2014 | (11,300) |
| Loan interest received | 32,100 |

The loan was made for a non-trading purpose.

### Working 3 – Dividends received

| | £ |
|---|---:|
| From unconnected UK companies | 20,700 |
| From a 100% UK subsidiary company | 8,762 |
| Dividends received | 29,462 |

These figures were the actual cash amounts received.

### Working 4 – Capital allowances

| | Main pool £ | Motor car £ | Special rate pool £ | Allowances £ |
|---|---:|---:|---:|---:|
| WDV brought forward | 2,400 | | 13,500 | |
| Additions | | | | |
| Machinery | 8,300 | | | |
| Motor car [1] | 13,800 | | | |
| Motor car [2] | | 11,800 | | |
| | 24,500 | | | |
| Annual investment allowance | (24,500) | | | 24,500 |
| Disposal proceeds | | | (9,300) | |
| | | | 4,200 | |
| Balancing allowance | | | (4,200) | (4,200) |
| WDA – 18% | | (2,124) | × 50% | 1,062 |
| WDV carried forward | 0 | 9,676 | | |
| Total allowances | | | | 21,362 |

(1) Motor car [1] has a $CO_2$ emission rate of 110 grams per kilometre.

(2) Motor car [2] has a $CO_2$ emission rate of 155 grams per kilometre. This motor car is used by the sales manager and 50% of the mileage is for private journeys.

(3) All of the items included in the special rate pool at 1 April 2013 were sold for £9,300 during the year ended 31 March 2014. The original cost of these items was £16,200.

### Other information

From your files, you note that Clueless Ltd has one associated company (the 100% UK subsidiary company mentioned in working 3).

*Required*

Prepare a corrected version of Clueless Ltd's corporation tax computation for the year ended 31 March 2014.

*Notes:*

1.    You should indicate by the use of zero any items in the computation of the trading profit for which no adjustment is required.

2.    In answering this part of the question you should ignore value added tax. **(16 marks)**

(b)    The managing director of Clueless Ltd understands that for the year ended 31 March 2014 the company will have to file its self-assessment corporation tax return online, and that the supporting accounts and tax computations will have to be filed using the inline eXtensible Business Reporting Language (iXBRL). The managing director is concerned about how the company will be able to produce documents in this format.

*Required*

(i)    State the date by which Clueless Ltd's self-assessment corporation tax return for the year ended 31 March 2014 should be filed. **(1 mark)**

(ii)    Explain the options available to Clueless Ltd regarding the production of accounts and tax computations in the iXBRL format. **(3 marks)**

(c)    Clueless Ltd is registered for value added tax (VAT), but currently does not use any of the special VAT schemes. The company has annual standard rated sales of £1,200,000 and annual standard rated expenses of £550,000. Both these figures are exclusive of VAT and are likely to remain the same for the foreseeable future. Clueless Ltd is up to date with all of its tax returns, including those for corporation tax, PAYE and VAT. It is also up to date with its corporation tax, PAYE and VAT payments. However, the company often incurs considerable overtime costs due to its employees working late in order to meet tax return filing deadlines.

Clueless Ltd pays its expenses on a cash basis, but allows customers two months credit when paying for sales. The company does not have any impairment losses.

Clueless Ltd is planning to purchase some new machinery at a cost of £22,000 (exclusive of VAT). The machinery can either be purchased from an overseas supplier situated outside the European Union, or from a VAT registered supplier situated in the European Union. Clueless Ltd is not a regular importer and so is unsure of the VAT treatment for this purchase.

*Required*

(i)    Explain why Clueless Ltd is entitled to use both the VAT cash accounting scheme and the VAT annual accounting scheme, and why it will probably be beneficial for the company to use both schemes.

**(6 marks)**

(ii)    Explain when and how Clueless Ltd will have to account for VAT in respect of the new machinery if it is purchased from (1) a supplier situated outside the European Union, or (2) a VAT registered supplier situated elsewhere within the European Union. **(4 marks)**

**(Total = 30 marks)**

# 3 Acebook Ltd (TX 12/12)

(a) Explain how limited companies can obtain relief for capital losses. **(3 marks)**

*Note:* you are not expected to explain how groups of companies can obtain relief for capital losses.

(b) Acebook Ltd sold the following assets during the year ended 31 December 2013:

    (1) On 10 March 2013 Acebook Ltd sold its entire shareholding of 50p ordinary shares in Oogle plc for £3.20 per share. The company had originally purchased 8,000 shares in Oogle plc on 28 June 2003 for £25,200. On 31 October 2006 Oogle plc made a 2 for 1 bonus issue. Then, on 14 February 2008, Oogle plc made a 1 for 5 rights issue. Acebook Ltd took up its allocation under the rights issue in full, paying £4.30 for each new share issued.

    Indexation factors are as follows:

| | |
|---|---|
| June 2003 to October 2006 | 0.105 |
| June 2003 to February 2008 | 0.166 |
| June 2003 to March 2013 | 0.369 |
| October 2006 to February 2008 | 0.055 |
| October 2006 to March 2013 | 0.239 |
| February 2008 to March 2013 | 0.174 |

    (2) On 30 June 2013 three acres of land were sold for £192,000. Acebook Ltd had originally purchased four acres of land, and the indexed cost of the four acres on 30 June 2013 was £196,000. The market value of the unsold acre of land as at 30 June 2013 was £53,000. During June 2013 Acebook Ltd spent £29,400 clearing and levelling all four acres of land. The land has never been used for business purposes.

    (3) On 1 October 2013 an investment property owned by Acebook Ltd was destroyed in a fire. The indexed cost of the property on that date was £138,400. Acebook Ltd received insurance proceeds of £189,000 on 20 October 2013, and on 31 October 2013 the company paid £172,400 for a replacement investment property. Acebook Ltd has made a claim to defer the gain arising from the receipt of the insurance proceeds.

*Required*

Calculate Acebook Ltd's chargeable gains for the year ended 31 December 2013. **(12 marks)**

**(Total = 15 marks)**

# 4 Sophia Wong and Andrew Zoom (TX 12/12 and TX 06/09 )

(a) **You should assume that today's date is 15 March 2013.**

Sophia Wong (born in 1977) is self-employed as a lawyer. For the year ended 5 April 2014 Sophia has forecast that her tax adjusted trading profit will be £80,000. This will be her only income for the tax year 2013/14, and Sophia's total income tax liability and national insurance contributions (NIC) for this year if she continues to trade on a self-employed basis will be £25,766 as follows:

|  | £ |
|---|---|
| Income tax | 21,822 |
| Class 2 NIC | 140 |
| Class 4 NIC | 3,804 |
|  | 25,766 |

Sophia understands that she could save tax and NIC if she instead traded as a limited company, and she is therefore considering incorporating her business on 6 April 2013. The forecast taxable total profits of the new limited company for the year ended 5 April 2014 are unchanged at £80,000 (before taking account of any director's remuneration).

*Required*

Assuming that Sophia Wong incorporates her business on 6 April 2013, advise her whether or not there will be an overall saving of tax and national insurance contributions (NIC) for the tax year 2013/14 if she withdraws all of the profits from the new company as:

(i) director's remuneration (after allowing for employer's class 1 NIC, gross director's remuneration will be £71,232); or **(6 marks)**

(ii) dividends (after allowing for corporation tax, net dividends will be £64,000). **(5 marks)**

*Note:*

For both alternatives, you are expected to calculate the corporation tax liability (if any) of the new limited company for the year ended 5 April 2014, the income tax payable by Sophia Wong, and the class 1 NIC (if any) payable by Sophia and the new company.

(b) Andrew Zoom is a cameraman who started working for Slick-Productions Ltd on 6 April 2013. The following information is available in respect of the year ended 5 April 2014:

(1) Andrew works a set number of hours each week and is paid an hourly rate for the work that he does. When Andrew works more than the set number of hours he is paid overtime.

(2) Andrew is under an obligation to accept the work offered to him by Slick-Productions Ltd, and the work is carried out under the control of the company's production manager. He is obliged to do the work personally, and this is all performed at Slick-Productions Ltd's premises.

(3) All of the equipment that Andrew uses is provided by Slick-Productions Ltd.

Andrew has several friends who are cameramen, and they are all treated as self-employed. He therefore considers that he should be treated as self-employed as well in relation to his work for Slick-Productions Ltd.

*Required*

List those factors that indicate that Andrew Zoom should be treated as an employee in relation to his work for Slick-Productions Ltd rather than as self-employed.

*Note:* you should confine your answer to the information given in the question. **(4 marks)**

**(Total = 15 marks)**

# 5 Rosie Rohan, Sam Shire and Tom Tirith (TX 12/12)

**You should assume that today's date is 15 February 2014.**

(a) Rosie Rohan, born in 1966, is the managing director of Hornburg plc. During the tax year 2013/14 Rosie was paid gross director's remuneration of £220,000. She has made the following gross personal pension contributions:

| Tax year | Pension contribution |
|----------|---------------------|
|          | £                   |
| 2009/10  | 33,000              |
| 2010/11  | 41,000              |
| 2011/12  | 26,000              |
| 2012/13  | Nil                 |

Rosie was a member of a pension scheme for the tax year 2012/13.

*Required*

Advise Rosie Rohan of the total amount of pension scheme annual allowances that she has available for the tax year 2013/14, the method by which tax relief will be given for any personal pension contributions that she makes during that year, and the tax implications if she makes contributions in excess of the available annual allowances.

*Notes:*

1. You are not expected to calculate Rosie Rohan's income tax liability.
2. You are not expected to consider the situation where pension contributions do not attract tax relief.

**(6 marks)**

(b) Sam Shire, born in 1982, has already invested £4,000 into a cash individual savings account (ISA) during the tax year 2013/14. He now wants to invest into a stocks and shares ISA.

*Required*

Advise Sam Shire of the maximum possible amount that he can invest into a stocks and shares ISA for the tax year 2013/14, and the tax advantages of holding stocks and shares within an ISA. **(2 marks)**

(c) Tom Tirith, born in 1938, made a cash gift of £200,000 to his daughter on 20 December 2012. He is now going to make a cash gift of £450,000 to a trust on 20 February 2014.

The nil rate band for the tax year 2012/13 is £325,000.

*Required*

(i) Calculate the lifetime inheritance tax that will be payable in respect of Tom Tirith's gift of £450,000 to a trust if:

(1) the trust pays the tax arising from the gift; or
(2) Tom pays the tax arising from the gift.

The total marks will be split equally between each part. **(3 marks)**

(ii) Assuming that Tom Tirith pays the tax arising from the gift of £450,000, calculate the additional inheritance tax that would be payable in respect of the gift if Tom were to die on 30 June 2018.

*Note:* you should assume that the nil rate band of £325,000 remains unchanged. **(4 marks)**

**(Total = 15 marks)**

# Answers

DO NOT TURN THIS PAGE UNTIL YOU HAVE
COMPLETED THE MOCK EXAM

# A plan of attack

What's the worst thing you could be doing right now if this was the actual exam paper? Sharpening your pencil? Wondering how to celebrate the end of the exam in about 3 hours time? Panicking, flapping and generally getting in a right old state?

Well, they're all pretty bad, so turn back to the paper and let's sort out a **plan of attack**!

## First things first

You have fifteen minutes of reading time. Spend this looking carefully through the questions and deciding the order in which you will attempt them. As a general rule you should attempt the questions that you find easiest first and leave the hardest until last. Depending on how confident you are we recommend that you follow one of the following two options:

## Option 1 (if you're thinking 'Help!')

If you're a bit worried about the paper, do the questions in the order of how well you think you can answer them. You may find the shorter questions less daunting than the longer questions. Alternatively, you may feel better prepared for questions 1 and 2 and wish to start there.

- Question 1 is an income tax question. There are plenty of easy marks available in this question but there is a lot of information to deal with so make sure you mark off each item as you include it in your answer.

- Question 2 is a slightly unusual corporation tax question in which you are given a computation that contains lots of errors which you need to spot and correct.

- Question 3 is on corporate chargeable gains including shares in a share pool. Using the correct pro forma for computing the cost of the shares sold is key to getting good marks on this question.

- Question 4 part (a) is about withdrawing income from a company either as salary or as dividend. Although this looks a bit complicated, the actual computations are quite straightforward. Part (b) is about the tests for employment versus self-employment.

- Question 5 is a three part question on pensions, individual savings accounts and inheritance tax. It is very important that you attempt all three parts of the question to obtain a reasonable number of marks.

Lastly, what you mustn't forget is that you have to **answer all of the questions in the paper. They are all compulsory**. Do not miss out any questions or you will seriously affect your chance of passing the exam.

## Option 2 (if you're thinking 'It's a doddle')

It never pays to be over confident but if you're reasonably confident about the exam then it is best to work through the questions sequentially starting with question 1.

## No matter how many times we remind you....

Always, always **allocate your time** according to the marks for the question in total and then according to the parts of the question. And **always, always follow the requirements** exactly.

## You've got spare time at the end of the exam.....?

If you have allocated your time properly then you **shouldn't have time on your hands** at the end of the exam. But if you find yourself with five or ten minutes to spare, check over your work to make sure that there are no silly arithmetical errors.

# Forget about it!

And don't worry if you found the paper difficult. More than likely other candidates did too. If this were the real thing you would need to **forget** the exam the minute you leave the exam hall and **think about the next one**. Or, if it's the last one, **celebrate**!

# 1 Josie Jones

## Marking scheme

| | | | Marks |
|---|---|---|---|
| **(a)** | *Trading income* | | |
| | Profit for year ended 30 April 2013 | | ½ |
| | Profit for period ended 30 June 2013 | | ½ |
| | Overlap profits | | 1 |
| | *Capital allowances* | | |
| | Period ended 30 June 2013 | - Addition | ½ |
| | | - Proceeds | ½ |
| | | - Balancing allowance | ½ |
| | *Employment income* | | |
| | Salary | | 1 |
| | Removal expenses | | 1 |
| | Beneficial loan | | 1½ |
| | Staff canteen | | ½ |
| | Car benefit   - Percentage | | 1½ |
| | | - Benefit | 1 |
| | *Property income* | | |
| | Property one | | 1 |
| | Property two | | 1 |
| | *Investment income* | | |
| | Building society interest | | ½ |
| | Gilt interest | | 1 |
| | Premium bond prize (exempt) | | ½ |
| | Dividends | | ½ |
| | *Taxable income* | | |
| | Personal allowance not available | | 1 |
| | *Tax payable* | | |
| | Increase in limits for gift aid donations | | 1 |
| | Tax liability | | 2 |
| | Tax credits/tax deducted at source | | 1½ |
| | | | 20 |

|       |      |                          |     | Marks |
|-------|------|--------------------------|-----|-------|
| (b)   | (i)  | Balancing payment        | 1½  |       |
|       |      | Payment on account       | 1½  |       |
|       |      |                          |     | 3     |
|       | (ii) | PAYE                     | 1   |       |
|       |      | Reduced to cover other income | 1 |    |
|       |      |                          |     | 2     |
|       |      |                          |     | 25    |

(a)   **Josie Jones – Income tax computation 2013/14**

|                               | Non-savings income | Savings income | Dividend income | Total    |
|-------------------------------|--------------------|----------------|-----------------|----------|
|                               | £                  | £              | £               | £        |
| Trading income (W1)           | 64,000             |                |                 |          |
| Employment income (W3)        | 126,754            |                |                 |          |
| Property business income (W5) | 5,100              |                |                 |          |
| BSI £8,000 × 100/80           |                    | 10,000         |                 |          |
| Gilt interest (received gross)|                    | 1,200          |                 |          |
| Premium bond prize (exempt)   |                    | 0              |                 |          |
| Dividends £6,480 × 100/90     |                    |                | 7,200           |          |
| Net income                    | 195,854            | 11,200         | 7,200           | 214,254  |
| Less personal allowance (N)   | (0)                |                |                 | (0)      |
| Taxable income                | 195,854            | 11,200         | 7,200           | 214,254  |

**Tax**

|                                                      | £      | £       |
|------------------------------------------------------|--------|---------|
| *On non-savings income*                              |        |         |
| £37,510 (W6) @ 20%                                    |        | 7,502   |
| £117,990 @ 40%                                        |        | 47,196  |
| £155,500 (W6)                                         |        |         |
| £40,354 @ 45%                                         |        | 18,159  |
| £195,854                                             |        |         |
| *On savings income*                                  |        |         |
| £11,200 @ 45%                                         |        | 5,040   |
| *On dividend income*                                 |        |         |
| £7,200 @ 37.5%                                        |        | 2,700   |
| Income tax liability                                 |        | 80,597  |
| Less:  dividend tax credit £7,200 × 10%              | 720    |         |
|        PAYE                                           | 41,577 |         |
|        BSI tax deducted at source £10,000 × 20%      | 2,000  |         |
|                                                      |        | (44,297)|
| Income tax payable                                   |        | 36,300  |

*Tutorial notes:*

1   Only £8,000 of the relocation costs is exempt.

2   The provision of meals in a staff canteen does not give rise to a taxable benefit.

3   The furnished holiday letting loss from property one can only be carried forward against future furnished holiday letting profits.

4   Premium bond prizes are exempt from income tax.

5   No personal allowance is available as Josie's adjusted net income of £(214,254 – 5,500) = £208,754 exceeds £118,880.

*Workings*

1    *Trading income*

|  | £ | £ |
|---|---|---|
| *Year ended 30 April 2013* | | |
| Trading profit | | 95,560 |
| *Period ended 30 June 2013* | | |
| Trading profit | 10,440 | |
| Less   capital allowances (W2) | (300) | |
| | | 10,140 |
| Less   overlap profits | | (41,700) |
| Trading income | | 64,000 |

2    *Capital allowances*

|  | Main pool £ | Allowances £ |
|---|---|---|
| *Period ended 30 June 2013* | | |
| WDV b/f | nil | |
| Addition | 2,000 | |
| Proceeds | (1,700) | |
| | 300 | |
| Balancing allowance | (300) | 300 |

3    *Employment income*

|  | £ |
|---|---|
| Salary £15,100 × 8 | 120,800 |
| Removal expenses £(11,600 – 8,000) | 3,600 |
| Loan £33,000 @ 4% × 7/12 | 770 |
| Staff canteen (exempt) | 0 |
| Car benefit (W4) | 1,584 |
| Employment income | 126,754 |

4    *Car benefit*

Amount by which $CO_2$ emissions exceed base level: (135 (rounded down) − 95) = 40 ÷ 5 = 8.
Car benefit percentage is 8 + 11 + 3 (diesel supplement) = 22%.
Car available from October 2013 to 5 April 2014 = 6 months.
Car benefit is £14,400 (list price) × 22% × 6/12 = £1,584.

5    *Property business income*

|  | £ |
|---|---|
| *Property one* | |
| £(6,600 − 9,700) = £(3,100) loss c/f against FHL income | 0 |
| *Property two* | |
| £(7,200 − 2,100) | 5,100 |
| | 5,100 |

6    *Tax rate limits*

Josie's basic and higher rate tax limits are increased by (£4,400 × 100/80) = £5,500 to £(32,010 + 5,500)  = £37,510 and £(150,000 + 5,500) = £155,500.

(b)   (i)   Josie's balancing payment for 2013/14 due on 31 January 2015 is £(36,300 − 34,400) = £1,900.

Her payments on account for 2014/15 will be £(36,300 × 50%) = £18,150. These will be due on 31 January and 31 July 2015.

(ii)   For 2014/15 the tax on Josie's employment income will be collected under PAYE.

Therefore a claim can be made to reduce the payments on account so that they just cover any remaining income tax that is payable, such as that on the property business profit.

# 2 Clueless Ltd

## Marking scheme

|  |  | Marks |
|---|---|---|
| (a) | *Trading profit* | |
| | Depreciation | ½ |
| | Donations to political parties | ½ |
| | Qualifying charitable donations | ½ |
| | Accountancy | ½ |
| | Legal fees | ½ |
| | Repairs | ½ |
| | Entertaining suppliers | ½ |
| | Entertaining customers | ½ |
| | Gifts to customers - pens | ½ |
| | Gifts to customers – food hampers | ½ |
| | Capital allowances | ½ |
| | *Capital allowances computation* | |
| | WDV b/f | 1 |
| | AIA | 1 |
| | Motor car [1] addition to main pool | ½ |
| | Motor car [2] addition to special rate pool, no adjustment for private use | 1 |
| | Disposal proceeds | ½ |
| | WDA @ 18% | 1 |
| | WDA @ 8% | ½ |
| | *Loan interest* | 1 |
| | *Qualifying charitable donation* | ½ |
| | *Franked investment income* | |
| | Grossed up dividends | 1 |
| | Group dividend | ½ |
| | *Upper limit* | ½ |
| | *Corporation tax* | |
| | Main rate on taxable total profits | ½ |
| | Marginal relief | <u>1</u> |
| | | 16 |

| | | | | Marks |
|---|---|---|---|---|
| (b) | (i) | Tax return submission date | | 1 |
| | (ii) | Using HMRC software | 1 | |
| | | Use of other software | 1 | |
| | | Tagging | 1 | |
| | | | | 3 |
| (c) | (i) | Eligible for both schemes on turnover | 1½ | |
| | | Up to date with payments for both schemes | 1 | |
| | | Up to date with returns for cash accounting scheme | ½ | |
| | | Output tax under cash accounting scheme | 1 | |
| | | Input tax under cash accounting scheme | 1 | |
| | | Annual accounting scheme – one return | 1 | |
| | | | | 6 |
| | (ii) | (1) Payment on importation | 1 | |
| | | Input tax recovery | 1 | |
| | | (2) Output tax on date of acquisition | 1 | |
| | | Input tax recovery | 1 | |
| | | | | 4 |
| | | | | 30 |

---

(a) **Clueless Ltd – Corporation tax computation for the year ended 31 March 2014**

| | £ |
|---|---|
| Taxable trading profit (W1) | 355,760 |
| Loan interest receivable | 32,800 |
| Total profits | 388,560 |
| Less   qualifying charitable donations | (900) |
| Taxable total profits | 387,660 |
| Add   franked investment income (W3) | 23,000 |
| Augmented profits | 410,660 |
| Marginal relief applies (W4) | |
| £387,660 @ 23% | 89,162 |
| Less marginal relief 3/400 (750,000 – 410,660) × 387,660/410,660 | (2,403) |
| Corporation tax liability | 86,759 |

*Workings*

1   *Taxable trading profit for the year ended 31 March 2014*

| | £ |
|---|---|
| Profit before taxation | 345,966 |
| Add:   Depreciation | 15,740 |
| Donations to political parties | 400 |
| Qualifying charitable donations | 900 |
| Accountancy | 0 |
| Legal fees | 0 |
| Repairs | 0 |
| Entertaining suppliers | 3,600 |
| Entertaining employees | 0 |
| Gifts to customers (pens) | 0 |
| Gifts to customers (food hampers) | 1,650 |
| | 368,256 |
| Less:   Capital allowances (W2) | (12,496) |
| Taxable trading profit | 355,760 |

*Tutorial notes:*

1   The only exception to the non-deductibility of entertainment expenditure is when it is in respect of employees.

2      Gifts to customers are an allowable deduction if they cost less than £50 per recipient per year, are not of food, drink, tobacco or vouchers for exchangeable goods, and carry a conspicuous advertisement for the company making the gift.

2   *Capital allowances*

| | AIA | Main pool | Special rate pool | Allowances |
|---|---|---|---|---|
| | £ | £ | £ | £ |
| WDV brought forward | | 2,400 | 13,500 | |
| Addition qualifying for AIA | | | | |
|   Machinery | 8,300 | | | |
| Annual investment allowance | (8,300) | | | 8,300 |
| Additions not qualifying for AIA | | | | |
|   Motor car [1] | | 13,800 | | |
|   Motor car [2] | | | 11,800 | |
| Disposal proceeds | | | (9,300) | |
| | | 16,200 | 16,000 | |
| WDA – 18% | | (2,916) | | 2,916 |
| WDA – 8% | | | (1,280) | 1,280 |
| WDV carried forward | | 13,284 | 14,720 | |
| Total allowances | | | | 12,496 |

*Tutorial notes:*

1      Motor car [1] has $CO_2$ emissions between 96 and 130 grams per kilometre and therefore qualifies for writing down allowances at the rate of 18%.

2      Motor car [2] has $CO_2$ emissions over 130 grams per kilometre and therefore qualifies for writing down allowances at the rate of 8%. The private use of a motor car is irrelevant, since such usage will be assessed on the employee as a benefit.

3   *Franked investment income*

Franked investment income is £20,700 × 100/90 = £23,000.

The dividends from the 100% subsidiary company are not franked investment income as they are group dividends.

4   *Upper limit*

Clueless Ltd has one associated company, so the upper limit is reduced to £(1,500,000/2) = £750,000.

(b)   (i)      Clueless Ltd's self-assessment tax return for the year ended 31 March 2014 must be submitted by 31 March 2015.

      (ii)      If Clueless Ltd has straightforward accounts, it could use the software provided by HM Revenue and Customs. This automatically produces accounts and tax computations in the iXBRL format.

            Alternatively, other software that automatically produces iXBRL accounts and computations could be used.

            A tagging service could be used to apply the appropriate tags to the accounts and tax computations, or Clueless Ltd could use software to tag documents itself.

(c)   (i)      Clueless Ltd can use both schemes because its expected taxable turnover for the next 12 months does not exceed £1,350,000 exclusive of VAT.

            In addition, for both schemes the company is up to date with its VAT payments, and for the cash accounting scheme it is up to date with its VAT returns.

            With the cash accounting scheme, output VAT will be accounted for two months later than at present as the date of the cash receipt determines the return in which the transaction is dealt with rather than the invoice date.

The recovery of input VAT on expenses will not be affected as these are dealt with on a cash basis.

With the annual accounting scheme, the reduced administration in only having to file one VAT return each year should save on overtime costs.

(ii) (1) **Supplier situated outside the European Union**

Clueless Ltd will have to pay VAT of £22,000 @ 20% = £4,400 to HM Revenue and Customs at the time of importation.

This will then be reclaimed as input VAT on the VAT return for the period during which the machinery is imported.

(2) **Supplier situated elsewhere within the European Union**

VAT will have to be accounted for according to the date of acquisition. This will be the earlier of the date that a VAT invoice is issued or the 15th day of the month following the month in which the machinery comes into the UK.

The VAT charged of £4,400 will be declared on Clueless Ltd's VAT return as output VAT, but will then be reclaimed as input VAT on the same VAT return.

# 3 Acebook Ltd

**Text references.** Capital losses are included in Chapter 22. Chargeable gains for companies are covered in Chapter 21. Part disposals and compensation are dealt with in Chapter 13.

**Top tips.** Use the three column pro forma for the company's share pool and take care to add the indexation allowance to the cost in the pool to obtain the indexed cost.

**Easy marks.** Part (a) was a straightforward statement of the use of capital losses for companies. The part disposal in part (b) was not difficult, in particular as the indexed cost was given.

**Examiner's comments.** Although there were many perfect answers to section (a), a number of candidates discussed trading losses, explained that capital losses could be utilised in a similar manner to trading losses, covered the rules for individuals rather than companies, or discussed groups - despite being told not to do so. Section (b) was generally very well answered, and there were many high scoring answers. One common mistake with the ordinary shares was to index the share pool prior to the bonus issue. Despite being told that the entire shareholding was disposed of, some candidates complicated the calculation by making a part disposal. Many candidates wasted time by calculating the CGT liability (often for an individual rather than a company) despite being instructed to just calculate chargeable gains.

**Marking scheme**

|  |  | **Marks** |
|---|---|---|
| (a) | Set off against gains in same accounting period | 1½ |
|  | Carry forward against first available gains | 1½ |
|  |  | 3 |

(b) **Oogle plc shares**

| | Marks |
|---|---|
| Purchase June 2003 | ½ |
| Bonus issue October 2006 | 1 |
| Indexation to February 2008 | 1 |
| Rights issue February 2008 | 1½ |
| Indexation to March 2013 | 1 |
| Disposal proceeds | 1 |
| Indexed cost | 1 |
| **Land** | |
| Disposal proceeds | ½ |
| Indexed cost | 1½ |
| Enhancement expenditure | 1 |
| **Investment property** | |
| Gain immediately chargeable | 2 |
| | 12 |
| | 15 |

(a) When a limited company has a capital loss, it is first set off against any chargeable gains arising in the same accounting period.

Any remaining capital loss is then carried forward and set off against the first available chargeable gains of future accounting periods.

(b) **Acebook Ltd – Chargeable gains for the year ended 31 December 2013**

**Oogle plc**

| | No of shares | Cost £ | Indexed cost £ |
|---|---|---|---|
| Purchase June 2003 | 8,000 | 25,200 | 25,200 |
| Bonus issue October 2006 2: 1 | 16,000 | | |
| | 24,000 | | |
| Indexed rise to February 2008 0.166 × £25,200 | | | 4,183 |
| Rights issue February 2008 1:5 @ £4.30 | 4,800 | 20,640 | 20,640 |
| | 28,800 | 45,840 | 50,023 |
| Indexed rise to March 2013 0.174 × £50,023 | | | 8,704 |
| | | | 58,727 |
| Disposal | (28,800) | (45,840) | (58,727) |

The gain is computed as follows:

| | £ |
|---|---|
| Proceeds 28,800 × £3.20 | 92,160 |
| Less indexed cost | (58,727) |
| Indexed gain | 33,433 |

**Land**

| | £ |
|---|---|
| Proceeds | 192,000 |
| Less cost $\dfrac{192,000}{192,000+53,000} \times £196,000$ | (153,600) |
| enhancement expenditure (clearing and levelling land) | |
| $\dfrac{192,000}{192,000+53,000} \times £29,400$ | (23,040) |
| Indexed gain | 15,360 |

**Investment property**

An amount equal to the insurance proceeds not reinvested of £(189,000 – 172,400) = £16,600 is an immediate chargeable gain for the year ended 31 December 2013.

*Tutorial note:*

The balance of the gain of £([189,000 – 138,400 = 50,600] – 16,600) =£34,000 is deferred by deducting it from the cost of the replacement property.

# 4 Sophia Wong and Andrew Zoom

**Text references.** Computation of income tax is covered in Chapter 2. Employment income is in Chapter 3. National insurance contributions are the subject of Chapter 12.

**Top tips.** Lay out your computations clearly so the marker knows which scenario you are dealing with. Make sure that you use these computations to answer the question in part (a) which is to advise on whether or not there will be an overall saving of tax and national insurance contributions.

**Easy marks.** There were some easy marks in this question for basic computations of income tax and national insurance contributions.

**Examiner's comments.** For part (a), many students did not seem to notice that they had been given some of the information (employer's NIC when withdrawing profits as director's remuneration, and corporation tax when withdrawing profits as dividends) and wasted time trying to calculate the figures themselves. As regards withdrawing profits as director's remuneration, very few candidates appreciated that there would be no taxable profit and hence no corporation tax liability. As regards withdrawing profits as dividends, far too many candidates did not appreciate that no NIC would be payable. Some candidates even attempted to answer this section with just one calculation combining the director's remuneration and dividend, and very few marks were available with this approach. For part (b), only a few students pointed out that the taxpayer did not take any financial risk or profit from sound management.

## Marking scheme

|  |  |  | Marks |  |
|---|---|---|---|---|
| (a) | (i) | Employer's NICs | 1 | |
| | | No corporation tax liability | 1 | |
| | | Personal allowance | ½ | |
| | | Income tax:   basic rate | ½ | |
| | |          higher rate | ½ | |
| | | Employee's NICs | 1½ | |
| | | Total tax and NICs compared with sole trader | 1 | |
| | | | | 6 |
| | (ii) | No Class 1 NICs | ½ | |
| | | Corporation tax | 1 | |
| | | Grossed up dividends | ½ | |
| | | Personal allowance | ½ | |
| | | Income tax:   basic rate | ½ | |
| | |          higher rate | ½ | |
| | | Tax credit | ½ | |
| | | Total tax and NICs compared with sole trader | 1 | |
| | | | | 5 |

| | | | Marks |
|---|---|---|---|
| (b) | Control | | ½ |
| | Financial risk | | ½ |
| | Basis of remuneration | | 1 |
| | Sound management | | ½ |
| | Required to do the work personally | | ½ |
| | Obligation to accept work offered | | ½ |
| | Equipment | | ½ |
| | | | 4 |
| | | | 15 |

(a)  (i)  **Profits withdrawn as director's remuneration**

Employer's class 1 NIC will be £(80,000 – 71,232) = £8,768.

There is no corporation tax liability for the new company as taxable total profits are nil as a result of the payment of director's remuneration and associated employer's class 1 NIC which are deductible expenses.

*Tax and NIC implications for Sophia*

Sophia's income tax liability for 2013/14 will be:

| | £ |
|---|---|
| Director's remuneration | 71,232 |
| Less personal allowance | (9,440) |
| Taxable income | 61,792 |

*Income tax*

| | £ |
|---|---|
| £32,010 × 20% | 6,402 |
| £29,782 × 40% | 11,913 |
| £61,792 | |
| Income tax liability/income tax payable | 18,315 |

Sophia's employee class 1 NICs for 2013/14 will be:

| | £ |
|---|---|
| £(41,450 – 7,755) = 33,695 × 12% | 4,043 |
| £(71,232 – 41,450) = 29,782 × 2% | 596 |
| Employee class 1 NICs | 4,639 |

The total tax and NIC cost if all of the new company's profits are withdrawn as directors remuneration is £(8,768 + 18,315 + 4,639) = £31,722.

This is £(31,722 – 25,766) = £5,956 more than the cost on a self-employed basis.

(ii)  **Profits withdrawn as dividends**

There will be no class 1 NICs.

The corporation tax liability of the new company ended 5 April 2014 will be £(80,000 – 64,000) = £16,000.

Sophia's income tax liability for 2013/14 will be:

| | £ |
|---|---|
| Dividends £64,000 × 100/90 | 71,111 |
| Less personal allowance | (9,440) |
| Taxable income | 61,671 |

|  | £ |
|---|---|
| *Income tax* | |
| £32,010 ×10% | 3,201 |
| £29,661 × 32.5% | 9,640 |
| £61,671 | |
| Income tax liability | 12,841 |
| Less tax credit £61,671 × 10% | (6,167) |
| Income tax payable | 6,674 |

The total tax and NIC cost if all of the new company's profits are withdrawn as dividends is £(16,000 + 6,674) = £22,674.

This is £(25,766 – 22,674) = £3,092 less than the cost on a self-employed basis.

(b) **Factors for employment rather than self-employment**

- Andrew is under the control of Slick-Productions Ltd.
- Andrew is not taking any financial risk.
- Andrew works a set number of hours, is paid by the hour and is paid for overtime.
- Andrew cannot profit from sound management.
- Andrew is required to do the work personally.
- There is an obligation to accept work that is offered.
- Andrew does not provide his own equipment.

# 5 Rosie Rohan, Sam Shire and Tom Tirith

**Text references.** Personal pensions are covered in Chapter 5. Individual savings accounts are dealt with in Chapter 2. Inheritance tax is the subject of Chapter 18.

**Top tips.** Remember that there is useful information contained in the Tax Tables provided in the examination. In this question, the annual allowance amount, the ISA limits and the taper relief percentages were vital and could be found in the Tax Tables.

**Easy marks.** There were easy marks in all three parts of the question, for example, a description of the tax relief on personal pensions, the ISA tax exemptions and the calculation of inheritance tax on cash lifetime transfers. It was important to keep your answer brief and to the point in part (b) which was only worth 2 marks.

**Examiner's comments.** Section (a) was generally well answered, with many candidates correctly calculating the amount of available annual allowances. However, it was often not appreciated that basic rate tax relief is given by contributions being made net, and also that an annual allowance charge is subject to tax at the taxpayer's marginal rate. Section (b) was also well answered. Surprisingly, very few candidates stated that ISAs offer exemption from both income tax and CGT – only mentioning one or the other. Most candidates answered section (c) extremely well, often gaining all of the available marks. However, the PET was sometimes incorrectly included in the workings for the first requirement – not only losing marks, but also complicating the otherwise straightforward calculations.

### Marking scheme

| | | **Marks** |
|---|---|---|
| (a) | Annual allowance 2009/10 | ½ |
| | Annual allowance 2012/13 | ½ |
| | Unused allowances | 2 |
| | Basic rate tax relief | ½ |
| | Higher and additional rate tax relief | 1 |
| | Identification of annual allowance charge | ½ |
| | Annual allowance charge at marginal rates of income tax | 1 |
| | | 6 |

| | | | | | Marks |
|---|---|---|---|---|---|
| (b) | | | Maximum investment into stocks and shares ISA | 1 | |
| | | | Tax exemptions for ISAs | 1 | |
| | | | | | 2 |
| (c) | (i) | (1) | Annual exemption 2013/14 | ½ | |
| | | | IHT liability at 20% | 1 | |
| | | (2) | IHT liability at 20/80 | ½ | |
| | | | Gross chargeable transfer | 1 | |
| | | | | | 3 |
| | (ii) | | Gross chargeable transfer (from (i) (2) above) | ½ | |
| | | | Available nil rate band      potentially exempt transfer | 1 | |
| | | |                               amount available for CLT | ½ | |
| | | | IHT liability at 40% | ½ | |
| | | | Taper relief | 1 | |
| | | | Lifetime tax paid | ½ | |
| | | | | | 4 |
| | | | | | 15 |

---

(a) **Rosie Rohan**

*Annual allowances*

The unused annual allowance for 2009/10 cannot be brought forward as this is more than three years prior to 2013/14.

Rosie was a member of a pension scheme for 2012/13, so the full annual allowance for that year is available.

She has unused allowances of £(50,000 – 41,000) = £9,000 from 2010/11, £(50,000 – 26,000) = £24,000 from 2011/12, and £50,000 from 2012/13, so the available annual allowances for 2013/14 are therefore £(50,000 + 9,000 + 24,000 + 50,000) = £133,000.

*Tax relief*

Personal pension contributions are made net of basic rate tax.

Higher and additional rate tax relief is given by increasing Rosie's basic and higher rate tax limits for 2013/14 by the gross amount of the pension contributions.

*Excess contributions*

If pension contributions are made in excess of the available annual allowances, then there will be an annual allowance charge.

This charge will be subject to income tax at Rosie's marginal rate(s) of income tax by treating the excess contributions as an extra amount of non-savings income received by Rosie.

(b) **Sam Shire**

Since Sam has already invested £4,000 into a cash ISA, he can invest a maximum of £(11,520 – 4,000) = £7,520 into a stocks and shares ISA for 2013/14.

Dividend income received within a stocks and shares ISA is exempt from income tax and chargeable gains are exempt from capital gains tax.

(c) **Tom Tirith**

    (i)    (1)    *Inheritance tax (IHT) paid by donee (the trustees)*

| | £ |
|---|---|
| Gift (value transferred) | 450,000 |
| Less annual exemption 2013/14 | (3,000) |
| Gross transfer of value | 447,000 |

|       |          |         | £ |
|-------|----------|---------|---|
| IHT   | £325,000 | × 0%    | Nil |
|       | £122,000 | × 20%   | 24,400 |
|       | £447,000 |         | 24,400 |

(2)    *Inheritance tax (IHT) paid by donor (Tom)*

|                              | £ |
|------------------------------|---|
| Gift (value transferred)     | 450,000 |
| Less  annual exemption 2013/14 | (3,000) |
| Net transfer of value        | 447,000 |

|       |          |         | |
|-------|----------|---------|---|
| IHT   | £325,000 | × 0%    | Nil |
|       | £122,000 | × 20/80 | 30,500 |
|       | £447,000 |         | 30,500 |

Gross transfer of value £(447,000 + 30,500)          477,500

*Tutorial note*

The gift made on 20 December 2012 utilises the annual exemption for 2012/13.

(ii)   *Additional liability arising on death if donor (Tom) pays the tax*

|                                               | £ |
|-----------------------------------------------|---|
| Gross transfer of value (from (i) (2) above)  | 477,500 |

|       |               |       | |
|-------|---------------|-------|---|
| IHT   | £131,000 (W)  | × 0%  | Nil |
|       | £346,500      | × 40% | 138,600 |
|       | £477,500      |       | 138,600 |
| Less taper relief @ 40% (death between 4 and 5 years after transfer) | | | (55,440) |
| Death tax                                     | | | 83,160 |
| Less  lifetime tax paid                       | | | (30,500) |
| Additional liability                          | | | 52,660 |

*Working*

The potentially exempt transfer made on 20 December 2012 will utilise £(200,000 − 6,000 [annual exemptions for 2012/13 and 2011/12]) = £194,000 of the nil rate band of £325,000 for 2018/19.

Therefore only £(325,000 − 194,000) = £131,000 is available against the chargeable lifetime transfer to the trust.

# ACCA

# Paper F6

# Taxation (United Kingdom)

# Mock Examination 2

| Question Paper | |
|---|---|
| Time allowed | |
| Reading and Planning | 15 minutes |
| Writing | 3 hours |
| **ALL FIVE questions are compulsory and MUST be attempted.** | |

**During the reading and planning time only the question paper may be annotated.**

**DO NOT OPEN THIS PAPER UNTIL YOU ARE READY TO START UNDER EXAMINATION CONDITIONS**

# ALL FIVE questions are compulsory and MUST be attempted

## 1 John and Rhonda Beach (TX 06/13)

John and Rhonda Beach are a married couple. The following information is available for the tax year 2013/14:

**John Beach**

(1) John was born in 1955 and is employed by Surf plc as a sales director. During the tax year 2013/14, he was paid gross director's remuneration of £184,000.

(2) During the tax year 2013/14, John contributed £28,000 into Surf plc's HM Revenue and Customs' registered occupational pension scheme. The company contributed a further £12,000 on his behalf. Both John and Surf plc have made exactly the same contributions for the previous five tax years.

(3) During the period 6 April to 31 October 2013, John used his private motor car for both private and business journeys. He was reimbursed by Surf plc at the rate of 60p per mile for the following mileage:

|  | Miles |
|---|---|
| Normal daily travel between home and Surf plc's offices | 1,180 |
| Travel between Surf plc's offices and the premises of Surf plc's clients | 4,270 |
| Travel between home and the premises of Surf plc's clients (none of the clients' premises were located near the offices of Surf plc) | 510 |
| Total mileage reimbursed by Surf plc | 5,960 |

(4) During the period from 1 November 2013 to 5 April 2014, Surf plc provided John with a petrol powered motor car which has a list price of £28,200 and an official $CO_2$ emission rate of 201 grams per kilometre. Surf plc also provided John with fuel for both his business and private journeys.

(5) During 2010 Surf plc provided John with a loan which was used to purchase a yacht. The amount of loan outstanding at 6 April 2013 was £84,000. John repaid £12,000 of the loan on 31 July 2013, and then repaid a further £12,000 on 31 December 2013. He paid loan interest of £1,270 to Surf plc during the tax year 2013/14. The taxable benefit in respect of this loan is calculated using the average method.

(6) During the tax year 2013/14, John made personal pension contributions up to the maximum amount of available annual allowances, including any unused amounts brought forward from previous years. These contributions were in addition to the contributions he made to Surf plc's occupational pension scheme (see note (2)). John has not made any personal pension contributions in previous tax years.

(7) John owns a holiday cottage which is let out as a furnished holiday letting, although the letting does not qualify as a trade under the furnished holiday letting rules. The property business profit for the year ended 5 April 2014 was £6,730.

**Rhonda Beach**

(1) Rhonda was born in 1947 and during the tax year 2013/14 she received pensions of £8,040.

(2) In addition to her pension income, Rhonda received gross building society interest of £21,400 during the tax year 2013/14.

*Required*

(a) Calculate John Beach's income tax liability for the tax year 2013/14. **(14 marks)**

(b) Calculate the class 1 and class 1A national insurance contributions that will have been suffered by John Beach and Surf plc in respect of John's earnings and benefits for the tax year 2013/14. **(4 marks)**

(c) Calculate Rhonda Beach's income tax liability for the tax year 2013/14. **(4 marks)**

(d) State the tax advantages of a rental property qualifying as a trade under the furnished holiday letting rules. **(3 marks)**

**(Total = 25 marks)**

# 2 Greenzone Ltd (TX 06/13)

(a) Greenzone Ltd runs a business providing environmental guidance. The company's summarised statement of profit or loss for the year ended 31 March 2014 is as follows:

|  | Note | £ | £ |
|---|---|---|---|
| Gross profit |  |  | 404,550 |
| Operating expenses |  |  |  |
| Depreciation |  | 28,859 |  |
| Repairs and renewals | 1 | 28,190 |  |
| Other expenses | 2 | 107,801 |  |
|  |  |  | (164,850) |
| Operating profit |  |  | 239,700 |

### Note 1 – Repairs and renewals

Repairs and renewals are as follows:

|  | £ |
|---|---|
| Repainting the exterior of the company's office building | 8,390 |
| Extending the office building in order to create a new reception area | 19,800 |
|  | 28,190 |

### Note 2 – Other expenses

Other expenses are as follows:

|  | £ |
|---|---|
| Entertaining UK customers | 3,600 |
| Entertaining overseas customers | 1,840 |
| Political donations | 740 |
| Donation to a charity where Greenzone Ltd received free advertising in the charity's newsletter. This was not a qualifying charitable donation | 430 |
| Gifts to customers (pens costing £30 each, not displaying Greenzone Ltd's name) | 660 |
| Gifts to customers (clocks costing £65 each and displaying Greenzone Ltd's name) | 910 |
| Balance of expenditure (all allowable) | 99,621 |
|  | 107,801 |

### Note 3 – Plant and machinery

On 1 April 2013 the tax written down values of Greenzone Ltd's plant and machinery were as follows:

|  | £ |
|---|---|
| Main pool | 48,150 |
| Special rate pool | 9,200 |

The following motor cars were purchased during the year ended 31 March 2014:

|  | Date of purchase | Cost £ | $CO_2$ emission rate |
|---|---|---|---|
| Motor car [1] | 10 April 2013 | 10,800 | 92 grams per kilometre |
| Motor car [2] | 10 June 2013 | 20,400 | 110 grams per kilometre |

The following motor cars were sold during the year ended 31 March 2014:

|  | Date of purchase | Proceeds £ | Original cost £ |
|---|---|---|---|
| Motor car [3] | 8 March 2014 | 9,100 | 8,500 |
| Motor car [4] | 8 March 2014 | 12,400 | 18,900 |

The original cost of motor car [3] has previously been added to the main pool, and the original cost of motor car [4] has previously been added to the special rate pool.

*Required*

Calculate Greenzone Ltd's tax adjusted trading profit for the year ended 31 March 2014.

Note: Your computation should commence with the operating profit figure of £239,700, and should also list all of the items referred to in notes (1) and (2), indicating by the use of zero (0) any items that do not require adjustment. **(10 marks)**

(b) Greenzone Ltd has held shares in four trading companies throughout the year ended 31 March 2014. All four companies prepare accounts to 31 March. The following information is available for the year ended 31 March 2014:

|  | Are Ltd | Be Ltd | Can Ltd | Doer Co |
|---|---|---|---|---|
| Residence | UK | UK | UK | Overseas |
| Percentage shareholding | 60% | 40% | 90% | 70% |
| Trading profit/(loss) | £(74,800) | £68,900 | £(64,700) | £22,600 |
| Dividends paid to Greenzone Ltd | £36,180 | £35,100 | £29,400 | £16,650 |

The dividend figures are the actual cash amounts received by Greenzone Ltd during the year ended 31 March 2014.

*Required*

(i) State, giving reasons, which of the four trading companies will be treated as being associated with Greenzone Ltd. **(2 marks)**

(ii) Calculate the maximum amount of group relief that Greenzone Ltd can claim for the year ended 31 March 2014. **(2 marks)**

(iii) Calculate Greenzone Ltd's corporation tax liability for the year ended 31 March 2014.

*Note:* you should assume that Greenzone Ltd will claim the maximum possible amount of group relief. **(5 marks)**

(c) **Note that in answering this part of the question, you are not expected to take account of any of the information provided in parts (a) and (b) above unless otherwise indicated.**

The following information is available in respect of Greenzone Ltd's value added tax (VAT) for the quarter ended 31 March 2014:

(1) Output VAT of £38,210 was charged in respect of sales. This figure includes output VAT of £400 on a deposit received on 29 March 2014, which is in respect of a contract that is due to commence on 20 April 2014.

(2) In addition to the above, Greenzone Ltd also charged output VAT of £4,330 on sales to Are Ltd and Can Ltd (see part (b) above). These two companies and Greenzone Ltd are not currently registered as a group for VAT purposes.

(3) The managing director of Greenzone Ltd is provided with free fuel for private mileage driven in his company motor car. Greenzone Ltd wishes to use the fuel scale charge. The relevant quarterly scale charge is £303. This figure is inclusive of VAT.

(4) On 31 March 2014, Greenzone Ltd wrote off an impairment loss in respect of a sales invoice that was issued on 15 September 2013. This invoice was due for payment on 31 October 2013. Output VAT of £640 was originally paid in respect of the sale.

(5) Input VAT of £12,770 was incurred in respect of expenses. This figure includes the following input VAT:

|  | £ |
|---|---|
| Entertaining UK customers | 210 |
| Entertaining overseas customers | 139 |
| Repainting the exterior of the company's office building | 1,678 |
| Extending the office building in order to create a new reception area | 3,300 |

For the quarters ended 31 December 2011 and 30 September 2013, Greenzone Ltd was two months late in submitting its VAT returns and in paying the related VAT liabilities. All of the company's other VAT returns have been submitted on time, and the related VAT liabilities have been paid on time.

*Required*

(i) Calculate the amount of value added tax (VAT) payable by Greenzone Ltd for the quarter ended 31 March 2014.

*Note:* your calculation should clearly refer to all of the items of input VAT listed in note (5), indicating by the use of zero (0) any items that do not require adjustment. **(7 marks)**

(ii) Advise Greenzone Ltd of the default surcharge implications if it is two months late in submitting its VAT return for the quarter ended 31 March 2014 and in paying the related VAT liability. **(2 marks)**

(iii) State the advantages if Greenzone Ltd, Are Ltd and Can Ltd (see part (b) above) were to register as a group for VAT purposes. **(2 marks)**

**(Total = 30 marks)**

# 3 Ginger, Aom, Innocent and Nigel (TX 06/13)

**You should assume that today's date is 1 March 2014.**

(a) Ginger has a holding of 10,000 £1 ordinary shares in Nutmeg Ltd, an unquoted trading company, which she had purchased on 13 February 2004 for £2.40 per share. The current market value of the shares is £6.40 per share, but Ginger intends to sell some of the holding to her daughter at £4.00 per share during March 2014. Ginger and her daughter will elect to hold over any gain as a gift of a business asset.

For the tax year 2013/14, Ginger will not make any other disposals, and has therefore not utilised her annual exempt amount.

*Required*

Explain how many £1 ordinary shares in Nutmeg Ltd Ginger can sell to her daughter for £4.00 per share during March 2014 without incurring any capital gains tax liability for the tax year 2013/14.

Note: Your answer should be supported by appropriate calculations. **(4 marks)**

(b) Aom is in business as a sole trader. On 3 February 2014, she purchased a freehold factory for £168,000. Aom also owns two freehold warehouses, and wants to sell one of these during March 2014. The first warehouse was purchased on 20 March 2010 for £184,000, and can be sold for £213,000. The second warehouse was purchased on 18 July 2003 for £113,000, and can be sold for £180,000.

All of the above buildings have been, or will be, used for business purposes by Aom. She will make a claim to roll over the gain on whichever warehouse is sold against the cost of the factory.

*Required*

Calculate the chargeable gain, if any, that will arise in the tax year 2013/14 if either (1) the first or (2) the second freehold warehouse is sold during March 2014. **(5 marks)**

(c) Innocent and Nigel, a married couple, both have shareholdings in Cinnamon Ltd, an unquoted trading company with a share capital of 100,000 £1 ordinary shares.

Innocent has been the managing director of Cinnamon Ltd since the company's incorporation on 1 July 2005, and she currently holds 20,000 shares (with matching voting rights) in the company. These shares were subscribed for on 1 July 2005 at their par value.

Nigel has never been an employee or a director of Cinnamon Ltd, and he currently holds 3,000 shares (with matching voting rights) in the company. These shares were purchased on 23 April 2009 for £46,200.

Either Innocent or Nigel will sell 2,000 of their shares in Cinnamon Ltd during March 2014 for £65,000, but are not sure which of them should make the disposal. For the tax year 2013/14, both Innocent and Nigel have already made disposals which will fully utilise their annual exempt amounts, and they will each have taxable income of £80,000.

*Required*

Calculate the capital gains tax saving if the disposal of 2,000 shares in Cinnamon Ltd during March 2014 is made by Innocent rather than Nigel.

**(6 marks)**

**(Total = 15 marks)**

# 4 Dominic, Katie, and Opal Ltd (part (c) TX 06/13)

(a)    Dominic started a sole trader business as a personal trainer on 6 April 2013. He wishes to use the cash accounting basis for small businesses in relation to his income tax liability.

The following information is relevant for the year to 5 April 2014.

    (1)    Dominic issued invoices totalling £65,000. Unpaid invoices at 5 April 2014 amounted to £3,000.

    (2)    A motor car was acquired on 15 April 2013 for £13,000. Dominic drove 16,000 miles in the car during the year to 5 April 2014 of which 4,000 miles were for private journeys. Dominic wishes to use the fixed rate mileage expense for motoring which is 45p per mile for the first 10,000 miles, then 25p per mile after that.

    (3)    Exercise equipment was acquired on 2 May 2013 for £6,000.

    (4)    Other allowable expenses amounted to £8,200. This amount includes an invoice for £200 for energy drinks provided to clients which Dominic paid on 28 April 2014.

*Required*

    (i)    Explain why Dominic can use the cash accounting basis to compute his taxable trading profit.

**(1 mark)**

    (ii)    Calculate Dominic's taxable trading profit for the year ended 5 April 2014.    **(5 marks)**

(b)    Katie has been in business as a sole trader for many years, preparing accounts to 31 December each year. In the year to 31 December 2013 she made a loss of £230,000.

In the tax year 2013/14 Katie also had employment income of £300,000 and she made gross personal pension contributions of £30,000.

Katie expects to make a trading profit of £110,000 in the year to 31 December 2014. She will also have employment income of £300,000 in 2014/15 but will make no personal pension contributions.

*Required*

    (i)    Calculate Katie's taxable income for the tax year 2013/14 assuming that she claims relief for her trading loss against general income in that tax year.    **(3 marks)**

    (ii)    State the amount of the loss for the year to 31 December 2013 Kate will be able to carry forward and relieve in the tax year 2014/15.    **(1 mark)**

(c)    Opal Ltd has prepared accounts for the 14-month period ended 31 May 2014, and its trading profit for this period is £434,000. This figure is **before** taking account of capital allowances.

The tax written down value of Opal Ltd's capital allowances main pool at 1 April 2013 was £62,000. On 10 April 2014, Opal Ltd purchased machinery for £75,700.

*Required*

Calculate Opal Ltd's taxable total profits for each of the accounting periods covered by the 14-month period of account ended 31 May 2014.

*Note:* you should assume that the capital allowance rates and allowances for the financial year 2013 apply throughout.

**(5 marks)**

**(Total = 15 marks)**

# 5 Pere Jones and Phil Jones (TX 06/13)

On 23 August 2008, Pere Jones made a gift of a house valued at £420,000 to his son, Phil Jones. This was a wedding gift when Phil got married.

## Pere Jones

Pere died on 20 March 2014 aged 76, at which time his estate was valued at £880,000. Under the terms of his will, Pere divided his estate equally between his wife and his son, Phil. Pere had not made any gifts during his lifetime except for the gift of the house to Phil.

The nil rate band for the tax year 2008/09 is £312,000.

## Phil Jones

Phil was born in 1966. The house which he received as a wedding gift from Pere, his father, was always let out unfurnished until it was sold on 5 April 2014. The following income and outgoings relate to the property for the tax year 2013/14:

|  | £ |
|---|---|
| Rent received | 23,000 |
| Sale proceeds | 504,000 |
| Cost of new boundary wall around the property (there was previously no boundary wall) | (5,300) |
| Cost of replacing the property's chimney | (2,800) |
| Legal fees paid in connection with the disposal | (8,600) |
| Property insurance | (2,300) |

Phil has no other income or outgoings for the tax year 2013/14.

*Required*

(a)  (i)  Calculate the inheritance tax that will be payable as a result of Pere Jones' death. **(6 marks)**

(ii)  State who will be responsible for paying the inheritance tax arising from Pere Jones' gift of the house, and when this will be due. **(2 marks)**

(b)  Calculate Phil Jones' income tax and capital gains tax liabilities for the tax year 2013/14. **(7 marks)**

**(Total = 15 marks)**

# Answers

DO NOT TURN THIS PAGE UNTIL YOU HAVE
COMPLETED THE MOCK EXAM

# A plan of attack

What's the worst thing you could be doing right now if this was the actual exam paper? Sharpening your pencil? Wondering how to celebrate the end of the exam in about 3 hours time? Panicking, flapping and generally getting in a right old state?

Well, they're all pretty bad, so turn back to the paper and let's sort out a **plan of attack**!

## First things first

You have fifteen minutes of reading time. Spend this looking carefully through the questions and deciding the order in which you will attempt them. As a general rule you should attempt the questions that you find easiest first and leave the hardest until last. Depending on how confident you are we recommend that you follow one of the following two options:

## Option 1 (if you're thinking 'Help!')

If you're a bit worried about the paper, do the questions in the order of how well you think you can answer them. You may find the shorter questions less daunting than the longer questions. Alternatively, you may feel better prepared for questions 1 and 2 and wish to start there.

- Question 1 is an income tax question. Presentation is a key aspect of this type of question so make sure that you set out your computations neatly and use workings for computations of more than one line.

- Question 2 is a corporation tax and value added tax question which is divided into a number of parts. It is important to attempt each part to ensure you gain reasonable marks.

- Question 3 is about chargeable gains for individuals. It involves some simple tax planning.

- Question 4 is a three part question dealing with the cash basis, restriction for loss relief, and a long period of account for a company. The first two aspects are new for 2013/14 and therefore highly examinable in the 2014 exams.

- Question 5 concerns a father and son and involves inheritance tax, income tax and capital gains tax. It is important to deal with each tax separately.

Lastly, what you mustn't forget is that you have to **answer all of the questions in the paper. They are all compulsory**. Do not miss out any questions or you will seriously affect your chance of passing the exam.

## Option 2 (if you're thinking 'It's a doddle')

It never pays to be over confident but if you're reasonably confident about the exam then it is best to work through the questions sequentially starting with question 1.

## No matter how many times we remind you....

Always, always **allocate your time** according to the marks for the question in total and then according to the parts of the question. And **always, always follow the requirements** exactly.

## You've got spare time at the end of the exam.....?

If you have allocated your time properly then you **shouldn't have time on your hands** at the end of the exam. But if you find yourself with five or ten minutes to spare, check over your work to make sure that there are no silly arithmetical errors.

## Forget about it!

And don't worry if you found the paper difficult. More than likely other candidates did too. If this were the real thing you would need to **forget** the exam the minute you leave the exam hall and **think about the next one**. Or, if it's the last one, **celebrate**!

# 1 John and Rhonda Beach

## Marking scheme

|  |  |  | Marks |
|---|---|---|---|
| (a) | Director's remuneration | ½ | |
| | Mileage allowance | | |
| |     Amount received | ½ | |
| |     Tax free amount | 1 | |
| |     Taxable benefit | ½ | |
| | Occupational pension contributions | 1 | |
| | Car benefit | | |
| |     Relevant percentage | 1 | |
| |     Available for 5 months | 1 | |
| | Fuel benefit | 1 | |
| | Beneficial loan | | |
| |     Outstanding loan at end of tax year | 1 | |
| |     Average loan | 1 | |
| |     Interest paid | ½ | |
| | Property business profit | ½ | |
| | Personal allowance – not available | 1 | |
| | Personal pension contributions | | |
| |     Unused allowance each year | ½ | |
| |     Available allowance for 2013/14 | 1 | |
| |     Increase in basic and higher rate band limits | 1 | |
| | Tax liability | | |
| |     Basic rate | ½ | |
| |     Higher rate | ½ | |
| | | | 14 |
| (b) | Employee Class 1 NIC | 2 | |
| | Employer Class 1 NIC | 1 | |
| | Employer Class 1A NIC | 1 | |
| | | | 4 |

|  |  | Marks |
|---|---|---|
| (c) | Pensions | ½ |
|  | Building society interest | ½ |
|  | Personal allowance |  |
|  | Personal allowance born between 6 April 1938 and 5 April 1948 | ½ |
|  | Restriction | 1 |
|  | Income tax liability |  |
|  | Starting rate | 1 |
|  | Basic rate | ½ |
|  |  | **4** |
| (d) | Capital allowances | 1 |
|  | Relevant earnings | 1 |
|  | Capital gains reliefs | 1 |
|  |  | $\underline{3}$ |
|  |  | $\underline{\underline{25}}$ |

(a) **John Beach – Income tax computation 2013/14**

|  | £ | Non-savings income £ |
|---|---|---|
| Employment income |  |  |
| Director's remuneration |  | 184,000 |
| Mileage allowance (W1) |  | 1,425 |
|  |  | 185,425 |
| Less: occupational pension contributions |  | (28,000) |
|  |  | 157,425 |
| Car benefit (W2) | 3,760 |  |
| Fuel benefit £21,100 × 32% × 5/12 | 2,813 |  |
| Beneficial loan (W3) | 1,610 |  |
|  |  | 8,183 |
| Property business profit |  | 6,730 |
| Net income |  | 172,338 |
| Less: personal allowance |  | (0) |
| Taxable income |  | 172,338 |

*Tutorial note*

No personal allowance is available as John's adjusted net income of £(172,338 – 40,000) = £132,338 exceeds £118,880.

**Tax**

|  | £ |
|---|---|
| *On non-savings income* |  |
| £72,010 (W4) @ 20% | 14,402 |
| £100,328 @ 40% | 40,131 |
| £172,338 |  |
| Income tax liability | 54,533 |

*Workings*

1   *Mileage allowance*

The mileage allowance received by John was 5,960 × 60p = £3,576.

Ordinary commuting does not qualify for relief, so the tax free amount is (4,270 + 510) = 4,870 × 45p = £2,151.

The taxable benefit is therefore £(3,576 – 2,151) = £1,425.

2     *Car benefit*

The relevant percentage for the car benefit is 11% + 21% (200 − 95 = 105/5) = 32%.

The motor car was available during the period 1 November 2013 to 5 April 2014, so the benefit for 2013/14 is £(28,200 × 32% × 5/12) = £3,760.

3     *Beneficial loan*

John repaid £(12,000 + 12,000) = £24,000 of the loan during 2013/14, so the outstanding balance at 5 April 2014 is £(84,000 − 24,000) = £60,000.

The benefit calculated using the average method (specified in the question) is as follows:

|  | £ |
|---|---|
| $\dfrac{84,000+60,000}{2} \times 4\%$ | 2,880 |
| Less: interest paid | (1,270) |
| Taxable benefit | 1,610 |

4     *Effect of personal pension contributions on tax limits*

Both employee and employer pension contributions count towards the annual allowance, so the amount of the unused allowance each year is £(50,000 − (28,000 + 12,000)) = £10,000.

Unused allowances can be carried forward for three years, so the available annual allowances for 2013/14 are £10,000 × 4 = £40,000.

John's basic and higher rate limits will be increased by his gross personal pension contributions of £40,000 to £(32,010 + 40,000) = £72,010 and £(150,000 − 40,000) = £190,000.

(b)     **John Beach and Surf plc − National insurance contributions 2013/14**

*Class 1 Employee contributions*

|  | £ |
|---|---|
| £(41,450 − 7,755) = 33,695 × 12% | 4,043 |
| £(185,425 − 41,450) = 143,975 × 2% | 2,879 |
|  | 6,922 |

*Class 1 Employer contributions*

| £(185,425 − 7,696) = 177,729 × 13.8% | 24,527 |
|---|---|

*Class 1A Employer contributions*

| £8,183 × 13.8% | 1,129 |
|---|---|

*Tutorial notes*

1     Earnings for Class 1 contributions include mileage allowance.
2     Occupational pension scheme contributions are not deductible for NIC purposes.

(c)     **Rhonda Beach − Income tax computation 2013/14**

|  | Non-savings income £ | Savings income £ | Total £ |
|---|---|---|---|
| Pensions | 8,040 |  |  |
| Building society interest |  | 21,400 |  |
| Net income | 8,040 | 21,400 | 29,440 |
| Less: personal allowance (W) | (8,040) | (790) | (8,830) |
| Taxable income | 0 | 20,610 | 20,610 |

**Tax**

| | | £ |
|---|---|---|
| *On savings income* | | |
| £2,790 @ 10% | | 279 |
| £17,820 @ 20% | | 3,564 |
| £20,610 | | |
| Income tax liability | | 3,843 |

*Working*

Personal allowance

| | £ | £ |
|---|---|---|
| Born between 6 April 1938 and 5 April 1948 | | 10,500 |
| Adjusted net income | 29,440 | |
| Less: income limit | (26,100) | |
| | 3,340 | |
| Divided by 2 | | (1,670) |
| Available personal allowance | | 8,830 |

(d) **Furnished holiday lettings**

Furniture and equipment purchased for use in the furnished holiday letting will qualify for capital allowances instead of the 10% wear and tear allowance.

The profit from the furnished holiday letting will qualify as relevant earnings for pension tax relief purposes.

Capital gains tax entrepreneurs' relief, relief for replacement of business assets and gift relief for business assets will potentially be available on a disposal of the furnished holiday letting.

# 2 Greenzone Ltd

**Text references.** Computing taxable total profits is covered in Chapter 19. The basics of adjustment of trading profit and capital allowances are dealt with in Chapters 7 and 8 respectively. The computation of the corporation tax liability, including the definition of associated companies, will be found in Chapter 20. Look in Chapter 23 for details of group relief. VAT aspects are dealt with in Chapters 25 and 26.

**Top tips.** Watch out for the difference between entertaining UK customers and overseas customers. Both types of entertaining are disallowed in the corporation tax computation, but input VAT is recoverable for entertaining overseas customers.

**Easy marks.** There were plenty of easy marks for standard items in the adjustment of profit. Don't forget to use a zero to show that there is no adjustment required. This approach was also required in part (c)(i).

**Examiner's comments.** Part (a) was well answered by the majority of candidates, with no aspect causing particular problems. The first requirement of part (b) was generally well answered, although some candidates incorrectly applied a 75% threshold. The second requirement of part (b) caused more problems, with many candidates including the loss from a group company where the shareholding was only 60%. Some candidates produced confused workings involving all four group companies, and therefore wasted quite a bit of time. The third requirement of part (b) was generally well answered, although the franked investment income was often omitted or incorrectly calculated. The first requirement of part (c) was generally well answered. Common mistakes included not appreciating that VAT figures were given (rather than supply figures), that no adjustment was required on a deposit (given that the tax point was the date of payment) and that no relief was available for the impairment loss (as less than six months had passed from the time that payment was due). The second requirement of part (c) was the one section on this paper that was inadequately answered by the vast majority of candidates, with few being able to explain the correct surcharge position. The third requirement of part (c) was generally well answered, although many candidates often wrote at length to explain a couple of fairly straightforward points.

**Marks**

| | | | |
|---|---|---|---|
| (a) | | Depreciation | ½ |
| | | Repainting | ½ |
| | | Reception area | ½ |
| | | Entertaining UK customers | ½ |
| | | Entertaining overseas customers | ½ |
| | | Political donations | ½ |
| | | Non-qualifying charitable donations | ½ |
| | | Pens | ½ |
| | | Clocks | ½ |
| | | Capital allowances deducted | ½ |
| | | Capital allowances | |
| | |     WDV b/f | 1 |
| | |     Addition – motor car [2] | ½ |
| | |     Disposal – motor car [3] | 1 |
| | |     Disposal – motor car [4] | ½ |
| | |     Balancing charge on special rate pool | ½ |
| | |     WDA on main pool | ½ |
| | |     Addition – motor car [1] | ½ |
| | |     FYA | ½ |
| | | | **10** |
| (b) | (i) | Associated company definition | ½ |
| | | Are Ltd and Can Ltd | ½ |
| | | Doer Ltd | 1 |
| | | | **2** |
| | (ii) | Maximum group relief | **2** |
| | (iii) | Trading profit | ½ |
| | | Group relief | ½ |
| | | Franked investment income | |
| | |     Gross up dividend | 1 |
| | |     Group dividends ignored | 1 |
| | | Upper limit | ½ |
| | | Corporation tax at main rate | ½ |
| | | Marginal relief | 1 |
| | | | **5** |
| (c) | (i) | Sales | 1 |
| | | Group sales | 1 |
| | | Fuel scale charge | 1½ |
| | | Impairment loss | 1 |
| | | Expenses | |
| | |     Entertaining UK customers | ½ |
| | |     Entertaining overseas customers | 1 |
| | |     Repainting office building | ½ |
| | |     New reception area | ½ |
| | | | **7** |
| | (ii) | Quarter ended 31 December 2011 | ½ |
| | | Quarter ended 31 March 2014 | 1 |
| | | Extension of surcharge period | ½ |
| | | | **2** |
| | (iii) | Ignore supplies between group members | 1 |
| | | One VAT return | 1 |
| | | | **2** |
| | | | **30** |

**(a)    Greenzone Ltd – Trading profit for the year ended 31 March 2014**

| | £ |
|---|---:|
| Operating profit | 239,700 |
| Add:    Depreciation | 28,859 |
| Repainting office building | 0 |
| New reception area | 19,800 |
| Entertaining UK customers | 3,600 |
| Entertaining overseas customers | 1,840 |
| Political donations | 740 |
| Non-qualifying charitable donation | 0 |
| Gifts to customers:    pens | 660 |
| clocks | 910 |
| | 296,109 |
| Less: capital allowance (W) | (18,409) |
| Trading profit | 277,700 |

*Tutorial notes*

1    The extension of the office building is not deductible as it is capital in nature. The building has been improved rather than repaired.

2    Gifts to customers are only an allowable expense if they cost less than £50 per recipient per year, are not of food, drink, tobacco or vouchers exchangeable for goods, and carry a conspicuous advertisement for the company.

*Working*

*Capital allowances*

| | FYA £ | Main pool £ | Special rate pool £ | Allowances £ |
|---|---:|---:|---:|---:|
| WDV brought forward | | 48,150 | 9,200 | |
| *Addition not qualifying for AIA/FYA* | | | | |
| Motor car [2] | | 20,400 | | |
| | | 68,550 | | |
| *Disposals* | | | | |
| Motor car [3] | | (8,500) | | |
| Motor car [4] | | | (12,400) | |
| Balancing charge | | | 3,200 | (3,200) |
| | | 60,050 | | |
| WDA @ 18% | | (10,809) | | 10,809 |
| *Addition qualifying for FYA* | | | | |
| Motor car [1] | 10,800 | | | |
| FYA @ 100% | (10,800) | | | 10,800 |
| WDV carried forward | | 49,241 | | |
| Allowances | | | | 18,409 |

*Tutorial notes*

1    Motor car [1] has $CO_2$ emissions up to 95 grams per kilometre and therefore qualifies for the 100% first year allowance.

2    Motor car [2] has $CO_2$ emissions between 96 and 130 grams per kilometre and therefore is added to the main pool.

3    The disposal value for motor car [3] is restricted to the original cost figure of £8,500.

(b)  (i)  Greenzone Ltd is associated with those companies in which it has a shareholding of over 50%.

Are Ltd and Can Ltd are therefore associated companies.

For associated company purposes, it does not matter where a company is resident, so Doer Co is also an associated company despite being resident overseas.

(ii)  The maximum amount of group relief that can be claimed is Can Ltd's trading loss of £64,700.

*Tutorial note*

Greenzone Ltd cannot claim group relief from Are Ltd as this company is not a 75% subsidiary.

The group relief claim is limited to the lower of Can Ltd's loss and Greenzone Ltd's taxable total profits (equal to trading profits of £277,700) ie Can Ltd's loss of £64,700.

(iii)  **Greenzone Ltd – corporation tax computation for the year ended 31 March 2014**

|  | £ |
|---|---|
| Taxable trading profit (from part (a)) | 277,700 |
| Less  group relief | (64,700) |
| Taxable total profits | 213,000 |
| Add  franked investment income (W1) | 39,000 |
| Augmented profits | 252,000 |
| Marginal relief applies (W2) | |
| £213,000 @ 23% | 48,990 |
| Less marginal relief 3/400 (375,000 – 252,000) × 213,000/252,000 | (780) |
| Corporation tax liability | 48,210 |

*Workings*

1  *Franked investment income*

Franked investment income is £(35,100 × 100/90) = £39,000

The dividends from Are Ltd, Can ltd and Doer Co are group dividends and are therefore not franked investment income.

2  *Upper limit*

Greenzone Ltd has three associated companies, so that the upper limit is reduced to £(1,500,000/4) = £375,000.

(c)  (i)  **Greenzone Ltd – VAT return for the quarter ended 31 March 2014**

|  | £ | £ |
|---|---|---|
| *Output VAT* | | |
| Sales | | 38,210 |
| Group sales | | 4,330 |
| Fuel scale charge £303 × 20/120 | | 50 |
| *Input VAT* | | |
| Impairment loss | 0 | |
| Expenses (W) | 12,560 | |
| | | (12,560) |
| VAT payable | | 30,030 |

*Tutorial notes*

1  The tax point for the deposit is the date of payment, so no adjustment is required to the output VAT figure of £38,210.

2  Relief is not available for the impairment loss as less than six months has passed from the time that payment was due.

*Working - Expenses*

|  | £ |
|---|---:|
| Total input VAT | 12,770 |
| Entertaining UK customers | (210) |
| Entertaining overseas customers | 0 |
| Repainting office building | 0 |
| New reception area | 0 |
|  | 12,560 |

*Tutorial note*

Input VAT on business entertaining is not recoverable unless it relates to the cost of entertaining overseas customers.

(ii) The late submission for the quarter ended 31 December 2011 is irrelevant, as it was followed by the submission of four consecutive VAT returns on time.

The late payment of VAT for the quarter ended 31 March 2014 occurs during the surcharge period relevant to the late return and payment for the quarter ended 30 September 2013. Therefore, it will result in a surcharge of £(30,030 × 2%) = £601 since it is the first default in the surcharge period.

In addition, the surcharge period will be extended to 31 March 2015.

*Tutorial note*

The surcharge of £601 is payable as it exceeds the *de minimis* amount of £400.

(ii) There will be no need to account for VAT on goods and services supplied between group members. Such supplies will simply be ignored for VAT purposes.

It will only be necessary to complete one VAT return for the three companies, so there could be a saving in administration costs.

# 3 Ginger, Aom, Innocent and Nigel

**Text references.** Chapter 13 covers the basics of computing chargeable gains. Chapter 15 deals with business reliefs.

**Top tips.** In part (c) think why the disposals by Innocent and Nigel would give rise to different capital gains tax liabilities. Are there different rates of capital gains tax? When do those rates apply?

**Easy marks.** There were some easy marks for basic computations in parts (b) and (c), even if you were not entirely sure about the operation of the reliefs.

**Examiner's comments.** Although there were a number of correct answers to part (a), it caused difficulty for many candidates. The main problem was not appreciating that the annual exempt amount should be used, despite a fairly heavy hint to this effect being given in the question. Part (b) was reasonably well answered by the majority of candidates, although the rollover relief aspects for the first warehouse often caused difficulty. Part (c) was another well answered section, with many candidates achieving maximum marks.

### Marking scheme

|  |  | **Marks** |
|---|---|---:|
| (a) | Chargeable to extent consideration exceeds cost | 1 |
|  | Amount chargeable | 1 |
|  | Annual exempt amount | ½ |
|  | Number of shares to sell | 1½ |
|  |  | 4 |

(b) *Sale of first warehouse*

| | |
|---|---|
| Disposal proceeds | ½ |
| Cost | ½ |
| Rollover relief | 1½ |

*Sale of second warehouse*

| | |
|---|---|
| Disposal proceeds | ½ |
| Cost | ½ |
| Rollover relief | 1½ |
| | **5** |

(c) *Innocent makes disposal*

| | |
|---|---|
| Disposal proceeds | ½ |
| Cost | 1 |
| CGT | 1½ |

*Nigel makes disposal*

| | |
|---|---|
| Disposal proceeds | ½ |
| Cost | 1 |
| CGT | 1½ |
| | **6** |
| | **15** |

(a) **Ginger**

The disposal is at an undervalue, so only the gift element of the gain can be deferred under gift relief. The consideration paid for each share will be immediately chargeable to capital gains tax to the extent that it exceeds the allowable cost. The chargeable amount is therefore £(4.00 – 2.40) = £1.60 per share.

Ginger's annual exempt amount for 2013/14 is £10,900.

She can therefore sell (10,900/1.60) = 6,812 shares to her daughter without this resulting in any capital gains tax liability for 2013/14.

(b) **Aom**

*Sale of first warehouse*

| | £ |
|---|---|
| Disposal proceeds | 213,000 |
| Less: cost | (184,000) |
| Gain before rollover relief | 29,000 |
| Less: rollover relief | (0) |
| Gain left in charge after rollover relief | 29,000 |

No rollover relief is available because the amount not reinvested of £(213,000 – 168,000) = £45,000 exceeds the chargeable gain.

*Sale of second warehouse*

| | £ |
|---|---|
| Disposal proceeds | 180,000 |
| Less: cost | (113,000) |
| Gain before rollover relief | 67,000 |
| Less: rollover relief £(67,000 – 12,000) | (55,000) |
| Gain left in charge after rollover relief | 12,000 |

The sale proceeds are not fully reinvested and so £(180,000 – 168,000) = £12,000 of the chargeable gain cannot be rolled over.

(c) **Innocent and Nigel**

*Innocent makes disposal*

|  | £ |
|---|---|
| Disposal proceeds | 65,000 |
| Less: cost | (2,000) |
| Gain | 63,000 |
| | |
| CGT on £63,000 @ 10% | 6,300 |

*Nigel makes disposal*

|  | £ |
|---|---|
| Disposal proceeds | 65,000 |
| Less: cost | (30,800) |
| Gain | 34,200 |
| | |
| CGT on £34,200 @ 28% | 9,576 |

*Capital gains tax saving*

The capital gains tax saving if Innocent makes the disposal rather than Nigel is therefore £(9,576 – 6,300) = £3,276.

*Tutorial notes*

1 A disposal by Innocent will qualify for entrepreneurs' relief as she is an officer (director) of Cinnamon Ltd which is a trading company and her personal company (she owns at least 5% of the ordinary share capital). These conditions have been satisfied throughout the period of one year ending with the date of the disposal.

2 A disposal by Nigel will not qualify for entrepreneurs' relief as he is not an officer or employee of Cinnamon Ltd. He also does not own at least 5% of the ordinary share capital of Cinnamon Ltd. Both of these conditions must be satisfied for entrepreneurs' relief to be available.

# 4 Dominic, Katie, and Opal Ltd

**Text references.** The cash basis is covered in Chapter 7. Trading losses are the subject of Chapter 10. Capital allowances are dealt with in Chapter 8. Computing taxable total profits is covered in Chapter 19.

**Top tips.** In part (c), remember that you must work out capital allowances separately for each accounting period.

**Easy marks.** The calculation of trading profits under the cash basis is reasonably straightforward.

**Examiner's comments.** Candidates generally achieved reasonable marks for part (c), but this was often only because the capital allowance marks were awarded as long as the workings followed whatever basis was adopted for the 14-month accounting period. It was unsatisfactory that the 12 month/2 month split was not more widely appreciated given that this aspect has now been examined several times in past F6(UK) papers.

**Marking scheme**

|  |  |  |  | Marks |
|---|---|---|---|---|
| (a) | (i) | Unincorporated business below threshold | | 1 |
| | (ii) | Cash received | 1 | |
| | | Fixed rate mileage expense | 2 | |
| | | Capital expenditure | 1 | |
| | | Expenses paid | 1 | |
| | | | | 5 |

|  |  |  |  | **Marks** |
|---|---|---|---|---|
| (b) | (i) | Net income | ½ | |
| | | Taxable income | ½ | |
| | | Maximum amount relievable | ½ | |
| | | Adjusted total income | 1 | |
| | | 25% of adjusted total income | ½ | |
| | | | | 3 |
| | (ii) | Loss relievable in 2014/15 | | 1 |
| (c) | | Trading profits | 1 | |
| | | Capital allowances | | |
| | | y/e 31.3.14 | | |
| | | WDV c/f | ½ | |
| | | WDA | ½ | |
| | | p/e 31.5.14 | | |
| | | Acquisition | ½ | |
| | | AIA | 1½ | |
| | | WDA | 1 | |
| | | | | 5 |
| | | | | 15 |

(a) **Dominic**

(i) The cash basis can be used by Dominic because he is carrying on an unincorporated business whose receipts for the tax year do not exceed the value added tax (VAT) registration threshold (currently £79,000).

(ii) **Dominic – taxable trading profit for the year ended 5 April 2014**

| | £ | £ |
|---|---|---|
| Receipts £(65,000 – 3,000) | | 62,000 |
| Less: Fixed rate mileage expense | | |
| 10,000 × 45p | 4,500 | |
| 2,000 × 25p | 500 | |
| | | (5,000) |
| Exercise equipment | | (6,000) |
| Expenses paid £(8,200 – 200) | | (8,000) |
| Taxable trading profit | | 43,000 |

*Tutorial notes*

1   Receipts and expenses are computed on the actual amounts received and paid during the period of account.

2   Fixed rate mileage expense is only given for business mileage which is (16,000 – 4,000) = 12,000 miles.

3   The cost of the exercise equipment is allowable under the cash basis as there is no distinction between revenue and capital expenditure for plant and machinery.

(b) (i) **Katie – taxable income 2013/14**

| | Non-savings income £ |
|---|---|
| Employment income/total income | 300,000 |
| Less: loss relief against general income (W) | (67,500) |
| Net income | 232,500 |
| Less: personal allowance | |
| (adjusted net income clearly exceeds £118,880) | (0) |
| Taxable income | 232,500 |

*Working*

The maximum loss relief against general income for 2013/14 is the higher of £50,000 and 25% of adjusted total income for that tax year.

Adjusted total income is calculated as follows:

|  | £ |
|---|---|
| Total income | 300,000 |
| Less: personal pension contributions | (30,000) |
| Adjusted total income | 270,000 |
|  |  |
| 25% of adjusted total income | 67,500 |

(ii) The remainder of the loss is £(230,000 − 67,500) = £162,500.

However, only £110,000 of the loss can be carried forward and relieved in the tax year 2014/15 as it is limited to the profits of the same trade.

(c) **Opal Ltd**

**Taxable total profits for the accounting periods ended 31 March 2014 and 31 May 2014**

|  | Year ended 31 March 2014 £ | Period ended 31 May 2014 £ |
|---|---|---|
| Trading profit 12:2 | 372,000 | 62,000 |
| Less: capital allowance (W) | (11,160) | (44,213) |
| Taxable total profits | 360,840 | 17,787 |

*Working*

Capital allowances

|  | AIA £ | Main pool £ | Allowances £ |
|---|---|---|---|
| *Year ended 31 March 2014* |  |  |  |
| WDV brought forward |  | 62,000 |  |
| WDA @ 18% |  | (11,160) | 11,160 |
| WDV brought forward |  | 50,840 |  |
| *Period ended 31 May 2014* |  |  |  |
| *Addition qualifying for AIA* |  |  |  |
| Machinery | 75,700 |  |  |
| Less: AIA £250,000 × 2/12 | (41,667) |  | 41,667 |
| Balance to main pool | 34,033 | 34,033 |  |
|  |  | 84,873 |  |
| WDA @ 18% × 2/12 |  | (2,546) | 2,546 |
| WDV carried forward |  | 82,327 |  |
| Allowances |  |  | 44,213 |

# 5 Pere Jones and Phil Jones

**Text references.** Inheritance tax is dealt with in Chapter 18. Property income is covered in Chapter 6 and the income tax computation in Chapter 2. Chargeable gains and the computation of capital gains tax are in Chapter 13. The points on distinguishing between revenue and capital expenditure are covered in Chapter 7.

**Top tips.** You don't need to know names of tax cases in the F6 exam, but you are expected to know, and be able to apply, the principles decided, as in part (b) here.

**Easy marks.** There were easy marks in part (a)(ii) for stating that the donee is responsible for IHT on a potentially exempt transfer and also the due date of payment.

**Examiner's comments.** The first requirement of part (a) was generally very well answered, with many candidates achieving maximum marks. The only aspect that consistently caused problems was taper relief, with either the incorrect rate being used or relief being given at the wrong point in the computation. The second requirement of part (a) was often not so well answered, with a number of candidates not being able to provide the correct due date. There were again many sound answers to part (b). Obviously, those candidates that included every item of income and expenditure in both the income tax and the capital gains tax computations could not expect to achieve many marks.

## Marking scheme

|  |  |  |  | Marks |
|---|---|---|---:|---:|
| (a) | (i) | Lifetime gift | | |
| | | Marriage exemption | 1 | |
| | | Annual exemption – current year | ½ | |
| | | Annual exemption – brought forward | ½ | |
| | | Potentially exempt transfer | ½ | |
| | | IHT @ 0% | ½ | |
| | | IHT @ 40% | ½ | |
| | | Taper relief | 1 | |
| | | Death estate | | |
| | | Spouse exemption | 1 | |
| | | IHT @ 40% | ½ | |
| | | | | 6 |
| | (ii) | Donee pays tax on PET | 1 | |
| | | Due date | 1 | |
| | | | | 2 |
| (b) | | Income tax computation | | |
| | | Rent receivable | ½ | |
| | | Repairs | ½ | |
| | | Insurance | ½ | |
| | | Personal allowance | ½ | |
| | | Income tax @ 20% | ½ | |
| | | Capital gains tax computation | | |
| | | Disposal proceeds | ½ | |
| | | Cost | 1 | |
| | | Enhancement | 1 | |
| | | Disposal costs | ½ | |
| | | Annual exempt amount | ½ | |
| | | Capital gains tax @ 18% | ½ | |
| | | Capital gains tax @ 28% | ½ | |
| | | | | 7 |
| | | | | 15 |

(a) **Pere Jones**

(i) Inheritance tax (IHT) arising on death

*Lifetime transfer 23 August 2008*

|  | £ |
|---|---|
| Gift | 420,000 |
| Less: marriage exemption | (5,000) |
| annual exemption 2008/09 | (3,000) |
| annual exemption 2007/08 b/f | (3,000) |
| Potentially exempt transfer | 409,000 |
| *IHT* |  |
| £325,000 @ 0% | 0 |
| £84,000 @ 40% | 33,600 |
| £409,000 |  |
| Less: taper relief (5 to 6 years @ 60%) | (20,160) |
| IHT payable | 13,440 |

*Tutorial note*

The potentially exempt transfer becomes chargeable as a result of Pere dying within seven years of making it.

Death estate

|  | £ |
|---|---|
| Value of estate | 880,000 |
| Less: spouse exemption £880,000/2 | (440,000) |
| Chargeable estate | 440,000 |
|  |  |
| IHT on £440,000 @ 40% | 176,000 |

(ii) Phil Jones, the donee will be responsible for paying the inheritance liability of £13,440 arising from the gift of the house.

The due date is 30 September 2014, being six months after the end of the month in which the donor died.

(b) **Phil Jones**

**Income tax computation 2013/14**

|  | £ |
|---|---|
| Property business income | 23,000 |
| Rent receivable |  |
| Less: repairs | (2,800) |
| insurance | (2,300) |
| Net income | 17,900 |
| Less: personal allowance | (9,440) |
| Taxable income | 8,460 |
|  |  |
| Income tax on £8,460 @ 20% | 1,692 |

**Capital gains tax computation 2013/14**

|  | £ |
|---|---|
| Disposal proceeds | 504,000 |
| Less: cost | (420,000) |
|     enhancement expenditure | (5,300) |
|     disposal costs | (8,600) |
| Gain | 70,100 |
| Less: annual exempt amount | (10,900) |
| Taxable gain | 59,200 |
|  |  |
| CGT on £23,550 (32,010 – 8,460) @ 18% | 4,239 |
| CGT on £35,650 (59,200 – 23,550) @ 28% | 9,982 |
|  | 14,221 |

*Tutorial note*

The cost of replacing the property's chimney is revenue expenditure because the chimney is a subsidiary part of the house (see *Samuel Jones & Co v CIR 1951*). The cost of the new boundary wall is capital expenditure as the wall is a separate, distinct, entity (see *Brown v Burnley Football and Athletic Club 1980*).

# ACCA

# Paper F6

# Taxation (United Kingdom)

# Mock Examination 3

# (December 2013 paper)

| Question Paper | |
|---|---|
| Time allowed | |
| Reading and Planning | 15 minutes |
| Writing | 3 hours |
| **ALL FIVE questions are compulsory and MUST be attempted.** | |

During reading and planning time only the question paper may be annotated.

**DO NOT OPEN THIS PAPER UNTIL YOU ARE READY TO START UNDER EXAMINATION CONDITIONS**

# ALL FIVE questions are compulsory and MUST be attempted

# 1 Richard Feast (TX 12/13)

(a) On 6 April 2013, Richard Feast, born in 1971, commenced in self-employment, running a restaurant. Richard's statement of profit or loss for the year ended 5 April 2014 is as follows:

|  | Note | £ | £ |
|---|---|---|---|
| Gross profit |  |  | 73,440 |
| Expenses |  |  |  |
| Motor expenses | 1 | 7,660 |  |
| Property expenses | 2 | 16,200 |  |
| Repairs and renewals | 3 | 6,420 |  |
| Other expenses | 4 | 10,960 |  |
|  |  |  | (41,240) |
| Net profit |  |  | 32,200 |

*Note 1 – Motor expenses*

Motor expenses are as follows:

|  | £ |
|---|---|
| Cost of running Richard's motor car | 4,710 |
| Cost of running a motor car used by the restaurant's chef | 2,670 |
| Parking fines incurred by Richard | 280 |
|  | 7,660 |

Richard's motor car is used 70% for private journeys and the chef's motor car is used 20% for private journeys.

*Note 2 – Property expenses*

Richard lives in an apartment which is situated above the restaurant, and one-fifth of the total property expenses of £16,200 relate to this apartment.

*Note 3 – Repairs and renewals*

Repairs and renewals are as follows:

|  | £ |
|---|---|
| Decorating the restaurant | 5,100 |
| Decoration the apartment | 1,320 |
|  | 6,420 |

The property was in a useable state when it was purchased.

*Note 4 – Other expenses*

The figure of £10,960 for other expenses includes legal fees of £2,590 in connection with the purchase of the restaurant property. The remaining expenses are all allowable.

**Additional information**

*Plant and machinery*

The following motor cars were purchased during the year ended 5 April 2014:

|  | Date of purchase | Cost | $CO_2$ emission rate |
|---|---|---|---|
|  |  | £ |  |
| Motor car [1] | 6 April 2013 | 14,000 | 104 grams per kilometre |
| Motor car [2] | 6 April 2013 | 16,800 | 118 grams per kilometre |

Motor car [1] is used by Richard and motor car [2] is used by the restaurant's chef.

*Required*

Calculate Richard Feast's tax adjusted trading profit for the year ended 5 April 2014.

*Notes:*

1.  Your computation should commence with the net profit figure of £32,200, and should list all of the items referred to in notes (1) to (4), indicating by the use of zero (0) any items which do not require adjustment.

2.  In answering this part of the question you are not expected to take account of any of the information provided in parts (b), (c) or (d) below. **(7 marks)**

(b)  Richard had three employees working for him in his restaurant during the tax year 2013/14 as follows:

(1)  A chef who was employed throughout the tax year 2013/14 on a gross annual salary of £46,000. The chef was provided with a petrol powered motor car (see the plant and machinery information in part (a) above) throughout the tax year. The list price of the motor car is the same as its cost. Richard did not provide any fuel for private journeys.

(2)  A part-time waitress who was employed for 20 hours per week throughout the tax year 2013/14 on a gross annual salary of £7,600.

(3)  An assistant chef who was employed for eight months from 6 August 2013 to 5 April 2014 on a gross monthly salary of £2,200.

*Required*

Calculate the employers' class 1 and class 1A national insurance contributions which Richard Feast would have incurred in respect of his employees' earnings and benefit for the tax year 2013/14.

*Note:* you are not expected to calculate the national insurance contributions suffered by the employees or by Richard in respect of his self-employment. **(6 marks)**

(c)  Richard has not previously filed a self-assessment tax return, and therefore wants to know when he will have to file his return for the tax year 2013/14. He is not sure whether to file a paper tax return or to file the return online.

As this will be his first self-assessment tax return, Richard is concerned that HM Revenue and Customs might carry out a compliance check.

*Required*

(i)  Advise Richard Feast of the latest dates by which his self-assessment tax return for the tax year 2013/14 should be filed in order to avoid a penalty. **(2 marks)**

(ii)  State the period during which HM Revenue and Customs will have to notify Richard Feast if they intend to carry out a compliance check in respect of his self-assessment tax return for the tax year 2013/14, and the possible reasons why such a check would be made.

*Note:* you should assume that Richard will file his tax return by the filing date. **(3 marks)**

(d)  Richard's sales since the commencement of trading on 6 April 2013 have been as follows:

| | |
|---|---|
| April to July 2013 | £10,500 per month |
| August to November 2013 | £14,000 per month |
| December 2013 to March 2014 | £21,500 per month |

These figures are stated exclusive of value added tax (VAT). Richard's sales are all standard rated.

As a trainee Chartered Certified Accountant you have advised Richard in writing that he should be registered for VAT, but he has refused to register because he thinks his net profit is insufficient to cover the additional cost which would be incurred.

*Required*

(i)   Explain from what date Richard Feast was required to be compulsorily registered for value added tax (VAT) and the VAT implications of continuing to trade after this date without registering.

*Note:* you are not expected to explain the VAT penalties arising from late VAT registration. **(4 marks)**

(ii)  Briefly explain from an ethical viewpoint the issues you, as a trainee Chartered Certified Accountant, should consider in order for your firm to deal with Richard Feast's refusal to register for VAT.

**(2 marks)**

(iii) State the circumstances in which a trader can issue a simplified (or less detailed) VAT invoice, when such an invoice should be issued, and FIVE pieces of information which such an invoice must show where the supply is entirely standard rated. **(4 marks)**

(iv)  Explain how and when VAT registered businesses have to submit their quarterly VAT returns and pay any related VAT liability.

*Note:* you are not expected to cover annual VAT returns, the election for monthly returns or substantial traders. **(2 marks)**

**(Total = 30 marks)**

# 2 Softapp Ltd (TX 12/13)

Softapp Ltd is a software developer. The company's summarised statement of profit or loss for the year ended 31 March 2014 is as follows:

| | Note | £ |
|---|---|---|
| Operating profit | 1 | 770,553 |
| *Other income* | | |
| Income from property | 2 | 36,700 |
| Loan interest receivable | 3 | 8,100 |
| Profit on disposal of shares | 4 | 64,900 |
| *Finance costs* | | |
| Interest payable | 5 | (67,200) |
| Profit before taxation | | 813,053 |

*Note 1 – Operating profit*

Depreciation of £10,170 and amortisation of leasehold property of £2,500 have been deducted in arriving at the operating profit of £770,553.

*Note 2 – Income from property*

Since 1 November 2013, Softapp Ltd has let out one floor of a freehold office building which is surplus to requirements. The income from property figure of £36,700 is made up of the following income and expenditure:

| Date received/paid | | £ |
|---|---|---|
| 23 October 2013 | Advertising for tenants | (600) |
| 25 October 2013 | Security deposit of two months rent | 10,400 |
| 25 October 2013 | Rent for the quarter ended 31 January 2014 | 15,600 |
| 1 November 2013 | Insurance for the year ended 31 October 2014 | (1,200) |
| 2 February 2014 | Rent for the quarter ended 30 April 2014 | 15,600 |
| 20 March 2014 | Repairs following a flood | (12,800) |
| 4 April 2014 | Insurance claim in respect of the flood damage | 9,700 |
| | | 36,700 |

*Note 3 – Loan interest receivable*

The loan was made for non-trading purposes on 1 July 2013. Loan interest of £5,600 was received on 31 December 2013, and interest of £2,500 was accrued at 31 March 2014.

*Note 4 – Profit on disposal of shares*

The profit on disposal of shares is in respect of the sale of Softapp Ltd's entire (2%) shareholding in Networked plc on 28 February 2014 for proceeds of £94,900. The shares were acquired on 15 July 2010 at a cost of £30,000. The RPI for July 2010 was 223.6 and the RPI for February 2014 was 255.3.

*Note 5 – Interest payable*

The interest payable is in respect of the company's 4% loan stock. Interest of £33,600 was paid on 30 September 2013 and again on 31 March 2014. The loan stock was used to finance the company's trading activities.

**Additional information**

*Leasehold property*

On 1 January 2014, Softapp Ltd acquired a leasehold office building, paying a premium of £100,000 for the grant of a ten-year lease. The office building was used for business purposes by Softapp Ltd throughout the period 1 January to 31 March 2014.

*Plant and machinery*

The tax written down value of Softapp Ltd's plant and machinery as at 1 April 2013 was nil.

On 1 September 2013, Softapp Ltd purchased computer equipment at a cost of £225,000.

During October 2013 Softapp Ltd had an extension constructed adjacent to its existing freehold office building, which is used by the company's employees as a staff room . The total cost of £100,000 is made up as follows:

|                                    | £       |
|------------------------------------|---------|
| *Integral to building*             |         |
| Building costs of extension        | 61,000  |
| Heating system                     | 3,600   |
| Ventilation system                 | 4,600   |
| *Not integral to building*         |         |
| Furniture and furnishings          | 29,400  |
| Refrigerator and microwave cooker  | 1,400   |
|                                    | 100,000 |

The full annual investment allowance of £250,000 is available to Softapp Ltd.

*Subsidiary company*

Softapp Ltd owns 100% of the ordinary share capital of Byte-Size Ltd. On 4 March 2014, Byte-Size Ltd disposed of its entire (1%) shareholding in Cloud Ltd, and this resulted in a capital loss of £48,200. For the year ended 31 March 2014, Byte-Size Ltd made no other disposals and will pay corporation tax at the small profits rate of 20%.

*Required*

(a)    Calculate Softapp Ltd's corporation tax liability for the year ended 31 March 2014.

     *Notes:*

     1.     Your computation should commence with the operating profit figure of £770,553.

     2.     In answering this part of the question, you should assume that no election is made between Softapp Ltd and Byte-Size Ltd in respect of chargeable gains. **(19 marks)**

(b)    State the due date for filing of Softapp Ltd's self assessment corporation tax return for the year ended 31 March 2014 and the penalty that would be payable if the return is filed four months after the due date. Softapp Ltd has always submitted its returns on time for previous accounting periods.

**(2 marks)**

(c)    Advise Softapp Ltd as to the joint election it should make with Byte-Size Ltd, regarding their respective chargeable gain and capital loss, including the date by which the election must be made, and explain how such an election will reduce the group's overall corporation tax liability for the year ended 31 March 2014.

     *Note:* you are not expected to perform any calculations. **(4 marks)**

**(Total = 25 marks)**

*BPP note*

This question has been slightly altered by BPP from that originally set, due to syllabus changes for the exams in 2014. It has been reviewed by the F6 examiner.

# 3 Delroy, Marlon and Leroy (TX 12/13)

(a) On 10 June 2013, Delroy made a gift of 25,000 £1 ordinary shares in Dub Ltd, an unquoted trading company, to his son, Grant. The market value of the shares on that date was £240,000. Delroy had subscribed for the 25,000 shares in Dub Ltd at par on 1 July 2003. Delroy and Grant have elected to hold over the gain as a gift of a business asset.

Grant sold the 25,000 shares in Dub Ltd on 18 September 2013 for £240,000.

Dub Ltd has a share capital of 100,000 £1 ordinary shares. Delroy was the sales director of the company from its incorporation on 1 July 2003 until 10 June 2013. Grant has never been an employee or a director of Dub Ltd.

For the tax year 2013/14 Delroy and Grant are both higher rate taxpayers. Neither of them has made any other disposals of assets during the year.

*Required*

(i) Calculate Grant's capital gains tax liability for the tax year 2013/14. **(3 marks)**

(ii) Explain why it would have been beneficial for capital gains tax purposes if Delroy had instead sold the 25,000 shares in Dub Ltd himself for £240,000 on 10 June 2013, and then gifted the cash proceeds to Grant. **(2 marks)**

(b) On 12 February 2014, Marlon sold a house for £497,000, which he had owned individually. The house had been purchased on 22 October 1998 for £146,000. Marlon incurred legal fees of £2,900 in connection with the purchase of the house, and legal fees of £3,700 in connection with the disposal.

Throughout the period of ownership the house was occupied by Marlon and his wife, Alvita, as their main residence. One-third of the house was always used exclusively for business purposes by the couple. Entrepreneurs' relief is not available in respect of this disposal.

For the tax year 2013/14 Marlon is a higher rate taxpayer, but Alvita did not have any taxable income. Neither of them has made any other disposals of assets during the year.

*Required*

(i) Calculate Marlon's chargeable gain for the tax year 2013/14. **(3 marks)**

(ii) Calculate the amount of capital gains tax which could have been saved if Marlon had transferred 50% ownership of the house to Alvita prior to its disposal. **(2 marks)**

(c) On 2 April 2014, Leroy sold 12,000 £1 ordinary shares in Jerk-Chic plc for £83,400. He has had the following transactions in the shares of the company:

| | |
|---|---|
| 1 March 2005 | Purchased 20,000 shares for £19,800 |
| 20 July 2009 | Purchased 8,000 shares for £27,800 |
| 23 October 2013 | Made a gift of 4,000 shares |

The gift of 4,000 shares on 23 October 2013 was to Leroy's daughter. On that date the shares were quoted on the Stock Exchange at £7.80–£8.20. There were no recorded bargains. Holdover relief is not available in respect of this disposal.

Neither disposal of Jerk-Chic plc shares during the tax year 2013/14 qualifies for entrepreneurs' relief.

For the tax year 2013/14 Leroy is a higher rate taxpayer, and will remain so for the tax year 2014/15. Leroy regularly makes disposals of other investments, so no annual exempt amount is available for either of the tax years 2013/14 or 2014/15.

*Required*

(i) Calculate the chargeable gains arising from Leroy's disposals of Jerk-Chic plc shares during the tax year 2013/14. **(4 marks)**

(ii) State why it would have been beneficial if Leroy had delayed the sale of the 12,000 shares in Jerk-Chic plc until 6 April 2014. **(1 mark)**

**(Total = 15 marks)**

# 4 Fang, Hong, Kang, Ling and Ming (TX 12/13)

(a) Fang commenced self-employment on 1 August 2011. She has a trading profit of £45,960 for the year ended 31 July 2012, and a trading profit of £39,360 for the year ended 31 July 2013.

*Required*

(i) Calculate the amount of trading profit which will have been assessed on Fang for each of the tax years 2011/12, 2012/13 and 2013/14, and state the amount of any overlap profit. **(3 marks)**

(ii) Explain how Fang would have obtained relief for trading expenditure incurred prior to 1 August 2011 and for computer equipment which Fang already owned which was brought into business use on 1 August 2011. **(2 marks)**

(b) Hong has been in self-employment since 2002, preparing accounts to 5 April. For the year ended 5 April 2014 she made a trading loss of £45,800, and has claimed this against her total income and chargeable gain for the tax year 2012/13.

For the year ended 5 April 2013 Hong made a trading profit of £29,700. She also has a property business profit of £3,900 for the tax year 2012/13. Hong has an unused trading loss of £2,600 brought forward from the tax year 2011/12.

During the tax year 2012/13 Hong disposed of an investment property and this resulted in a chargeable gain (before the annual exempt amount) of £17,800. Hong has unused capital losses of £6,200 brought forward from the tax year 2010/11.

*Required*

After taking account of the loss relief claims made, calculate Hong's taxable income and taxable gain for the tax year 2012/13, and state the amount of any trading loss carried forward.

*Note:* you should assume that the tax allowances for the tax year 2013/14 apply throughout. **(5 marks)**

(c) Kang, Ling and Ming have been in partnership since 2004, preparing accounts to 30 June. Ming left the partnership on 31 October 2012. Profits have always been shared equally.

The partnership had a trading profit of £148,800 for the year ended 30 June 2012, and a profit of £136,800 for the year ended 30 June 2013. Each partner has unused overlap profits brought forward of £29,400.

*Required*

Calculate the trading income assessments of Kang, Ling and Ming for each of the tax years 2012/13 and 2013/14. **(5 marks)**

**(Total = 15 marks)**

# 5 Afiya

Afiya died on 29 November 2013. She had made the following gifts during her lifetime:

(1)     On 13 April 2012, Afiya made a cash gift of £32,000 to her husband.

(2)     On 2 May 2012, Afiya made cash gifts to her three nieces. The first niece was given £100, the second niece was given £200, and the third niece was given £400.

(3)     On 14 September 2012, Afiya made a gift of 6,500 £1 ordinary shares in Cassava Ltd, an unquoted investment company, to her daughter.

Before the transfer Afiya owned 8,000 shares out of Cassava Ltd's issued share capital of 10,000 £1 ordinary shares. On 14 September 2012, Cassava Ltd's shares were worth £3 each for a holding of 15%, £7 each for a holding of 65%, and £8 each for a holding of 80%.

(4)     On 27 January 2013, Afiya made a cash gift of £400,000 to a trust. Afiya paid the inheritance tax arising from this gift.

On 29 November 2013, Afiya's estate was valued at £620,000. Under the terms of her will Afiya left £150,000 to her husband, a specific legacy of £40,000 to her sister, and the residue of the estate to her children.

The nil rate band for the tax year 2012/13 is £325,000.

*Required*

(a)     Calculate the inheritance tax which will be payable as a result of Afiya's death.          **(12 marks)**

(b)     State the due dates of payment for the inheritance tax arising from the gift made to the trust on 27 January 2013.

*Note:* your answer should cover both the lifetime inheritance tax paid and the additional tax payable as a result of Afiya's death.          **(2 marks)**

(c)     Calculate the amount of the inheritance which will be received by Afiya's children.          **(1 mark)**

**(Total = 15 marks)**

# Answers

DO NOT TURN THIS PAGE UNTIL YOU HAVE
COMPLETED THE MOCK EXAM

# A plan of attack

What's the worst thing you could be doing right now if this was the actual exam paper? Sharpening your pencil? Wondering how to celebrate the end of the exam in about 3 hours time? Panicking, flapping and generally getting in a right old state?

Well, they're all pretty bad, so turn back to the paper and let's sort out a **plan of attack**!

## First things first

You have fifteen minutes of reading time. Spend this looking carefully through the questions and deciding the order in which you will attempt them. As a general rule you should attempt the questions that you find easiest first and leave the hardest until last. Depending on how confident you are we recommend that you follow one of the following two options:

## Option 1 (if you're thinking 'Help!')

If you're a bit worried about the paper, do the questions in the order of how well you think you can answer them. You may find the shorter questions less daunting than the longer questions. Alternatively, you may feel better prepared for questions 1 and 2 and wish to start there.

- Question 1 covers a number of taxes: income tax, national insurance and value added tax. It is important to attempt all parts of the question.

- Question 2 is a corporation tax question. There is a lot of information to process in this question, but don't panic! Work through each item carefully and mark off each one to ensure you don't miss one out.

- Question 3 is on capital gains tax for individuals. There are a number of straightforward computations required in this question as well as an appreciation of basic CGT planning.

- Question 4 is about aspects of business income tax including the basis of assessment and loss relief. There are some easy marks in this question but the extension of loss relief to capital gains is a bit more difficult.

- Question 5 is a comprehensive inheritance tax question. It is vital that you deal with each transfer in a methodical manner.

Lastly, what you mustn't forget is that you have to **answer all of the questions in the paper. They are all compulsory**. Do not miss out any questions or you will seriously affect your chance of passing the exam.

## Option 2 (if you're thinking 'It's a doddle')

It never pays to be over confident but if you're reasonably confident about the exam then it is best to work through the questions sequentially starting with question 1.

### No matter how many times we remind you....

Always, always **allocate your time** according to the marks for the question in total and then according to the parts of the question. And **always, always follow the requirements** exactly.

### You've got spare time at the end of the exam.....?

If you have allocated your time properly then you **shouldn't have time on your hands** at the end of the exam. But if you find yourself with five or ten minutes to spare, check over your work to make sure that there are no silly arithmetical errors.

### Forget about it!

And don't worry if you found the paper difficult. More than likely other candidates did too. If this were the real thing you would need to **forget** the exam the minute you leave the exam hall and **think about the next one**. Or, if it's the last one, **celebrate!**

# 1 Richard Feast

**Text references.** The adjustment of profit is covered in Chapter 7 and capital allowances in Chapter 8. National insurance contributions are the subject of Chapter 12. Self assessment and compliance checks are dealt with in Chapter 17. Value added tax registration and payment of VAT will be found in Chapter 25 and VAT invoices in Chapter 26. Ethical considerations are covered in Chapter 1.

**Top tips.** Remember to use the standard pro-forma computations in part (a) for adjustment of profit and capital allowances.

**Easy marks.** The adjustment of profit in part (a) should have yielded good marks. The national insurance computations in part (b) were not too difficult. The due dates for filing returns in part (c) should have been well known. In part (d), the calculation of the date for registration for VAT was straightforward.

## Marking scheme

|  |  |  | Marks |
|---|---|---|---|
| (a) | *Adjustment of profit* | | |
| | Motor expenses: Richard | 1 | |
| | Motor expenses: chef | ½ | |
| | Parking fines | ½ | |
| | Property expenses | 1 | |
| | Decorating: restaurant | ½ | |
| | Decorating: apartment | ½ | |
| | Other expenses | ½ | |
| | Capital allowances: motor car [1] addition | ½ | |
| | motor car [2] addition | ½ | |
| | motor car [2] WDA | ½ | |
| | motor car [1] WDA | 1 | |
| | | | 7 |
| (b) | *Chef* | | |
| | Class 1 | 1 | |
| | Class 1A: car benefit percentage | 1 | |
| | car benefit | ½ | |
| | NICs | ½ | |
| | *Waitress* | | |
| | No NICs | ½ | |
| | *Assistant chef* | | |
| | Monthly secondary threshold | 1 | |
| | NICs | 1½ | |
| | | | 6 |
| (c) | (i) Paper return | 1 | |
| | Electronic return | 1 | |
| | | | 2 |
| | (ii) Compliance check notification date | 1 | |
| | Random basis | 1 | |
| | Other reasons | 1 | |
| | | | 3 |

(d) (i)
| | |
|---|---|
| Compulsory registration limit | ½ |
| Date registration required | 1½ |
| Date registration effective | 1 |
| Consequences of non-registration | 1 |
| | 4 |

(ii)
| | |
|---|---|
| Honest and integrity | ½ |
| Cease to act and inform HMRC | 1 |
| Money laundering notification | ½ |
| | 2 |

(iii)
| | |
|---|---|
| Simplified invoice | 1 |
| Request for invoice | ½ |
| Details on invoice: ½ mark per item to maximum | 2½ |
| | 4 |

(iv)
| | |
|---|---|
| Online filing and electronic payment | 1 |
| Due date | 1 |
| | 2 |
| | 30 |

---

(a) **Richard Feast – Trading profit for the year ended 5 April 2014**

| | £ |
|---|---|
| Net profit per accounts | 32,200 |
| Add: motor expenses – Richard £4,710 × 70% (private use) | 3,297 |
| motor expenses – Chef | 0 |
| parking fines for Richard | 280 |
| property expenses – apartment £16,200 × 1/5 (private use) | 3,240 |
| decorating – restaurant | 0 |
| decorating – apartment (private use) | 1,320 |
| other expenses – legal fees (capital) | 2,590 |
| | 42,927 |
| Less: capital allowances (W) | (3,780) |
| Tax adjusted trading profit | 39,147 |

*Tutorial note*

The redecoration of the restaurant is a trading expense since the property was in a useable state when it was purchased (*Odeon Associated Theatres Ltd v Jones 1971*).

*Working – capital allowances*

| Additions | Main pool £ | Private use motor car £ | Allowances £ |
|---|---|---|---|
| Motor car [1] | | 14,000 | |
| Motor car [2] | 16,800 | | |
| WDA @ 18% | (3,024) | | 3,024 |
| WDA @ 18% | | (2,520) × 30% | 756 |
| TWDV c/f | 13,776 | 11,480 | |
| Allowances | | | 3,780 |

*Tutorial note*

Both motor cars have $CO_2$ emissions between 96 and 130 grams per kilometre, and therefore qualify for writing down allowances at the rate of 18%. The private use of a motor car by an employee is irrelevant, since such usage will be assessed on the employee as a benefit.

(b) **Richard Feast – National insurance contributions (NIC) as employer**

*Chef*
Employer's Class 1 NIC for 2013/14 £(46,000 – 7,696) = £38,304 × 13.8%                     £5,286

Employer's Class 1A NIC for 2013/14  £2,520 (W) × 13.8%                     £348

*Working – Car benefit*

Amount by which $CO_2$ emissions exceed base level: (115 (rounded down) – 95) = 20 ÷ 5 = 4.
Car benefit percentage is 4 + 11 = 15%.
Car benefit is £16,800 (list price) × 15% = £2,520.

*Waitress*

No NICs were payable as the waitress earned less than the secondary earnings threshold of £7,696.

*Assistant chef*
Employer's Class 1 NIC for 2013/14 £(2,200 – 641(W)) = £1,559 × 13.8% × 8                     £1,721

*Working – Monthly secondary threshold*

£7,696 ÷ 12 = £641

*Tutorial note*

The alternative approach using the annual earnings threshold and then taking 8/12ths of an annual NIC figure is acceptable.

(c)    (i)    **Richard Feast – Self-assessment**

Unless the return is issued late, the latest date that Richard can file a paper self-assessment tax return for 2013/14 is 31 October 2014.

However, again unless the return is issued late, he has until 31 January 2015 to file his self-assessment tax return for 2013/14 online.

(ii)    **Richard Feast – Compliance checks**

If HM Revenue and Customs intend to carry out a compliance check enquiry into Richard's 2013/14 tax return, it will have to notify him by the first anniversary of the actual filing date.

HM Revenue and Customs have the right to carry out a compliance check enquiry as regards the completeness and accuracy of any return and some returns are selected for a compliance check enquiry at random.

Other returns are selected for a particular reason, for example, if HM Revenue and Customs believes that there has been an underpayment of tax due to the taxpayer's failure to comply with tax legislation.

(d)    **Richard Feast – Value added tax (VAT)**

(i)    Richard would have been liable to compulsory VAT registration when his taxable supplies during any 12-month period exceeded £79,000.

This happened on 31 October 2013 when taxable supplies were £([10,500 × 4]+ [14,000 × 3]) = £84,000.

Registration is required from the end of the month following the month in which the limit is exceeded, so Richard should have been registered from 1 December 2013.

If Richard continued to trade after 1 December 2013 without registering for VAT, he would still have to pay the VAT due from the time he should have been registered.

(ii) The matter is one of professional judgement and a trainee Chartered Certified Accountant would be expected to act honestly and with integrity.

If Richard refuses to register for VAT, you should cease to act for him. You must notify HM Revenue and Customs that you no longer act for Richard although you should not provide any reason for this.

You would also be obliged to make a report under the money laundering regulations.

(iii) A simplified (or less detailed) VAT invoice can be issued by a trader where the VAT inclusive total of the invoice is less than £250.

Such an invoice should be issued when a customer requests a VAT invoice.

A simplified VAT invoice must show the following information:

- The supplier's name and address
- The supplier's registration number
- The date of the supply
- A description of the goods or services supplied
- The rate of VAT chargeable
- The total amount chargeable including VAT

(iv) VAT registered businesses must file their VAT returns online and make payments electronically.

The time limit for submission and payment is one month plus seven days after the end of the VAT quarter. For example, a business which has a VAT quarter ending 31 March 2014 must file its VAT return and pay the VAT due by 7 May 2014.

# 2 Softapp Ltd

**Text references.** The computation of taxable total profits is covered in Chapter 19 and the corporation tax liability in Chapter 20. Corporation tax returns are dealt with in Chapter 24. Capital gains groups are covered in Chapter 23.

**Top tips.** Watch out for the accruals basis in the computation of interest and property business income.

**Easy marks.** There were some easy marks for the calculation of capital allowances and property business income.

## Marking scheme

|  |  |  | Marks |
|---|---|---|---|
| (a) | Operating profit | ½ | |
| | Depreciation | ½ | |
| | Amortisation | ½ | |
| | Deduction for lease premium: | premium received | ½ | |
| | | amount not assessed on landlord | 1 | |
| | | deduction for trader | 1½ | |
| | Loan stock interest | 1 | |
| | Capital allowances: | building costs | ½ | |
| | | heating system | ½ | |
| | | ventilation system | ½ | |
| | | AIA on special rate pool expenditure | 1 | |
| | | computer equipment | ½ | |
| | | furniture and furnishings | ½ | |
| | | fridge and cooker | ½ | |
| | | AIA on main rate pool expenditure | ½ | |
| | | WDA | ½ | |
| | | c/f | | 10½ |

|  | b/f | 10½ |
|---|---|---|
| Property business profit: rent received | 1 | |
| security deposit | ½ | |
| advertising | ½ | |
| insurance | 1 | |
| repairs | 1 | |
| Interest income | 1 | |
| Chargeable gain: proceeds | ½ | |
| cost | ½ | |
| indexation allowance | 1 | |
| Corporation tax: main rate | ½ | |
| upper limit | ½ | |
| marginal relief | ½ | |
|  | | 19 |

| (b) | | |
|---|---|---|
| Due date for filing return | 1 | |
| Penalty for filing four months late | 1 | |
|  | | 2 |

| (c) | | |
|---|---|---|
| Election – effect | 1 | |
| Date for election | 1 | |
| Use of loss | 1 | |
| Balance of gain at small profits rate | 1 | |
|  | | 4 |
|  | | 25 |

---

(a) **Softapp Ltd – Corporation tax computation for the year ended 31 March 2014**

|  | £ |
|---|---|
| Operating profit | 770,553 |
| Add: depreciation | 10,170 |
| amortisation | 2,500 |
|  | 783,223 |
| Less: deduction for lease premium (W1) | (2,050) |
| loan stock interest payable (trading loan relationship) | (67,200) |
| capital allowances (W2) | (252,520) |
| Trading profit | 461,453 |
| Property business profit (W3) | 21,800 |
| Interest income (non-trading loan relationships) £(5,600 + 2,500) | 8,100 |
| Chargeable gain (W4) | 60,647 |
| Taxable total profits | 552,000 |

| *Corporation tax* |  |
|---|---|
| £552,000 × 23% | 126,960 |
| Less: marginal relief (W5) | |
| 3/400 × £(750,000 – 552,000) | (1,485) |
| Corporation tax liability | 125,475 |

*Workings*

1 *Deduction for lease premium*

The amount assessed on the landlord is £82,000, calculated as follows:

|  | £ |
|---|---|
| Premium | 100,000 |
| Less: £100,000 × 2% × (10 – 1) | (18,000) |
| Assessable as property business income on landlord | 82,000 |

This is deductible by a business tenant over the life of the lease so the deduction for Softapp Ltd for the year ended 31 March 2014 is £(82,000/10 × 3/12) = £2,050.

2    Capital allowances

| | AIA | Main pool | Special rate pool | Allowances |
|---|---|---|---|---|
| | £ | £ | £ | £ |
| Additions qualifying for AIA | | | | |
| Building costs | 0 | | | |
| Heating system | 3,600 | | | |
| Ventilation system | 4,600 | | | |
| | 8,200 | | | |
| AIA (part) | (8,200) | | | 8,200 |
| Transfer to SR pool | 0 | | 0 | |
| | | | | |
| Computer equipment | 225,000 | | | |
| Furniture and furnishings | 29,400 | | | |
| Fridge and cooker | 1,400 | | | |
| | 255,800 | | | |
| AIA (balance) | (241,800) | | | 241,800 |
| Transfer to main pool | 14,000 | 14,000 | | |
| WDA @ 18% | | (2,520) | | 2,520 |
| TWDVs c/f | | 11,480 | 0 | |
| Allowances | | | | 252,520 |

*Tutorial notes*

1    The expenditure which is integral to the building is special rate pool expenditure.

2    It is beneficial to claim the annual investment allowance of £250,000 against this expenditure in priority to main pool expenditure, as it would otherwise only qualify for writing down allowance at the rate of 8% in the special rate pool.

3    *Property business profit*

| | £ |
|---|---|
| Rent accrued to 31.3.14 | |
| Quarter to 31.1.14 | 15,600 |
| Quarter to 30.4.14 £15,600 × 2/3 | 10,400 |
| Security deposit | 0 |
| | 26,000 |
| Less: advertising | (600) |
| insurance accrued to 31.3.14 £1,200 × 5/12 | (500) |
| repairs £(12,800 − 9,700) | (3,100) |
| Property business profit | 21,800 |

*Tutorial note*

A security deposit, less the cost of making good any damage, is returned to the tenant on the cessation of a letting. It is therefore initially not treated as income.

4    *Chargeable gain*

| | £ |
|---|---|
| Proceeds | 94,900 |
| Less: cost | (30,000) |
| Unindexed gain | 64,900 |
| Less: indexation allowance | |
| $\dfrac{(255.3 - 223.6)}{223.6} \times £30,000$ | (4,253) |
| Indexed gain | 60,647 |

5    *Upper limit for corporation tax*

Softapp Ltd has one associated company, so the upper limit is reduced to
£(1,500,000/2) = <u>£750,000</u>.

(b)    **Softapp Ltd – Corporation tax return filing**

The due date for filing of Softapp Ltd's corporation tax corporation tax return for the year ended
31 March 2014 is 31 March 2015.

The penalty for filing a return between three and six months late is £200.

(c)    **Softapp Ltd – Joint election with Byte-size Ltd**

A joint election should be made so that Byte-Size Ltd is treated as having made Softapp Ltd's chargeable
gain.

The election must be made within two years of the end of the accounting period in which Softapp Ltd made
the disposal ie by 31 March 2016.

This will mean that Byte-Size Ltd's otherwise unused capital loss of £48,200 can be set against Softapp Ltd's
chargeable gain of £60,647.

It may also be beneficial for the balance of the chargeable gain to arise in Byte-Size Ltd if it will be taxed at
the small profits rate of 20%.

*Tutorial note*

The balance of the gain is £(60,647 – 48,200) = £12,447 and this will be taxed at the small profits rate of
20% provided it does not take Byte-Size Ltd's augmented profits over the lower limit of £(300,000/2) =
£150,000.

# 3 Delroy, Marlon and Leroy

**Text references**. Computing chargeable gains and computation of the CGT liability are covered in Chapter 13.
Principal private residence relief is dealt with in Chapter 14. Business reliefs are the subject of Chapter 15. Shares
are covered in Chapter 16.

**Top tips.** Basic CGT planning involves making sure that the annual exempt amount is utilised, ensuring the lowest
possible rate of tax applies, and delaying payment of CGT. All three appeared in this question – can you spot
where?

**Easy marks.** There were some easy marks for basic computation of gains and the share pool.

|  |  |  | Marks |
|---|---|---|---|
| (a) | (i) | Proceeds | ½ |
|  |  | Cost | 1 |
|  |  | Annual exempt amount | ½ |
|  |  | Capital gains tax | 1 |
|  |  |  | 3 |
|  | (ii) | Entrepreneurs' relief | 1 |
|  |  | Rate of CGT | ½ |
|  |  | Cash gift: no CGT consequences | ½ |
|  |  |  | 2 |
| (b) | (i) | Proceeds | ½ |
|  |  | Disposal costs | ½ |
|  |  | Cost | 1 |
|  |  | PPR exemption | 1 |
|  |  |  | 3 |
|  | (ii) | Tax saving: annual exempt amount | 1 |
|  |  | basic rate band | 1 |
|  |  |  | 2 |
| (c) | (i) | Gift: proceeds | 1 |
|  |  | Sale: proceeds | ½ |
|  |  | Share pool: c/f at 20.7.09 | ½ |
|  |  | disposal 23.10.13 | 1 |
|  |  | disposal 2.4.14 | 1 |
|  |  |  | 4 |
|  | (ii) | Delay disposal | 1 |
|  |  |  | 15 |

(a) **Delroy and Grant**

(i) **Grant – Capital gains tax liability 2013/14**

|  | £ |
|---|---|
| *Ordinary shares in Dub Ltd* |  |
| Proceeds | 240,000 |
| Less: cost | (25,000) |
| Gain | 215,000 |
| Less: annual exempt amount | (10,900) |
| Taxable gain | 204,100 |
|  |  |
| CGT: £204,100 × 28% | 57,148 |

*Tutorial notes*

1   The effect of the gift relief election is that Grant effectively took over Delroy's original cost of £25,000.

2   The disposal does not qualify for entrepreneurs' relief as Grant was neither an officer nor an employee of Dub Ltd and, in any case, had only owned the shares for just over three months (the minimum period for the conditions for the relief to be satisfied is one year).

(ii)   Delroy's disposal would have qualified for entrepreneurs' relief because for at least one year prior to the disposal:

- Dub Ltd was Delroy's personal company as he owned at least 5% of the ordinary share capital
- Dub Ltd was a trading company
- Delroy was an officer or employee of Dub Ltd

The rate of capital gains tax payable by Delroy would therefore have been 10%.

There are no capital gains tax implications of a gift of cash.

(b) **Marlon and Alvita**

(i) **Marlon – Chargeable gain 2013/14**

|  | £ |
|---|---:|
| *House* | |
| Proceeds | 497,000 |
| Less: disposal costs | (3,700) |
| Net disposal proceeds | 493,300 |
| Less: cost £(146,000 + 2,900) | (148,900) |
| Gain before PPR relief | 344,400 |
| Less: PPR relief (W) | (229,600) |
| Gain after PPR relief | 114,800 |

*Working*

One-third of Marlon's house was always used exclusively for business purposes, so the principal private residence relief exemption is restricted to £(344,400 × 2/3) = £229,600.

(ii) The capital gains tax saving if 50% ownership of the house had been transferred to Alvita prior to its disposal would have been £6,253, calculated as follows:

|  |  | £ |
|---|---|---:|
| Annual exempt amount | £10,900 @ 28% | 3,052 |
| Basic rate band | £32,010 @ (28 – 18)% | 3,201 |
| Total tax saving | | 6,253 |

*Tutorial notes*

1   The 50% ownership of the house would have been transferred from Marlon to Alvita on a no gain, no loss basis. The effect of this is that 50% of the gain on disposal would accrue to Marlon and 50% to Alvita.

2   Transferring 50% ownership of the house to Alvita prior to its disposal would have enabled her annual exempt amount and basic rate tax band for 2013/14 to be utilised.

(c) **Leroy**

(i) **Leroy – Chargeable gains 2013/14**

|  | £ |
|---|---:|
| *Gift of ordinary shares in Jerk-Chic plc* | |
| Deemed proceeds (market value) (W1) | 31,600 |
| Less: cost (W2) | (6,800) |
| Gain | 24,800 |
| *Sale of ordinary shares in Jerk-Chic plc* | |
| Proceeds | 83,400 |
| Less: cost (W2) | (20,400) |
| Gain | 63,000 |

*Workings*

1   *Market value of gifted shares*

£7.80 + ¼ × £(8.20 – 7.80) = £7.90 × 4,000 = £31,600

2   *Share pool*

|  |  | Number | Cost |
|---|---|---:|---:|
|  |  |  | £ |
| Acquisition | 1.3.05 | 20,000 | 19,800 |
| Acquisition | 20.7.09 | 8,000 | 27,800 |
| c/f |  | 28,000 | 47,600 |

| | | | |
|---|---|---|---|
| Disposal | 23.10.13 | (4,000) | (6,800) |
| c/f | | 24,000 | 40,800 |
| Disposal | 2.4.14 | (12,000) | (20,400) |
| c/f | | 24,000 | 20,400 |

(ii) Delaying the sale of the 12,000 shares in Jerk-Chic plc until 6 April 2014 would have deferred the due date for the related capital gains tax liability from 31 January 2015 to 31 January 2016.

# 4 Fang, Hong, Kang, Ling and Ming

**Text references.** The basis of assessment for sole traders is covered in Chapter 9. Relief for pre-trading expenditure is described in Chapter 7 and capital allowances in Chapter 8. Trading losses are dealt with in Chapter 10. Chapter 11 covers partnerships.

**Top tips.** It is important to identify the relevant tax years when dealing with the basis of assessment, not just whether that the year is 'year 1' or the 'final year'.

**Easy marks.** The calculation of overlap profits in part (a) should have been easy marks as they were the same as the assessable profits in the first year of the trade. In part (b), the calculation of taxable income was straightforward. In part (c), the allocation of profits was not difficult as there were no salaries or interest to deal with, simply profit sharing ratios.

**Marking scheme**

| | | | Marks | |
|---|---|---|---|---|
| (a) | (i) | 2011/12 | 1 | |
| | | 2012/13 | ½ | |
| | | 2013/14 | ½ | |
| | | Overlap profits | 1 | |
| | | | | 3 |
| | (ii) | Pre-trading expenditure | 1 | |
| | | Capital allowances | 1 | |
| | | | | 2 |
| (b) | | Trading profit | ½ | |
| | | Loss relief b/f | ½ | |
| | | Property business profit | ½ | |
| | | Loss relief c/b against general income | ½ | |
| | | Personal allowance | ½ | |
| | | Chargeable gain | ½ | |
| | | Loss relief c/b against chargeable gain | 1 | |
| | | Annual exempt amount | ½ | |
| | | Loss c/f | ½ | |
| | | | | 5 |
| (c) | | Allocation of profits y/e 30.6.12 | ½ | |
| | | Allocation of profits y/e 30.6.13 | 1½ | |
| | | Trading income y/e 30.6.12 for all partners | ½ | |
| | | Trading income p/e 31.10.12 for Ming | 1 | |
| | | Relief for overlap profits | 1 | |
| | | Trading income y/e 30.6.13 for Kang and King | ½ | |
| | | | | 5 |
| | | | | 15 |

(a) **Fang**

(i) **Assessments 2011/12, 2012/13 and 2013/14**

| Tax year | Basis of assessment | £ |
|---|---|---|
| 2011/12 | Actual – 1 August 2011 to 5 April 2012 | |
| | £45,960 × 8/12 | 30,640 |
| 2012/13 | 12 months to accounting date in tax year | |
| | y/e 31 July 2012 | 45,960 |
| 2013/14 | Current year basis | |
| | y/e 31 July 2013 | 39,360 |

In 2012/13 there are overlap profits of £30,640 (the eight-month period from 1 August 2011 to 5 April 2012).

(ii) The trading expenditure will be treated as incurred on 1 August 2011 provided it was incurred within the previous seven years and would have been allowable if the trade had already commenced.

The computer equipment which Fang already owned will be an addition for capital allowances purposes based on its market value at 1 August 2011.

(b) **Hong**

**Taxable income 2012/13**

| | £ |
|---|---|
| Trading profit | 29,700 |
| Less: trading loss brought forward | (2,600) |
| | 27,100 |
| Property business profit | 3,900 |
| | 31,000 |
| Less: trading loss carried back | (31,000) |
| Net income | 0 |
| Less: personal allowance | (0) |
| Taxable income | 0 |

**Taxable gain 2012/13**

| | £ |
|---|---|
| Gain | 17,800 |
| Less: trading loss carried back (W) | (11,600) |
| Net gain | 6,200 |
| Less: annual exempt amount (restricted) | (6,200) |
| Taxable gain | 0 |

*Working*

Loss relief against gains is the lower of:

1 Loss remaining after relief against income £(45,800 – 31,000) = £14,800
2 Net gains ignoring annual exempt amount £(17,800 – 6,200) = £11,600

| | |
|---|---|
| Trading loss carried forward is £(45,800 – 31,000 – 11,600) | £3,200 |

(c) **Kang, Ling and Ming**

**Allocation of profits**

| | Kang £ | Ling £ | Ming £ |
|---|---|---|---|
| *Y/e 30 June 2012* | | | |
| £148,800 × 1/3 | 49,600 | 49,600 | 49,600 |
| *Y/e 30 June 2013* | | | |
| 1 July 2012 to 31 October 2012 | | | |
| £136,800 × 4/12 × 1/3 | 15,200 | 15,200 | 15,200 |
| 1 November 2012 to 30 June 2013 | | | |
| £136,800 × 8/12 × 1/2 | 45,600 | 45,600 | 0 |
| | 60,800 | 60,800 | 15,200 |

**Trading income assessments**

| | Kang £ | Ling £ | Ming £ |
|---|---|---|---|
| *2012/13* | | | |
| Y/e 30 June 2012 | 49,600 | 49,600 | 49,600 |
| P/e 31 October 2012 | | | 15,200 |
| | | | 64,800 |
| Less: overlap profits relief | | | (29,400) |
| | | | 35,400 |
| *2013/14* | | | |
| Y/e 30 June 2013 | 60,800 | 60,800 | |

*Tutorial note*

The cessation rules apply to Ming for 2012/13 since she ceased to be a partner on 31 October 2012.

# 5 Afiya

**Text references**. Inheritance tax is covered in Chapter 18.

**Top tips.** The small gifts exemption only applies for gifts up to £250 per tax year per donee. It does not exempt part of a larger gift.

**Easy marks.** The use of exemptions should have been well known. The due dates for payment were easy marks.

**Marking scheme**

| | | | Marks |
|---|---|---|---|
| (a) | *Lifetime transfers* | | |
| | 13 April 2012 | Exempt transfer to spouse | ½ |
| | 2 May 2012 | Small gifts exemption on gifts to two nieces | ½ |
| | | Transfer to third niece | ½ |
| | | Annual exemption 2012/13 (part) | ½ |
| | 14 September 2012 | Value of shares before transfer | 1 |
| | | Value of shares after transfer | 1 |
| | | Annual exemption 2012/13 (remainder) | 1 |
| | | Annual exemption 2011/12 brought forward | ½ |
| | 27 January 2013 | Nil rate band | ½ |
| | | Balance @ 20/80 | 1 |
| | | c/f | 7 |

|  | | Marks |
|---|---|---|
| | b/f | 7 |

*Additional liabilities arising on death*

| | | |
|---|---|---|
| 14 September 2012 | Potentially exempt transfer now chargeable | 1 |
| 27 January 2013 | Gross chargeable transfer | ½ |
| | Nil rate band | 1 |
| | Balance @ 40% | ½ |
| | Lifetime tax already paid | ½ |

*Death tax*

| | | |
|---|---|---|
| Value of estate | | ½ |
| Spouse exemption | | ½ |
| Charge @ 40% | | ½ |
| | | 12 |

| | | | |
|---|---|---|---|
| (b) | Due date for lifetime tax | 1 | |
| | Due date for additional tax on death | 1 | |
| | | | 2 |
| (c) | Residue of estate | | 1 |
| | | | 15 |

---

(a) **Afiya – Inheritance tax on death**

**Lifetime transfers**

*13 April 2012*

Exempt transfer to spouse.

*2 May 2012*

First and second nieces: exempt transfer (small gifts).

Third niece

| | £ |
|---|---|
| Transfer of value | 400 |
| Less: annual exemption 2012/13 (part) | (400) |
| | 0 |

*14 September 2012*

| | £ |
|---|---|
| Value of shares held before transfer 8,000 × £8 | 64,000 |
| Less: value of shares held after transfer 1,500 × £3 | (4,500) |
| Transfer of value | 59,500 |
| Less: annual exemption 2012/13 (remainder) £(3,000 – 400) | (2,600) |
| annual exemption 2011/12 b/f | (3,000) |
| Potentially exempt transfer | 53,900 |

*27 January 2013*

| | £ |
|---|---|
| Net chargeable transfer | 400,000 |

| *IHT* | |
|---|---|
| 325,000 × 0% | 0 |
| 75,000 × 20/80 (donor pays tax) | 18,750 |
| 400,000 | 18,750 |
| | |
| Gross chargeable transfer £(400,000 + 18,750) | 418,750 |

**Additional tax on lifetime transfer on death of donor**

*14 September 2012*

Potentially exempt transfer of £53,900 becomes chargeable as donor dies within seven years.

Within nil rate band at death, no tax to pay.

*27 January 2013*

Nil rate band available £(325,000 – 53,900) = £271,100.

|  | £ |
|---|---|
| Gross chargeable transfer | 418,750 |

*IHT*

| | £ |
|---|---|
| 271,100 × 0% | 0 |
| 147,650 × 40% | 59,060 |
| 418,750 | 59,060 |
| No taper relief (death within three years of transfer) | |
| Less: lifetime tax paid | (18,750) |
| Additional tax payable on death | 40,310 |

**Death estate**

|  | £ |
|---|---|
| Value of estate | 620,000 |
| Less: exempt legacy to spouse | (150,000) |
| Chargeable estate | 470,000 |
|  |  |
| IHT liability £470,000 × 40% | 188,000 |

(b) The due date for the IHT liability of £18,750 payable by Afiya was 31 July 2013, (later of 30 April following the transfer and six months from the end of the month in which the transfer was made).

The due date for the additional liability of £40,310 is 31 May 2014, (six months after the end of the month in which the donor, Afiya, died).

(c) Afiya's children will inherit the residue of £(620,000 – 150,000 – 40,000 – 188,000) = £242,000.

# Tax tables

## SUPPLEMENTARY INFORMATION

1.  Calculations and workings need only be made to the nearest £.
2.  All apportionments may be made to the nearest month.
3.  All workings should be shown.

## TAX RATES AND ALLOWANCES

The following tax rates and allowances are to be used in answering the questions.

### Income tax

|  |  | Normal rates | Dividend rates |
|---|---|---|---|
|  |  | % | % |
| Basic rate | £1 – £32,010 | 20 | 10 |
| Higher rate | £32,011 – £150,000 | 40 | 32.5 |
| Additional rate | £150,001 and over | 45 | 37.5 |

A starting rate of 10% applies to savings income where it falls within the first £2,790 of taxable income.

### Personal allowance

|  | £ |
|---|---|
| **Personal allowance** | |
| Born on or after 6 April 1948 | 9,440 |
| Born between 6 April 1938 and 5 April 1948 | 10,500 |
| Born before 6 April 1938 | 10,660 |
| **Income limit** | |
| Personal allowance | 100,000 |
| Personal allowance (born before 6 April 1948) | 26,100 |

### Residence status

| Days in UK | Previously resident | Not previously resident |
|---|---|---|
| Less than 16 | Automatically not resident | Automatically not resident |
| 16 to 45 | Resident if 4 UK ties (or more) | Automatically not resident |
| 46 to 90 | Resident if 3 UK ties (or more) | Resident if 4 UK ties |
| 91 to 120 | Resident if 2 UK ties (or more) | Resident if 3 UK ties (or more) |
| 121 to 182 | Resident if 1 UK tie (or more) | Resident if 2 UK ties (or more) |
| 183 or more | Automatically resident | Automatically resident |

### Child benefit income tax charge

Where income is between £50,000 and £60,000, the charge is 1% of the amount of child benefit received for every £100 of income over £50,000.

### Car benefit percentage

The base level of $CO_2$ emissions is 95 grams per kilometre.

The percentage rates applying to petrol cars with $CO_2$ emissions up to this level are:

|  | % |
|---|---|
| 75 grams per kilometre or less | 5 |
| 76 grams to 94 grams per kilometre | 10 |
| 95 grams per kilometre | 11 |

### Car fuel benefit

The base figure for calculating the car fuel benefit is £21,100.

### Individual savings accounts (ISAs)

The overall investment limit is £11,520, of which £5,760 can be invested in a cash ISA.

# Pension scheme limits

| | |
|---|---|
| Annual allowance | £50,000 |

The maximum contribution that can qualify for tax relief without any earnings is £3,600.

# Authorised mileage allowances: cars

| | |
|---|---|
| Up to 10,000 miles | 45p |
| Over 10,000 miles | 25p |

# Capital allowances

| **Plant and machinery** | % |
|---|---|
| Main pool | 18 |
| Special rate pool | 8 |

| **Motor cars** | |
|---|---|
| New cars with $CO_2$ emissions up to 95 grams per kilometre | 100 |
| $CO_2$ emissions between 96 and 130 grams per kilometre | 18 |
| $CO_2$ emissions over 130 grams per kilometre | 8 |

| **Annual investment allowance** | |
|---|---|
| First £250,000 of expenditure (since 1 January 2013) | 100 |

# Cap on income tax reliefs

Unless otherwise restricted, reliefs are capped at the higher of £50,000 or 25% of income.

# Corporation tax

| **Financial year** | **2011** | **2012** | **2013** |
|---|---|---|---|
| Small profits rate | 20% | 20% | 20% |
| Main rate | 26% | 24% | 23% |
| Lower limit | 300,000 | 300,000 | 300,000 |
| Upper limit | 1,500,000 | 1,500,000 | 1,500,000 |
| Standard fraction | 3/200 | 1/100 | 3/400 |

## Marginal relief

Standard fraction $\times$ (U – A) $\times$ N/A

# Value Added Tax (VAT)

| | |
|---|---|
| Standard rate | 20.0% |
| Registration limit | £79,000 |
| Deregistration limit | £77,000 |

# Inheritance tax: tax rates

| | | |
|---|---|---|
| £1 – £325,000 | | Nil |
| Excess – | Death rate | 40% |
| – | Lifetime rate | 20% |

# Inheritance tax: taper relief

| **Years before death** | % reduction |
|---|---|
| Over 3 but less than 4 years | 20 |
| Over 4 but less than 5 years | 40 |
| Over 5 but less than 6 years | 60 |
| Over 6 but less than 7 years | 80 |

# Capital gains tax

| Rates of tax | – | Lower rate | 18% |
| | – | Higher rate | 28% |
| Annual exempt amount | | | £10,900 |
| Entrepreneurs' relief | – | Lifetime limit | £10,000,000 |
| | – | Rate of tax | 10% |

## National insurance contributions
### (not contracted-out rates)

| | | % |
|---|---|---|
| Class 1 Employee | £1 – £7,755 per year | Nil |
| | £7,756 – £41,450 per year | 12.0 |
| | £41,451 and above per year | 2.0 |
| Class 1 Employer | £1 – £7,696 per year | Nil |
| | £7,697 and above per year | 13.8 |
| Class 1A | | 13.8 |
| Class 2 | £2.70 per week | |
| | Small earnings exception | £5,725 |
| Class 4 | £1 – £7,755 per year | Nil |
| | £7,756 – £41,450 per year | 9.0 |
| | £41,451 and above per year | 2.0 |

### Rates of interest (assumed)

| | |
|---|---|
| Official rate of interest | 4.0% |
| Rate of interest on underpaid tax | 3.0% |
| Rate of interest on overpaid tax | 0.5% |

## Review Form – Paper F6 Taxation (UK) (01/14)

**Name:** _____ **Address:** _____

_____

_____

**How have you used this Kit?**
*(Tick one box only)*

☐ Home study (book only)

☐ On a course: college _____

☐ With 'correspondence' package

☐ Other _____

**Why did you decide to purchase this Kit?**
*(Tick one box only)*

☐ Have used the complementary Study text

☐ Have used other BPP products in the past

☐ Recommendation by friend/colleague

☐ Recommendation by a lecturer at college

☐ Saw advertising

☐ Other _____

**During the past six months do you recall seeing/receiving any of the following?**
*(Tick as many boxes as are relevant)*

☐ Our advertisement in *Student Accountant*

☐ Our advertisement in *Pass*

☐ Our advertisement in *PQ*

☐ Our brochure with a letter through the post

☐ Our website www.bpp.com

**Which (if any) aspects of our advertising do you find useful?**
*(Tick as many boxes as are relevant)*

☐ Prices and publication dates of new editions

☐ Information on product content

☐ Facility to order books off-the-page

☐ None of the above

*Which BPP products have you used?*

| | | | | | |
|---|---|---|---|---|---|
| Text | ☐ | *Success CD* | ☐ | *i-Learn* | ☐ |
| Kit | ☑ | *i-Pass* | ☐ | *Home Study Package* | ☐ |
| Passcards | ☐ | | | | |

*Your ratings, comments and suggestions would be appreciated on the following areas.*

| | Very useful | Useful | Not useful |
|---|---|---|---|
| *Passing F6* | ☐ | ☐ | ☐ |
| *Planning your question practice* | ☐ | ☐ | ☐ |
| *Questions* | ☐ | ☐ | ☐ |
| *Top Tips etc in answers* | ☐ | ☐ | ☐ |
| *Content and structure of answers* | ☐ | ☐ | ☐ |
| *Mock exam answers* | ☐ | ☐ | ☐ |

*Overall opinion of this Kit*     Excellent ☐     Good ☐     Adequate ☐     Poor ☐

**Do you intend to continue using BPP products?**     Yes ☐     No ☐

**The BPP author of this edition can be e-mailed at: AlisonPriest@bpp.com**

**Please return this form to: Amber Cottrell, ACCA Range Manager, BPP Learning Media Ltd, FREEPOST, London, W12 8BR**

**Review Form (continued)**

**TELL US WHAT YOU THINK**

Please note any further comments and suggestions/errors below.